ARTIGAS AND THE EMANCIPATION OF URUGUAY

PLATE I

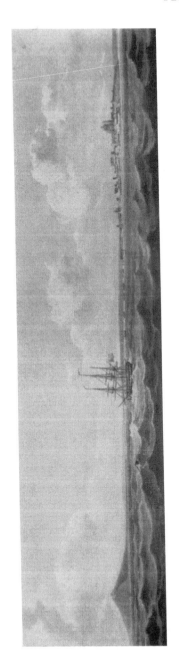 

Montevideo and Buenos Aires from the sea

ARTIGAS AND THE EMANCIPATION OF URUGUAY

BY

JOHN STREET

CAMBRIDGE
AT THE UNIVERSITY PRESS
1959

CAMBRIDGE UNIVERSITY PRESS

Cambridge, New York, Melbourne, Madrid, Cape Town, Singapore, São Paulo, Delhi

Cambridge University Press
The Edinburgh Building, Cambridge CB2 8RU, UK

Published in the United States of America by Cambridge University Press, New York

www.cambridge.org
Information on this title: www.cambridge.org/9780521065634

First published 1959
This digitally printed version 2008

A catalogue record for this publication is available from the British Library

ISBN 978-0-521-06563-4 hardback
ISBN 978-0-521-08693-6 paperback

In Memoriam

J. B. TREND

CONTENTS

ILLUSTRATIONS

PLATES

Plates 1-3 are reproduced from E. E. Vidal, *Picturesque Illustrations of Buenos Ayres and Montevideo*, London 1820.
The photographs on Plate 4 are by the author.

MAPS

PREFACE

THIS book is a study of the origins of Uruguayan nationality, in the development of which the career of Artigas was one of the most important forces. Yet the life of the hero does not suffice to explain all those forces, nor indeed to describe the erection of Uruguay into a separate state, since at the crucial period he was in exile. Consequently I have been obliged to write at length about matters in which Artigas was not directly involved, such as imperial rivalry in South America, and the British interest there. The book is not a biography of Artigas, and its unity is to be found in the greater theme of the birth of a new nation.

I wish here to express my deep gratitude to the many who have freely given their help, and especially to Sir Eugen Millington-Drake, K.C.M.G., the Friends of Uruguay Society and the Comisión Nacional de Homenaje a Artigas for making it possible for me to visit Argentina and Uruguay to collect material. Without their aid this book could not have been written. My stay in Uruguay was made agreeable by the friendliness of many, among whom I remember with gratitude Carlos Caurant Aguirre, Jon E. Jones, the British Council officers J. G. Bruton and D. de Boinville, J. R. Peet of the Royal Bank of Canada, and the historian Edmundo M. Narancio. The services of archive and library staffs in four countries deserve my best thanks; and the Uruguayans J. C. Gómez Alzola of the Archivo General de la Nación, Dionisio Trillo Pays of the Biblioteca Nacional, and Juan E. Pivel Devoto of the Museo Histórico Nacional, who bore the brunt of my enquiries, were particularly kind to me. I also acknowledge my debt to the following scholars: Professor R. A. Humphreys of University College, London, and the late Professor J. B. Trend of Christ's College, Cambridge, who made valuable suggestions, and

Professor J. H. Parry, now of the University College of Ibadan, and my wife, who read and criticised the complete typescript. Their generosity with their time and encouragement is beyond thanks.

The opinions expressed in this book and any errors it may contain are my own.

J.S.

CAMBRIDGE
December 1958

ABBREVIATIONS

USED IN CITATIONS OF REFERENCES

A.A. = Comisión Nacional Archivo Artigas, *Archivo Artigas*, vol. 1–, 1950–.

A.G.I., Seville, B.A. = Archivo General de Indias, Seville; Audiencia de Buenos Aires.

A.G.I., Seville, I.G. = Archivo General de Indias, Seville; Sección Indiferente General.

AGN, B.A., Div. Col., Sec. Gob. = Archivo General de la Nación, Buenos Aires; División Colonial, Sección Gobierno.

AGN, B.A., Div. Nac., Sec. Gob. = Archivo General de la Nación, Buenos Aires; División Nacional, Sección Gobierno.

AGN, B.A., *Doc. ref. guerra* = Archivo General de la Nación, Buenos Aires, *Documentos referentes a la guerra de la independencia y emancipación política* . . .

AGN, B.A., *Pap. Arch.* = Archivo General de la Nación, Buenos Aires, *Papeles del Archivo*.

Arch. Adm. = Archivo General de la Nación, Montevideo; Fondo ex-Archivo Administrativo.

Congreso . . . 1813 = Comisión Nacional de Homenaje a Artigas, *El Congreso de Abril de 1813* . . .

H.N.A. = R. Levene, ed., *Historia de la nación argentina desde sus orígenes hasta la organización definitiva en 1862*.

M.H.N. = Museo Histórico Nacional, Montevideo; Biblioteca Pablo Blanco Acevedo, Documentos del Consulado de Comercio.

xiii

P.R.O., Adm. = Great Britain, Public Record Office; archives of the Admiralty.

P.R.O., F.O. = Public Record Office; archives of the Foreign Office.

P.R.O., W.O. = Public Record Office; archives of the War Office.

CHAPTER I

THE ENVIRONMENT

I. THE LAND AND THE PEOPLE

URUGUAY is one of the smallest countries of Latin America, although it covers an area considerably larger than that of England and Wales; and it is among the most peaceful and progressive of all the twenty Latin American republics. But until the beginning of the twentieth century, this was one of the most turbulent districts of a turbulent region.[1] The reasons for that chronic state of instability can be traced, for the most part, to the origins of Uruguayan nationhood in the first decades of the nineteenth century, and even as far as the beginnings of Uruguay as a settled territory in the time of the Spanish Empire in America.

The country's full name, the Eastern Republic of the Uruguay, describes its situation in that corner of South America tucked in between the River Uruguay and the Atlantic Ocean. On the north Uruguay has a frontier with Brazil; while on the south the River Plate, into which the Uruguay flows, forms a natural boundary with Argentina. This position has great strategical importance, since it commands the entrance to the River Plate and with it the shipping routes to Buenos Aires and up the affluents of the Plate, the Paraná and the Uruguay, leading to the Argentine and Brazilian interiors and to Paraguay. Uruguay's friendship is important, too, to any nation with interests in the South Atlantic. Finally, she is a buffer state between two considerable powers, Brazil and Argentina, which tower in strength above their South American neighbours, and which are now taking their place among the influential countries of the world.

This position as a buffer was, indeed, the first great factor in Uruguay's history. In colonial times the Banda Oriental, as the

[1] S. G. Hanson, *Utopia in Uruguay*, p. 3.

territory was called (the Eastern Bank, that is, of the River Uruguay), became a bone of contention between the owners of the two empires in South America, Portugal and Spain. Uruguay's fertile soil and the great herds of wild cattle and horses which grazed over her rolling ranges and drank at the wooded banks of

South America Today

her streams combined with her strategic position to form the in-
centives behind the struggle for what was in other respects an
empty land.

Uruguay is fortunate in her topography and climate. She is well

Latin America about 1800: The Viceroyalties

watered, provided with good ports and water communications on all but her Brazilian frontier, and she has no great mountains, deserts or swamps (features only too apparent in other Latin American countries) to impede internal communication. The climate varies from temperate to sub-tropical as one goes from south-east to north-west, from the Atlantic seaboard open to the Antarctic winds and current, to the hot interior of the continent. But nowhere is it impossible for white men and for cattle to live in all seasons; and cattle especially throve in the past in a country of good grass lacking large predatory animals. The 'native' or 'creole' unimproved cattle were in fact not indigenous, but were the wild descendants of the few released by early Spanish visitors, and they found the Banda Oriental so favourable that they had increased to millions, it was said, before the middle of the eighteenth century.[1]

Yet the Banda Oriental, although discovered by the Spanish explorer Solís in 1516, was not settled even in part for over a hundred years. The Spanish conquistadores were not deeply interested in this land because it was inhabited by primitive and warlike Indians (Solís himself was killed by men of the Charrúa tribe at the moment of discovery), and, more to the point, because neither the country nor the Indians possessed or produced anything of value: no gold, silver, domestic animals, fruits, crops, nor even useful slaves.

The Banda Oriental, however, had water and wood for the ships arriving from Spain on their way up the rivers to Paraguay, where the Spaniards had settled by the middle of the sixteenth century. So the authorities in the Paraguayan capital, Asunción, made attempts to establish small posts on the Uruguayan coast, though they were at first unsuccessful owing to the bitter hostility of the natives. Nothing was known of the interior, since no explorer had ventured beyond the coastal district. But with the rise

[1] P. Blanco Acevedo, *El gobierno colonial en el Uruguay y los orígenes de la nacionalidad*, pp. 35-6.

of Buenos Aires on the other bank of the River Plate, towards the end of the sixteenth century, settlement began in the Banda Oriental.

Spain realised at the beginning of the seventeenth century that the administrative area of Paraguay was too large, embracing as it did all the River Plate besides Paraguay proper. Buenos Aires had been founded in 1580 after an abortive attempt forty years before, and so in 1618 the whole territory was divided into two *gobernaciones:* Paraguay, ruled from Asunción, and the River Plate, with Buenos Aires as capital. The Banda Oriental fell within the province of Buenos Aires, though we may well wonder how the tiny Spanish colonial population had the energy to undertake its settlement.[1]

Friendly relations with the Indians were at first fostered by means of gifts and entertainment, and then a few peaceful missionaries, Franciscans, were sent to prepare the way for more permanent contacts. In 1624 they set up a church and missionary village at a place which they called Santo Domingo Soriano, on the lower Uruguay, near the mouth of the Río Negro, and here the small local tribe, the Chanás, accepted Christianity and Spanish rule with it. An attempt to impose the strict discipline of the Jesuit mission, the *reducción*, which was having such success in the Paraguay Missions, failed here since Spanish settlers too quickly followed the missionaries and occupied the neighbourhood; and then Spaniards and Indians living in a community inevitably mixed their blood, so that quickly the Chanás lost their tribal identity together with their language and customs. Other missions were established by the Franciscans at Las Víboras and Espinillo, but that typical device of the Spanish conquistadores, the *encomienda* system of ensuring native tribute and labour, did not grow up here since tribes which were not completely assimilated,

---

[1] The population of the *Gobernación del Río de la Plata* at this time was 2730 whites and 4899 friendly Indians, for an area including the present Argentine provinces of Buenos Aires, Santa Fe and Entre Ríos, as well as Uruguay (J. Torre Revello, *Los gobernadores de Buenos Aires (1617-1777)*, p. 468, in H.N.A., vol. III, part 2, chap. VIII).

as were the Chanás, were too wild for any form of civilised life, and lived in liberty and more or less intermittent hostility towards the settlers.

It was the wealth of cattle which they found that attracted the Spaniards and led them to explore the rest of the Banda Oriental and slowly spread the area of occupation. Before this discovery, the people of Buenos Aires had regarded the Banda Oriental as a source of wood and charcoal, which they badly needed since the Argentine side of the Plate was bare of natural timber. Now that the wild descendants of the cattle brought by early explorers had multiplied throughout the country, Buenos Aires found that the Banda Oriental was even more profitable as a source of hides, tallow, fat and other products of cattle-killing than as a fuel reserve. Cattle formed the only important economic resource of the River Plate area, and the Banda Oriental was discovered to be the richest in them of all the districts of the *gobernación*.[1]

A Scottish traveller of the first years of the nineteenth century, J. P. Robertson, gives the atmosphere of this primitive industry in a description of one of its centres, typical of many, although this one was in the Argentine province of Santa Fe. The place

might have been called the Golgotha of cattle; for I found it strewed not only with their skulls, but their carcases. It was quite surrounded by slaughter-grounds and corrales; or rather, instead of these *surrounding* the town, they constituted part of it. The ground was soaked with the blood of the animals; and the effluvia from their offal, from large piles of hides, and from manufactories of tallow, emitted under the hot rays of a burning sun with tenfold intensity, were nearly insupportable. The air over the site of those corrales was almost darkened by birds of prey. Vultures, carrion-crows, and carrion-gulls, hovered, skimmed, and wheeled their flight round the carcases of the slain. Here were a dozen clamorous assailants fixing their talons, and thrusting their curved beaks into the yet warm flesh of an animal, which had yielded its hide and tallow (all for which it was deemed valuable) to the Gaucho executioners of the matadero [slaughter-ground]. There, so many pigs were

---

[1] For the spread of cattle see Blanco Acevedo, *op. cit.* pp. 33-5, and *A.A.*, tomo 11, prologue by J. E. Pivel Devoto, pp. ix-x.

contending for mastery in the revels, and close by, some ravenous dogs were usurping and maintaining an exclusive right to the prey. Ducks, fowls, turkeys, all seemed to prefer beef to anything else; and such a cawing, cackling, barking, and screaming, as were kept up by the heterogeneous family of quadrupeds and winged creatures which were voraciously satisfying the cravings of nature, was never heard out of Babel. [1]

Buenos Aires drew revenue from the new industry by establishing a system of taxes on it. The slaughtering parties which left the Argentine side to make a bloody harvest in the Banda Oriental had to obtain licences from the Buenos Aires Cabildo (town council) for a specified number of animals, and a third of their supposed value was paid in tax. The wild cattle were considered Crown property, in the same category as the precious mines of other parts of America, and therefore they could not legally be used without some payment, such as this, to the Crown. The inevitable result was that the Banda Oriental came to be regarded as a sort of large ranch leased to Buenos Aires; and this attitude and the exploitation which sprang from it continued to the end of colonial days, and in some respects beyond. The reaction of the people of the Banda Oriental, as they grew more numerous and more conscious of themselves as a community, caused friction between the two sides of the River Plate, especially after the beginning of the eighteenth century. The whole question, indeed, encouraged the growth of what may be termed a community persecution-mania in the Banda Oriental, which led directly to attempts at emancipation from Buenos Aires even before the revolutions of the early nineteenth century, and to the autonomous designs of Uruguayan leaders, particularly the national hero, Artigas, during these later struggles. This feeling is clearly the second great factor in the development of the country.

Some of the more immediately apparent effects of the cattle boom were also far-reaching. They included the exploration of the

---

[1] J. P. and W. P. Robertson, *Letters on Paraguay*, vol. I, pp. 226-7.

country by the marauding parties of cattle-hunters from Buenos Aires or from local settlements and from Brazil to the north, which led to the establishment of villages, at first makeshift but later more permanently built, in convenient places on the coast or on rivers: the *Arroyos* (streams) de Pando, Solís Grande, Maldonado Grande and Maldonado Chico, the *Laguna* (lake) de Rocha, and other natural features attracted communities in this way, and as this movement went forward, so the country was opened up and these features named.

Another result of the boom, and one which was sinister from the point of view of the Spaniards, was an increase in the interest in the Banda Oriental shown by the Portuguese established in Brazil. Equally sinister, though, as things turned out, less dangerous, was a change in the customs of the wild Indians, who quickly learned the value of the wild cattle as sources of food and of various useful materials, and the use of the wild horses which had spread with them. The Indians had acquired something new which helped them to withstand the Spanish advance more easily and for longer than they could have done in their primitive state: they could now attack swiftly and effectively, and disappear just as swiftly before their pursuers. Now, too, they could find better food, and with less trouble than they had had before as hunters, on foot, of small game. There was little temptation to come to terms with the invaders, so that the outcome was a long series of Indian wars, in which the settlers and their friends gradually annihilated the savages, though the process lasted well into the nineteenth century, and at times whites and Indians became allies in the face of a common foe.[1]

Perhaps the most important result of the cattle exploitation was its social effect on the people who lived by it – who were the large majority of the people of the Banda Oriental until near the end of colonial times. Agriculture was neglected for the easier life and more immediate profits of ranching or merely killing the wild

---

[1] Blanco Acevedo, *op. cit.* p. 9.

cattle.[1] Consequently the population grew slowly, since ranching needs far fewer men than does agriculture, apart from the influence on the rate of natural increase of the free, nomadic, bachelor life of the cowboy and the settled, domestic life of the farmer. The Uruguayan historian Bauzá, writing towards the end of the nineteenth century, blamed on this lack of people much of his country's instability until his day;[2] and in this he followed the Argentine Sarmiento's idea that the large, almost empty tracts of land of those countries created barbarism. He believed, with another, slightly earlier, Argentine thinker, J. B. Alberdi, that 'gobernar es poblar' – to govern is to populate.

Not only the quantity of people, but their quality as human beings was deeply affected. 'La agricultura es sedentaria y civil; la ganadería es ecuestre y guerrera', writes an acute Uruguayan observer[3]: it was the old contrast between Cain and Abel. Ranching, especially the mere exploitation of the early centuries of Uruguayan history – and the same could be said for Argentina and large areas of Venezuela and of Mexico, not to go beyond the Spanish world – made the individual free, independent, and irresponsible. Food was plentiful, and to get it was simply a matter of lassoing the nearest cow, or bringing it down with the *boleadoras* (thongs loaded with heavy balls which were thrown so as to entangle the animal's legs), killing it, cutting out a choice part, roasting it over the camp fire and eating it with knife and fingers. The hides of cattle and horses supplied almost every other need of the early Uruguayan – as, indeed, of many other Latin Americans – clothing, boots, saddlery, bed, even tents and huts, doors and windows. They also supplied the medium of exchange for buying the few necessities which a man could not make for himself: tobacco, drink, knives. Education, and even the rudiments of civilised living, were neglected. They were impossible where the population

---

[1] F. de Azara, *Memoria sobre el estado rural del Río de la Plata y otros informes*, pp. 3–5.

[2] F. Bauzá, *Historia de la dominación española en el Uruguay*, vol. I, p. 145. He added that the land only supported 50 persons where it should support 2,000.

[3] A. Zum Felde, *Evolución histórica del Uruguay*, p. 14.

was so sparse, and where men cared for nothing but their own manliness. The dangers and fatigues of hunting and killing cattle inured the countrymen to a life of perpetual campaigning. In fact, Indian attacks, and brushes with the Portuguese or occasionally with the Spanish authorities created a perilous state of anarchy. Men brought up to such a life made perfect material for revolution or war, whether civil or against a foreign enemy.

Life was primitive in the scattered settlements and even in the capital, Montevideo, newly founded in 1724. Until well on in that century it was the roughness and rural simplicity of life which gave the dominant note of colonial Uruguay, and it will be best to examine the country districts closely before going on to describe the development of the most important city and of the Banda Oriental's complicated relations with Buenos Aires and Brazil.

The basis of the population was Spanish, with a not very large admixture of Indian blood. Some Portuguese came and stayed, particularly after their foundation of Colónia do Sacramento on the shore of the River Plate opposite Buenos Aires, in 1680. There were almost no other foreigners, since, apart from the exclusion laid down in Spanish law, there was little in the country to attract them. The Spaniards' descendants were called *criollos*, creoles, as elsewhere in Spanish America, and they formed the bulk of the population, which was therefore mainly white. By the end of the eighteenth century there was possibly more African than Indian blood in the Banda Oriental, after the introduction of black slaves which began about 1756. However, negroes and mulattoes were more common in and near Montevideo than in the country districts, where more *mestizos* (half-breed of white and Indian) than mulattoes existed.[1]

The owners of ranches had a degree of rude comfort in their estancia houses. The Scot, J. P. Robertson, as a young merchant, dined in an affluent country house in a place near the Uruguayan frontier, a part of present-day Argentina which had much in

[1] H. Arredondo, *Civilización del Uruguay*, tomo I, pp. 35-9.

common with the Banda Oriental in the old days; and he described it:

A deal table was covered with a splendidly-tamboured table-napkin; most of the supper utensils were of silver; sparkling water glittered in a crystal caraff; wine, water-melons, peaches, honey, and cigars, stood upon a side-table; and after a two hours' repast I stretched myself upon a luxurious, albeit uncurtained bed, and slept soundly . . .

You must not run away with the idea, however, that we were seated in anything like an English dining-room. The floor of our apartment was of mud; so were the walls. The thatch of the roof was but too apparent. Here, in one corner, stood my bed,– there, in another, lay strewed the cumbrous saddle-gear of three or four horses. In two large earthen pitchers stood the water; and the copper-coloured servants that waited on us were dressed in half-naked Indian simplicity. We had change of neither knives, plates, nor forks. [The rancher], his head capataz, or overseer, and the curate of a neighbouring capilla [chapel], ate off the same dish. The chairs were antiquated leather-bottomed chairs, with backs five feet high from the ground. The door stood open, with half a dozen horses saddled, and tied to stakes around it. No pictures graced the walls, no sashes, nay, not even shutters protected the windows, nor did glass make a part of them. Everything around us, even our savoury and abundant cheer, bespoke that we were supping with a nomadic chief. His welcome was primitive and hearty; his wealth consisted in flocks and herds; and his domestic arrangements were rough and simple as the habits of the master . . . The basin in which, like the Jews, we washed hands after meals, was carried round by a *China* or Indian female servant; and a tall mulatto taking off my boots, struck the adhesive clay from them, and put them down by the side of my bed . . . Just as the day began to dawn, a mate [Paraguayan tea] and cigar were brought to me . . .; the saddle-gear was carried out of the room, and put on the backs of several magnificent horses, which stood ready at the door to be saddled; and in ten minutes, [the rancher], his capataz, my servant, and eight peones, followed by six large dogs, were mounted, and ready to ride the round of the estancia . . . [1]

The sort of life which was lived in the country districts varied comparatively little in all the interior of the River Plate area, although it differed radically from life in the towns, and especially

[1] J. P. and W. P. Robertson, *Letters on Paraguay*, vol. I, pp. 233-5.

in the capital, Buenos Aires; and this difference was fundamental
in shaping the political development of the River Plate countries,
and forms yet another essential factor in the making of Uruguay.

Félix de Azara, a scientifically-minded Spanish officer who
travelled widely in the Plate region towards the end of the
eighteenth century, gives us the most complete picture of country
life.[1] Cowboys, he wrote, were usually employed at the rate of
two per thousand head of cattle. The foremen were usually
married, but the others were not, and therefore women were
scarce and in great demand. Herding consisted simply of galloping
round the ranges once a week, collecting the cattle together,
keeping them so for a short time, and then letting them go. (By
this time most of the cattle nominally belonged to some large
rancher, though hundreds of thousands were still wild, and therefore were royal property.) The aim of the manoeuvre was to keep
the animals from straying too far off the vaguely defined, unfenced
estancias of at least four to five square leagues each – a league being
about three miles.

The cowboys spent the rest of the week breaking horses and
doing other necessary tasks, or simply idling. They lived far apart:
sometimes four, ten, or even thirty leagues from each other, and
communal life could hardly be said to exist. Religion, for instance,
was only rarely practised, so that many were only baptised if they
married, and then only because baptism was a necessary preliminary. If they went to church, they sat on their horses outside,
listening. But they had a superstitious desire to be buried in con-
secrated ground, and when they died their relatives and friends
fulfilled the wish, even if they had to leave the flesh to rot or cut it
off the bones before undertaking the long journey to the cemetery.
In illness, the cowboys' normal resource was the local, possibly
Indian, *curandero*, the witch-doctor, or even the advice of a casual
passer-by.

[1] See his *Estado rural*, and his *Voyages dans l'Amérique méridionale, depuis 1781 jusqu'en
1801*, vol. II, particularly chap. XV.

PLATE 2

An *estancia* on the Río San Pedro

Furniture in the huts normally consisted of a keg for fetching water, a drinking horn, wooden spits for roasting the inevitable beef, and a little copper pot for heating water and infusing the tea made from *hierba mate*. Some had a cauldron, perhaps a bench, and a bed, which was made of four poles with a hide stretched across them resting on four posts stuck in the ground in a rectangular pattern. It was more common, however, for the bed to be a hide laid on the mud floor. The people normally sat crouched on their haunches or on the skull of a cow or a horse.

These people ate no vegetables, calling them 'hay', and laughing at European-born Spaniards for eating 'horse food'. Indeed, they ate almost nothing else but beef roasted after the Charrúa style on a stick leaning at an angle over an open fire, and they did not even use salt. They had no fixed meal times, and after eating they wiped their mouths with the backs of their knives and cleaned their greasy fingers on their legs or on their soft leather boots. The ground round the cowboys' huts was always covered with bones and rotting carcases, since they ate only delicacies such as the ribs or the flesh of the belly, which they called *matambre*, kill-hunger. The rest of the animal would be wasted, and about four times the amount of meat used was left to rot in filth which bred disease.

In Azara's day the country dress showed some distinction between classes. The ranchers and foremen wore a coarse jacket, waistcoat, breeches, drawers, hat, shoes and poncho. This garment, still used in parts of South America, was like a thick blanket with a hole in the middle for the wearer's head, and was worn draped shapelessly but protectively over shoulders and body. It was a good dress for men who spent most of their lives on horseback. The ordinary hands, the peones, wore no shoes, jacket or breeches, and simply girded their loins with loose, coarse white drawers – a garment called a *chiripá* – and wore a hat, poncho and *botas de potro*: soft boots made by stripping the skin whole from the leg of a horse and curing it. Few had a shirt. There were no barbers: men let their hair grow, occasionally tidying up with their knives. The women were barefoot and sluttish, like their men. They never learned to sew or spin, and merely swept out the huts, roasted the beef and boiled the water for mate. Neither sex had a change of clothing. Azara wrote that if it rained, the men would protect their clothing by taking it off and putting it under their saddles, and dressed again when the weather cleared.

The huts themselves were usually made of mud and thatched with straw. They were not even whitewashed, inside or out, and the whole family slept in the one room, if there were a family. Children never learned anything of manners or discipline: they never saw such a thing as a clock, but only lakes, rivers, deserts and a few wandering naked men hunting wild animals and cattle.[1] They grew up completely untrammelled and independent, knowing no law and disliking the society of men. These people had no respect for morality, decency, comfort or any sort of learning or education: in a word, they were barbarians, killing a man as coolly as they would a cow, and, according to this observer, they were scarcely superior to the pagan Indians in anything.

This type of life made the cowboy, the gaucho, as he was beginning to be called in the latter half of the eighteenth century, extremely tough physically and callous spiritually.[2] These men did not complain at sickness, injury, or even at cruel death. They seemed indifferent to life or death, for themselves as well as for others. They would never work indoors, but did not mind the hardships of their chosen cattle-hunting. And yet Azara notes that their sense of personal liberty was so great that however well a master treated them, they never became attached to him, and would leave him for a whim or for the sake of a change. But the gaucho showed in the revolutionary wars of the early nineteenth century that he could be unshakeably loyal to a leader whose qualities appealed to him and which he could respect since they were his own on a heroic scale.

[1] *Estado rural*, pp. 3-5.
[2] Concolorcorvo, *El Lazarillo de ciegos caminantes desde Buenos Aires hasta Lima*, pp. 37-9, and M. W. Nichols, *The Gaucho*.

Like all primitive, scattered peoples, the gauchos were hospitable to any chance visitor, especially if he were a notable guitarist and extempore versifier; but they were so isolated that they made few friendships and became distrustful and cunning. Their pastimes were their vices: drinking, gambling and women, occasionally varied by hunting partridge, deer or ostriches on horseback. Robbery was commonplace: gauchos would steal horses and other things of little account, but generally could be trusted with important things. They enjoyed killing animals, even without reason, as do some other hunters. They hated doing anything they could not do on horseback, and would meet and sit talking to one another for hours on their horses, or fish and draw water from the same position. Consequently, they were consummate horsemen from the age of five or six on, who could ride and break any animal, and rarely hurt themselves in the frequent falls on rough ground.

Gauchos malos, true outlaws for one reason or another, existed in numbers, especially in the no-man's-land near the Brazilian frontier. Bougainville, about 1767, learned that there was a 'tribe' of these men consisting of about six hundred refugees from justice and their offspring by Indian women, and that they spent their time rustling cattle to sell across the Brazilian border.[1] The *gauderios* described by Concolorcorvo a few years later were not far from this state. It was among such people that Artigas was to make his name, first as their leader, and later as their tamer.

2. THE DEVELOPMENT OF A NO-MAN'S-LAND

THIS semi-barbarous cattle-hunting country needed few towns or centres of population for the business of civilised life. Towns were slow to appear, and were at first as primitive as the country itself. The establishment of towns, indeed, came as a conscious attempt to settle the question of ownership of the Banda Oriental: whether it was to be Spanish or Portuguese. In this way it was the secular

[1] L. A. de Bougainville, *Viaje alrededor del mundo*, vol. I, pp. 49–50.

rivalry between the two peoples which to begin with encouraged civilisation in the Banda Oriental, in default of any economic reason for its further development. The economy of the country tended to produce a kind of barbarism; and it may appear strange to some that imperial rivalry should have had the opposite effect. The Treaty of Tordesillas (1494) was intended to settle the question of the spheres of influence of Spain and Portugal throughout the world. Portugal's sphere was made to include part of the as yet unexplored and probably undiscovered continent of South America; and that part roughly included all of the coast and interior of Brazil to the east of a line joining the sites of the future towns of Pará and São Vicente. It did not include the Banda Oriental, nor indeed the present west and south of Brazil, that is, over half of Brazil's territory now; but as the Portuguese and the colonists of Brazil had little respect for the Tordesillas line, an artificial boundary backed by scanty forces, they explored and occupied land wherever they could roam, making constant annexations of nominally Spanish territory not effectually occupied by the Spaniards.

In the Banda Oriental, this advance came up against the true frontier of Spanish occupation, and nevertheless passed it in the course of a long drawn out effort to win access to the rivers Plate, Uruguay and Paraná, to occupy the fertile and well-stocked lands in between, and to reach channels of communication with the interior of the continent. The process was a natural expansion of a colonising people, not necessarily at first or for many years a national policy. Settlers, or adventurers, found the Banda Oriental brimming with cattle waiting to be killed for their hides, or to be ranched on the spot or driven back home to Brazil. They were not the people to waive such prosperity for the sake of an out-of-date and unrealistic treaty, and they exploited an almost unpeopled country.

The Spanish authorities were aware of the danger; and it is a measure of its importance as an influence on the development of the whole Plate region that almost every new governmental institution created there owed its origin to the need to check the Portuguese advance. The first expedition, in 1535, to establish a colony on the Plate, the creation of the *gobernaciones* of Paraguay and Río de la Plata in 1617, the temporary creation of an Audiencia or higher law court at Buenos Aires in 1661, the establishment there of a new viceregal capital in 1776 to supervise the whole area from Bolivia to Patagonia, all had as one of their main motives the Spanish fear of Portuguese expansion, as had the creation of Montevideo itself.

Apart from the unofficial operations of Portuguese rustlers, and of smugglers who found a ready market for European goods among the Spanish settlers of the Plate, no penetration into the Banda Oriental itself came until 1680, when a Portuguese fleet sailed up the River Plate and impudently founded a fortified town, Colónia do Sacramento, on the Banda Oriental of the estuary, exactly opposite Buenos Aires. Portuguese families were installed, houses built and farms cultivated, and Colónia began to flourish. Here was an ordered and planned attempt to colonise the Banda Oriental, under the very noses of the Spanish officials who had never considered such a thing worth doing.

The governor of Buenos Aires reacted with energy and captured the fortress and town within the same year; but when the news of this reached the Peninsula, Portugal, at the time the stronger power, threatened to invade Spain unless Colónia were returned. Spain gave in.[1] The treaty of 1681 which arranged the return of Colónia also stipulated the setting up of a joint commission to fix the limits of Spanish and Portuguese possessions in America. The commission met several times, and the Pope was finally asked to give the decision, but nothing definite came of it. In fact, Portugal held Colónia: further expansion was possible, and even likely.

Colónia flourished in the period of peace. The Portuguese, good

---

[1] Bauzá, *op. cit.* vol. I, pp. 175-6.

settlers, made the land around like a 'vast garden covered with trees, vineyards and dovecotes'.[1] The city quickly became an important port and centre of the contraband between Brazil and the Plate, as merchants established themselves and gained contacts with the nearby Spanish colonists. Negro slaves, tobacco, wines and spirits, textiles and other goods from Brazil and Europe were illegally traded for flour, dried and salt meat and Peruvian silver. Portuguese merchants had infiltrated even as far as Peru, where their suspected Jewish backgrounds brought them the too close attention of the Inquisition; and the contraband had grown to such proportions even before the foundation of Colónia that an Audiencia had been established in Buenos Aires to check it – but had been dismantled very shortly since it was found that the proliferation of officials had not stopped smuggling, nor could it be expected to. A land frontier and internal customs barrier was set up towards the end of the seventeenth century, first at Córdoba and later at Jujuy, on the way from the River Plate to Peru, to check the illegal trading and the supposedly dangerous drain of silver.

The Spanish merchants of Lima, with vested interests in the maintenance of the legal trade system, had urged the government to adopt these measures, for under that system Buenos Aires was not even open as a port for trade with Spain, much less with foreign countries: all goods had to come with the Spanish fleets through the port of Cartagena in the Caribbean, over the Isthmus of Panamá by mule train, down the South American coast to Callao, and then by mule again across Peru, over the Andes and through the pampas. Immense profits were made by the merchants engaged in this trade, but great expense was caused to the consumers at the far end of the line, and much damage to the goods in transit was almost unavoidable.[2] The smuggler usually

---

[1] *Ibid.* p. 117.

[2] Bauzá, *ibid.;* see also M. Lastarria, *Colonias orientales* (1805), in *Documentos para la historia argentina,* t. III; and for general trade system C. H. Haring, *The Spanish Empire in America,* chap. XVI, especially pp. 324, 329–31.

had the advantage in price and quality. Those merchants of Buenos Aires who stayed faithful to the legitimate Spanish trade, and who had the most influence on the Cabildo, now began to find their profits cut down, while some hitherto unknown traders engaged in some untraceable form of commerce began to make fortunes. The contraband with Colónia must be responsible for this injustice, and it must be stopped. The Spanish monopoly was being broken. So in 1699 the Cabildo of Buenos Aires petitioned the King of Spain for permission to undertake the reconquest of Colónia. It had become obvious that either Colónia or Buenos Aires was to dominate the Plate and the ways to the interior, and it was vital for the people of Buenos Aires to stamp out the competition from the opposite bank. But Spain was then in no state to provoke trouble in South America, and instead she made a treaty with Portugal ceding Colónia definitely to her.

This policy was soon reversed when the Portuguese began to increase their hold in South America by invading the Misiones territory, in the interior, between Brazil and Paraguay. In 1703 Buenos Aires was ordered to capture Colónia and expel the Portuguese, and this was done in 1705, after a five months' siege. The next few years were spent in fighting and pacifying the Indians of the Banda Oriental, who had been roused by the Portuguese in 1701 to attack the Spanish settlements. Yet the Spanish triumph was short, for the Treaty of Utrecht in 1713, as part of the general division of spoils after the War of the Spanish Succession, stipulated the return of Colónia to the Portuguese. The wound made in the body of the Spanish trade system was widened by a treaty granting the slave *asiento* (the contract to supply negro slaves to the Spanish colonists) to a British company. British ships and merchants had now a pretext for frequenting various Spanish American ports, including Buenos Aires, with the result that a great increase in illegal trade helped to weaken Spain's economy at a time when the new Spanish Bourbons were making attempts to improve it. A blunder, too, had been made in the wording of the cession of Colónia to Portugal: the treaty mentioned 'Colónia and her territory', which might be taken to mean the whole Banda Oriental, not merely the immediate surroundings within cannon-shot which the Spaniards had intended.[1] There was no saying where the Portuguese expansion might stop after this. When, however, in 1716 the Portuguese re-occupied Colónia, the alert Spanish authorities restricted their holding strictly to the land within a cannon-shot of the fortress. Madrid, tardily, ordered a close watch to be kept to prevent the Portuguese from trading with the Spanish territories, or establishing themselves at such favourable points as Montevideo and Maldonado. At last Spain, revitalised, it seemed, by the new régime, made serious efforts to contain the Portuguese. A notable soldier, Bruno Mauricio de Zabala, was sent to govern the Plate, with orders to undertake the establishment of Spanish settlements at Montevideo and Maldonado so as to ensure that the Portuguese should not spread. Both of these places were ports which commanded the main channel into the Plate estuary, and which thus cut off the Portuguese in Colónia from sea communication with Brazil; and in fact Montevideo was the best natural port in the whole region from São Vicente to the south.

Zabala took over the government in 1717, but evidently could not find the means in Buenos Aires to establish new colonies, so that the Portuguese were left to spread for a few more years. Orders for founding a settlement at Montevideo were repeated by Spain in 1720 and 1723; she was becoming more anxious. As it was, the Portuguese got there first, establishing a small fort at Montevideo in 1723. This stung Zabala to action, and within a few weeks he had dislodged the invaders and set up a Spanish garrison in their place. Finally seven families from Buenos Aires were persuaded to join the fifteen families of colonists brought from the Canary Islands and start the civilian population of Montevideo in 1726. They amounted to about a hundred souls.[2]

[1] Bauzá, *op. cit.* pp. 191-3.
[2] Blanco Acevedo, *op. cit.* pp. 24-8.

This strategic move was the beginning of the future capital of a future state. The new 'city' was laid out by military engineers on the plans recommended in the Spanish Laws of the Indies, and in 1730 Zabala appointed a Cabildo from among the colonists. At first the new citizens were maintained by a daily ration, just as were the one hundred and fifty soldiers and one hundred serving Indians of the garrison.[1]

An open clash with the Portuguese seemed bound to come now that the rivalry between Spain and Portugal was concentrated on the tense situation in the Banda Oriental. An attempt to capture Colónia during hostilities in 1735 failed; but the next move was an offer by Spain to exchange an equivalent for Colónia, as Utrecht had provided. Negotiations culminated in the Treaty of Madrid of 1750, by which Spain was to receive Colónia in exchange for the title, which she was to give to Portugal, to a large tract of land to the north, between the Atlantic coast and the River Uruguay. This included a large part of the territory of the Jesuit Missions of Paraguay. It was a heavy price to pay for a doubtful peace, and it proves the ability of the Portuguese diplomats and the weakness of the Spanish.[2] The price was inflated by the condition that Spain should enforce this change on the Missions, a clause which led to a long and costly campaign by the Spanish army against the peaceful and loyal Missions Indians.

It was soon realised that the exchange was impossible owing to this opposition, so that in 1761 the Spaniards, taking advantage of a general European war, repudiated it; and at the same time Cevallos, Governor of Buenos Aires, was ordered to seize Colónia by force. Spain's attitude was hardening again. Colónia was taken by storm after a siege, in 1762, but once again it was returned almost with apologies, under the Treaty of Paris of 1763: it was Spain's misfortune to be on the losing side throughout the century in nearly all her wars.

---

[1] L. E. Azarola Gil, *Los orígenes de Montevideo, 1607-1749*, p. 133.
[2] Blanco Acevedo, *op. cit.* pp. 29-30.

Portugal took another step towards the Plate when in 1776 she conquered the territory of Rio Grande do Sul, just to the north of the Banda Oriental. Again, Spain was stung to activity, and this time she made a complete re-organisation of her southern dominions so as to end the Portuguese advance. The great Spanish imperial administrator, José de Gálvez, put forward a scheme for unifying the command and improving the government in all the territories under the Audiencia of Charcas (now Bolivia, Paraguay and Eastern Argentina) and in the region of Cuyo (Western Argentina). Lima had until then been the nearest vice-regal headquarters for these areas, and the distance had lessened the efficiency of administration, particularly in meeting the Portuguese military and commercial penetration. Now Buenos Aires was to be the capital of a new Viceroyalty of the River Plate, ruling these lands. The office of Viceroy was at first to be temporary, for the duration of a campaign against the Portuguese, but it was made permanent by the appointment of successors to the first Viceroy, who was the successful soldier Cevallos. He sailed from Spain in November 1776, in command of a large army of regular troops.[1]

Cevallos quickly dealt with the Portuguese threat. He captured their island of Santa Catarina, off the Brazilian coast, while on the way, and then went on to land at Montevideo. Thence he took 7,000 men to attack Colónia, which capitulated in July 1777. Operations stopped here, for the diplomats in the Peninsula arranged a peace at San Ildefonso, whereby Colónia became Spanish at last, and a boundary in the area was agreed on in principle, and on paper. A boundary commission was to be sent out to go over the ground, set up marks, draw maps, and settle for ever the question of Brazil's limits.

The Spanish commissioners had all arrived in South America by 1781 – a mere four years' hiatus – but the Portuguese raised so

---

[1] E. Ravignani, *El Virreinato del Río de la Plata (1776–1810)*, in *H.N.A.*, vol. IV, section I, part I, chap. I.

many difficulties and caused such delays that the limits were not
fixed before the next war between the two countries, in 1801,

Banda Oriental: Main Settlements at the End of the 18th Century

while the Spanish commissioners grew old waiting to begin work.[1]
A real loss to Uruguay was caused, however, by Cevallos' decision to raze Colonia del Sacramento so as to remove the cause of

[1] See Azara, *Estado rural*, introduction by J. C. González.

any future Portuguese incursion. The growing country lost its best town – a sizeable one, elegant for the place and period, containing some 2,600 inhabitants – and a strong fortress. The true emporium of River Plate trade was thus destroyed,[1] to the joy, no doubt, of the rival merchants of Buenos Aires.

The upshot was that the immediate Portuguese threat was removed, and Buenos Aires became supreme in the Plate, while Montevideo became the one town of any importance in the Banda Oriental. A similar commercial rivalry was soon to arise between these two cities, owing to Montevideo's better port facilities and hinterland rich in cattle and to Buenos Aires' jealous hold over the Banda Oriental. Even with the checkmate of the Portuguese, the merchants of Buenos Aires did not achieve peace of mind.

3. MONTEVIDEO

CIVILISATION spread slowly through the Banda Oriental. Till after the middle of the eighteenth century the only towns were on the coast: Soriano, Colonia, Montevideo, Maldonado, with the villages Las Víboras and Espinillo. Then as people gradually accumulated at convenient points in the interior, spreading out from the coastal centres, by 1810 some thirteen small towns had been established in the interior, together with three frontier fortresses in the north, facing Brazil.[2] Yet the entire population was still small by the turn of the century – perhaps something over forty thousand, of whom about fifteen thousand lived in the city of Montevideo.[3] Life even there was primitive to begin with, for the city lived as a farming community locked up in a fortress. The early settlers had house plots within the walls, and small farms and

[1] Blanco Acevedo, *op. cit.* p. 32, and Bauzá, *op. cit.* vol. I, p. 320.

[2] Azara, *Voyages*, vol. II, facing page 328. See also Blanco Acevedo, *op. cit.* p. 37.

[3] Azara, *ibid.* gives a list of all the towns and villages in the province of Buenos Aires (which included the Banda Oriental) and their populations. From this the population of the Banda Oriental can be roughly worked out at about 35,000 to 40,000; but this takes no account of the less settled people, who must have amounted to a considerable number; therefore I take the higher figure as being more reasonable.

larger cattle estancias were allotted to them in the surrounding country.[1] Besides, the city was immediately surrounded by its common pastures and public lands to be leased to raise public revenue. All the organisation was carried out according to the Laws of the Indies dealing with colonisation. Naturally the new settlement was poor at first, and people tried to raise a little ready money by selling hard biscuit to the local garrison. Later, commerce developed, though always subordinated to the need for maintaining the supremacy of Buenos Aires. Many families began as small farmers and ranchers, and increased their fortunes during the century by gaining large grants of cattle-range in the interior. The sons would take grants further inland, and so the city helped to settle the country.[2]

At first there had been room inside the walls for gardens, but by the end of the century the space was taken up by houses, and more were built outside the walls. The streets were on the familiar Spanish colonial gridiron plan, and were unpaved owing to lack of public funds and of public spirit. An English visitor in 1799 remarked that the streets of Montevideo were 'by far the worst for travelling that imagination can conceive, for being compounded of rock-stones and sand, the large cavities make it very disagreeable for man and beast, especially in rainy weather'; and 'to fill up a hole they have killed one of the team [of horses drawing a cart] to assist the wheel in passing over'.[3]

Public works developed late in Spanish America because of the citizens' unwillingness to tax themselves for the public good. Sanitation was incredibly bad. In 1783 the *Síndico Procurador* (public proctor) of the Cabildo had to complain of the danger to public

[1] A farm lot (*chacra*) was about 200 to 400 yards by 3 miles, and an estancia 3,000 yards by four and a half miles. Blanco Acevedo, *op. cit.* p. 40.

[2] Arredondo, *op. cit.* pp. 61-3.

[3] Rev. W. Gregory, *Visible display of Divine Providence*, pp. 171-2. In 1783 the Governor had complained to the Cabildo that the streets were 'absolutely impassable', and had urged them to consider ways and means of paving them. The Cabildo replied that the citizens were too poor to bear the whole cost and that the King (i.e., his local representative) should help by providing labour. Nothing was done. (Arch. Adm., caja 126; 6; 13 and 14).

health of the number of burials of negroes who died aboard the slave ships in the port. The cemetery of the main church was used for this, and it was now so full that the fetid smell it gave out made people fear for their health. The danger was increased by the filth of the main square, which resembled a dung-heap, since rotting stuff of all kinds was thrown there – vegetables and meat, hides and hooves. The man who was supposed to clean the square did nothing but draw his pay. The *Síndico* also described the streets, which were equally filthy with garbage, especially where a vacant plot could be used as a dumping-place. Children who had fallen into the noisome morasses on these plots had been drowned, and the whole city was daily becoming more unhealthy. The reason for these complaints was the temporary presence in Montevideo of the Viceroy of the River Plate and his court: these people had been disgusted at the state of the city, and but for this visit probably no complaint would have been made public. As a result of the publicity a number of such scandals was ventilated and some action was taken.[1] By 1787 street crossings were paved, and water was drained off the streets by gutters running towards the river.[2]

Little permanent good was done, for in 1800 the Governor called a conference of the five medical men in the city, to determine the causes of the frequency of epidemics. The doctors unanimously declared that one of the main causes was the swampy filth of the streets and vacant plots of the city, whose pestilent stench polluted the atmosphere. The harm would be irremediable unless the place were cleansed, especially as the population was increasing. However, no extraordinary measures were taken, even

[1] Report of *Síndico Procurador General* to Cabildo, 14 Jan., 1783, in Arch. Adm., caja 126; 6; 4; also *ibid.* doc. no. 6, a complaint from a citizen to the *Síndico*, d. 18 Jan. 1783. This man complained of a vacant plot next to his house which overflowed its contents onto the whole street, and was full of garbage, dead cats and dogs, rotting meat, hides, etc. One distracted housewife also complained that the Cabildo itself had neglected its earth privy so badly that its contents had burst through the wall between the Town Hall and her house and flooded her kitchen. It was nearly a year before anything was done to remedy this situation. (*Ibid.* caja 141; 5; 16).

[2] Blanco Acevedo, *op. cit.* p. 49.

though a report was sent to the Viceroy.[1] J. P. Robertson, as late as 1807, found the streets at night 'infested with voracious rats', since there was no public cleansing department, and the heaps of filth in the streets, carried off occasionally by rain water, attracted legions of rats which were so fierce and large that they often chased the Scottish merchant down the streets.[2] It was not only the people of the country districts who were ignorant of the advantages of cleanliness.

The houses were unimpressive, even up to the third decade of the nineteenth century. Few had more than one storey then, and the majority were built in the Spanish colonial style: flat roofed, round an interior patio, with rooms opening into each other, and with large and solid outside doors. The outside walls were generally plain, whitewashed, with windows guarded by heavy iron grilles. The interiors were not very comfortable, since floors were of brick or earth, and ceilings showed the rough beams of the roof. The furniture was solid, even massive, built of imperishable Paraguayan woods. Heating, necessary for comfort in winter, was provided by the Spanish charcoal brazier, and was probably not adequate. Foreign travellers' descriptions make the houses sound cheerless, though no doubt the local society did not find them so.[3] The Montevideans were fond of parties with dancing and singing to the guitar, and were hospitable to strangers.[4]

In fine, the dominating architectural note was military, and it was supplied by the citadel and the defensive walls. Montevideo was a strong point, the key to the Plate, and so was first and foremost a garrison city, a defence particularly against the Portuguese. The fortifications were the strongest in the whole Viceroyalty,[5] and even, with the possible exception of those of Cartagena, in the whole of South America.

[1] Arch. Adm., caja 243; 2; 57.

[2] J. P. and W. P. Robertson, *op. cit.* vol. I, pp. 107-8.

[3] Blanco Acevedo, *op. cit.* pp. 50-2. Also J. E. Pivel Devoto, *Raíces coloniales de la revolución de 1811*, pp. 97-8.

[4] J. P. and W. P. Robertson, *op. cit.* vol. I, pp. 104-7.

[5] Blanco Acevedo, *op. cit.* p. 53.

Montevideo's importance as the main administrative centre in the Banda Oriental began in 1749 with the appointment of the first Governor of the city and its district. Before this, there had been considerable conflict of authority between the civil power, the Cabildo, and the military commander of the forces. This problem was solved by making the new Governor both military and civil chief. But the supreme authority, now as before, was the Governor of Buenos Aires, and the orders which came from him tended to depress the importance of Montevideo and increase that of Buenos Aires. Even after the creation of the Viceroyalty and the establishment, in 1783, of the Intendant system copied from the famous and successful French local government (reforms meant by Charles III of Spain to improve administration), the Governor of Montevideo remained under the authority of the Viceroy, and no intendant was appointed to the Banda Oriental.[1] The constant aim was apparently to avoid the creation of a separate administrative unit in the Banda Oriental, and so to keep the district under the control of Buenos Aires. This arrangement naturally upset the people of the Banda Oriental, particularly since it had an adverse effect on their prosperity.

Montevideo could not help becoming the capital city of the Banda Oriental, since the territory formed a natural division of the Spanish Empire. Also, even the early Cabildo had exercised administration over a vaguely defined district allotted to it. For instance, what order there was emanated from the Cabildo, which was also the local minor law-court. The Cabildo it was which forbade gambling, persecuted vagabonds and Portuguese and other foreigners, organised the cattle industry, kept the streets empty and respectable at night, took measures against cattle-rustlers and men who caused public danger by burning over the prairies before the right season of the year. And it was the Cabildo which punished these and other offences according to the law.[2] The country was

---

[1] Blanco Acevedo, *op. cit.* chap. VII.

[2] Eg. *Bandos de Buen Gobierno* of the Cabildo in Arch. Adm., 19 Jan. 1735, caja 1;15;1; 17 Jan. 1739, 1; 24; 1; 11 Nov. 1742, 1; 36; 2; 10 Jan. 1751, 2; 29; 1; etc., etc.; and *Bando* of 28 Jan. 1747, 2; 8; 1.

mainly colonised by families spreading from Montevideo, and the majority of trade flowed through it too.

Trade was vital to the bourgeois of Montevideo, though less so to the self-supporting people of the country districts. The citizens, especially the Cabildo, did everything possible to protect and encourage the country's economic resources, and often came into conflict with the men of Buenos Aires as a result. Consequently much bad feeling was created, which helped to exacerbate the anger felt in Montevideo at what was though to be the selfish oppression imposed by Buenos Aires. The Cabildo made orders forbidding excessive killings of cattle, especially of cows with calves, since even in the early eighteenth century it was feared that the cattle population was decreasing owing to indiscriminate slaughtering for hides. Cattle and horse rustlers, especially Portuguese, and also Spanish renegades driving stolen herds into Brazil, were opposed with what slight means the city possessed.[1]

This in itself suited the policy of Buenos Aires too, and her Governor in 1747 urged the Cabildo of Montevideo to take more efficacious steps, organising the estancieros in parties to scour the country and eliminate the rustlers. Therefore, with what at first sight appears to be a reversal of the usual policy, the people of the Banda Oriental were encouraged to look after their personal interests and not to expect help from the government; but it was no reversal, for the Orientals were simply being urged to defend the interests of Buenos Aires merchants at the same time as their own. The Governor reminded them that 'none is more obliged to guard his herds than the owner himself', but this did not prevent the royal authorities both of Buenos Aires and of Montevideo from giving what help they could spare to protect the cattle, and from admonishing and urging the people to greater efforts. It seemed a real danger that unrestricted killing of cattle would wipe out the Banda Oriental's only, and Buenos Aires' richest, source of wealth.[2]

[1] *Ibid.* Also *Autos contra unos ladrones de Cavallos, ibid.* caja 2; 7A; 1.
[2] *Ibid.* caja 45; 3; 2 (1775); 118; 3; 5 and 16 (1782); 118; 3; 24 (1782).

The Environment

In 1785, indeed, the Governor of Montevideo had to order that in future no-one should make boots of the skin of the legs of cows or calves, but only of mares. Any boots made of the forbidden leather were to be sent to Montevideo from all parts of the district and burned by the public executioner.[1] However, the authorities' efforts were always nullified by the lack of troops to use as police.[2] For this reason, the Viceroy himself in 1778 created a special force of twenty-four men and three officers, to supervise the cattle industry in the Banda Oriental and stop all 'exportation, slaughtering and flaying of all cattle by all persons of whatever condition and rank without licence from this superior Government. . . .'[3]

Sea-borne contraband, welcome enough to the ordinary people on both banks of the Plate, met the united opposition of established Spanish merchants and governors. Again, it was the Portuguese who were mainly culpable, and although many smugglers were caught and punished, many more must have evaded the thin screen of coastguards or bribed their way in.[4] Brazilian tobacco and sugar-cane spirit were favourite smuggling goods. English smugglers, as heretics and special enemies of Spain and allies of Portugal, were particularly obnoxious to the authorities. Visits by English ships were always treated with the utmost suspicion, and no goods were allowed to be unloaded from them on whatever pretext.[5] The ordinary folk of Montevideo, however, were glad to profit by the smuggling and to buy luxuries which had not paid the heavy Spanish taxes.[6]

Legitimate trade became quite prosperous, especially after the reform in Spanish colonial trade established in 1778 by Charles III. By his so-called 'Regulations for Free Trade' a considerable improvement in conditions of trade was permitted, and in particular

[1] *Ibid.* caja 140; 2; 1 (1785).
[2] *Ibid.* caja 64; 4; 38 (1777).
[3] *Ibid.* caja 79; 2; 1.
[4] *Ibid.* caja 25; 6; 43; 45; 4; 1 (1775); and 51; 5; 14 and 16 (1776).
[5] *Ibid.* caja 79; 6; 5 and 7 (1778); 156; 4; 48, 50, 52, 53 and 55; 162; 5; 6; 169; 4; 81 (1787-1789).
[6] *Ibid.* caja 51; 5; 16.

the Plate benefited by being at last allowed full use of its ports in trading with Spain.[1] Both Buenos Aires and Montevideo became busy emporiums. Montevideo was suddenly endowed with a customs house and local branches of the Royal Treasury and the Accountancy Department, and it seemed a foregone conclusion that most ships from Spain would sail to Montevideo and that their cargoes would be transhipped there for Buenos Aires or other Argentine ports. As Montevideo moved more swiftly towards self-sufficiency, inevitably Buenos Aires strove to retain and enforce her grasp.[2]

Montevideo had long had a local trade in products such as stone, wood, sand, fruits and vegetables, mainly with Buenos Aires. From the middle of the eighteenth century, too, Spanish register ships had taken some of the cattle products across the ocean. After 1778, however, trade became prosperous, and with it the city itself grew rapidly. For example, on one day in 1781, 25 ships sailed from Montevideo carrying 432,000 hides.[3] Trade in other articles flourished as Montevideo became an entrepôt on the route to Peru: vicuña wool, chinchilla furs, copper, cacao, wool and coinage were exported together with local pastoral products, animal skins, and seal furs and whalebone from local and Patagonian fishing-grounds.[4]

A new industry, preparing salt meat, grew up with the opening of the port.[5] This industry, the basis of the first great export trade of the Plate countries, was started on a big scale by one Francisco de Medina in the Banda Oriental in 1786. He had made a fortune as a purveyor to the Spanish expedition against the Portuguese in 1777, and to increase it went into whale fishing off the Patagonian coast, using skilled English fishers. This was forbidden by the

[1] See Haring, *op. cit.* chap. XVII; and especially *Reglamento y aranceles reales para el comercio libre de España a Indias*, in *Docs. para la historia argentina*, t. VI, pp. 3-132, and Introducción by R. Levene.

[2] Blanco Acevedo, *op. cit.* pp. 69-71; Pivel Devoto, *op. cit.* pp. 100-3.

[3] Pivel Devoto, *op. cit.* pp. 98-9, 104-5; Blanco Acevedo, *op cit.* pp. 105-6.

[4] Pivel Devoto, *op. cit.* pp. 106-7. Also list given in Gregory, *op. cit.* pp. 173-4.

[5] Blanco Acevedo, *op. cit.* pp. 106-7; Bauzá, *op. cit.* vol. I, pp. 336-7.

Viceroy, so Medina established a big *saladero* (meat salting establishment) at Colla, near Colonia, bred his own pigs and collected stock of over 30,000 cattle. He used salting methods he had seen the English whalers use. His aim was to get a government contract to supply the Spanish navy, whose local headquarters was at Montevideo. Just as his enterprise was beginning to progress he died, and the establishment was allowed to go to ruin. However, other landowners followed his example, and the industry enjoyed a moderate prosperity. Dried meat became in the 1780s a staple export from Montevideo to Havana in Cuba, where it was used to feed the slaves, and Montevideo received sugar and spirits in return. Tallow and flour were sent to the same destination. The trade was encouraged by the government, which levied no export tax on meat, and in turn it encouraged stock-raisers to increase their herds and the quality of the cattle. This type of inter-Spanish colonial trade was itself a new departure from the old system, and the prosperity it brought in this single example illustrates the success of the Bourbon reforms. Now, also, for the first time meat was of some economic importance in the Plate, whereas before only the quality of the hides had counted, since these alone were exported. The price of cattle rose, and general well-being in the region increased: even the population increased since the industry needed labour. Between 1785, when this trade began, and 1793, 41 ship-loads totalling 138,815 quintals of a hundred pounds each of dried meat had been exported from Montevideo to Havana. It was recognised that this trade, if continued, would soon make the Banda Oriental wealthy.[1]

Unfortunately, at the end of the century, all the Spanish American trade was too often cut off because of the wars in which Spain sided with France against Britain, whose fleet controlled the Atlantic. The state of affairs in 1799 was described by the missionary Gregory, whose ship had been captured by French corsairs and taken to the allied port of Montevideo: 'No ships come regu-

---

[1] Arch. Adm., caja 209; 2; 70, *Expediente* on dried meat trade with Cuba.

larly to this port, and only three or four make an annual voyage to Europe, and during the war even this small number has decreased. Cloathing of every description, and articles of household utensils are excessively dear, and though the houses are uncomfortable in many respects the rent is high. Notwithstanding the cargo of the Duff [the missionaries' ship] was prohibited to be sold, the town was never so plentifully supplied by any ship, nor so well stocked with those necessaries which the inhabitants so much wanted. Most articles of apparel was of four times more value than in England, and even higher. Having lost my tea-kettle, I enquired the price of two which held about two quarts, one with, and the other without a lid: six dollars was the price of the one, three and a half of the other. The rent of a room without window or fire-place, was forty-eight dollars, and one hundred per annum for an house, consisting of two rooms and a yard; four flat-irons twelve, and one ounce of pins in English money three shillings and six-pence'.[1]

But even so, Montevideo was better off at the end of the century than ever before: the landowners and merchants grew rich, life became more luxurious and civilised, even though smuggling was in large measure responsible for the improvement; and even the negro slaves were able to demand high rates of pay.[2] When war cut off legitimate trade, some foreign ships took advantage of Spanish orders of 1795 and 1797 allowing some trade between Spanish American and foreign ports, and in this way, as well as through smuggling and the selling of captured prizes, Montevideo was supplied to some degree with manufactured goods in ex-change for her cattle products and other exports.[3]

[1] Gregory, *op. cit.* pp. 173-4.

[2] Blanco Acevedo, *op. cit.* pp. 107-10; Pivel Devoto, *op. cit.* pp. 105-10.

[3] Eg. Arch. Adm., caja 228; 4; 37, concerning captured English goods; and 243; 3; 35, 42 and 44, concerning five United States merchant ships in the port.

4. THE FEELING BETWEEN MONTEVIDEO
    AND BUENOS AIRES

It has been stressed that Montevideo's interests were normally subordinated to those of the viceregal capital; but nowhere was this
more evident, or more galling to the people of Montevideo, than
in the question of trade. Montevideo's situation, to sum up, was
that she was the only natural port in the Plate, and was the first
port of call for ships coming from Europe, and so after Colonia's
demise seemed due to become a rival emporium to Buenos Aires,
with a good chance of taking over the leadership as a port. But
Buenos Aires was the capital, and besides the institutions of government, she had the majority of the merchants connected with
European trade. An economic conflict was bound to come when
Montevideo became dangerously prosperous. The increased use of
Montevideo as a trading centre seemed to mean a necessary decline of Buenos Aires in the same function, because both ports
served the same hinterland, which was in effect not much more
than the province of Buenos Aires, since the interior of the Viceroyalty still traded more naturally with Chile and Peru; and the
Banda Oriental was in natural resources the richest part of the
Plate hinterland.

Spain herself seemed to encourage the growth of Montevideo as
a port rather than Buenos Aires. This was only common sense,
since Montevideo was a reasonable harbour and Buenos Aires was
not. For instance, in 1770 Montevideo, and not Buenos Aires, was
made the terminal for Spanish mails to southern South America;
from 1776 all ships sailing from Spain to Peru had to call at Montevideo for possible orders and for inspection of their cargo lists. In
1779 customs were established at Montevideo. Two orders of 1779
and 1781 created a coastguard authority, with headquarters at
Montevideo, for all the Atlantic coast of the Viceroyalty. Montevideo's importance and prosperity and Buenos Aires' jealousy
were further increased when in 1797 the former was made the

34

only port of entry for negro slaves for the Viceroyalty and for Chile and Peru – a rich prize for this upstart port.[1]

Rightly or wrongly, the people of Montevideo had for long, even before the new prosperity, opposed economic direction from the authorities in Buenos Aires, in the same spirit as they had opposed their own early governors. These people had developed a sense of independence, very largely owing to their pioneering origins and their sense of the importance of their city as the military key to the Plate.[2] This sturdy independence – very Spanish – extended to matters of political government. Montevideo protested whenever she felt her due rights were being attacked by the superior authority in Buenos Aires.[3] None of these protests, of course, foreshadowed revolt against Spanish rule: they were rather expressions of localist feeling so common in the Spanish world, and so fatal to its unity. They did, however, weaken Spanish authority in the Plate, and helped to bring the welter of ill-feeing and administrative chaos which both complicated and helped on the revolutionary movement in the Plate in the early years of the next century.

The establishment by Royal Order of a Consulado (merchants' guild) in Buenos Aires in 1794 brought the economic rivalry between the two cities to a head. The Buenos Aires merchants who formed the body of the Consulado insisted on doing everything possible to damage Montevideo's trade and increase their own, or that is what it seemed to the people of Montevideo. Although at first the Consulado appeared to be trying to help Montevideo,

---

[1] Blanco Acevedo, *op. cit.* chap. xii. Pivel Devoto, *op. cit.* pp. 112-14 gives details of the controversy over the introduction of slaves.

[2] E.g. Arch. Adm., caja 10; 1B; 1, *expediente* on the proposed cancellation of the application of the *alcabala* (sales tax) in Montevideo, 1762. The Cabildo of Montevideo protested against a measure instituted by the royal treasury officers of Buenos Aires to apply the *alcabala* to Montevideo. The Cabildo claimed that this tax had been specifically remitted by the Crown at the foundation of the city, so as to encourage the pioneers; also Montevideo was 'la llabe, o la puerta, que deve Zerrar la entrada alos enemigos en Ql Qra acontecimto,' and the people deserved to be well treated for the sake of their loyalty.

[3] Eg. Arch. Adm., caja 118; 3; ?, letter of the governor to the Cabildo of Montevideo, 12 Aug. 1782.

asking its deputy in that city for suggestions on the improvement of the port and its approaches, by the end of 1795 its tone was hostile. It forbade its deputy to let the merchants of Montevideo meet and decide on their own commercial affairs, since this was the prerogative of the parent body. Obviously, any sign of independence in the Montevideo merchants was to be crushed;[1] and in fact the Consulado ended by doing nothing for Montevideo. Trade organisation in Montevideo was to be kept as simple (not to say mean) as possible. On the 17th of March 1796 the Consulado gave its Montevideo deputy a list of the establishment he was allowed. He could have in his office one table, two chairs (one for himself and one for his clerk), and two extra chairs for additional judges in complicated commercial cases. There was to be no lavishness, no *asesor* (legal assistant), no salaries for clerks, scriveners, or servants apart from one clerk and one scrivener when needed.

To effect positive harm to Montevideo was the tendency, if not the intention, of most moves of the Buenos Aires Consulado. In 1797 the Consulado petitioned the King to cancel his decree of the 4th of March 1795 allowing the exportation from the Empire to foreign colonies of any surplus local products not taken off by the trade with Spain; and similar action was taken against a kindred order of 1797 allowing the same sort of trade with neutral nations. The decrees were liberal, and Montevideo profited from them since she produced a great surplus of pastoral products, which had been unsaleable within the Empire. But the Consulado, composed of merchants established in the monopoly trade with Spain, argued, for example, that the measure of 1795 was against the spirit of the laws (which was only too true), would decrease the sale of Spanish goods because of the foreign goods imported in exchange, would encourage contraband because foreign ships would have a legal pretext to be in Spanish waters, and would in general help foreigners and harm the Spanish Empire.

The Montevideo Cabildo counter-petitioned for the orders to be

[1] M.H.N., carpeta I, 1794-1797.

kept in effect (as in fact they were), especially because the prosperity and increased population brought by the increased trade would ensure that Montevideo and its district would be a strong bulwark against Portuguese aggression. There was much truth in this: it was largely because the Banda Oriental was wild, underpopulated and unexploited that the Portuguese had been able to advance and were to do so again in the future. The Cabildo refused to believe that smuggling would increase, since hides would be too bulky to be exported clandestinely, or that Spain's industries would be hurt, since she would be able to concentrate on the lines she produced best instead of trying to supply everything. Also, since profit depends on greater numbers of inhabitants consuming greater quantities of goods, Spain would profit if she saw to it that the Banda Oriental's population increased and became more prosperous, as these orders were ensuring. The men of Montevideo were up-to-date with their political economy, though perhaps a little disingenuous over the absence of the possibility of more smuggling. They were deeply involved in smuggling anyway, and would view more opportunities with pleasure. The Consulado had had occasion before to censure Montevideo for smuggling so much.[1] A basic point had been touched, however: the monopolists of the old Spanish system, rooted in Buenos Aires, believed in selling little, but gaining a large profit from each article sold. It was safer that way. The merchants of Montevideo were looking forward to a new era in their wish for a large turnover with perhaps not so large a profit on each article.

The irony of this situation is that just over a decade later the creole merchants and landowners of Buenos Aires were themselves calling for concessions in trade which would end the Spanish monopoly. They were opposed by the same class of Spanish merchants who were now opposing a limited freedom for Montevideo. Yet at the later date Montevideo was to be ultra-loyal to

---

[1] Arch. Adm., caja 221; 2; 73, *expediente* on the export of the products of the country, 1797; M.H.N., *loc. cit.;* Pivel Devoto, *op. cit.* pp. 114-19.

Spain, and Buenos Aires was on the way to revolution. What had happened by then to turn Montevideo from the same path was that she had gained her wish, of which this struggle is the symbol, to be independent of Buenos Aires; in fact, by 1808 she had become the mainstay of Spanish authority in the Plate, owing to a series of incidents which will be mentioned in due course. But the countryside of the Banda Oriental was to split off from Montevideo and go over to the revolutionary side, as will also be explained later.[1]

The commercial rivalry between the two cities, however, came to a head over the question of the port of Montevideo, which was undeniably the 'principal key to Peru and this Province', as the Consulado's deputy in Montevideo wrote in 1799. Yet the Consulado did nothing to improve the port, so that in this year two warships, six merchant ships, two naval launches and over sixty launches and boats were driven ashore in the port by a storm. The Consulado should have had life-boats and other auxiliary vessels built and stationed in such an important port in case of such calamities, but it had done nothing: there were not even spare cables and anchors or a completed mole for boats to come alongside in safety.[2] This neglect must have seemed like a deliberate attempt to give the port of Montevideo a bad name among seamen.

The Consulado concentrated on improvements on its own side of the river, even decreeing in 1799 the establishment of a school of navigation in Buenos Aires.[3] But the measure which really upset Montevideo was one of 1801, a decree of the Viceroy's ordering the little uninhabited 'port' of Ensenada de Barragán, some twelve leagues down-stream from Buenos Aires, to be opened as an

[1] In the *expediente* in Arch. Adm., caja 221; 2; 73, *cit.* a report of *Síndico Procurador* of the Cabildo of Montevideo shows that the city's merchants were well satisfied with Spanish rule now that the trade reforms of the last quarter century had opened their port and brought them prosperity. They were, however, very critical of the old trade system and strongly opposed to anything like a return to it, as was suggested by the Consulado.

[2] M.H.N., *loc. cit.*, letter of the deputy to the Consulado, d. 24 September, 1799.

[3] *Ibid.*, *carpeta* 11, 1798-1805, edict of the Consulado, 6th April, 1799.

international port, including the building of a new town there, 'because of its situation preferable to that of all the other' ports, and at the petition of the sinister Consulado.[1]

The Cabildo of Montevideo had a year before protested without result to the King against the Consulado's scheme, which would naturally damage Montevideo's economic interests.[2] Their case was publicised in the new Buenos Aires journal, the *Telégrafo Mercantil*, by a correspondent who attacked Buenos Aires and Ensenada as impossible ports for big ships because of their shallowness and treacherous sandbanks. Ensenada, even when built, would hold only sixty ships, which would still be exposed. The port would be distant from Buenos Aires, and the roads were bad. Another correspondent defended the Consulado's action on the grounds that the capital needed to have a port nearer than Montevideo (some two hundred miles away), and that transhipment into launches at Montevideo for the crossing to Buenos Aires was stupid and costly. Also, to have one port alone open to international trade gave that port a monopoly, which was harmful to the merchants and consumers of the rest of the Viceroyalty, who were dependent on it.[3]

Again in 1802 the Cabildo protested, using reasonable arguments. Montevideo again showed her consciousness of her vital problem by pointing out that her prosperity and population should be encouraged by all means so as to provide the necessary bulwark against the Portuguese. It was stressed that since the opening of the port, twenty-five years before, much of the hinterland had been made into cattle-ranches, and the city had filled to overflowing. These remarks were added to the testimony of an expert witness: the naval commander of the Montevideo station, who declared that Montevideo was a better harbour than Ensenada; and it was also alleged that all owners of ships sent them for safety

[1] *Ibid.*, letter of the Consulado to the deputy in Montevideo, 21st April, 1801.

[2] Arch. Adm., caja 243; 2; 7, letter of Echevarría to the Cabildo, d. Madrid, 8th Feb. 1800; and 243; 2; 15, letter *id.* to *id.*, 9th April 1800.

[3] Blanco Acevedo, *op. cit.* pp. 124-7.

to Montevideo, not elsewhere in the Plate: 'no ship-owner who is not a citizen of Buenos Aires sends his ship to Ensenada'.[1]

Both sides were right in some ways, and were conscious of their rectitude; and, as is so often the case, each could see only malice and selfishness in the other side. The harm was that the publicity which the argument received made it an affair between the peoples of the two cities. The Governors of Montevideo consistently supported the claims of the city's Cabildo, so that about the turn of the century the rivalry between the two cities became almost an official matter.[2] It was this support by the Governors which kept Montevideo loyal to Spain when Buenos Aires was slipping towards revolution.

In 1802 feeling in Montevideo was so high that the Cabildo gathered evidence and opinions to support a petition to the King for the establishment of a Montevideo body to regulate commerce separate from the Buenos Aires Consulado.[3] As early as 1794, when the creation of the Consulado was in the air, the merchants of Montevideo had met and declared their trade to be distinct from that of Buenos Aires, demanding their own organisation to look after their own interests.[4] Events had proved them right, and now all the Consulado's omissions and iniquities were paraded: the eight years' neglect of Montevideo's port and its safety, and of the district's resources and industries; the inadequacy of the landing facilities, which were all that the merchants of Montevideo could afford, and for which the Consulado had given no funds at all in spite of the *avería* tax it levied on goods entering Montevideo, the product of which should have been applied to works of public utility in the port of Montevideo as well as in that of Buenos Aires. The Montevideo merchants had constantly complained, fruitlessly, about this imposition. Not even cranes had been provided, and all the loading and unloading of ships was done by

[1] Arch. Adm., caja 260; 2; 2, report of the Cabildo to the Viceroy, d. 25th Jan. 1802.
[2] Blanco Acevedo, *op. cit.* pp. 127-8.
[3] Arch. Adm., libro 150, *expendiente* of the Cabildo d. 1802; and *ibid.*, caja 261; 3; 63.
[4] Pivel Devoto, *op. cit.* pp. 121-3.

hand. But if Montevideo were allowed to keep her own *avería* money for her own use, the necessary improvements could and would be made. Various officials, including the captain of the port, testified to the excellence of Montevideo as a harbour, and to its need for maintenance and improvement.

The petition was turned down in 1803, although the merchants of Montevideo did win the right they had exercised in this affair: that of meeting formally in their own Junta. The Consulado, fearing that its powers were in this way restricted, had protested about such meetings, but in 1804 Spain decreed that they were legal.[1] So a first measure of independence from Buenos Aires was won by Montevideo: a first move in the direction which within a few years was to lead to complete independence from both the old viceregal capital and the metropolis itself. Meanwhile the prosperity of Montevideo and her district continued and increased.

Not only in trade, but even in government Montevideo's aspirations to fend for herself became stronger about the beginning of the new century. Indeed, claims for administrative independence from the rival city were the natural consequence of the reality of the economic rivalry between them. The situation foreshadowed with uncanny accuracy, although on a smaller scale, the future emancipation of the Plate from Spain.

Montevideo had never been allowed to extend her jurisdiction over the whole of the Banda Oriental: she was kept in the position of a subordinate town. In 1726 Montevideo was given for the limits of her territory the River Plate from the Arroyo Cufré to the Sierras de Maldonado; on the east the Cerro Pan de Azúcar and the River Cebollatí; and on the north the Cuchilla Grande: in all, about a quarter of the Republic's present area. The estancias between the Rivers Negro and Uruguay and the Arroyo Tacuarembó belonged to the jurisdiction of the Misiones town of Yapeyú, itself under the authority of Buenos Aires; and all the rest of the Banda Oriental came directly within the jurisdiction of

[1] Blanco Acevedo, *op. cit.* pp. 131-2.

Buenos Aires.[1] No geographical, climatic or economic differences
made these divisions natural: indeed, all these factors tended to
unite the Banda Oriental around Montevideo. Therefore the
settlers from Montevideo pressed on into the interior, settling new
estancias and spilling into the other jurisdictions; while the people
at home tried to have the city's territory extended to match her
activity and the energy of her sons. But nothing came of the
attempts.

Even the installation of the Viceroyalty and of the Intendant
system in the Plate had not changed Montevideo's situation. The
city's jurisdiction was still much restricted, and the Banda Oriental
was still divided into three when all the dangers of the proximity
of the Portuguese and all the conveniences of united command
demanded the establishment of a single government for all the
Banda Oriental in Montevideo. Because of these reasons the Viceroy in 1784 had in fact extended the military command of the
Governor of Montevideo to include the port of Maldonado and
the frontier forts of Santa Teresa and Santa Tecla. The Governor
himself, the next year, asked for the whole jurisdiction to be extended to Colonia and Castillos, that is from opposite Buenos
Aires to the point on the Atlantic coast where the Banda Oriental
and Brazil met; and he asked for this area to be made an Intendancy. This proposal was rejected in Madrid because it was felt
there that the Banda Oriental was not important enough to merit
promotion to an Intendancy, and this was perhaps true as far as
the number of inhabitants was concerned. Yet the whole development of the Plate region for the next fifty years was one long proof
that the Spanish government had been mistaken in failing to
recognise the importance of the Banda Oriental as the key to the
south of the continent. However, in 1788, because of the special
circumstances uniting all the Spanish territory east of the Uruguay,
it was found necessary to extend to all of it the jurisdiction of the
Governor of Montevideo in his capacity as Subdelegate of the

---

[1] Pivel Devoto, *op. cit.* p. 131.

Royal Treasury.[1] Geographical, climatic, economic and military facts were beginning to be dimly recognised. The first step towards an autonomous Uruguay had now been taken.

The problem of unification of administration became urgent as the No-man's-land between the Rivers Yí and Negro (that is, the gap left between the limits of the jurisdictions of Montevideo and Yapeyú) was occupied. By 1797 over two hundred men had established estancias there, and were living without justice, law and order. Therefore Montevideo decided to petition the King again for wider limits, and this time asked for almost all of what is now Uruguay, except for the part administered from Yapeyú. The Uruguayan historian Pivel Devoto has pointed out that this move, coming at the same time as Montevideo's economic revolt against Buenos Aires and the Consulado and also an attempt to make the Church in the Banda Oriental independent of the See of Buenos Aires, shows that Montevideo was ripe for autonomy.[2] Probably few, even in Montevideo, thought clearly on these lines; but the forces driving the rival cities further apart soon became irresistible.

[1] Pivel Devoto, *op. cit.* pp. 133-40.
[2] *Ibid.* pp. 140-4.

CHAPTER II

THE ARTIGAS STOCK

I. A PIONEER FAMILY

I T W A S the obscure army captain José Gervasio Artigas who eventually brought Montevideo and the Banda Oriental together to seek independence of both Spain and Buenos Aires. His family had distinguished itself in the service of Montevideo since the very foundation of the city, so that Artigas was born a member of the directing class. His grandfather Juan Antonio Artigas, a native of Zaragoza in Aragón, had fought for Philip v in the Spanish War of Succession, enlisting at the age of sixteen in a cavalry regiment. Although the eldest son of his father, this young man abandoned a comfortable heritage consisting of a farm at Albortón and a house in Zaragoza, and in 1717 embarked as a reinforcement for the garrison of Buenos Aires, seeking a fortune in the Indies as had many Spaniards for over two hundred years. He soon married the daughter of Captain Salvador Carrasco, twenty-four of whose relatives, including this Artigas and his wife and their four small daughters, figure in the list of thirty-four members of the first six families to settle in Montevideo in 1726. The running of Montevideo was a family affair from the start. If young Artigas was adventurous, how much more so was his wife, setting up house for her tender family on a bare, windswept peninsula, close to Indian and Portuguese enemies, and with none of the comforts of civilisation.

Juan Antonio Artigas was ennobled by the act of becoming an original settler of a new colonial town, as the Laws of the Indies provided in Ley 6, Título 6, Libro 4. He became an *hijodalgo de solar conocido* (one of the landed gentry), and like the other settlers, he was at once allotted a house plot on the very bank of the River Plate. A few months later, farm plots close at hand were allocated by the viceregal delegate, and Juan Antonio was given his farm of four hundred yards by one league. In 1728, when the cattle ranches were allotted, further away from Montevideo, one of three thousand yards by one and a half leagues was given to Captain Artigas, as he was by now (he was captain of the local militia) on the banks of the Arroyo de Pando. The same year another farm plot was granted to Artigas, now *Alcalde de la Santa Hermandad*, or chief officer of police in the rural jurisdiction of the new city – a sort of sheriff.

Thus arduous duties came to Artigas at the same time as the merited privileges of the frontier colonist, and the relative affluence of a farmer and rancher in a primitive country. At various times Juan Antonio held office in the Cabildo and exercised other police powers, spending his time scouring the wild interior in order to pacify, in the true sense of the word, hostile Indians, or to wipe out Spanish and Portuguese bandits and rustlers. He also took part in set raids against the Portuguese: he even went on a campaign near the Brazilian frontier in 1762, when he was sixty-nine or seventy years old. As a reward for his services, the patriarch was granted in 1768 another ranch, on the Arroyo de Casupá. He lived, with his numerous descendants about him, until 1775; and he was in his time one of the leaders of the struggling new community.

Juan Antonio's public spirit, activity and courage passed down to his son Martín José, father of the revolutionary leader José Gervasio. Young José himself, born in 1764 in Montevideo,[1] benefited from the teachings and reminiscences and above all the honourable fame of his grandfather, and from his earliest years knew that he belonged to a family foremost in service to the community. A kind of aristocracy of public service was growing in the city and its district, and to this class the Artigas belonged. They were primarily landowners and soldiers, and the influence of these

[1] The controversy about the date and place of birth is summed up by J. M. Traibel, *Artigas antes de 1811*.

45

two main family interests was always strong on José. It would be stretching the evidence to state that he could not bear city life, but he certainly spent most of his time on campaign or settling rural affairs in some country camp or village: he was forced to do this by all the circumstances of his character, his life and his times.

Martín José inherited his father's qualities and, as he matured, his father's offices and duties as a soldier-cum-policeman striving to bring some order and peace to the lawless chaos of the interior. Consequently, like his father, he spent much of his life on campaign or on the ranch he inherited. He married the daughter of another well-to-do landowner, and by her had six children, of whom José Gervasio was the third. Martín José retired from active military service in 1796, after forty-four years of meritorious activity as private, lieutenant and then captain of the Regiment of Cavalry Militia of Montevideo, a body frequently called out to deal with Indian or Portuguese threats. In his career he had at various times been *Alcalde de la Santa Hermandad, Alcalde Provincial* (another police officer for the interior), and in the Cabildo had been *Alférez Real* (an honorific post as royal standard-bearer, with some duties concerned with public order) and *Depositario General* (public trustee). He lived to see his son José lead the people of the Banda Oriental in revolution, to retreat with him in the famous Exodus of 1811 before a Portuguese occupying army, and even to see José finally defeated in 1820 by political rivals. He died between 1822 and 1824, at the age of about ninety.[1]

José Artigas, as José Gervasio Artigas always signed himself, almost went into the Church, but instead became a soldier and revolutionary. His paternal grandfather, his Artigas blood, won, while his maternal grandfather lost. The latter had left provision in his will for young José to be given a living if he became a priest. The obscurity of José's youth, passed mainly on estancias and herding cattle across country, gave his later powerful enemies room to

---

[1] All details concerning José Gervasio Artigas' father and grandfather are found in *A.A. t. I.*

46

build up a legend of the young man as a bandit. A *Porteño* (inhabitant of Buenos Aires, the 'port'), Pedro Feliciano Sáenz de Cavia, whom José Artigas had expelled in 1815 from the Banda Oriental and so caused to lose an important government post with the then occupying authority, Buenos Aires, was employed by Artigas' political enemies to write a defamatory pamphlet, published anonymously. In this work is painted a truly terrifying picture of Artigas as tyrant. The lies and errors of this pamphlet, and of the works of others who later wrote about Artigas, were only satisfactorily exposed and refuted in a well-documented study published by the Uruguayan historian Eduardo Acevedo in 1909.[1]

As with any man, great or not, the formative years of youth had a decisive influence on José Artigas. His family tradition, his father's and his grandfather's examples, his life in the insecurity of the country, all made the boy self-reliant, loyal to his country and people, tough, even wild. With his family prestige and his own pioneering training and tastes, he was in an admirable position to become a caudillo of the cowboys; and besides this, perhaps without realising it, he was an outstanding representative of the wealthy class with its hard ranching background and its growing commercial interests, so that his appeal to the majority of the Uruguayans was strong.

But José was not an illiterate barbarian. He was born in Montevideo and went to school there, while his father frequently went away on campaign – in 1776, for instance, to defend the frontier fortress of Santa Tecla against the Portuguese. José's companions at the school kept by the Franciscans in the monastery of San Bernardino included other future heroes of the independence movement: Larrañaga, Vedia, Viana, Rondeau (who rose to be Supreme Director of the United Provinces of the River Plate) and Otorgués. This was an establishment for the children of the well-

[1] Anon. (P. F. Sáenz de Cavia). *El Protector nominal de los Pueblos Libres D. José Artigas clasificado por El Amigo del Orden*; refuted by E. Acevedo, *José Artigas*. On Cavia see t. 1, pp. 43-7 of the official re-edition, Montevideo 1950.

to-do, who could afford to send their boys to a good school; though there was another school in Montevideo, run by the Jesuits, for poor boys. José went through the course, learning reading, writing and arithmetic, and acquiring some Latin and more religion. It was adequate for a boy destined to be a rancher and a soldier, or even for a merchant's son. It did not spoil the native simplicity of his style, which appears, phonetic spelling as well as directness, in his early despatches, before he employed secretaries.[1] Neither did it stifle his own thought and imagination, or his own clear view of his native country, as is evident from his practical aim as a leader in the revolution from 1811 to 1820, during his short period of power. It is very likely that Artigas thought more than he read, and certain that he learned more from his family and their responsibilities and from his years in the interior than from the Franciscans.[2]

José's early years must have been spent in the way normal for boys of his class and time: life in the family home in winter, with the days at school broken by occasional rides into the surrounding country for hunting or simply searching for adventures. In the summer, the free life of a family estancia, where a boy could learn to throw a lasso and the *boleadora*, to hunt and skin cattle, to respect the hardiness and lore of Indians and gauchos, and to love that life and that country. José became, as his father and grandfather before him, a pioneer, practising on his father's estates the arts of the gaucho, and becoming as expert as these 'new Centaurs'

[1] L. Barbagelata, *Artigas antes de 1810*. pp. 30–45. See e.g. despatch of Artigas to the Viceroy A. Olaguer Feliú, d. 'Aroyo depamaroti', 3 Oct., 1797., *A.A.*, t. ii, pt. ii, doc. 19.

[2] The Franciscans established a superior course, philosophy, in 1787, but by then Artigas was 23 and busy learning about his country in the practical way. (Barbagelata, *op. cit.* pp. 42–3.) His father in 1790, as *Depositario General* of Montevideo, had in his charge some books belonging to an official who was returning to Spain. Among them were many 'dangerous' titles, including 'la Ensiclopedia', 'Historia de Carlos dose' (Voltaire), 'Filosofia de Neuton', 'Derecho natural, y de Gentes', 'obras de Munsiur de Montesquieur', 'Historia de America por Mr Robertson', 'obras de Fonteneli', 'Carta Persas en frances' (Montesquieu), 'Quarenta tomos obras de Bolter' (Voltaire). See *A.A.*, to. i, pt. iii, c, doc. 74. But there is no proof that José or his father even opened these books, and the existence of this list merely underlines the well-known fact that such 'subversive' literature was not uncommon among the official class in Spanish America.

in riding and falling and in living rough. When it became time for José to strike out for himself and earn his living, as his brothers were already in charge of his father's estancias and no attractive place could be found for him on them, the young man found himself a congenial occupation. He became a purveyor of hides and cattle products, buying them from ranches in the interior, in the Misiones, Arapey, Queguay and Soriano (where he settled for some years), and hunting cattle himself on some estancias – with the owners' permission, it is to be supposed. He supplied hides to wealthy family friends and acquaintances who owned exporting businesses in Montevideo: the Latorres, the Otorgués, and others, some of whom were to follow him in the revolution.[1]

It is in this little-documented period of Artigas' life, the 1780s, that detractors place his alleged desertion of the family and his entry into the profession of outlaw, cattle-rustler and smuggler. But apparently he stayed on good terms with his father and the rest of the family, even though he had to find his livelihood away from them. Indeed, his father received loads of hides, tallow and such things, that José sent into the city from the interior; while José's own brother Manuel sold them for him.[2] Old Martín José showed his trust in his son, and his appreciation of his qualities, when in 1806 he made him joint executor of his will, together with his daughter Martina Antonia, passing over an elder son, José Nicolás, as well as a younger one, Manuel Francisco.[3] At the time when José was supposed to be turning renegade, his family thought him 'a great gad-about, very fond of society and paying visits as well as of dressing in fine clothes like a town-councillor or like the dandies; ... he gained people's good will by his affable and friendly manner': a very likeable young man, in short.[4]

Smuggler young José Artigas almost certainly was; but

[1] L. Barbagelata, *op. cit.* pp. 49-50; Traibel, *op. cit.* p. 32.
[2] Declaration of Josefa Ravia, José Artigas' cousin, to Justo Maeso, *cit.* in Traibel, *op. cit.* p. 32.
[3] *A.A.*, t. II, pt. v, doc. 1.
[4] Declaration of Josefa Ravia.

smuggling was not uncommon in the Banda Oriental at that time (or since), nor was it strictly dishonourable, and it was a useful economic activity when other means of attracting foreign trade were forbidden. On New Year's Day 1795 a Spanish officer reported that one Artiga was known to be nearing the Brazilian frontier driving four thousand 'animals' with eighty armed men, mostly Portuguese. Obviously this Artiga was a notable smuggler chief, though there is no hint that the cattle were stolen – indeed it was common for smugglers to get their cattle quite honestly from the creole owners. There is a hint that Artiga was prepared to resist with force the interference of authority, a more serious matter: 'these men will certainly defend their things to the last gasp'. Artiga was most likely Artigas. A year later, the Viceroy himself was informed of the movements of some smugglers on the Brazilian frontier, including one 'called Pepe [Joe] Artigas, a smuggler and a citizen of this city', and of the action taken by the authorities of Montevideo to stop their traffic. There can be little doubt that this 'Joe' Artigas was the future hero.[1]

The knowledge of the country, of the frontier, and of the routes, fords, pastures and men of the whole region that Artigas gained while plying this trade was invaluable to him later. It must be admitted that young Artigas was wild, but there is no proof that he was evil or vicious. Besides, in this life his spirit was forged, and he learned to lead his wild countrymen. Such a youth was essential to the revolutionary Artigas.[2]

---

[1] *A.A.*, t. II, pt. I, docs. I and 2; t. IV, Apéndice, docs. I and 5.

[2] A portrait of Artigas at this time written later by a political enemy, Vedia, was meant to show him in a bad light, but in fact shows him as a typical young caudillo, who was still an honest smuggler who bought his cattle and did not steal them: 'Don José Artigas era un muchacho travieso e inquieto y propuesto a sólo usar de su voluntad; sus padres tenían establecimientos de campaña, y de uno de estos desapareció a la edad como de 14 años, y ya no paraba en sus estancia, sino una que otra vez ocultándose a la vista de sus padres. Correr alegremente los campos, changuear y comprar en éstos ganados mayores y caballadas para irlos a vender a la frontera del Brasil, algunas veces contrabandear cueros secos, y siempre haciendo la primera figura entre los muchos compañeros, eran sus entretenimientos habituales. Jugaba mucho a los naipes, que es una de las propensiones más comunes entre los que llamaremos gauchos, tocaba el acordeón . . .' (Gen. N. de Vedia, *Apuntes biográficos sobre don José Artigas*, in Traibel, *op. cit.* p. 33.)

Another fruit of these years was a son, born in 1791 to Isabel Sánchez in Soriano. Artigas was a healthy and energetic young man, and evidently had his affairs as did other men with whom he mixed; and in the manner of those patriarchal times Artigas recognised his son, and later had him with him as an officer on his patriotic campaigns. Artigas even made this son, Manuel, his deputy as head of the family when he had to leave his native province at the approach of the disastrous end of the wars. Manuel was a true Artigas, and could safely be left in charge of his father's interests, including his mad wife and his small son by her.[1]

But in this period, Artigas' stature as a leader began to show itself. By the time he was thirty, Artigas was known to the cowboys by his force of personality and his prestige as a caudillo. Vedia, who was critical, recalled seeing him in 1793 'on the banks of the Bacacay, surrounded by many fascinated lads who had just arrived with a large herd of animals to sell'.[2] Artigas was soon to use this prestige in a way more in accordance with the tradition of his family, and probably too with his own inclination as he grew to maturity. Four years after this he was an officer in a Spanish force raised for the express purpose of ridding the country of outlaws, ensuring the safety of the Brazilian frontier, and bringing order, peace and civilisation to the interior of the Banda Oriental.

What caused this change may have been his realisation that the country was in chaos, worse than ever before, owing to the unchecked depredations of bands of outlaws, raiding Indians and the Portuguese. Artigas, it may be supposed, could not watch his own country ruined; and, possibly recognising his own part in adding to the unrest, he joined the side of civilisation and order in a characteristic gesture of patriotism. Certainly, by 1795, the country under Montevideo's jurisdiction was in such disorder that the ranchers sent a petition to the Cabildo pointing out the state of affairs and requesting protection against the roving bandits who

[1] Traibel, *op. cit.* pp. 33-4.
[2] Vedia, *Apuntes, ibid.*

preyed on their herds as well as on the unallotted royal cattle, attacking their ranches and their men. They rightly pointed out that the prosperity of Montevideo depended on the products of ranching, and that therefore the defence of these interests was vital to the province. The bandits continually carried off herds of cattle and horses – over two thousand head in one year – to sell to the Brazilians; 'they sack our houses, carry off married and single women; they roughly handle our cowhands, workers and slaves, leaving them tied up to posts so that they can make not the slightest resistance to their misdeeds; they commit cruel murders, and after all this those miscreants wander unpunished, with the most bare-faced assurance, about the very estancias where they did their execrable misdeeds, sheltered only by distance and by the fact that the authorities which are capable of punishing their abominable excesses are very far away'.[1] Since justice was so in-effective, the Portuguese had begun settling in the district in large numbers, attracted by the contraband.

All these lawless men, said the ranchers, acted as a bad example to peaceable cowboys, who were being drawn by the loose, ex-citing life to join them, so that the country was rapidly losing all its elements of stability. 'It is certain that the country districts have never been so much infected with pernicious men, yet we can find no cause for it', went on the petition. Perhaps, it was suggested, the troops used for the policing of the country were too inexpert: they were not used to riding, and so could never successfully pur-sue the gaucho outlaws. Certainly order used to be better main-tained when the policing was done by local men commanded by local militia officers. Though they did not say so outright, the ranchers were thinking of the leadership given by two generations of the Artigas family. It was time for a third to come forward.[2] Their picture of saddle-sore greenhorn Spanish mounted infantry gingerly plodding after the 'new Centaurs' is a clear indication

[1] *Solicitud* of 28 May 1795, A.A., t. II, doc. 3.
[2] Traibel, *op. cit.* p. 35.

of the creoles' scorn of their Peninsular masters. Self-sufficiency and complete independence are not far apart.

The petition was favourably received by the *Síndico Procurador* of the Cabildo, who urged the council to take action, adding force to the ranchers' arguments. He quoted the recent creation of two raiding parties for cattle-stealing, one by a Spaniard and one by a Portuguese officer who had a ranch on the Brazilian side of the border. In one raid this party had rustled twenty thousand head of cattle.[1] He recommended the creation of a local Regiment of *Blandengues* (a sort of Lancers) on the lines of the regiment recently formed in Buenos Aires in order to repel Indian raids, but this one to be used for keeping order in the Banda Oriental.

It took two years, however, for this regiment to be formed, and even then it was done as one of several defensive measures taken in the Banda Oriental in case of English attacks, since Spain and England were at war before the end of the century. But at length, in January 1797, the Viceroy, Melo de Portugal, gave orders for the creation of a *Cuerpo de Blandengues* in the Montevideo district, with headquarters at Maldonado. In February the Governor of Montevideo, Olaguer Feliú, published on the Viceroy's orders a special amnesty for certain classes of criminals who might enlist for eight years in the new regiment. These classes included smugglers, deserters from the army or fugitives from prisons (clearly regarded as the same thing), and 'those who have committed any other crime except that of murder and that of having used arms against agents of justice and rural police patrols'.[2] The aim was to have a specially tough force of gauchos who would be able to fight on equal terms with bandits, Indians and Portuguese. On the 10th of March 1797, Artigas joined this regiment as a trooper, taking advantage of the amnesty.[3]

---

[1] *Vista*, d. 30 June 1795, *A.A.*, t. II, doc. 3.

[2] L. Barbagelata, *op. cit.* pp. 59-64; *A.A.*, t. II, docs. 4 and 5. The establishment was for 8 companies of 100 men each, though in colonial days there were never more than 480 men in the regiment. Artigas himself brought in 200 recruits in its first two years of existence.

[3] *A.A.*, t. II, pt. III, doc. 33.

Artigas was already working for the Royal account, having been commissioned by Olaguer Feliú to recruit in the interior for the new regiment, and his activity and prestige brought success in this task. His superiors evidently respected him for his knowledge of the country and his influence over the gauchos, for although he was still technically only a trooper, he was in August sent out in command of a party of thirty others to pursue the outlaws wandering about the country. The stock-raisers, who knew Artigas even better than did the authorities, had in the previous May petitioned for him to be sent out in this way.[1] On this first armed mission in support of authority, Artigas took his men up to the Brazilian frontier and harried the smugglers who were killing cattle for hides. He returned impressed by the damage done by these outlaws to the country's main resource, reporting: 'It is pitiful to see the destruction they wreak in the country. Merely for the hides they kill the cows.' It was, of course, important to spare the cows for the sake of the calves they might produce: bulls could be killed in reasonable numbers without endangering the existence of the herds. Artigas had matured since his own smuggling days, for from this time on his concern for the economic welfare of the country developed, together with his other patriotic views. During this excursion, too, Artigas came off best in a brush with wild Indians: sufficient proof of his skill as a frontiersman and officer. In the course of a ride in pursuit of rustlers in the neighbourhood of the frontier post of Batoví, Artigas gained a knowledge of that district which was to be used three years later in a civilising mission undertaken by the naturalist and boundary commissioner Azara.[2]

In November 1797, still on mobile frontier patrol, Artigas had a clash with a band of smugglers bringing contraband tobacco in from Brazil. The *Blandengues* lost two men killed, and then Artigas himself, charging into a wood where the bandits had taken refuge,

[1] *A.A.*, t. II, pt. II, docs. 1-10.
[2] *Ibid.* docs. 15, 19.

54

captured one armed with a carbine and pistol, both loaded, and a fighting knife, who, on recognising the leader shouted out that he surrendered. He was a Portuguese well known as a murderer, who in this very action had killed one *Blandengue* and wounded another twice.[1]

When in January 1798 Artigas brought his detachment back into Montevideo, he returned as a captain of the Cavalry Militia, not as a trooper. His promotion had taken place in his absence, on the 27th of October, apparently in part fulfilment of a promise given by Olaguer Feliú, now Viceroy, before the detachment set out.[2] Artigas' loyalty to Spain and to Olaguer Feliú was complete, especially now that his wild oats were forgotten; and he was able to begin a career of honourable service, no doubt welcome to his father. The new captain of militia still commanded detachments of the regular *Blandengues*, and had only been given a militia commission because of his irregular entry into the army and his lack of seniority, which prevented his rapid promotion to match his extraordinary usefulness as an expert leader of frontier patrols. Meanwhile Artigas' name, given fresh importance by his rank, was submitted to the King for the appointment of *Ayudante Mayor* (adjutant) to the Regiment of *Blandengues* of Montevideo, and the new commission was signed in Madrid in January 1799.[3]

The Spanish government knew how to make use of loyal and active creoles as junior commanders; in fact, for nearly a year Artigas had been acting *Ayudante Mayor* of the *Blandengues*, with the rank of regular lieutenant, on the Viceroy's own nomination.[4]

---

[1] *Ibid.* doc. 28.

[2] *Ibid.* docs. 33 and 34; also doc. 31, letter of José Artigas to the Viceroy, d. 'Aroyo del sause. 10 de henero de 1798:' '. . . debe vm. estar persuadido qe recibo esta honra el mayor a precio y rendido por ella las mas debidas Gracias la ydea qe. tengo formado Sor. exmo. dela Grandeza del corazon de Ve. me hizo siempre concebir ciertas esperanzas de qe. en sufabor en Contraria el mas seguro anparo y pro ten cion y *la palabra qe. ami pro partid-amedio de faborecerme* No solo la beo Cumplida Con las honrosas Comisiones y enpleos Con qe. me ha destenguido sino qe. me haze Bibir en la firme cre en cia de qe. *me de algun lugar en los Cuerpos bibos que esta Criando y de ungol pe Meponga en carera de honor*', etc., etc. (Italics mine.)

[3] *Ibid.* pt. III, doc. 1.

[4] *Ibid.* docs. 2 and 3.

But the new Viceroy, Avilés, who took over from the friendly Olaguer in 1799, was a man who believed in seniority, and had no special respect for Artigas since he had no experience of the state of the country before Artigas had joined the side of law and order; it took thirteen years for the next promotion, to regular captain, even though a vacancy had occurred in 1798[1]. It may be guessed how those long years of waiting affected the creole's loyalty and prepared him to side with the revolution: he was kept subordinate in his own country, knowing and constantly proving himself to be one of the most useful tools of Spanish dominion in it. It was a common creole tragedy, which had much to do with arousing revolutionary feeling at this time in Spanish America.

Artigas' service career was active. He was rarely at regimental headquarters in Maldonado, as an adjutant might be expected to have been, but instead was usually out in command of some detachment fighting Indians, smugglers or rustlers, and patrolling the Brazilian frontier. Without the rank of captain he had all the duties and responsibilities of a veteran company commander on campaign. From October 1798 to June 1799 he was out with his *Blandengue* party, making full use of his expert knowledge of the country in frontier warfare with Brazilian tobacco smugglers, and marauding Minuán and Charrúa Indians who just then were very troublesome.[2]

The authorities were at their wits' end trying to bring some semblance of order to that turbulent frontier region, and the law-breakers were so numerous that many evaded arrest and carried on with their business untroubled while the *Blandengues* dealt legally with those they captured. The troops were too few, and detachments brought in for rest could not be replaced by fresh ones.[3] As a result, Artigas 'because of his great knowledge and the disposition he has to serve with advantage in those lands', was made

[1] *Ibid.* docs. 5, 29-35.
[2] *Ibid.* doc. 9.
[3] *Ibid.* doc. 17.

the chief hope of a captain sent out with a much reduced detachment, in which Artigas' skill was to balance the lack of troops.[1]
After a few months' duty in Maldonado and Montevideo, in
early 1800, the height of the southern summer, Artigas was out
again, chosen because of his skill, at the head of a detachment
ranging the wide uncivilised zone north of the Río Negro, keeping the peace and finding recruits among the gauchos to replenish
the ranks of the *Blandengues*. Artigas met his usual crop of frontier
incidents, capturing a smuggler, a *Blandengue* deserter, and various
Portuguese criminals, and freeing a woman who had been carried
off from Brazil.[2]

At this stage in his career Artigas had the good fortune to serve
under Félix de Azara, who had been in the Plate region for nine-
teen years, waiting to play his part in the settlement of the boundaries provided for in the treaty of 1777 between Spain and
Portugal. The experience could not but be helpful to the untrained
civiliser in Artigas, especially since the particular duty involved
was that of setting up a town to be a centre of civilisation for a part
of the frontier with Brazil covering the debated Misiones territory.

The frontier problem was important and delicate, as Artigas'
previous adventures bear witness; and it exercised the Spanish
authorities constantly. Azara hit on the idea of creating centres of
Spanish population on or near the frontier, so as to make it less
easy for lawbreakers on either side to cross over and cause international incidents as they pursued their various bandit callings in
the no-man's-land about the unmarked border. A settled frontier
zone, with a stable population owning property in the form of
houses, estancias and cattle, would be a great factor in discouraging
indiscriminate gaucho lawlessness. At the same time Azara meant to
do good to the viceregal treasury by offering to use as settlers
many families who had been sent from Spain and the Canary
Islands over twenty years before on the understanding that they

---

[1] *Ibid.* doc. 22.
[2] *Ibid.* docs. 36-42.

were to settle new towns in Patagonia, and that meanwhile until the towns were established and the lands divided among them, they were to receive substantial pensions from the local treasury. Only one small town had been founded, and the majority of the immigrants had lived for the whole time in centres such as Montevideo, Maldonado and Colonia, happily pensioned and idle. Now Azara ended this costly piece of inefficiency by offering the families the alternative of either settling the proposed new establishments on the Brazilian frontier, or staying where they were without pension. According to Azara, the families refused to move, which was what he wanted since they had become soft and useless as pioneers; and so he founded his new town of Batoví with more satisfactory volunteer settlers.[1] No doubt these were much better material, these eighty families of settlers whom Azara established at San Gabriel de Batoví on the River Yaguarí, near the frontier River Ibicuy. The other establishments planned to cover the frontier from Santa Tecla onwards never took shape.

Artigas played his part in this strategic and social enterprise, as an aide to Azara for some months from April 1800, helping to free the zone from Portuguese invaders before laying out the new town and dividing the lands. Here the future statesman received his only lesson, practical and theoretical, in formally civilising the country, a preoccupation with him from this time forward. In Batoví Azara wrote his *Memoria sobre el estado rural del Río de la Plata*, dating it the 9th of May, 1801. No doubt he talked over with his chief aide some of the problems he discussed in his memorandum: such as the low population of the interior, and the state of barbarism in which the cowboys lived; the absolute lack of schoolmasters and even churches between the banks of the Plate and the Uruguay and the newly established frontier towns of Cerro Largo and Batoví: that is, in the whole interior of the Banda Oriental; and the unfortunate fact that both Spanish and Portuguese settlers were equally willing to smuggle and to shelter outlaws,

---

[1] Azara, *Estado rural*, pp. 16-17.

The difficulty of any economic advance is clearly stated: there was no market for agricultural products nearer than Europe, and the cost of transport forbade real farming in the interior, away from the ports; and therefore there was no settled population in the interior, nor was there likely to be any. These problems, common to both sides of the Plate, were only solved gradually during the course of the nineteenth century, with the advent of railways, immigrants and refrigerator ships. But meanwhile, the only industry really suited to the conditions of the country and its people was ranching, which needed few men and no transport, and which gave fair returns for little labour. Besides, 'could one find any occupation so agreeable and suited to the whims, condition and tastes of these folk, whose delight is to be always on horseback and chasing after the bulls?' Trades and manufacturing were bound to fail, if introduced, because they could not bring in such large and easy profits. There were other factors which Azara did not admit, apart from the ones mentioned: such as, for instance, the excessive shortage of disposable capital in the region, which is a part of the unfortunate side of the Spanish heritage. But these things were only recognised a generation later.

As Azara saw it, what should be done to help the country's prosperity was to set up some kind of institution to study cattle-raising and give instruction on the best methods, so educating people not to waste this wealth. The wasteful methods used in cattle-hunting have been described. Yet, Azara was certain, the country could be the happiest on earth if the trade of the Plate had been thrown open and ranching carried on in a sensible way. This would have populated the interior, besides conserving the cattle, and it would also have ensured the safety of the frontier, and even the possession, he thought, of the Brazilian province of Rio Grande do Sul. Here he was coming close to the economic thought of the revolutionaries of the region some years later, which is possibly not surprising since he was himself a considerable figure in the Spanish Enlightenment.[1] At any rate, Artigas later took up exactly these ideas in throwing open Uruguayan trade, and even in attempting an invasion of Rio Grande.

But in any case, Azara continued, the cost of buying public land was too high for most individuals, so that only the very rich could ask for empty lands; and they bought vast tracts, which had the opposite effect to that intended, helping to keep the population low. These large estates should be split up into smaller, but still adequate, ranches for several families. Otherwise, as in the Banda Oriental beyond the Río Negro, many settlers had occupied lands without buying them and therefore without legal title, thus adding to the chaos and insecurity. Public lands should be divided among those with the skill and energy to use them. Artigas was to remember these curiously modern at the same time as eighteenth-century ideas when he himself came to face the problem of settling and civilising the country; and most Spanish American countries have faced or are still facing the great problem, caused in similar ways in colonial times, of the over-large estate with its social consequences. Artigas was always to remember, too, Azara's warning that unless the interior were settled, the Portuguese would gradually settle it from Brazil. The whole Batoví venture was based upon this fear. Here is the key to much of the conduct of the future *Jefe de los Orientales* (Leader of the Easterners). It was the need for strong measures to save his own *patria chica* from Portuguese-Brazilian expansion that caused Artigas to adopt many of his later attitudes, and not so much hatred and fear of Buenos Aires, except in so far as the leaders of that city showed a constant tendency to sacrifice the Banda Oriental to the aggressive Portuguese and Brazilians for the sake of a doubtful and unstable peace for themselves.

Azara's remedies were sensible, so far as they went, and they chimed in with the feelings of the people of the Banda Oriental.

---

[1] Azara, and more so his brother Nicolás, an anti-clerical Spanish ambassador to Rome, were among the elite, striving to bring Spain abreast of the times. See J. Sarrailh, *L'Espagne éclairée de la seconde moitié du XVIIIe siècle*, especially pp. 364-72.

Possibly Artigas was able to give the author an insight into the local state of mind, which was eventually to bring about complete independence for the Banda Oriental. Besides recommending a vast plan of settlements for the interior, with a centre of population possessing a church and a school every sixteen or twenty leagues, the treatment of the Indians in a way calculated to make them useful members of society, splitting up the land among families, and taking care of the herds, Azara very significantly proposed reforms in government and in the regulation of commerce. The frontier region, between the Rivers Negro and Ibicuy and the Uruguay and the Brazilian border, should have its own administration separate from that of Montevideo; and some trade over the border in products plentiful in the Banda Oriental should be encouraged for the sake of aiding local industry and, in the case of horses and mules, so as to gain profit from their sale instead of losing them altogether to Brazilian rustlers, who came to steal them because of their scarcity over the border. In sum, a measure of legal contact with Brazil was asked for, but the frontier was to be held strongly, and nothing should be done to help the Brazilians, but only to help the Uruguayans.[1]

In practice, it was Artigas who was entrusted by Azara with the details: the task of surveying the lands, in company with a naval officer, and that of dividing them up among the settlers. So the *Blandengue* officer came to know the practical difficulties of settling a turbulent area, gaining experience in overcoming such difficulties – experience which enabled him to make minute regulations later for similar efforts in his own period of government. Besides, he saw how the town itself was laid out in gridiron pattern, the public buildings placed round the square, and house lots given to the families. Artigas learned a great deal in this roundabout way from the Spanish Enlightenment and the Laws of the Indies.[2]

---

[1] For the conditions of land grants see *A.A.*, t. II, pt. IV, doc. 2.

[2] *Ibid.* pt. IV. Artigas' brother Manuel was on the 15 June 1801 given an estancia in the Batoví lands, but apparently did not occupy it. He was an absentee such as Azara was trying to keep out.

2. JOSÉ ARTIGAS AS A SPANISH OFFICER

Artigas' apprenticeship to Azara and the success of Batoví were equally brief, since one of the results of the declaration of war on Portugal in 1801 by a Spain bullied by Napoleon Bonaparte was the Portuguese occupation of the Misiones territory which Batoví had been founded to defend. When the news of war arrived, Artigas had refused to obey Azara's order to return to Montevideo, preferring to stay 'demonstrating the most ardent and lively desire, which has always fired my mind, to give my best service to defend the State'.[1] But his patriotism served no purpose, for the commandant of the fortress of Batoví, who was in league with the Portuguese, handed it over to them without resistance. It was of no interest to that officer who owned the frontier lands, so long as he could do profitable business with their master. Artigas' hurt national pride became eloquent in his account of this disgraceful episode, showing his increasing distrust of Brazil, although he still wrote and apparently felt like a loyal Spanish colonial officer. Still, it is clear that to him it was his own country which was being attacked, and that this attack hit directly at his deepest feelings: he never mentioned the larger issues of the war even in America, much less in Europe. But he still had a long way to go before love of his Banda Oriental would force him to turn traitor to his military oath and training and send him to join the revolutionary movement in 1811.

Artigas withdrew to Cerro Largo, where the Spanish forces were concentrated, to join an expedition under Colonel Quintana which marched into Misiones, to the region of the Ibicuy, and made contact with the enemy in November 1801. Almost at once came the order to countermarch to the base at Melo, on the other side of the country, since the Portuguese had broken through there. Arriving too late to save Melo, Quintana's column joined large forces which came forward under the Sub-inspector General

[1] *A.A.*, t. II, pt. v, doc. 5.

of the Viceroyalty in person, Sobremonte, a good civil servant but an inept soldier. The Portuguese, made nervous rather than beaten, withdrew beyond the frontier of the Yaguarón again, and their authorities in Rio Grande prepared for a Spanish counter-invasion. But Sobremonte would not risk his army, and instead he remained still and ordered another expedition to proceed to Misiones, this time under Colonel Lecoq, but again with the co-operation of Artigas as chief guide and organiser of the march. Artigas was by now feared by the Portuguese as the most active of their opponents.[1] News of the peace signed in Badajoz came in time to prevent action, though a party of a hundred still went on to pacify the Indians of the frontier. The Misiones lands east of the River Uruguay were lost, therefore, and they remained in Portuguese and later Brazilian hands.[2] This was another object lesson for Artigas: a lesson which reaffirmed his distrust of the strong neighbour to the north and also began to shake his confidence in Spain's representatives in America. Sobremonte had gained nothing and had lost a potentially rich piece of Spanish territory, which Artigas years later tried to regain for his country.

It is possible that these severe marches and arduous campaigns strained Artigas' previously robust health; but the fact is that he returned to Montevideo and spent the greater part of 1802 and 1803 and part of 1804 on what was described as sick leave.[3] It seems more likely, however, in view of his future good health when on campaign during the revolutionary wars, that the disaster of the loss of the Eastern Misiones and the bungling of Sobremonte had disgusted the patriot and decided him to take the only course open to a man of honour in order to withdraw from service with the Spanish army. More convincing, perhaps, is the tone of

[1] See the petition of Raimundo Santiago to the Portuguese authorities claiming a reward for services against the Spanish Misiones, including the care and vigilance with which he had opposed the designs of the 'Castelhano Pepe Artigas' in 1801 and 1802. *A.A.*, t. III, appendix, doc. 3.
[2] *A.A.*, t. II, pt. v, doc. 21.
[3] *Ibid.* docs. 12-20; Traibel, *op. cit.* p. 38.

Artigas' application in October 1803 for permission to retire in view of his 'broken health'. The application was rejected by Madrid, even though Artigas had produced a medical certificate stating that he was suffering from 'pertinacious and stubborn rheumatic Arthritic pains' in all his body, including his lungs, and that his troubles were incurable and might be fatal if made worse by another attack. Artigas blamed his ailments on his six years' active service, campaigning in all weathers, and particularly on the last expedition to Misiones.[1]

Artigas perforce continued in the army. His reputation as an enforcer of order was, in fact, so great that the Guild of Stock-raisers petitioned Sobremonte, who had succeeded to the Vice-royalty, to send him out on a special expedition to sweep the interior clean of outlaws. As they wrote afterwards, the condition of the country at this time was worse than ever, most likely because of the increased aggressiveness of the Portuguese since the last war and the spread of lawlessness encouraged by the fluctuations of the border.[2] The mission was given to Artigas, who found himself once more engaged in the hard but inspiring labour of civilising his own country. He had been asked for by his own countrymen, and while protecting them he could feel himself largely independent of Spanish supervision. No inkling of this kind of reflection has come to us from Artigas' pen, but he may well have felt something of this when he rode out of the city at the head of his men at the beginning of winter, in April 1804, forgetting the mortal sickness his doctor had described a few months before. He accomplished his task with his usual zeal and energy: as the Stock-raisers wrote in 1810 when finally rewarding him with the five hundred pesos they had promised him after his success in 1804, 'he conducted himself with such efficacy, zeal and discipline that, as he captured the bandits and terrorised those who escaped falling into his hands by running away, we experienced within a short time

[1] *Ibid.* docs. 21–6.
[2] *Ibid.* docs. 125 and 126.

the benefits we hoped for, seeing peace of spirit and the security of our ranches substituted for timorousness and alarm'.

In 1804 Artigas first became a public figure among his country-men, and not only a leader of gauchos, but an admired represen-tative of order. His appearance in 1811 as leader of the revolution in the Banda Oriental had therefore been prepared for years: he was the logical choice since he had been accepted as the leading native soldier, with great experience of campaigns and of con-ditions in the district. This campaign of 1804 brought incidents similar to those which he had met before. He scoured the frontier, and drawn as he always would be by that precious piece of land lost to the Portuguese, he made his way up towards the Misiones, crossing the Arapey. Here he captured some men and horses from a cattle-hunting expedition commanded by a Portuguese militia captain, who, he understood, had been marauding thereabouts for over a year; and he learned of two other such parties existing in the field, which had joined forces with wild Indians. This incident was important to Artigas' future development because of the trouble he got into over it. This lieutenant of *Blandengues* wrote a hasty note to Colonel Rocamora, the officer in command of a large force covering the border, outlining a plan for the two de-tachments to attack the Portuguese jointly and recover the stolen cattle and horses, and so perform 'a memorable deed for the sake of the Fatherland'.

This wounded Rocamora's pride, which had already been pricked by a previous despatch in which Artigas demanded re-inforcements without troubling to explain the nature of his mission from the Viceroy. Artigas was not the man to explain when he was in the right and when he was in independent com-mand. But as a result he was now made to realise his real depen-dence on the Spanish military hierarchy, and the experience no doubt deepened his disgust. Rocamora ordered Artigas not to attack, but instead to come and report to him, since his informa-tion did not tally with what Artigas had written. Artigas had not been circumspect, had not shown the respect due to a superior officer, and was to be put in his place. The colonel picked holes in Artigas' despatches, scornfully hinted that he had learned less from them than from the despatch-riders, and pointed out that for the sake of regular discipline a visit by Artigas was necessary and normal. He went on to accuse Artigas of impetuosity, and stated that this attack required mature deliberation and preparation: he meant that it needed the professional touch, not Artigas' amateurish folly. Rocamora then insisted that his own scouts had reported that the Portuguese had not been near for a year, and ended by threatening to report all this to the Viceroy himself, so that any faults caused by Artigas' military laxness would be punished. In this way Artigas came to know the tiresomeness and worse of the routine military mind, while the outlaws were given the time to escape. It was not his last clash with the hierarchy, since a similar incident in 1811 helped him to make up his mind to join the revolution. Meanwhile, his dissatisfaction with things in his native land was increased by such obstruction.[1]

To justify himself, Artigas reported his own version of the story to Sobremonte and advised him to place the military headquarters for the frontier much further forward in order to stop the slow absorption of the country and its resources by Portuguese bands. He went on to say that the six hundred wild Indians living in the district were in league with the Portuguese, as were by now the Guaraní Indians from the former Spanish mission villages. The local Charrúas stole Spanish cattle to sell to the Portuguese for spirits, cloth, tobacco, *hierba mate* and knives.[2]

The only answer was to find more men like Artigas to pacify the frontier lands and keep out the Portuguese, as the Governor of Montevideo, Ruiz Huidobro, agreed. He sent out seventy-five

---

[1] It was true that the Portuguese had not been the whole year in the district, but only two or three months, as was later elicited by questioning the prisoners in Montevideo. (*A.A.* doc. 40.) Artigas had misunderstood or been misled when he first questioned them in the heat of the chase.

[2] *A.A.*, doc. 36.

men to reinforce Artigas' detachment of forty, allowing him to face the various enemies on more even terms.[1] A letter that Ruiz Huidobro sent to the Portuguese Governor of Rio Grande, complaining of the aggressions and calling on him to have them stopped in accordance with the treaties in force, waited from July to September for a reply;[2] but the reply justified Artigas' activity, for the Portuguese promised to forbid their subjects to settle on the Spanish side of the border, or to have dealings with the wild Indians. The Governor also, with a show of good will, promised to have the prisoners taken by Artigas and Rocamora punished as an example if the Spaniards would return them to him; but the Spanish authorities refused, believing (possibly with cause) that the prisoners would simply be released if they were sent back. By this time the suspicion and veiled hostility of both sides were apparent.

Meanwhile, all through the winter of 1804, Artigas remained near the border. In six weeks he patrolled from Batoví to Santa Tecla, but then he withdrew a few miles, since he could find no cattle on which to feed his troops, as the Portuguese had driven off the herds which used to abound there. On the other hand, he found and destroyed many Portuguese boundary marks set up well within Spanish territory, and some months later he had the satisfaction of learning of his Viceroy's approval.[3] On a search for trouble somewhat further from the border, Artigas had an encounter with a raiding party of Charrúas sent by the Portuguese. One of his men was killed in this skirmish, and Artigas again lost patience with authority and wrote a scathing report to the Governor of Montevideo showing that several large expeditions under various high-ranking officers (including Rocamora) had done nothing to pacify the country, while he, constantly searching with a small party, as constantly found danger and did his duty. When once he had succeeded to the command of a larger party of over

---

[1] *Ibid.* doc. 39.
[2] *Ibid.* docs. 44 and 91.
[3] *A.A.*, docs. 50 and 53.

a hundred men on the death of its captain, he had 'done in the Interior whatever he wished on behalf of the King's Forces and the Country, exterminating the Indians and driving them back as far as Misiones: so that the people all lived free of care on their estancias'. Artigas' progress towards revolution was becoming more rapid as he realised the extent of the authorities' incompetence.[1]

As a result of Artigas' discovery of the Portuguese rustling and colonising establishments, the Viceroy ordered in July a larger expedition to be sent, under Lieutenant-colonel Viana, second-in-command of the Montevideo garrison, to take over the supervision of the frontier. But Artigas still scouted independently all that winter, and the seventy-five militiamen who had already been sent to reinforce him were increased by another twenty-five, although in fact only fourteen ever reached him. The authorities, especially Ruiz Huidobro, as well as the local people, clearly had great confidence in Artigas' ability, and so it is perhaps only to be expected that the enquiry ordered by the Viceroy as a result of Rocamora's complaint was, Spanish fashion, allowed to be quietly forgotten.[2]

In spite of the Viceroy's order in July, by the middle of August Viana's expedition had still not left, and Artigas was the only active leader in the frontier region. Again the Guild of Stockraisers complained about the length of time it took to give them and their property full protection, while they praised Artigas for all he had done with his limited means. Surely, they wrote, it was time to halt the expansion of Brazil, especially since the Treaty of Badajoz was still fresh. They pointed out, with the wisdom of expert ranchers who had spent a life of enforced contemplation of the chaotic state of their country, that the true reason for the Portuguese expansion was simply that the Spanish frontier lands were unoccupied, still awaiting the plan of settlement promised

[1] *Ibid.* doc. 51.
[2] *Ibid.* docs. 42, 45, 61-3, 65.

years before by the *Señores Virreyes*, and, they might have added, given an abortive start by Azara and Artigas. Therefore Portuguese expeditions openly entered and plundered the lands, and had even taken over a large part of them, as Artigas had proved. South of the Ibicuy the Portuguese had settled their own new estancias, and they already believed the whole country as far south as the headwaters of the Río Negro to be theirs; and all this was besides the Misiones, which they had unjustly kept at the last peace. There was no saying how far the advance might continue. Accordingly, the Stock-raisers advised Sobremonte to send a prudent envoy to Brazil to show the injustice of the case to the Portuguese, and if these peaceful means failed, to have resort to arms. Sobremonte sent a curt reply saying that international affairs were entirely his province, but that Viana's expedition had been prepared. No doubt preparations were hastened after this, but it was November before Viana and his men arrived to take over from Artigas.[1]

A remarkable document, which shows Artigas' mettle and his attitude in the question of the welfare of the Banda Oriental is a letter he wrote to Ruiz Huidobro in October, while still on this campaign, refuting Rocamora's charges.[2] He cut the ground from under Rocamora's feet at the very start by proving the independence of his command, a thing always dear to him; and then in the rest of the letter he destroyed his superior officer's detailed complaints at the same time as he tore his military reputation to shreds with his heavy irony. Although Artigas began: 'I confess in good faith that all this paper work is a very difficult subject for my intelligence', he nevertheless proved that he could argue ruthlessly, and knew what he was arguing about: in fact this document shows clearly that he considered himself to be at least the equal of any man in his country, and goes a long way towards showing that he was.

Artigas argued that to visit Rocamora while in action would

---

[1] *Ibid.* docs. 66 and 93.
[2] *A.A.*, doc. 71.

have taken up two precious days for what was 'a mere courtesy'. Indeed, Rocamora had himself disobeyed orders in failing to provide Artigas with help and support, as his general orders for the campaign had stated, whereas Artigas had carried out his to the letter. Also, Artigas' orders from the Viceroy authorised him to operate independently, and therefore he was right to avoid taking orders from a colonel, or accepting reinforcements from him led by a captain who, by his superior rank, must take over the command of Artigas' expedition. It was a case of obeying the orders of the supreme chief and disobeying the contrary orders of a subordinate one.

In any case, Artigas continued, he had disobeyed Rocamora not merely out of independence of spirit, but also because Rocamora's dispositions would have been opposed to the success of the expedition. 'I shall speak of this matter in the light of the knowledge I have gained from the interior; since if I cannot brag of being so military as the Colonel, at least without boasting I can affirm that I have more experience of our backwoods than he has.' Here the expert frontiersman showed his scorn, born of injured patriotism and pride, for the hidebound, parade-square notions of the hierarchy, as represented by this colonel, so much out of his element among the savage skirmishes and running fights of the untamed interior. Rocamora had, 'together with other things of his well-known military science', ordered Artigas to report to him for orders for an attack, when it was obvious that for Artigas to lead his men round the enemy to the Colonel's position would have exposed them to danger or made a long detour essential. Again, Artigas had prudently retreated, which the Colonel thought cowardice, but Artigas had done so because his scouts warned him of an enemy force of three times the size of his detachment hotly following his trail. By retreating, Artigas avoided a complete disaster such as happened soon after to a less skilled officer. Artigas did not believe in forlorn hopes: 'I am of the same opinion as any rational man; that is, the greater strength in every case triumphs over the lesser.' He was uttering a prophecy of the main cause of his own eventual disaster.

No doubt, Artigas continued, Rocamora would insist that the prisoners Artigas had taken had told him that the Portuguese force consisted of only forty men. 'This exposition would be a convincing reason to order the attack for any man who possessed that Military Science which I am sure the Colonel has; but since I do not possess it in the same degree as his honour', wrote Artigas, he did not believe his prisoners, suspecting that they meant to lead him into a trap. Since he did 'flee', as Rocamora said, he was not crushed as was the detachment of seventy sent by the Colonel later.

Artigas then attacked the Colonel, pointing out that he had a large force, including artillery, 'all at the disposition and under the command of a leader so Military as the Señor Don Tomás' [Rocamora], and yet five or six Portuguese rustling expeditions did as they liked in the region around him, even using slow bullock carts since they felt so safe, without any of at least four scouting parties from Rocamora's force seeing them or even suspecting their presence. Anybody in the interior should scout round his neighbourhood carefully every day to watch for any movement, as did Artigas; and if Rocamora did the same then all his scouts must have been blind, 'because herding cattle together disturbs a wide expanse of country, since the cattle flee, the herds of wild horses flee, the ostrich, the deer and various other wild animals flee, and in this flight, which does not occur unless there are men close by, any intelligent watcher finds a clue to the motive which causes it'. With that lesson in fieldcraft Artigas left his accuser deflated. Artigas was indispensable to the authorities, who must have read his blunt words with a smile and a shrug and then filed it, leaving him the freedom of his independent ideas.

If Artigas was disgusted with the authorities' neglect of even the elementary safety of the Banda Oriental, the Stock-raisers were no less so, and they even petitioned the King, in October 1804, to do something to bring tranquillity to their estancias, asking him to take up with Lisbon the whole question of the Portuguese advances and raids in the frontier lands. They were becoming exasperated, but as yet were far from revolutionary in feeling.[1] In November Artigas renewed his petition to be allowed to retire, since his old illness had returned: indeed, he affirmed, throughout the campaign he had been suffering from the after-effects of the last attack. Perhaps we may conjecture that the illness was not so severe as Artigas suggested, and that his recent clashes with authority had renewed his intention to retire and be truly independent. This view is reinforced by the fact that Viana took over command of the frontier expedition in November, and had either already done so when Artigas petitioned, or was due to arrive soon and take away what independence Artigas had as chief of his own detachment.[2]

Yet when Viana at length arrived with his large and unwieldy expedition, it was Artigas who was the most helpful in doing what he could to scour the denuded country for cattle to feed the troops, and in performing other services. When it came to the point, he could not let down these men who had come to defend the country: he could not cut off his nose to spite his face. As Viana reported to Sobremonte, Artigas had done all in his power, in spite of his sufferings and bad health; and he mentioned Artigas' 'well-known love for the Royal Service' as something familiar to the Viceroy and all the authorities. But still Viana found that he had not enough active men to 'guard his headquarters, contain the Portuguese, pursue the Barbarians, punish the rustlers, and clean up the country so as to give peace and tranquillity to the ranchers', as his orders stipulated.[3]

The truth is that the large and necessarily unwieldy expedition of those days could not live in that country and at the same time

---

[1] *A.A.*, doc. 89.
[2] *A.A.*, docs. 92 and 93.
[3] *Ibid.* doc. 97.

have the energy to spare to pacify it. The only possible police force was the small, highly mobile party such as Artigas had led, composed entirely of gauchos and under the command of an expert frontiersman. No doubt Viana realised this fact, and he certainly thought of forming a company of fifty gauchos especially enlisted – a scheme which received the Viceroy's approval in April 1805. In June the company was formed, put under Artigas' command as a matter of course, and sent on an expedition against the Indians.[1]

Meanwhile the large expedition had undertaken a long march, and had been badly shaken by the rough going of the thicket-clad untracked country and by the shortage of provisions. Where before cattle had lived in thousands, it was now necessary to search ten or twelve leagues for enough to feed the troops every day. The horses suffered too, because of this hard service on top of the normal marches and unsuitable camping sites and the hazards of storms and jaguars. Nevertheless, Artigas scouted out the Indians, who defended themselves fiercely when hopelessly taken by surprise. One Indian earned the praise of Viana by charging with his lance straight for twenty soldiers standing ready for him, and by dying still 'embracing his lance'. On this expedition further evidence of the depredations of Brazilian settlers was found, in several large stretches of country covered with the skeletons of four to six thousand cattle slaughtered by them, and in the spearheads made in Portugal used by their Indian allies. Viana's troops lost all semblance of military order because of their privations. They did not even look like soldiers, since their uniforms and poor equipment had quickly rotted, and now they had to cover their nakedness with their horse-blankets. This expedition in its present state could do nothing against the Portuguese.[2]

Perhaps it is not surprising that in March 1805 Artigas once again petitioned to be allowed to retire because of his state of health, and this time without even pressing for a pension. His

---

[1] *Ibid.* docs. 100, 101, 103 and 104.
[2] *Ibid.* doc. 105.

doctor's certificate showed that he suffered from a general stiffness in all his body and dropsy in both legs, caused no doubt by his rough service, and that he could not ride without suffering a dangerous decline in health. This was conclusive enough: Artigas could not continue in active service.[1] The petition went its long journey through the usual channels, but meanwhile at the end of June Viana was forced or prevailed upon to grant Artigas sick leave to recuperate in Montevideo.[2]

There has been a suggestion that Artigas' sickness and petitions for retirement were subterfuges for a different purpose. One historian, who traced his early life, wrote: 'we believe that Artigas hid the true cause, as his sickness was not physical but moral'; but this author believed that the true cause was a passion which Artigas conceived for his cousin Rafaela Rosalía Villagrán. This may have contributed to his desire to leave the service, but the completely mature age of both (Artigas was forty-one and Rafaela thirty when they married in December 1805) argues against the hypothesis that Artigas threw up his career at the height of a sudden passion, as also does the length of time (since late 1802) that Artigas had been spending long periods on sick leave. Also, in Artigas' petition to the ecclesiastical authorities asking for licence to marry his first cousin, the main reason for setting aside the rule against consanguinity was given as Rafaela's advanced age, which made it 'very difficult for her now to find a husband to maintain her in the condition in which the Petitioner is able to owing to his comfortable circumstances'. Rafaela's father was dead and her mother was poor, so in this marriage Artigas was acting as a loyal and charitable member of his family.[3] Indeed, he was praised at this time by the clergy who granted the licence as a man of known merit in the Royal service, and of 'good disposition, and love for his family'. This does not sound like passion.

[1] *Ibid.* docs. 111 and 112.

[2] *Ibid.* docs. 107 and 108.

[3] L. Barbagelata, *op. cit.* pp. 82-6; Traibel, *op. cit.* p. 39; see also the documents on Artigas' marriage in *A.A.*, t. III, pt. VI, especially doc. 1.

In any case, in November, a month before his marriage, Artigas was petitioning the Viceroy for a certain post which would allow him to recuperate yet at the same time be on the active list. The post was that of commander of the remount depot, usually reserved for meritorious officers needing rest. It was occupied, and Artigas was given no post. So he repeated his application in April, only to meet the same rebuff.[1] Apparently Artigas was in need of money at this time, and he therefore applied for employment so as to keep his expenses down while awaiting the result of his application for retirement. This impression is strengthened by his insistence on trying to get the five hundred pesos promised him by the Guild of Stock-raisers as a reward for his successes in the last campaign. He spoke to the Viceroy about this in August 1804, when visiting Buenos Aires, and wrote asking him about it in May and December 1806.[2] On the latter occasion he wrote: 'I have now been living for two years in this Fortress [Montevideo], and up to now I have not received any money at all', and that his illnesses 'have caused me much expense, and this is the reason why I am embarrassed and am respectfully troubling Your Excellency'. Through all this Artigas was learning to have ever less respect for the way things were done in his country.

Even as an invalid and bridegroom Artigas was not left in peace, for in December 1805 the Plate Viceroyalty was shocked into mobilisation by the news that a threatening British fleet, accompanied by troop transports, was watering in Rio de Janeiro, and seemed to be on its way to try to make a surprise attack on the Spanish territory. The troops and militia were called out and volunteer bands of citizens were formed. Artigas married on the 23rd of December, and only the day before he had been given the command of one of these bands. A large proportion of his particular band was formed by prisoners released on condition that they would join. Many of this tough body of men must have been

---

[1] *A.A.*, t. III, pt. v, docs. 116-120.
[2] *A.A.*, docs. 1211-25.

captured by Artigas himself in his various expeditions. Their crimes bear witness to their toughness; but Artigas was able to lead them, and not by his own sheer toughness, but by his humanity. When some of the worst characters were to be taken from him and not freed (men guilty of treacherous murders, rapes and arson), he pleaded to be allowed to keep them because he had given his word that if they served under him they would be freed, pointing out that if after that they were not freed, they would blame him and take any future opportunity of revenging themselves upon him. He won his point, and kept his men.[1]

This party left Montevideo on the 29th of December to do its part, but it was back again in a few days. Before the end of January 1806, however, Artigas was again out on his usual service of keeping order in the country, and he led his normal active life until his return to the capital in March, and again in May he was out for a short time.[2] Artigas had a short honeymoon and an undomestic marriage.

If in fact Artigas' passion for Rafaela had been overpowering at first, it soon met a tragic and insurmountable obstacle. His only legitimate son, José María, was born a year after the marriage, and after the birth his wife began to suffer from intermittent attacks of lunacy, probably increased by the deaths of two daughters, within a few months of their births, in 1808 and 1810. Artigas was always tender towards her and his son, as his letters of 1815 and 1816, in the middle of his great struggles, testify; but he was resigned to his intimate loneliness, and after 1806 became restless, as though he could not bear the sadness in his home. This must have turned such an active man outwards towards the problems which had claimed his attention before, and which now must have become his ruling passion. But to begin with, Artigas returned to the Spanish service, glad of the opportunity it gave him for long absences in his beloved country, in spite of the continuance of the unsatisfactory

---

[1] *A.A.*, t. III, pt. VI, doc. 10; pt. VII, docs. 1-5.
[2] *Ibid.*, docs. 6-20, 24.

hierarchy which had disheartened him before. This continued link with the Spanish authorities at once explains Artigas' tardiness in joining the revolutionary movement in May 1810, and his violent independence once he had thrown in his lot.

In the middle of 1806 Ruiz Huidobro employed Artigas as a preventive officer in the capital, and here the future Chief of the Orientals showed in one instance what has been taken as a remarkable gentleness, in contrast to the brutality attributed to him by his detractors of a few years later. A militia sergeant beat his wife, who ran away and took refuge with an ensign, perhaps her lover. The sergeant went to fetch her, but she refused to go with him and he drew his sword on the officer. Artigas sent a party of men to arrest him, but when it became clear that the sergeant would resist, he withdrew his men and wrote a note to the Governor asking permission to shoot if the sergeant resisted arrest at the next attempt; 'for I am informing Your Honour of this so that if the arrest of the said Sergeant should lead to serious trouble, there shall follow no charges against me'.[1] Is this an unwillingness to shed blood, or rather an unwillingness to take the responsibility? The most likely explanation is that Artigas, not feeling independent and free to do as he would have done in the interior, wanted to be sure that he was doing the right thing in going to the utmost limits to impose order in Montevideo. One can imagine that this doubt would rankle in Artigas' mind and force him to reassure himself of the legality of his act. The incident at any rate does go to prove Artigas' respect for the law, if further proof were needed after this survey of his early efforts on its behalf.

A few weeks after this incident, there occurred another which besides involving Artigas was to have great repercussions on the state of affairs in the River Plate: it was the first English Invasion, a most important formative force during the growth of the Plate countries.

---

[1] E. Acevedo, *op. cit.* vol. I, p. 147; cf. also L. Barbagelata, *op. cit.* pp. 86-7; *A.A.*, t. III, pt. VII, doc. 25.

CHAPTER III

THE DIVISION OF THE WAYS

I. THE VICEROYALTY THREATENED:
THE ENGLISH INVASIONS

ONE of the most far-reaching effects of the English Invasions (always given capital letters by River Plate historians) of 1806 and 1807 was to increase the mutual jealousy and hostility of Buenos Aires and Montevideo, a fact which has not been sufficiently stressed. The growth of these sentiments had continued since the port question of the first years of the century, and any piece of administration or business which involved both of the cities was by now bound to lead to attempts by one to get the better of the other, or at least was bound to create suspicions that this was happening. The burghers of Montevideo were particularly sensitive to these attempts and suspicions, since they were in an inferior position to the citizens of the viceregal capital. Hence, for instance, in 1803 the Cabildo of Montevideo made public the information gathered by the Guild of Stock-raisers on the chaotic state of the interior,[1] showing how the Portuguese had defied the Treaty of Badajoz and had occupied all the region between the Uruguay and the Ibicuy.

The Montevideans blamed the state of affairs they described on the neglect of the authorities of Buenos Aires, and wrote: 'The interior is at the present day the practical school of all sorts of crime, and the refuge of all classes of delinquents. The distance from the Capital [that is, Buenos Aires]: the multiplicity and importance of the affairs of the Superior Government, the consequent delay in its measures: the division of jurisdictions, the lack of guarding, the asylum and protection given to the Portuguese, the slowness and inertia of the last expedition and the jealousy with

[1] *Informe* of Cabildo, 23 August 1803, *Arch. Adm.*, 272; 2; 29.

which the Capital observes the growth of this people and their commerce, all unite to destroy and annihilate the happiness of these countries . . .' Jealousy of the people of Buenos Aires for the progress of a possible rival: it was the port question over again. As a result of this intentional neglect, 'it can be affirmed with certainty that the Interior is in the same state as Savage Countries in which strength and passions alone command'; and the only remedies were to throw out the Portuguese and settle the interior – as Azara had proposed in 1801, the Stock-raisers might have added.

Now came the English Invasions, episodes which on the surface appear to give evidence of an approximation of the rival cities and their hinterlands for common defence and mutual help; yet in fact the very help given by each to the other at certain times became later the source of bitter recrimination and jealousy, whilst the British occupation of Montevideo in 1807 gave the Orientals ideas of prosperity through trade which clashed with the ambitions of Buenos Aires.

An English invasion of some part of Spanish America was nothing new: such things had been taking place since the sixteenth century, caused by golden dreams of the supposed wealth of the Spanish possessions. British pirates, smugglers, merchants and slave-traders had seen visions of unlimited profit in Spanish America. The British Government at times dallied with schemes for invading parts of the Spanish Empire even in the eighteenth century, not to mention Cromwell's ideas in the previous century, and had lately been encouraged in this flirtation by Miranda, the Venezuelan 'Great Precursor' of the Spanish American Revolution. Spain, when the Napoleonic Wars upset the world, became a useful satellite of France, and the wealth – especially the silver, it was suspected – drawn from her America might be a potent weapon against Britain. Therefore Pitt, the Prime Minister, was willing to support Miranda and the adventurous English naval captain, Sir Home Riggs Popham, in a scheme they brought forward in 1804 for invading various parts of South America, including the River Plate,[1] for the sake of emancipating the Spanish colonies and setting up friendly creole governments there. The operation was postponed owing to more urgent needs nearer home, but Popham did not forget, and when he had helped to capture the Cape of Good Hope from the Dutch in 1805, he recalled that the supposedly rich and certainly strategically placed Viceroyalty of the River Plate was only a step away over the South Atlantic. Borrowing a few troops from the military commander at the Cape and a few more from St. Helena, he sailed to make an unauthorised attack on Montevideo, the fortress city, the key to the Plate, with its fifteen thousand inhabitants and its strong garrison; but he changed his mind when he heard of a rich consignment of treasure lying at Buenos Aires, and he decided to go straight for the capital, with its forty thousand people. His own landing force consisted of one thousand six hundred and thirty-five men under General Beresford, later famous in the Peninsular War. The attack was a startling and swift success. The convoy arrived in the River Plate on the 10th of June, the troops landed near Buenos Aires on the 26th, and they occupied the city the next day after a little skirmishing.

The Spanish Viceroy there was now Sobremonte, the able administrator, who should not have let himself be surprised in this way. Apart from the presence of the convoy in the river since the 10th of June, he had had warning the year before of possible invasion, for the expedition to the Cape, which Popham had convoyed, had watered in Brazil, and news had been brought to Buenos Aires, where it was thought that an attack was imminent. Certain precautions which, as has already been mentioned, involved José Artigas at the start of his married life, had been taken in the area. However, the first fright had worn off, and Sobremonte

[1] J. Street, *La influencia británica en la independencia de las Provincias del Río de la Plata, con especial referencia al período comprendido entre 1806 y 1816*, chap. 1, in *Revista Histórica*, año XLVII (2a. ép.), t. XIX, nos. 55-57; R. A. Humphreys, *Liberation in South America 1806-1827. The career of James Paroissien*, chap. 1.

had done very little to organise defence against the British this time. He had even, together with his family, left his capital before the British attack, and when it came he had fled to Córdoba, some hundreds of miles inland. This act and his later weakness soon made Sobremonte unpopular with all classes in his capital and led to his deposition – the first of a series of revolutionary acts which culminated in the Revolution of May 1810.

Beresford's well-meaning military government of Buenos Aires hardly had time to impress the creoles with British enlightenment, as was the intention, before it was overwhelmed by a popular creole reaction. Beresford offered the people continuance of their own law and religion, a considerable degree of self-government, and the great advantages of *comercio libre:* that is, trade with any friendly nation, as opposed to the Spanish closed system. It was the standard British régime of those days, as the ex-Spanish colonists of Trinidad were discovering to their benefit. Free trade in this sense was what the creole ranchers had been desiring for many years, in order to sell their hides and tallow in a profitable market and gain consumer goods cheaply in return. Beresford and Popham had every reason to think that the creoles would welcome the change of government, particularly since Miranda had given voluble assurances that the creoles of Spanish America had had enough of Spanish domination and were ripe for emancipation.

But it was emancipation that the creoles wanted, not a change of masters, even a change including greater wealth as one of its benefits, and so they failed to support the British, in the way that the people of 'liberated' territories almost invariably turn against the occupying 'liberator'. The creoles joined with the Spanish authorities and the Spanish merchants with vested interests in the old régime in throwing out the invaders. Beresford, since he had had no orders from the British Government, could give no promise of emancipation, and had to rule as he would a normal occupied district. The new Whig Government, which had succeeded to power after Pitt's death in January 1806, had no ideas at all on the treatment of South Americans, and after recovering from their shock at learning of the unexpected gift Popham and Beresford offered them, they took the line of making a normal British colony of it. Pitt had been wiser: he had been convinced that only emancipation would do, and if he had survived it is possible that the Invasions might have eased considerably the process of the emancipation of at any rate the southern Spanish American dominions.

In any case, by the time Britain heard of the conquest of Buenos Aires, that city was back under Spanish rule and the British occupiers were prisoners of war. Within two days of the conquest a resistance group started work in the capital, and began to dig mines under the British barracks and to enlist volunteer troops in the surrounding countryside. Sobremonte in Córdoba began futile preparations for counter-attack, and the fortress city of Montevideo came into its own as the base of Spanish operations. There, plans for a reconquering expedition were made, and the command was given to Santiago Liniers, a Frenchman serving as an officer in the Spanish navy. He took his men across the Plate, landing on the 4th of August, incorporated into his force the body of volunteers commanded by Pueyrredón, a local worthy who later became Supreme Director of the new state, and marched on Buenos Aires. He took it on the 12th, after Beresford had lost three hundred men and had realised the hopelessness of further resistance against the whole people. The importance of this victory lay in the self-confidence it instilled into the creoles who formed the basis of the troops. Now they began to see that they were better than the Spanish hierarchy, who had not been able to keep the British out.

Artigas played a minor part in this new campaign. During the scare of 1805 he had, though still officially sick, been given command by the Governor, Ruiz Huidobro, of a force of two hundred cavalry raised and maintained by a rich *saladerista* (owner of a meat-salting establishment). When in June 1806 there came news of the approach of the British fleet, Artigas was again put in command of a troop of volunteers. At the fall of Buenos Aires, Montevideo prepared the Reconquest (as River Plate historians call the recovery of the viceregal capital), and Artigas volunteered to go with the expedition in any capacity, since his own regiment, the *Blandengues*, was not able to go, having been detailed to guard various parts of the country. Ruiz Huidobro trusted Artigas with a message for Liniers, on the other side of the Plate, and Liniers gave Artigas a place in one of the attacking columns outside Buenos Aires. Artigas noted that his detachment behaved with the greatest spirit and valour, as did a number of *Porteños* who joined them, but he can have done little else but observe as he had no command. At the victory he was sent back to Ruiz Huidobro with the good news, and was almost drowned on the journey when his boat capsized.[1]

The perhaps surprising loyalty to Buenos Aires of the people of the persecuted and neglected Montevideo may be explained by the presence of the very orthodox Spanish Governor Ruiz Huidobro, a good soldier and a good governor, who had spent his energies doing all in his power to help the prosperity of Montevideo and the Banda Oriental. He had won the respect and affection of the people of all the region, and now it would hardly be too strong to say that he became the soul of the reconquest of Buenos Aires. He organised the expedition and distributed the loans and gifts generously subscribed by the merchants and landowners in his district. But it should be remembered, too, that the Reconquest was popular from the start, and roused the enthusiasm of all the people. Probably the Orientals gave their services and money for the campaign to free Buenos Aires mainly because of their fear of the British, and also partly because of their vanity, which was agreeably tickled by their being in a position to rescue the capital, which had fallen so ignominiously before a very small army. Certainly a

[1] Certificate of services of José Artigas, 10 June 1808, Arch. Adm., libro 165, doc. 12. See also E. Acevedo, *op. cit.* vol. I, pp. 159–160; and *A.A.*, t. III, pt. VII, docs. 27-30.

contemporary Montevidean diarist could sneer about 'the domineering men of Buenos Aires' having fallen in their pride, and yet at the same time offer a large sum of money to help to pay the costs of the reconquering expedition.[1]

Historians have pointed out that possibly the citizens of Montevideo saw in this reconquest a means of wiping out Buenos Aires' supremacy and asserting their own.[2] At any rate, at this time of danger the merchants and ranchers, who had been loudest in their condemnation of the policies of Buenos Aires, were quick and generous in their support.[3] But that they were still critical of Buenos Aires is shown in the Cabildo's loyal letter to the King, written on the 4th of July 1806, when the news of the fall of Buenos Aires was fresh. Amid offers and reports of help for the capital appears this: 'the Capital has surrendered without firing a shot: but Montevideo, Sire, is more fearful of losing for one single instant her vassaldom to the Catholic Crown than of shedding all her blood for its glorious conservation'.[4] And the declaration of the intention of reconquering Buenos Aires is accompanied by the heavy hint that it would have been done already 'if the wearisome subjection, the humiliating dependence of this Government and Commerce to those of Buenos Aires did not forbid [Montevideo] the freedom even of preparing against her own needs. Ah Sire! How certain it is that the dumb eloquence of events reaches where reason does not.'

This was striking while the iron was hot, and the Cabildo went on to point out that Montevideo had not even been made an Intendancy, whilst lesser cities in the interior of the Viceroyalty had, and that Montevideo felt the 'enormous weight against her progress'

---

[1] A. I. Gómez Ferreyra, S. J., *La Invasión Inglesa vista desde Montevideo*.

[2] Blanco Acevedo, *op. cit.* p. 141; Pivel Devoto, *Prólogo*, in *A.A.*, t. III, p. LXVIII.

[3] The merchants and ranchers offered to impose on all exports a tax of 2 % ,calculated to raise 100,000 pesos to pay the troops and supply horses. The Governor asked them to make it specie, not paper money, which the troops would not accept as they were unused to it. (Letter of Ruiz Huidobro to the Montevideo Deputy of the Buenos Aires Consulado, 7 July 1806, in M.H.N., vol. III.)

[4] Arch. Adm., *borradores*, caja 304; I; 110.

of this 'servitude' to Buenos Aires. The old grudges against the Consulado of Buenos Aires were resuscitated to show how Montevideo had been left without official resources. Now, in the moment of danger, Montevideo had to rely on the patriotism of her citizens. Finally, the Cabildo openly asked the King to make the city the headquarters of an Intendancy and to give her a Consulado of her own. These authorities would in the future, boasted the Cabildo, ensure the tranquillity of the Plate and take effective measures against further attacks. The inference was that Buenos Aires was lax and unworthy, but the key to the Plate, Montevideo, if given some autonomy, would make up for the capital's defects.

It is clear that the Cabildo had in view the autonomy which had been Montevideo's aim for years, and took the conquest of Buenos Aires as an argument in favour of its thesis. At the same time the Cabildo took this opportunity of asserting another old claim: the letter asked the King to extend the limits of the proposed new Intendancy so as to include the whole Banda Oriental, for the purpose of making the whole a reasonable administrative district. Autonomy of the Banda Oriental and unity within it: the claims were sensible, and were supported by strong reasons of efficient government, as has been seen, for example, in the question of preserving the frontier. But also, the claims were near to the heart of the people of the Banda Oriental, who showed by now marked signs of separate regional, almost national, characteristics, which in due time Artigas was to utilise in his effort to attain the country's freedom.

After the reconquest of the capital, Liniers, the leader, became the city's popular hero, and Montevideo's help was remembered in medals struck in her honour. But this honeymoon soon ended, for although Liniers remained popular, and was even made military commander of the Viceroyalty in place of Sobremonte, who was still skulking on the pampa, the *Porteños* soon began to quarrel with the Montevideans over the relative importance of their efforts towards the Reconquest. The *Porteños* claimed that they had risen *en masse* when the army from Montevideo had arrived, and so it was they who had really won the victory, whereas the Montevideans counter-claimed that they had raised and equipped the army, without which Buenos Aires would never have been freed. The Cabildo of Montevideo, supported by the Governor of the city, claimed to be given possession of the British flags taken as trophies. Buenos Aires, supported by the popular idol Liniers, refused to part with them. The old rancours between the cities flared up again, especially in Montevideo, ever the more susceptible since she was weaker and subordinate. The result was that Montevideo decided to press as strongly as she could her claims to autonomy, and her Cabildo sent two delegates to Spain to forward the negotiations. It was a decisive move, since Montevideo now put forward her claims in an active campaign, without relying, as she had done in the past, merely on petitions. The first Invasion and the Reconquest had their first important result in the open moves by Montevideo to 'free' herself from Buenos Aires.

Besides announcing the Reconquest, which was the official motive of the mission, the delegates were to ask for various rewards. The most important was the creation of an Intendancy which should include all the Banda Oriental; then came the creation of a Consulado because that of Buenos Aires merely taxed the Montevideo trade and used the proceeds in Buenos Aires, doing nothing for Montevideo. Other privileges requested included the granting of some means of raising money to spend on necessary works, and also of special dignities for the city, such as the use of mace-bearers, additions to the coat of arms as honours of the Reconquest, and other things. Montevideo intended to put Buenos Aires in her place,[1] and all her people were agreed on this. But the delegates had a hard time of it when they got to Madrid, because apart from the difficulties normal in getting anything done at the Spanish court, there were the additional delays caused by

[1] Blanco Acevedo, *op cit.* pp. 155-7; Pivel Devoto, *Prólogo, op. cit.,* pp. lxviii-lxx, lxxxi-xcviii,

events in Spain in the next few years, and the opposition of a counter-delegation sent by Buenos Aires a few months after the departure of that from Montevideo. However, some concessions were made at length, especially since Montevideo's merit in Spanish eyes continued to be raised by further acts of loyalty in succeeding years.

The months after the Reconquest, indeed, were filled with activity. Besides the embittering of the quarrel between Montevideo and Buenos Aires, there was the British danger to think about. More forces were to be raised to withstand a new attack which was expected, since the British fleet still blockaded the Plate; and at the same time the British prisoners of war used their enforced excursions to safe points of the interior to good effect by spreading ideas of constitutional monarchy, free trade, freemasonry and emancipation wherever they went.[1] Sobremonte in August tentatively approached his capital, to be met by a delegation with the news that Liniers was in command and he, the Viceroy, was not welcome. This was not yet revolution, but it was self-government in a way, and it was the creoles who had insisted on the change. Sobremonte therefore crossed the River Plate to install himself in Montevideo, ostensibly to organise the defence there; and he found himself only more welcome there than in Buenos Aires because he was in conflict with the capital.

Preparations for defence went on with enthusiasm in both the rival cities, but in Montevideo Sobremonte was distrusted as a leader, and the Governor and people soon became nervous. If it came to the point, Montevideo's morale would soon desert her because of Sobremonte's bad reputation. Buenos Aires was not so hampered, and she was united behind Liniers.

The second English Invasion commenced, then, in October,

---

[1] Street, *op. cit.* pp. 220, 224-5; A. Gillespie, *Gleanings and remarks collected during many months of residence at Buenos Ayres and within the upper country*, pp. 62-3; letters of Viola to Ogilvie and Patrick (British officer prisoners of war) of 8 November and 24 December 1806, AGN, B.A., Div. Col., Sec. Gob., legajo 30-3-6.

when reinforcements consisting of one thousand seven hundred men arrived from the Cape of Good Hope, tried with Popham to attack Montevideo, failed, and instead occupied Maldonado as a strong point where they could await a larger army from England. They had an uncomfortable time of it, for they were penned in by gaucho cavalry sent from Montevideo, and they learned to their surprise that the people of the country were not in the least ready to accept British rule, even with open ports, in exchange for Spanish.[1] Indeed, the Cabildo of Montevideo sent a delegation asking for help from Buenos Aires in view of the imminence of an attack, but Liniers realised that he could spare nothing, whilst the creole militia of Buenos Aires ordered the delegates to leave the capital on pain of death. Montevideo was suitably impressed by the sisterly spirit of Buenos Aires.[2] It was not the best augury for a defence or for a hazardous future. Thrown on her own resources, Montevideo continued feverishly preparing for the attack which was bound to come. Everything possible was done: what could not be done, which was to turn Sobremonte into a soldier, proved to be the fatal weakness.

In January 1807 there arrived in the Plate a convoy of reinforcements sent from Britain the previous September, when the Whig Government had decided to make a real effort to capture a large foothold in Spanish America in view of the unprecedented success at Buenos Aires. Heavy pressure from the merchants of Britain, who were badly in need of an outlet since the Continent was closed to them by Bonaparte, had helped to push the Whigs into this action; and the merchants themselves had been led on by a circular from Popham puffing up the magnificence of the market South America offered, and by the traditional belief in the inexhaustible wealth of the Spanish Empire. Indeed, had they not seen cart-loads of Spanish silver captured in Buenos Aires paraded

---

[1] Efforts to win help, even to get a minimum of food, are shown by the promises and threats contained in proclamations in bad Spanish distributed by these troops, AGN, B.A., Div. Col., Sec. Gob., legajo 30-3-6.

[2] Blanco Acevedo, *op. cit.* p. 162.

in triumph through the streets of the City? The Government, too, still believed Popham's hints that the creoles would help to overthrow the Spanish régime so as to place themselves under the 'mild British yoke' for the sake of trade and tolerance. Therefore Wellesley, the future Duke of Wellington, was set to draw up a plan for the invasion of Mexico, and in November an army was in fact embarked to make an attack on Chile and carry on into Peru. Things were not to be done by halves: even sepoys from India were to be called in at a certain stage.

All this imaginative scheming collapsed when General Auchmuty arrived in the Plate in January to find Buenos Aires freed, and a miserable, hungry detachment of British troops besieged in Maldonado. He proceeded to make what he could of the affair, and re-embarked the Maldonado party before sailing to attack Montevideo, which he quickly realised must be captured because of its strategic position. The British attack met fierce resistance from the fortress city, which had to be taken by the formal means of a siege followed by an assault. It was an operation costly to both sides, but it was successfully carried out on the 3rd of February, and quickly the city fell. Sobremonte had performed his familiar manoeuvre of beating a strategic retreat out of and away from the city when danger threatened. Fresh appeals for the help of Buenos Aires had been received with coolness in the capital, and Liniers had been allowed to leave with only a small auxiliary force too late to help Montevideo. Both these failures had their repercussions.

As in the first Invasion, Artigas did his duty. He had continued in employment in the security force of Montevideo, and his fine reputation had caused his Commanding Officer, Allende, to ask for Artigas to be posted as an aide of his when he was placed in command, in November 1806, of an expedition to dislodge the English from Maldonado. Sobremonte refused to allow Artigas to go, since he remained in command of the only troop of cavalry left on the coast – and they were his own men, whom he himself was maintaining.[1] Later, as the second Invasion approached, Artigas was sent on reconnaissances, and then was put in charge of a system of warning beacons which was set up. His outstanding local knowledge made him the automatic choice for a post where exact and rapid judgement of views, distances and angles was essential.[2]

When the battle started, Artigas took part with the *Blandengues* in various skirmishes round the city, ending up together with most of his regiment helping to man the walls. His Commanding Officer mentioned him and other officers by name in his report on the action, writing that they all 'carried themselves with the greatness boldness, without sparing themselves at all, encouraging the men who, however, needed no encouragement in view of the ardour with which they threw themselves into the enemy's fire'.[3] Artigas refused to give himself up to the invaders, and escaped by boat across the bay of Montevideo to continue the resistance. His part in this campaign increased the esteem in which he was held by the Spanish authorities and by his countrymen. He next tried to organise a party of *Blandengues* to roam the country round Montevideo and cut off the British from supplies, though his efforts had little success because he had no pay for his men.[4] His anger and grief at not being able to throw out the invaders was real: the fact was that he felt that it was his own native land which had been invaded, and he reacted as a patriot.

Sobremonte's second failure brought Buenos Aires perilously close to revolution. Within a week of the fall of Montevideo the Viceroy had been deposed by a *Cabildo abierto* (town council meeting attended by high officials and influential citizens especially invited for some important discussion) influenced by a yelling creole mob, and the Viceroyalty was placed under the joint government of Liniers and the Audiencia. Liniers, backed by his large creole militia, had the real power, and Spanish authority

[1] *A.A.*, t. III, pt. VII, docs. 32-5.
[2] *Ibid.* docs. 38-57.
[3] *Ibid.* doc. 76.
[4] *Ibid.* docs. 65-7.

received another blow. The resistance prepared against the expected British attack was largely a creole matter.

The British occupation of Montevideo, from February to
September 1807, continued the spreading of discontent with the
Spanish régime begun by Beresford the previous year. Once again
the virtues of British rule were publicised by official proclamations
and liberal legislation, by a bilingual newspaper (the first in
Montevideo), *The Southern Star, La Estrella del Sur,* and most of all
by the two thousand or so British merchants who flocked into the
city. But in spite of a policy of painstaking respect for local
authorities and religion, and in spite of the increased prosperity of
the city under liberal trade regulations,[1] no permanent change of
government could be made palatable because the British still
lacked the insight to realise that the creoles wanted independence,
not a change of masters. Beresford, escaped from captivity, had
realised this, but before his ideas could reach the British Government every chance of emancipation by British help had been lost
with the loss of the foothold in the Plate. The expedition to Chile
had been diverted to the Plate to help to recapture Buenos Aires,
and a new expedition with an incompetent but senior general,
Whitelocke, had been sent from England to complete the conquest. Whitelocke had attacked Buenos Aires in July, had been
thoroughly beaten by the brave and well organised creole resistance, and to extricate himself and his army he had had to capitulate,
handing back to the Spanish authorities all the territory occupied
in the Plate.

The general effect of the English Invasions was to shake creole
faith in Spanish efficacy, and at the same time to heighten the
creoles' confidence in their own ability. The mutterings of discontent, particularly with the economic régime, became louder
because the British rule had given an example of comparative
liberty and of the prosperity possible with a more open commercial organisation. A creole citizen army had been formed,

[1] See Blanco Acevedo, *op. cit.* chap. XVI.

trained, and tried in battle; and it was much stronger in numbers and in spirit than the Spanish regulars in the Plate. Indeed, the English Invasions left the Viceroyalty almost prepared for emancipation, and with concrete ideas concerning what it wanted from a change of government.

But the effect on relations between Montevideo and Buenos Aires was even more clear and specific at the time. If the First Invasion had made Montevideo openly appeal for separation from Buenos Aires, the Second almost caused hostilities between the cities. Montevideo felt that Buenos Aires had played her false in not sending help promptly, and then had made things worse by not accepting a prisoners' exchange suggested by the British, which would have freed many Montevideans languishing in British transports in the harbour, some of whom were at length sent to Britain. Meanwhile the British themselves were courteous, allowed the Cabildo and the laws of the country to operate unchanged, and became friendly with the Montevideans. Montevideo did not welcome a return of Buenos Aires' overlordship, and Buenos Aires was excessively suspicious of the loyalty of the people of Montevideo. This was a bad start for an era of disquieting events.

No case was more critical than that of open trade. British commerce had brought an unknown prosperity to Montevideo, turned into a vast emporium after having been almost ruined by the cost of the Reconquest and then her own defence. Although formerly the Spanish merchants settled in the city had been loud in their protests against allowing any British goods to enter the port, even in neutral ships,[1] the people in general were won over by the prosperity brought by British goods during the occupation. A fleet of sixty-six British merchantmen, attracted by Popham's circular of 1806, had sailed into Montevideo harbour with the warships convoying the attacking troops, and others continually

[1] M.H.N. book III: *Expediente* of 1806 on two cargoes of English goods; letter of Montevideo merchants to Consulado, 26 November 1806.

arrived. The merchants, some of them 'a dubious crew', established themselves wherever they could find room in the city, so that . . . 'it soon had more the appearance of an English colony than of a Spanish settlement'.[1] General Auchmuty cut the customs dues from an average of over fifty per cent. to twelve and a half per cent., with the result that goods to the value of three quarters of a million pounds entered before the middle of May, and were sold by the British merchants for one and a quarter million pounds. Activity went on at this rate until September, and it is obvious that a city which in peace-time had only fifteen thousand people could not absorb the goods represented by these figures at the values of those days. And in fact, there was a large contraband trade going on in the Banda Oriental between the people under British rule and those still under the Spanish, so that the whole Viceroyalty was a market for the goods.[2] The Spanish authorities could not stop this trade. An officer in charge of gaucho troops trying to do so reported of the people of the Banda Oriental: 'These people are not only disobedient, but most insolent, and when one tries to gain recruits, the least thing they reply is that now another King rules them [the British King].' Desertion was heavy: one sergeant lost all his men but one, whom he had to send to headquarters to report the fact.[3]

When on her evacuation by the British troops, Montevideo returned to the Spanish rule, in September 1807, it went very much against the grain for the Montevideans to accept again the closed system of trade, and to lose their fruitful contacts with Britain.

2. THE VICEROYALTY THREATENED: CRISIS OF THE RELATIONS BETWEEN BUENOS AIRES AND MONTEVIDEO

Buenos Aires and Liniers now seemed to go out of their way to hurt the feelings of the Montevideans, already raw after the British

---

[1] See J. P. and W. P. Robertson, *op. cit.*, vol. I, pp. 101–2.

[2] Letters Auchmuty to Windham, 2 March 1807, 27 April 1807, and custom return for Montevideo, in P.R.O., W.O. 1/162.

[3] Joaquín Alvarez to Allende, 8 and 9 February 1807, AGN, B.A., Div. Col., Sec. Gob., leg. 30-3-7.

occupation of their city and its evacuation arranged as an after-thought when Whitelocke capitulated before Buenos Aires.[1] Even before the British troops left Montevideo, Liniers, acting as provisional head of the Viceroyalty, appointed a young and vigorous new Governor over her to replace the lamented Ruiz Huidobro, who had been sent as a prisoner of war to England. The new Governor, Colonel Francisco Xavier de Elío, was a new-comer whose only recommendation, so far as was known in Montevideo, was that he had played a poor part in the fighting against the British. He was, however, a man of some intelligence and great patriotism and ambition, and he was a seasoned soldier who soon proved his mettle. At the moment his appointment was a double insult to Montevideo, for Liniers, not being a royally appointed Viceroy until May the following year, had no power to nominate governors; whilst in cases of absence of governors with-out duly appointed deputies, the Laws of the Indies stipulated that the Senior Alcalde of the chief city of the district should act as Governor pending the royal decision. Also, Elío was junior to other better-known and better-qualified officers who would have been more acceptable to Montevideo.[2]

This looked like a calculated slight on the loyalty and import-ance of Montevideo, and her Cabildo accordingly protested and even sent the case up to Madrid for settlement. Meanwhile, how-ever, they were persuaded to accept the Governor as a provisional appointment. They were not to regret it, for Elío soon became Montevideo's firmest protector against Buenos Aires. He began by showing a real interest in Montevideo's prosperity and defence, and worked in harmony with the Cabildo instead of merely giving them orders, as they had feared he would, with the result that soon the people of Montevideo were won over to ardent support of him.

[1] J. J. Biedma and A. S. Mallié, (eds.), *Acuerdos del extinguido Cabildo de Buenos Aires*, t. III, años 1807-1808, entry for 5 de julio de 1807; Blanco Acevedo, *op. cit.* chap. XVII.

[2] *Borrador* letter to the King from the Cabildo, 2 November 1807, in Arch. Adm., legajo 315; IA; 76.

Liniers, however, continued his foolish if not petulant interference. He ordered the officers of the militia artillery, which had won praise from the British for their brave defence of the city, to be replaced by complete strangers: another slight upon the people of Montevideo. He alienated Elío by taking over command of the Spanish naval base of the River Plate, a command always exercised by the Governor of Montevideo as the officer in charge of the fortress blocking the way up the Plate. This insult, with its implied slur on the quality of the port of Montevideo, made the Montevideans take Elío to their hearts as a joint martyr with them to the jealousy of the capital.

This bitterness was increased by the squabbling between the two cities over honours granted in recompense of their efforts against the British. Unofficial news came before the end of 1807 telling of the honours conferred on Montevideo for the reconquest of Buenos Aires. She was awarded the title of *Muy Fiel y Reconquistadora* (Most Faithful and Reconquering), and given certain rights. The more important rewards, the Intendancy and the Consulado, were still under consideration, and were delayed at first by Buenos Aires' representations about her own part in the Reconquest and her own victory over the British army commanded by Whitelocke. Buenos Aires, indeed, was thrown into a fury by the news of the honours given to her rival, and she began new representations for honours as a reward for the later victory, even going so far as to claim for her Cabildo the ridiculous title of *Conservador de la América del Sur y Protector Medianero de todos los demás Cabildos del Continente* (Conserver of South America and Mediating Protector of all the other Town Councils of the Continent). As a counterblast Montevideo felt obliged to prepare a dossier of her own services to the Crown in the current war against Britain, and particularly in the Reconquest.[1] The obvious silliness of these wrangles merely indicates the amount of passionate dislike which had arisen between the two cities.

[1] *Expediente* of 1808, beginning 8 January, in Arch. Adm., libro 166.

The Division of the Ways

In such an atmosphere the settlement of the question of Montevideo's trade with Britain was explosive. During the English Invasions the Buenos Aires Consulado, composed mainly of Spanish merchants and their agents, loyal to Spain and their own monopoly interests, had petitioned to have even neutral trade stopped, as indeed had the Spanish merchants of Montevideo, for fear of English goods. The claim was that all foreigners should be strictly excluded, and even certain business houses engaging in foreign trade should be closed. At the British occupation of Montevideo, the *Porteño* merchants requested the death penalty for any Spanish subject trading with the invaders.[1] Yet it will be recalled that floods of articles entered Montevideo during the occupation, and were smuggled out from there into the rest of the Viceroyalty.

With Whitelocke's defeat in July and the consequent evacuation of Montevideo in September, many British merchants were left with large unsold stocks on their hands, which they tried to liquidate at almost any price rather than be obliged to freight them back to Britain. The Cabildo of Buenos Aires, many of whose members were Spanish, hastily urged Liniers to ensure that while the British remained in Montevideo no-one from their city should be allowed to visit her, so as to avoid the smuggling which would certainly ensue. Yet many individuals in fact went, bought the goods at cut prices and sold them in Buenos Aires at great profit, to the equally great disadvantage of the Spanish merchants and the defrauded viceregal treasury. In August the Cabildo even suggested making a search of the houses of Montevideans known to have traded with the British, and confiscating any British goods found. In the end, however, it was discovered that so many prominent Montevideans were implicated that the Buenos Aires Consulado had to allow British goods bought while Montevideo was under British occupation to be circulated – on payment of duties of fifty-two and a half per cent.

[1] *Expediente* of Consulado on neutral trade, 17 September 1806, published in AGN, B.A. *Doc. ref. guerra*, pp. 160 ff. Also Biedma and Mallié, *op. cit.* año 1806, 25 de septiembre; año 1807, 11 de marzo.

96

Crisis between Buenos Aires and Montevideo

The strongest protests from Montevideo only gained a reduction in the duties to twenty-five per cent., and naturally the Montevideans regarded themselves as being under special victimisation intended to confirm the monopoly of the merchants of Buenos Aires, although in fact many Buenos Aires merchants were deeply involved too.[1] As a result, the British goods were not declared to the customs authorities, and were simply smuggled into use,[2] while at the same time the people and Governor of Montevideo made common cause to protest against the regulations. It is easy to understand the view of the Consulado: the goods had been bought at knock-down prices, and without some heavy duty they would undersell any other similar articles, to the exclusion of honest traders who had not suffered the misfortune of living under British occupation. In this case the Montevideans were goaded by their well-founded suspicions of Buenos Aires into upholding a weak case.

The matter was passed on to Nicolás de Herrera, Montevideo's agent in Spain, for him to negotiate with the government, and eventually, amid the upheavals of 1808 and 1809, the *Junta Central* then ruling in Spain declared in favour of Montevideo; but complete satisfaction was never given because new occurrences, in the Plate and in Spain, intervened to postpone decisive action until at length this special case became identified with Montevideo's other claims, those for an Intendancy and a Consulado of her own. Although all these things were apparently favourably viewed in Spain, they were held up until in 1810 Montevideo became permanently independent of Buenos Aires by the fact of the latter's rejection of a new loyalist Spanish government. Then the Consulado and the other organs of government were granted to her

---

[1] Biedma and Mallié, *op. cit.* año 1807, 28 de mayo and 9 de julio; also petition of Crespo and González, Buenos Aires merchants, published in AGN, B.A., *Papeles del Archivo*, pp. 125-32.

[2] Letter of Elío to Deputy of Consulado in Montevideo, 5 February 1808 in M.H.N., book III; also Biedma and Mallié, *op. cit.* año 1807, 28 de mayo and 9 de julio; and R. Levene, *Ensayo histórico sobre la Revolución de Mayo y Mariano Moreno*, vol. 1, pp. 155-7.

almost as a matter of course, although it still required two years
for the merchants' guild to be actually formed.[1]

Therefore for reasons of self-interest Montevideo, which later
stayed loyal to Spain, was the first to make efforts to bring more
open trade to the Plate, while Buenos Aires, working up already
towards revolution, at first opposed open trade. In both cities the
greater merchants were loyal Spaniards.

Self-interest, too, caused the merchants and Cabildo of Montevideo to protest in May and June 1808 against another measure
introduced by Buenos Aires, this time for placing comparatively
heavy taxation on imports and exports in order to raise additional
revenue for defence. The income was badly needed, but Montevideo as usual only saw in the decision a blow against her prosperity, for she had a large foreign trade, especially with Brazil.
Inevitably, feeling against the capital rose, since to Montevideo the
policies of the viceregal authorities and the interests of the *Porteños*
appeared to be identical. This measure, like the former one, was
never put into effect in Montevideo because the open rupture
came before the arguments had stopped crossing and re-crossing
the Plate.

Inside Buenos Aires, too, this project brought an important
result. The treasury was bankrupt in 1807 and 1808 because of the
expenses caused by the Invasions, and the new tax was clearly
necessary, though unpopular. The creole ranchers especially objected to it, since they, in common with most creoles of substance,
believed that open trade was essential for the prosperity of the
region, and that this tax would hit foreign trade particularly hard.
Foreign trade was in effect British trade, even though the British
goods might come in Portuguese ships via Brazil. On the other
hand, the loyal Spanish merchants stood to gain indirectly from
this tax, since it would help to concentrate commerce in their
hands, as the agents of Spanish firms and therefore supporters of

[1] M.H.N., correspondence of Herrera in book III; *expediente* on creation of Consulado, 1812, in book IV.

the closed system. Liniers, the creoles' nominee in office, showed himself in June 1808 to be on their side by decreasing the new tax in order to encourage foreign trade, and by establishing a *contribución patriótica*, an emergency levy, which bore heavily on Spaniards as well as on creoles. Consequently Liniers lost the already suspicious respect of the Spanish part of the population and the Spanish-dominated Cabildo and Consulado, and became even more popular than he had been before with the creoles. It was only a step from this to factional disturbances between creoles and Spaniards with their creole hangers-on, and but one more to revolution.[1]

And so because of self-interest the creoles of Buenos Aires insisted on open trade; but the identical aims of the majority of people both in Montevideo and in the capital did not bring them any closer towards a union to gain their ends. The split by 1808 was too deep and permanent: a feeling of nationhood was growing up on each bank of the River Plate. At this very stage the somewhat parochial squabbles between the two cities of the Plate became intermingled almost inextricably with certain wrangles on wider issues brought about by events in the Peninsula, which must now be introduced to complicate the issue. Both series of motives of disagreement continued to exacerbate the situation, and it is likely that to the men involved both series shaded imperceptibly into each other, in the manner in which quite distinct grievances frequently coalesce to form an aching and apparently homogeneous feeling of discontent with the opposing faction; but we must attempt to trace the separate strands in the tangle of this development.

Open hostility between Montevideo and Buenos Aires was brought about by the arrival, in August 1808, of the news of the Spanish rising the previous May against the French usurpers of Spain's Crown and government. At the end of 1807 the French had occupied Portugal, marching through Spain with her consent,

---

[1] Levene, *Moreno*, vol. I, pp. 210–19.

with the result that the Portuguese Royal Family had put itself under Britain's protection and had sailed across the Atlantic to set up a new court in Rio de Janeiro. The presence of the Portuguese government in Brazil in itself complicated affairs in the Plate, particularly in the Banda Oriental, where Portuguese pressure at once became stronger in response to the Rio government's policy of avenging the loss of Portugal in Spanish America.[1] Castlereagh, the British Foreign Secretary, in whose hands lay the future of Portugal and her Royal House, at first indeed expected the Portuguese to avenge themselves in this way.

Yet the Spanish people felt themselves humiliated by a French hegemony which went so far as the imposition of Napoleon's drunken brother Joseph as King in place of old Charles IV and his son Ferdinand VII, who had both been tricked into abdicating. Accordingly a series of popular risings against the French took place in the summer of 1808. The headquarters of the revolt soon became established at Seville, where a Junta was set up calling itself the *Junta Suprema de España y de las Indias*, and governing in the name of the ill-natured Ferdinand VII, curiously called *el Deseado*, 'the Desired'. Other regional Juntas arose and at first claimed equal authority, a fact which caused some confusion when they approached Britain for help against France and even more when they sent envoys to America claiming the loyalty of the Empire.

The Central Junta at Seville eventually came to be recognised as supreme in fact, and Britain treated it as the government of Spain and of the Spanish possessions, fighting the Peninsular War as Spain's ally. From this time Britain was forced to attempt to implement two incompatible policies: one of alliance with Spain and protection of her interests throughout the world, and the other of fostering trade relations with Spain's colonies (which rebelled soon and claimed self-government) – relations which were thought to be essential for British trade, and without which, it was hinted, it

[1] See J. Street, *Lord Strangford and Río de la Plata, 1808-1815*, in *The Hispanic American Historical Review*, vol. XXXIII, pp. 477-510 for details of the political relations between Britain, Portugal, Spain and the Spanish and Portuguese colonies.

would be impossible to pay for the defence of Spain, apart from other things. Hence Britain's desire not to offend the colonists, which was taken by them to be support of the Spanish American emancipation movement, and especially so in the case of the Plate countries owing to the activities of many British subjects in that region.

In the Plate Viceroyalty, then, these distant events began quickly to have results which directly contributed to the separation of Buenos Aires and Montevideo, because there was a difference in the reactions of the rival cities to the news from Spain. Confirmation of an earlier rumour that Charles IV had abdicated and passed his crown on to Ferdinand arrived in Montevideo on the 1st of August 1808, and therefore Elío and the Cabildo arranged for the official proclamation and oath-taking ceremony to take place on the 12th. Meanwhile, however, Liniers wrote with the un-official news that Charles IV had withdrawn his abdication and that Ferdinand was not to be proclaimed yet, and also that an emissary whom Liniers had sent to Madrid had had an interview with Napoleon and had been promised arms for the defence of the Plate against the British and the Portuguese. Meanwhile, again, an emissary sent by Napoleon to try to persuade the Plate authorities to throw in their lot with him arrived in Montevideo and gave out the startling news that Charles IV had now abdicated in favour of Napoleon. Elío took all this as incontrovertible proof that Liniers was playing some deep game with Napoleon, and doggedly went on with his proclamation of Ferdinand VII on the day he had arranged. Tension between the cities rapidly grew tighter, especially since the Spanish and pro-Spanish element of the population of Buenos Aires, led by the Senior Alcalde, Álzaga, having decided that Liniers and the creoles meant disloyalty, had therefore allied themselves with Elío and the apparently solidly pro-Spanish Montevideo.

But in fact, as a result of the Napoleonic mission, a council of the authorities called by Liniers decided to swear loyalty to Ferdinand

VII on the 21st of August as a gesture against French interference, instead of on the 30th as had been planned before. There is no real proof that Liniers ever meant to accept French rule, and certainly his creole supporters, who had already thrown out the British, refused to submit to the French either. Nevertheless, the damage was done to relations between Elío and Liniers and between the creoles and the Hispanophiles of Buenos Aires.[1]

Further confusion, estrangement and suspicion were caused by the arrival at Montevideo on the 19th of August of Goyeneche, an envoy of the local provincial Junta of Seville, with the news that Spain, now on Britain's side, had risen against the French and created Juntas in the name of Ferdinand VII, the captive King. Goyeneche also foolishly said that the creation of Juntas in the American Empire on the model of those at home was to be encouraged.[2] This idea was to be taken up, or re-invented, all over Spanish America when the colonies wanted to form their own governments in 1810. For the moment, Elío and Montevideo saw their forthright support of Spain and Ferdinand VII fully justified, and the hesitation of Buenos Aires and Liniers even further discredited. Elío carried the people of his city forward on a wave of exalted enthusiasm for Spain and the monarchy, while Liniers and the *Porteños* were looked upon as disloyal francophiles.[3] Yet in Buenos Aires Ferdinand VII was loyally proclaimed on the 21st, before Goyeneche arrived there with his news; and when the latter appeared, on the 22nd, the enthusiasm in the capital was as great as that in Montevideo. But, fatally, the split had been widened, and was made worse by Goyeneche himself, who had been violently denouncing Liniers while with Elío, but who once in Buenos Aires suddenly became Liniers' friend and denounced Montevideo.

Then there was the revival of the long-standing Portuguese threat to the Banda Oriental, as certain complicated intrigues, threats and

[1] See Biedma and Mallié, *op. cit.*, 13 de agosto de 1808 to 21 de agosto de 1808.
[2] Report on Goyeneche's remarks, quoted in Blanco Acevedo, *op. cit.* p. 213.
[3] See, for example, Anon., *Apuntes históricos sobre la Banda Oriental del Río de la Plata, desde el descubrimiento de ese territorio hasta el año de 1818* . . . , pp. 26-7.

feints were set in train by the Portuguese Minister for War and Foreign Relations, Souza Coutinho (later Count de Linhares), as soon as he arrived in Rio with the Court, in March 1808. The details of the manoeuvring would be out of place here, but Lord Strangford, the British Minister to the Portuguese Court, who also went to Rio, was able to keep the Banda Oriental free from Portugal during his residence in Brazil between 1808 and 1815, acting, it should be noted, in the interests of peace between nations who were allied against France, and not in the interests of the Spanish Americans in particular.[1]

The suspicions created in Buenos Aires by the intrigues, begun by a Portuguese agent sent to Montevideo, added to the Spanish residents' distrust of Liniers, who was after all a Frenchman by birth and therefore a suspicious character. The Portuguese agent in question, Curado, was aware of the ill-feeling between Buenos Aires and Montevideo, and did his best to add to it, hoping to gain something for his country from the discord. He bided his time, watching and helping on the progress of the Buenos Aires Cabildo's quarrel with Liniers and of Elío's and Montevideo's exasperation with the capital, and at exactly the right moment he shot his bolt. On the 6th of September Elío proclaimed the whole Banda Oriental to be in a state of war against France – thus uniting the country in fact; and, partly under the influence of Curado's insinuations, but also with the support of the Cabildo of Montevideo, on the 7th he demanded the removal of Liniers from the office of Viceroy. On the 10th there were delivered jointly to the Buenos Aires authorities a letter from the Cabildo of Montevideo and a note from Curado, timed by him so as to give the impression that the Cabildo were in league with the Portuguese agent. The first was a demand for the deposition of Liniers and the second a demand for the cession to Portugal of the Banda Oriental, on the grounds that the Prince Regent of Portugal wished to ensure peace between the Spanish colonies and considered this the best way of

[1] See Street, *Strangford*.

103

doing so.[1] Prudently, Curado waited for no reply, but started for Brazil as soon as he had sent his note. As it happened, Strangford's opposition to Portuguese expansion in view of the Anglo-Spanish alliance of 1808 prevented this scheme from coming to fruition, but Liniers and the other *Porteño* authorities were enraged at this apparent treachery of Elío and the Montevideans, and the state of hostility created by it split the Viceroyalty effectively enough without the need for foreign intervention.

To the Montevideans, Liniers seemed a traitor ready to hand over the Viceroyalty to Napoleon. If he stayed in power, it had been made clear by Curado that Portugal would invade the Banda Oriental so as to protect Brazil against French influence in the Plate. Montevideo was in a cleft stick,[2] and had to dispose of Liniers for her own safety as well as for the sake of loyalty to Spain. The break between Montevideo and Buenos Aires could hardly be more complete. Liniers and the Buenos Aires authorities demanded the presence of Elío before them to substantiate in person his accusations against the Viceroy, but Elío and the Cabildo of Montevideo refused to budge. Liniers, in a rage, declared Elío's appointment at an end; but the Montevideans took this as a challenge and supported their Governor in his refusal to vacate his position. The officer sent to replace Elío was met by the hostility of a mob shouting for his blood and demanding a *Cabildo Abierto* to decide the future of the city.[3]

The *Cabildo Abierto* met on the 21st of September. It was attended by all men of standing in Montevideo, including the members of the Cabildo, the higher officers of the armed forces and of the public service, and the dignitaries of the Church. They were mostly Spaniards, but they were not unaware of the influence of a mob of citizens gathered in the square outside the Cabildo building, and these were mostly creoles. Their own deputies, some of the

[1] Letter of Curado to Liniers, 2 September 1808, copy in P.R.O., W.O. 1/163. For this episode see also D. L. Molinari, *Antecedentes de la Revolución de Mayo*, III.

[2] Anon., *Apuntes históricos, loc. cit.*; see also Blanco Acevedo, chap. XVIII.

[3] *Ibid.* chap. XIX.

richer creoles, joined the *Cabildo Abierto*. All of them were, however, agreed on retaining Elío, the 'best and most loyal Spaniard we have known', as Governor.[1] Then, urged on by the mob's shouts of '¡Junta! ¡Junta como en España!' (A Junta! A Junta as in Spain!) the *Cabildo Abierto* turned itself on the spot into a governing Junta with Elío presiding, and 'formed after the example of those which have been ordered by the *Junta Suprema* of Seville to be created in all towns of the Kingdom which contain the number of two thousand citizens'.[2] The decision was not revolutionary in its objects, but was dangerously so in its form. The example of Spain, the ancient Spanish theory of popular sovereignty if the monarchy for any reason should fail,[3] and loyalty in the face of the French threat, were paradoxically responsible for Montevideo's secession from the Viceregal authority. In less than two years the same reasons would be used to explain the emancipation of Buenos Aires, though not of Montevideo, from Spain herself.

It forms an ironical postscript to record the effect of this schism on the question of open trade, which it will be recalled was being urged at this time by creole groups on both sides of the Plate. Very soon after Montevideo broke from dependence on Buenos Aires, British merchant vessels were allowed to enter both ports by the rival Spanish authorities, although no official regulation permitted this trade. Since Britain and Spain were now allies in the war against France, there seemed to be little harm in opening the ports, especially since the customs revenue was badly needed by both. Indeed, the rivals touted for the custom of British ships entering the estuary: the Viceroy's own son, a junior naval officer, cruised the river in a small boat, meeting what ships he could and advising them to sail into Buenos Aires, while Montevideo also tried to

[1] Public notice of Parodi, the Senior Alcalde, of 21 September 1808, *ibid.* p. 222.

[2] *Ibid*, p. 224. See also contemporary opinions in Montevideo on the propriety of following Spain's example, quoted by M. J. Ardao and A. C. de Castellanos in *Artigas: su significación en los orígenes de la nacionalidad oriental y en la Revolución del Río de la Plata*, pp. 12–13; and *Documentos relativos a la Junta montevideana de gobierno de 1808*.

[3] M. Giménez Fernández, in *Las doctrinas populistas en la independencia de Hispano-América*, discusses these theories.

attract the British merchantmen. Blockade and counter-blockade were established, and as Lord Strangford sardonically reported a few months after the split, British goods were 'the source of those supplies by which . . . [Montevideo and Buenos Aires] are mutually enabled to meet the expenses and exigencies of Civil War between one another'.[1] But at any rate, British commerce had now penetrated into the Plate on a large scale, and it remained the preponderant foreign trade for over a century.

3. REVOLUTION

It is clear from what has gone before that the rupture between Buenos Aires and Montevideo was more serious than was justified by the apparent cause, the hatred between Liniers and Elío. All Montevideo had some reason for wanting independence from the viceregal capital, and it was accidental that the independence should come in the guise of a passionate loyalty to Spain in the face of a supposed threat. The accident had its importance, for it put Montevideo and the Banda Oriental under the government of ardent Spanish patriots, committing the people to their loyalty to Spain, when in Buenos Aires the movement for emancipation from Spain was growing stronger and was soon to have the opportunity of showing its strength. When this came, in May 1810, the whole Banda Oriental found itself fighting against Buenos Aires (a thing which it in some ways found to its taste) for the wrong ideal.

Although the fundamental rivalry and hostility between Montevideo and Buenos Aires persisted and even grew stronger between 1808 and 1810, the superficial state of relations between them fluctuated between open war and mutual blockade, as at the end of 1808, and apparent reconciliation a year later, when Liniers was replaced by a new Spanish-born Viceroy. At first, after the formation of the Montevideo Junta, the Montevideans experienced

[1] Letter of Strangford to Canning, no. 3, 30 January 1809, P.R.O., F.O., 63/68. See also J. Luccock, *Notes on Rio de Janeiro and the southern parts of Brazil: . . . . . 1808-1818*, pp. 138-44.

a new feeling of freedom, and life became better and more pros-perous as British trade opened and flourished. No longer was the Banda Oriental a ranch for Buenos Aires to exploit. Liniers and the Audiencia of Buenos Aires fulminated uselessly against Elío and the Cabildo of Montevideo. Hostilities began at sea even before the end of September 1808. The Montevideo Cabildo in October urged the Cabildo of the capital to depose the Viceroy – another revolu-tionary act, though not in intention – and the ultra-Spanish Cabildo of Buenos Aires, led by Álzaga, prepared a revolt against Liniers for the 17th of October; but it failed because the creole militia, the only considerable military force in Buenos Aires, re-fused to countenance it. They supported Liniers, and in any case they were hostile to Montevideo.

But for the activity of Strangford in Rio de Janeiro, the isolation of Montevideo might, in the circumstances, have led to the occupation of the Banda Oriental by the watchful and vengeful Portuguese. But Strangford's restraining influence on Prince João, the Prince Regent, maintained the peace and gave the Banda Oriental a fleeting chance to enjoy a certain independent organisa-tion, though still under Spanish rule. In the same period Strang-ford scotched the plans of the Spanish princess Carlota Joaquina, wife of Dom João, and her younger brother Pedro, both of whom were installed at the Court in Rio and had conceived the idea of taking over the government of the Spanish American Empire as the only representatives of the Spanish Royal House not in captivity. The unauthorised support given to Carlota by the Admiral in command of the British naval squadron stationed in Brazil, Sir William Sidney Smith (who was soon quelled by Strangford), and the innocent help given her by the English adventurer Paroissien (who was soon double-crossed by Carlota herself), gave Spanish America for a time the mistaken impression that Britain was behind the intrigues.[1] In the event, nothing permanent came of all this, except that unrest and the general

---

[1] J. Street, *Strangford* p. 484; also Humphreys, *op. cit.* pp. 21-36.

decay of respect for the Spanish system and confusion over loyalties became worse in the Plate countries. Revolution was made slightly easier, especially since a nucleus of revolutionary creoles in Buenos Aires had at first dallied with Carlota's scheme and was now exposed to the Spanish authorities in a fit of pique by the schemer. Therefore everyone was forced to recognise the existence of a current of revolutionary feeling in the Viceroyalty.

Liniers believed Elío to be sympathetic towards Carlota's ambitions, and became even harsher towards Montevideo.[1] The city's continued disobedience led him to threaten hostilities by land, and he sent an expedition in November 1808 ready to reduce Montevideo to order. Montevideo merely closed her ranks and affirmed her loyalty to Elío and her hatred of the Frenchman.[2]

The example of the Junta of Montevideo was fruitful in Buenos Aires. The pro-Spanish clique had tried in October to get rid of Liniers and form a Junta loyal to Spain, and they tried again on the 1st of January 1809, taking advantage of the occasion when the retiring Cabildo met to elect the members for the New Year. But again the creole militia supported Liniers, and the attempt failed. It was becoming clear that the creoles were using Liniers as a figure-head for their anti-Spanish ideas, which were in fact soon to turn frankly revolutionary. The most effective members of the Cabildo, still under the influence of the staunch Álzaga, were arrested and deported to an uncomfortable exile on the coast of Patagonia, whence they were rescued by Elío and brought in triumph to Montevideo. The situation could not have been more paradoxical. All semblance of viceregal authority was destroyed in Montevideo, for motives of loyalty to Spain. For Liniers it was the end of his prestige: now even the Audiencia, tired of his bungling, joined their pleas for his replacement to those already despatched to the Junta at Seville by Montevideo, the Buenos Aires

---

[1] Blanco Acevedo, *op. cit.* p. 239.
[2] See the paper entitled 'Defensa de Montevideo', note 'contra Liniers', in Arch. Adm., legajo 333; 11; 8.

Cabildo and others. That Junta had in any case already decided, on the 1st of February 1809 and appointed Baltasar Hidalgo de Cisneros Viceroy of Buenos Aires in Liniers' stead.[1]

Cisneros' arrival at Montevideo from Spain at the end of June caused a superficial change in the situation in the Viceroyalty. The enthusiasm with which the Montevideans greeted the new Viceroy is proof not only of their hatred of Liniers but also of their loyalty to Spain.[2] There appears to be no reason to believe, as does one important Uruguayan historian,[3] that Elío and Montevideo had meant anything more than to oppose a Viceroy suspected of planning treason; both were loyal to Spain, and the Montevideans were possibly made ultra-loyal because they had regarded the government of Spain as a final arbiter to whom to appeal in their struggle against their immediate enemy, Buenos Aires. Cisneros, then, was accepted willingly by Montevideo, and not so willingly by Buenos Aires, but it seemed on the surface that the motive of the hostilities between the cities was now removed with the replacement of Liniers and the unification of the Viceroyalty under Cisneros.

The Montevideo Junta was at once dissolved, though with the thanks of the Junta in Seville for their patriotism. Elío was also thanked and promoted to be Inspector and Second-in-Command of the troops of the Viceroyalty. Liniers and the commanders of the Buenos Aires militia were made to swear their loyalty to the new Viceroy, and only after they had done so did Cisneros consent to enter his capital amid a show of rejoicing on the 29th of July. No real change in the situation had taken place. Montevideo, which had appeared to be taking revolutionary steps, had in fact imposed her Spanish loyalty on Buenos Aires. But at this humiliation, the movement towards true revolution in Buenos Aires became stronger, so that there seems to be a *volte-face* in the roles of

[1] Blanco Acevedo, *op. cit.* pp. 249-50.
[2] Anon., *Apuntes históricos*, pp. 28-9.
[3] Blanco Acevedo, *op. cit.* chap. XXI.

the two cities, although in fact neither changed its attitude, and the situation had simply become clearer with the removal of Liniers, the cat's-paw of the creoles. The creole militia of Buenos Aires was stung by the loss of its popular leader Liniers, and now would be ready to support a movement for emancipation, since it had no respect for Cisneros and the Spanish hierarchy. Also, Elío was the worst possible choice for a high command over the troops in Buenos Aires, since the militia regarded him as responsible for the fall of their idol and refused to obey him. Cisneros was therefore obliged to leave Elío as Governor of Montevideo, and the power of the creoles was confirmed. Again, the fact that the Junta of Montevideo and Elío had been officially thanked and rewarded, while Buenos Aires had been bereft of her Viceroy, was another source of rankling jealousy and bad feeling between the cities.[1] By now it seemed that nothing could truly reconcile them. Even worse, the example of the Junta of Montevideo received the stamp of official approbation: the creation of local Juntas would no longer seem dangerous or even strange, and Spain's prestige vanished almost entirely in Buenos Aires. Revolution was imminent, particularly in the viceregal capital, but it was to be revolution in the name of Ferdinand VII and in favour of defending Spanish America from French hegemony, for it was commonly believed there that the French were on the point of complete and permanent victory over Spain.

Elío soon showed signs of entering on a new round of insubordination in Montevideo, apparently believing himself to be the Spaniard destined by Providence to save the whole Empire, and Cisneros sent him back to Spain in 1810. The ex-Governor of Montevideo took with him the gratitude and good will of his city, and the Cabildo's commission to represent them in certain business in Spain. Thus Cisneros by his own act deprived himself of a man who would have been his most solid supporter in future

---

[1] *Ibid.* pp. 254-7.

troubles, and also forfeited Montevideo's sympathy, since she could not forgive the man who exiled her adopted champion.

The revolution, when it came, was not violent nor even clearly revolutionary. It bore no social implications, but merely envisaged a change of government. Several incidents since 1806 had shown that the creoles were willing to govern themselves, and had also given examples of the manner of doing it: using Juntas, after the Spanish method. In late 1809 and early 1810 Spain seemed to be tottering, and was expected to fall under French domination – hopefully expected by a minority of creoles, especially in Buenos Aires (not to speak of the other centres of government in Spanish America).When this happened, the Junta would be set up and the emancipation party would seize power and carry the apathetic majority with them, all in the name of Ferdinand VII and opposition to France. This was known and planned in Buenos Aires well in advance, and British protection had even been sought for the proposed creole government.[1]

As was expected, the revolution in Buenos Aires (and in several other Spanish American capitals) in fact began on the receipt of the news of the great French successes in Andalucía in the winter of 1809 to 1810, and of the setting up of a new Spanish government, a Council of Regency, in the fragment of territory left unoccupied. It was an English ship which brought the news to Montevideo, on the 13th of May 1810. The Viceroy, Cisneros, was warned at once and on the 18th he issued a proclamation giving the known details of the disasters, making them so lifelike, as one Montevidean complained, that the people were alarmed and agitated instead of calmed. Cisneros thus prepared his own fall,[2] even to the extent of hinting at a government by a Junta which might include representatives of the various provinces of the Viceroyalty 'in the un-

[1] Letter of Strangford to Wellesley (Foreign Secretary), no. 48, 10th June 1810, P.R.O., F.O. 63/84: 'Independence is desired; if possible under the protection of England; but at all events, Independence', wrote Strangford.

[2] Anon., *Apuntes históricos*, p. 30. Proclamation published in *Registro oficial de la República Argentina, de 1810 a 1873*, t. I, pp. 1-2.

fortunate event of the total loss of the Peninsula and in default of a supreme government'.

Within a week the creoles of Buenos Aires had organised themselves under the commanders of the militia troops: men who were also rich landowners or had some other interest in seeing their native country governed for its own benefit, men such as Saavedra and Belgrano. These schooled a mob to demand a *Cabildo Abierto* to discuss the future government of the Viceroyalty now that Spain was no longer free. They claimed that the new government of Spain was illegal, since it could not represent a majority of Spaniards (that is, the colonials, who had not been consulted about its formation, besides those Spaniards living under French occupation) nor, obviously, had it the Royal assent.

The *Cabildo Abierto* met on the 22nd of May, and of about four hundred and fifty substantial citizens and officials of Buenos Aires invited, only two hundred and sixty-two arrived; the rest, in the main Spaniards from Spain or their creole sympathisers, were clearly nervous of the creole mob and judged it prudent not to expose themselves to it. Whipped up into a frenzy by leaders of the emancipation party, the mob roared outside the hall throughout the day-long discussion, reminding the Spaniards where the real power in Buenos Aires lay. Finally the opinions of Saavedra and Belgrano won the majority vote in the assembly: that the Cabildo should govern until a Junta could be set up, formed as the Cabildo should decide. This meant emancipation, even though the Junta would rule in the name of the captive King.[1] A final attempt by the Spaniards to keep a degree of authority by including the Viceroy in the governing Junta was shattered by the creoles on the 25th, when they forced the Cabildo to name a Junta composed entirely of leaders of the emancipation party, with Saavedra, colonel of the most important militia regiment, as its president. The Junta, it was stated, would be completed as soon as possible by

[1] Biedma and Mallié, *op. cit.* t. IV, 21 and 22 de mayo de 1810. See also General Tomás Guido, *Reseña histórica de los sucesos de mayo*, published in R. Levene, (ed.), *Los sucesos de mayo, contados por sus actores C. Saavedra, M. Belgrano, M. Rodríguez, etc.*

the incorporation of deputies to be sent to the capital from the provinces.

Economic motives had played a large part in fostering a revolutionary spirit in the Viceroyalty, and it was fitting that some of the first steps taken by the new Junta of Buenos Aires should be to remove the colonial restrictions on trade and to write to Strangford telling him so, and requesting him to use every effort to gain for them Britain's trade and friendship. They wished to prove that their aim was not so much separation from Spain as extirpation of the evils which they believed were caused by Spanish rule, and at the same time they wished to make their country prosperous. For both of these things they needed Britain's good will.[1]

Cisneros' proclamation arrived to spread doubt in Montevideo on the 20th of May, but before any reaction could occur, there arrived the news of the movement in Buenos Aires which culminated in the *Cabildo Abierto* of the 22nd. The port was at once closed to prevent any ship taking the news to Brazil and so putting temptation in the way of the Rio de Janeiro government before the Banda Oriental had recovered from these shocks. The Montevideo Cabildo held arduous sessions on the 25th and 26th, inviting several important creoles to take part in the deliberations. Two parties made their appearance: an ultra-Spanish group led by an ambitious sailor, Salazar, commander of the Spanish naval forces in the Viceroyalty and a fitting heir to Elío's principles; and also a more moderate party. The Salazar group were all for rejecting the revolution of Buenos Aires, declaring Montevideo capital of the Viceroyalty and somehow bringing over the Viceroy himself to rule; but the others were much vaguer, and merely wanted to preserve peace and order and the rights of Ferdinand VII,[2] or in other words, to wait and see. It was still not clear that any revolution had taken place, although it was clear that the Viceroy's

---

[1] Letter of Strangford to Wellesley, no. 49, 20th June 1810, P.R.O., F.O. 63/84, enclosing letter of the Junta of Buenos Aires to Strangford, d. 28 May.

[2] Blanco Acevedo, *op. cit.* pp. 262-3.

H

authority had gone, and that a Spanish type of Junta had taken over the government.

Indeed the Junta of Buenos Aires never did proclaim independence. It ruled in the name of Ferdinand VII, although without doubt many of the leading creoles intended to gain independence eventually, and the Junta's troops came into conflict with loyal troops. However, on the 26th of May the Junta proclaimed its own installation and its loyalty to Ferdinand, and agreed to send circulars to all the authorities of the Viceroyalty telling the news, and to request them at the same time to recognise it as the provisional government.

Therefore Montevideo received letters from Buenos Aires on the 31st urging her people to recognise the Junta and thus help to maintain the Viceroyalty unified in its loyalty to Ferdinand and in its power of defence against any possible attack by the 'neighbouring power', Brazil.[1] The creoles of Buenos Aires made this appeal, as they had made their revolution, on the basis of popular sovereignty (a basis upheld by the sixteenth-century Spanish political theorists as well as by the French eighteenth-century philosophers), but in claiming Montevideo's adhesion the Junta forgot the corollary of popular sovereignty, self-government. Just as the Spanish liberals at that moment, thinking out an advanced constitution for Spain and her Empire, accepted popular sovereignty but forgot colonial autonomy because of their narrow concentration on Hispanic unity, so the revolutionaries of Buenos Aires forgot that the provinces of the Viceroyalty had the right to decide for themselves once the Spanish example was followed. In this way the wars of emancipation from Spain are foreshadowed by the movement of Montevideo and the Banda Oriental against Buenos Aires. Similar movements arose in other provinces of the Viceroyalty, giving rise to the so-called federal movement, which set itself up against the centralist system of the capital. In this light the struggle of the Banda Oriental, particularly under the leader-

---

[1] Blanco Acevedo, *op. cit.* chap. XXI.

ship of Artigas from 1813 onwards, can be seen as only the best and clearest example of a separatist tendency which appeared in all the Viceroyalty, and, indeed, throughout almost all of Spanish America. The reasons were deep-seated, but they were brought into the open by the assumption by Buenos Aires of the independent government of the Viceroyalty in May 1810. They were those which Montevideo had had for many years: envy, hurt pride, and especially economic interests in conflict with those of the capital.

At this early stage, however, the presence of a strong Spanish garrison and civil service in Montevideo, supported by a pro-Spanish party, confused the issue; and Montevideo was not herself sure in 1810 whether she meant to be ultra-loyal to Spain or whether she intended simply to cut herself off from Buenos Aires. Consequently, when hostilities broke out between Montevideo, left as a Spanish outpost on the east coast of South America, and Buenos Aires, the Montevideans, not quite understanding what it was all about, let themselves be led by their fear and hatred of Buenos Aires to support the tottering Spanish power in their country.[1] The *Cabildo Abierto* called in Montevideo on the 1st of June to consider the messages from Buenos Aires hesitantly decided to join with the Junta of Buenos Aires, since it claimed to govern in the name of Ferdinand VII, but no doubt suspected that the Junta would be even less well disposed towards Montevideo than the previous authorities had been. Therefore the news which arrived the next day from Spain, that the French advance had been stopped and the government of Spain was stable under a Regency, was seized upon by Salazar and his party and exaggerated; and a new *Cabildo Abierto* immediately, with great joy and doubtless relief too, decided to recognise the new Spanish government.

The Buenos Aires Junta refused to recognise a Spanish government which was, they claimed, completely unrepresentative and

---

[1] See Anon., *Apuntes históricos*, pp. 31-2, for this state of confusion. Also Pivel Devoto, *Raíces*, pp. 259-63.

unofficial. They were determined to rule themselves. Many creoles of Montevideo fell unresisting back into Spain's arms, not knowing what else to do to keep out of Buenos Aires' clutches, and therefore on the 6th of June replies were sent to the capital refusing to agree to the Junta's plans. From that time every action of the Junta confirmed the suspicions of the Montevideo Spaniards that what had happened in Buenos Aires was revolution, and that no reconciliation was possible. They were convinced by such things as the shipping of the Viceroy and Audiencia to the Canary Islands, and the despatch of a military expedition from Buenos Aires into the interior provinces in order to quell the opposition of Spanish sympathisers and officials. War broke out between Montevideo and Buenos Aires, and once again the Banda Oriental enjoyed a peculiar independence under Spanish leaders.

Yet in Montevideo too there was a nucleus of creoles of influence who were not swept off their feet by Salazar. Not that they were averse to cutting loose from Buenos Aires, which appealed to them for reasons unconnected with this particular crisis. They felt loyal to Spain, but, wanting self-government, they wavered between throwing in their lot with the Junta of Buenos Aires, which might bring them their desire, and accepting things as they were in Montevideo pending the arrival of an opportunity to set up a Junta for themselves. Nicolás Herrera, just returned from his mission in Spain, was a prominent member of this group, together with Lucas Obes and Pedro Feliciano Sáenz de Cavia, the future detractor of Artigas.[1]

These creoles adopted the theory of popular sovereignty, but their first impulse to join with the Junta of Buenos Aires had been defeated on the 2nd of June by Salazar and his supporters. On the 11th of July, Salazar gained another victory over them – a victory which eventually recoiled on him – when he and his sailors enforced the disbandment of two regiments of creole militia in Montevideo whose loyalty to his own extremist views he rightly

---

[1] Pievl Devoto, *op. cit.* pp. 227 ff.

doubted. As a level-headed observer wrote, Salazar and his men had not the vision to see that 'with this disciplined local soldiery there would in the future be formed in the interior the first hostile plans [against the Spanish régime], and that in the end they would come and lay siege to the fortress city'.[1] Meanwhile, Salazar and the sailors were left complete masters of Montevideo, although a Governor, Soria, was titular head of the administration. Salazar instituted a blockade of Buenos Aires, temporarily gaining acceptance of this hostile move from the commander of the British naval squadron stationed in the Plate with orders to supervise maritime affairs there. But British trade was too valuable to too many, and the British merchants already settled in Buenos Aires quickly, through Strangford, had British recognition of the blockade withdrawn. So it became ineffective in a few weeks,[2] although Montevideo's command of the Plate waters remained useful for purely military ends.

Yet while Montevideo remained in Spanish hands and working for Spanish objects, the forces at work in the country districts of the Banda Oriental prepared further complications of the situation.

[1] Anon., *Apuntes histórios*, p. 33.
[2] Street, *Strangford* pp. 495-6.

CHAPTER IV

THE RISE OF ARTIGAS

I. THE REVOLUTION OF THE BANDA ORIENTAL

THE work of the *Blandengues* of Montevideo in pacifying the whole of the Banda Oriental had been sadly interrupted during the English Invasions, when the troops were withdrawn from the interior to face the foreign attackers. Disorder returned to the country regions: smuggling, rustling, wild living came back to lands which had been made fit for peaceful settlement by the efforts of Artigas and a few others.[1] Artigas himself returned to active service, to the task of freeing the country of outlaws – a task which occupied him almost continuously from the end of 1807. The Buenos Aires revolution of May 1810 came while he was employed in this way, and he continued with his civilising mission, especially careful of the Brazilian frontier, whence might come the greatest threat to his country.[2] At last, in September 1810, Artigas was promoted captain and company commander upon the death of the officer who had been promoted in his stead at the last opportunity, in 1793.[3]

But a crisis in Artigas' life and in the development of the Banda Oriental was approaching. The country was infected with revolutionary feeling, and sporadic risings began to take place at the beginning of 1811. On the 12th of February Elío, now returned as Governor of Montevideo, declared war on the Junta of Buenos Aires, and on the 15th Artigas deserted from his post at Colonia and went over the river to Buenos Aires, joining the revolution. This was not merely the defection of a disgruntled junior officer of

[1] Pivel Devoto, *Raíces*, pp. 182-3.
[2] *A.A.*, t. III, pt. IX; t. IV, apéndice, docs. 7-10.
[3] *Ibid.* t. III, pt. IX, doc. 126, appointment dated 5 September 1810.

forty-six years of age, but the declaration for freedom of the gaucho leader who was best loved and respected by the people of the countryside. Artigas' campaigns had made him known and loved by honest creoles as much as he was feared by outlaws; and his commanding officers had constantly shown how greatly they valued his services.[1] He had made up his mind. He saw in the local revolts the beginning of a national movement which he could lead to independence, and he went to Buenos Aires to gain the help he needed.

Almost at the same time another future hero of the revolution went across: Captain José Rondeau, who was to be a rival and at times an opponent of Artigas. Rondeau was born in Buenos Aires in 1773, but as a child he went to live in Montevideo. He had joined the army at the age of twenty, and he served until 1807 in Buenos Aires and the Banda Oriental, attaining the rank of captain. Then he went to Spain and fought against the French until his return to Montevideo in 1810, where he served with apparent loyalty until 1811. There is no explanation for his decision to join the revolution except that he was a creole and therefore must have been convinced of the justice of the 'patriot' cause, as were many other creole officers who served at that time in Spain and talked matters over, as he did, in the clubs of Cádiz. The Argentine liberator San Martín had exactly the same experience. Rondeau was a man of honour and discipline, who now became completely faithful to his chosen party and to his superiors in Buenos Aires.

[1] See, for example, the opinion of Artigas' prestige given by a pro-Spanish creole in his 'Exposición sobre el estado de Montev⁰. y su Campaña', d. 4 August 1811, presented to the Cortes of Cádiz by the Montevideo deputy Zufriátegui, copy in Arch. Adm., libro 570, pp. 81-85. Zufriátegui wrote that Artigas and Rondeau had won the entire confidence of the people of the Banda Oriental and of their own commanders, '. . . por muy particular el Dⁿ. Jose Artigas para comisiones de la campaña por sus dilatados conocimientos, persecucion de Vagos Ladrones, Contrabandistas, Indios Charruas y Minuanes . . . [que] la infestan y causan males irreparables, é igualm.ᵗᵉ para contener álos Portugueses que en tiempo de paz acostumbran usurpar nuestro ganado, y abanzan impunem.ᵗᵉ. . . .' Also Joaquín de Soria, Military Governor of Montevideo, expressed a very high opinion of Artigas in a letter to the Cabildo d. 22 August 1810. Soria admitted that he could find no-one to replace Artigas as guardian of the frontier and the interior; no-one else had the complete confidence of the Governor and at the same time could do Artigas' job. (*A.A.*, t. III, pt. IX, doc. 125.)

His merits were quickly recognised, so that he rose rapidly to the highest rank, being promoted brigadier in May 1814. He went on to exercise many important government offices, becoming Supreme Director of the United Provinces of the River Plate for a few months in 1819; and he was made Governor of the Banda Oriental in 1829, when it was about to become a separate state permanently. He ended his career as Argentine Minister of War and Navy under the dictator Rosas, and retired from public life in 1840. It was a misfortune for Rondeau as well as for Artigas and the Banda Oriental that their paths crossed several times during the revolutionary wars.[1]

By the time of the outbreak of the revolution in Buenos Aires, the country districts of the Banda Oriental had begun to have some feeling of unity and even of embryo nationhood. Although the jurisdiction of Montevideo was still limited, all the Banda Oriental had much in common, even the part in the north along the River Uruguay, which was directly under the control of Buenos Aires. The Banda Oriental as a whole had its own style of life, and the common problems of under-population, lack of development, and the proximity of the aggressive Brazilians. The *Blandengues* had helped to spread an idea of unity since they had tried to cope with these problems for the whole of the territory east of the River Uruguay. Montevideo's claims to be made the capital of a new Intendancy which should include all the Banda Oriental had not been met, but in 1808 a step towards administrative unification of the territory had been taken – the first step since the unification of the Banda Oriental revenue system in 1788. Elío in 1808 had been made Governor of the whole Banda Oriental, an entirely new office. This meant that all military affairs of the territory were unified, which was a sensible and even, many thought, a necessary move, in view of the mounting tension on the Brazilian frontier. The new office was specifically made to

[1] See 'Autobiografía del Brigadier General Don José Rondeau', in Andrés Lamas, *Colección de memorias y documentos para la historia y la jeografía de los pueblos del Río de la Plata.*

include a general supervision of order in the Banda Oriental.[1] Elío actively encouraged the feeling of unity, particularly by attempting to renew the drive for the settlement of the whole territory, which had lapsed since the English Invasions. Azara and Artigas in Batoví had been engaged on this problem, which for years had worried the authorities and even more the individuals interested in the peaceful development of the country and its protection against the Portuguese.[2] Sobremonte in 1805 had seen fit to issue a *Reglamento de poblanza de terrenos fronterizos* (code of regulations for the settlement of frontier lands), aimed particularly at establishing new villages near the Brazilian border and so checking the Portuguese advance and the smuggling, but nothing more had come of the idea.[3] But in 1809, Elío called a meeting of deputies of the landowners of the Montevideo district to discuss and adopt measures for the common good. Later, with the Viceroy's permission, deputies from all the other districts making up the Banda Oriental joined the conference, and they all agreed on the setting up of a Junta to represent the interests of all the landowners. These things promoted a certain community spirit amongst the people of the Banda Oriental, even though, strictly speaking, Montevideo was not the capital of the whole territory.

When the Junta of Buenos Aires, on its installation, sent circulars to all the subordinate territories requesting their adherence, those parts of the Banda Oriental directly under the administration of Buenos Aires joined without hesitation. Therefore such places as Colonia, Maldonado, Santo Domingo Soriano, San Carlos, Santa Tecla and Mercedes declared for the Junta of Buenos Aires and naturally carried their own administrative districts with them. So by the middle of June 1810, Montevideo and her district were

[1] Pivel Devoto, *Raíces*, pp. 183-4. But see F. Ferreiro, *Orígenes uruguayos*, pp. 18-19, where the author argues that by 1810 no idea of nationhood had grown up in modern Uruguay, since Montevideo was not the official capital. But the evidence shows that the feeling of local unity at least was strong enough to cause a split with Buenos Aires in 1811.

[2] See, for example, Lastarria, *Colonias orientales*, cit., in *Documentos para la historia argentina*, t. III.

[3] AGN, Montevideo, Fondo ex-Archivo y Museo Histórico Nacional, caja 6, 'Reglamento', d. 6 May 1805.

ringed round by potentially hostile territory. The small settlements within the Montevideo district at first declared, as was logical, for the Spanish Regency and the status quo in Montevideo.[1]

Accordingly, the Junta of Buenos Aires took steps to attract to itself the other country districts of the Banda Oriental, in order to reduce Montevideo's following and power. It is ironical that in July Buenos Aires should have opened the port of Maldonado to international trade, with the aim of fostering a rivalry between Maldonado and the main port of the country, Montevideo, which, by its wealth, business and facilities, had suffocated Maldonado. The story of Montevideo's revolt against Buenos Aires was expected to repeat itself in miniature. The other, subordinate, aim of this measure was to provide the Banda Oriental with an alternative outlet, which would encourage the country people to desert from their allegiance to Montevideo without fear of economic disaster. The Junta also thought of making an attempt to ensure at last the safety of the Brazilian frontier by increasing vigilance there and helping the foundation of new settlements.

But whatever may have been the sympathies of the country people, the presence of a strong and active Spanish garrison in Montevideo had its effect, and towards the end of July Colonia, Soriano, and even, unwillingly, Maldonado, were brought to recognise the authority of the Governor of Montevideo as direct representative of the Spanish government. Temporarily the whole Banda Oriental now fell under Montevideo's rule, and the country people found themselves paying heavy taxes, billeting troops, and doing other things to help to make Montevideo the citadel of Spanish power in South America.[2]

For some years past, owing to lack of funds, the Spaniards had neglected every aspect of public activity in the Banda Oriental. Besides failing to provide adequate troops to defend the frontier, depending instead on Artigas' extraordinary success, the Spaniards

[1] Pivel Devoto, *Raíces*, pp. 233-8.
[2] *Ibid.* pp. 239-43.

had even allowed the few stone forts to fall into a ruinous state. Anything that had been achieved had been done by individual settlers or small groups, as happened in the case of the occupation and semi-civilisation of the parts of the Banda Oriental to the north of the Río Negro. Often people prospered through illegal enterprise – smuggling hides, tobacco and spirits. They had grown used to extra taxes and forced subventions in the emergencies since 1806, but the extremely heavy weight thrown on them, now that they were the only support of Spanish authority in the Viceroyalty and had to provide for all its machinery and also produce large donations to help Spain in her struggles, was too much for them.Trade was not good, and by October many citizens of the outlying townships were refusing to give or lend more.[1]

The authorities of Montevideo made themselves even more unpopular when, to raise money in this strait, they announced their intention of forcing all ranchers to prove their titles to their land. If it was found that they had no legal deeds, they were to be allowed to buy them, and if they did not do so the lands would be sold by auction as royal property. This hit a number of honest ranchers of the Banda Oriental who had simply occupied empty (and therefore legally royal) lands without fulfilling any or all of the legal requirements: notably, they had not paid for the lands. It touched the fundamental problem of the settlement of the Banda Oriental. Azara's answer to the same problem had been more humane: give the lands to those who would settle them. This final blow brought a considerable number of country people to revolution, both those who had paid for their lands but had not gone through all the legal formalities and those who were squatting on some absentee landlord's unexploited estate – for the King could be regarded as such a landlord. The summons to prove title had to be repeated before any notice was taken of it, and even then there were so many

---

[1] *Ibid.* pp. 243-6.

protests and incidents throughout the Banda Oriental that order
was shaken and revolution appeared to be the only possible
outcome.[1]

The new Governor, Mariscal del Campo Don Gaspar de
Vigodet, who arrived fresh from Spain on the 7th of October, was
another ultra-loyal Spaniard, and he increased the pressure on the
inhabitants of the Banda Oriental, striving to enforce the title-
proving decree, and creating a special *Junta de Hacienda* (Treasury
Council) to squeeze more contributions in money and in kind
from all the territory. It has been pointed out that this creation of a
new Junta in effect made an autonomous unit of the Banda
Oriental for the purposes of revenue, the sinews of peace as well as
of war.[2] It also increased unrest amongst the inhabitants of the
country districts, and so helped to destroy, almost before it was a
fact, the autonomy and unity so long desired, and gained in such
an unexpected way.

The completion of the Banda Oriental's administrative independence and unity came on the very eve of the revolution of the
country districts. Elío, so popular as a Governor in the past, was
made Viceroy by the Regency in August and arrived at the beginning of 1811 to make Montevideo the seat of his government.
How little he understood the truth of the situation in the Banda
Oriental, despite his aptitude for command and his interest in the
country, is proved by the steps he took to enforce the unwelcome
measures on the people of the interior, now ripe for revolution.
The interior towns were held down by Spanish troops, the taxes
were wrung from the people, military commanders were sent out
to set aside local Cabildos, gauchos were driven into the army, and
at length the ranchers, in February, received news of an even
harsher system of taxation to be imposed. Elío also weakened the
military situation by withdrawing well-placed forces, replacing a
commander expert in local conditions by a newcomer at the vital

[1] *Ibid.* pp. 246-9.
[2] *Ibid.* pp. 249-52.

port of Colonia, and, in February, he even hastened to declare war on the Buenos Aires Junta.[1]

This was the signal for the country districts of the Banda Oriental to join with the Junta of Buenos Aires in opposition to the Spanish authority. All their own motives of unrest and discontent were added to the propaganda of Buenos Aires in favour of independent government, though still in the name of the captive King. There were many tough gauchos (one estimate gives the number of unattached men as two thousand) roaming the interior, who were simply waiting for a leader to put himself at their head and give them something to fight for.[2] Artigas was that leader. He declared for independence under the Buenos Aires Junta, but he was not long in proclaiming the desire for complete independence of the Banda Oriental, and his devoted Orientals would fight and die for that ideal. Not only rough gauchos, but landowners too, for their own political and economic reasons, were ready for revolution and the prosperity they believed would come from self-government.[3]

The ideas of independence from Spain had been preached in the Banda Oriental as early as 1808 by future leaders of the country such as Joaquín Suárez, the rich estanciero and future member of the patriot government, Bauzá, Father Figueredo and Melo, members of important families. The movement was linked with one inside Montevideo, which continued underground after Montevideo had declared for Spain.[4] Others involved in this movement, or a similar one, included some of the Artigas family and others soon to become influential leaders: the priests Monterroso and Larrañaga (the former a future secretary of Artigas during that leader's period of power, and the latter a notable scholar),

[1] *Ibid.* p.. 252-7; see also letters of Salazar to the Secretario de Estado y del Despacho Universal de Marina, Madrid, no. 109, d. Montevideo 10 May 1811 and no. 268, d. 19 November 1811, in A.G.I., Seville, B.A., legajo 156.

[2] Pivel Devoto, *Raíces*, pp. 257-9.

[3] *Ibid.* pp. 260-1.

[4] J. Maeso, *Los primeros patriotas orientales de 1811* . . . , pp. 36-7. *A.A.*, t. IV, pt. XI, doc. 3, *expediente* of a case against certain inhabitants of Montevideo for attempted desertion to Buenos Aires in March 1811.

and Artigas' future lieutenants Otorgués and Barreiro. José Artigas himself had already been named at this time, by Father Monterroso, as the man who might lead his country to independence.[1] Men with these ideas were spread all over the Banda Oriental, and they were men of weight: the parish priests of Colonia, Paysandú, Canelones and San José were all involved. Their influence on their flocks was great, possibly, when it came to the point, decisive.[2]

Therefore, when Elío's pugnacity precipitated open war between the two factions in the Plate, the revolutionary movement spread almost explosively through the waiting Banda Oriental. Artigas himself, possibly because of his Uruguayan's mistrust of Buenos Aires, had not joined the movement in 1810 although his sympathies were in tune with the revolution; but Elío's restless bellicosity was soon responsible for sending him to join the movement. Salazar complained to Spain about Elío's clumsy way of dealing with the delicate situation in the Viceroyalty, and he put this down as his greatest mistake. One of Elío's reforms on taking over the government had been to replace the well-liked, shrewd and well-informed commander of Colonia by one Muesas 'to whom God has not granted the gift of command'. At once the men and even the officers of the garrison began to desert, until finally Muesas called Captain Artigas before him and gave him a harsh reprimand because some of his *Blandengues* had been accused

[1] Maeso, *op. cit.* pp. 39-41.

[2] Bauzá, *op. cit.* vol. III, pp. 29-30. The influence of the lower clergy in favour of the emancipation movement in various parts of Spanish America is a commonplace. In the case of the Plate region, and especially the Banda Oriental, contemporary opinion is very clearly stated by Salazar in his letters to the Spanish government: 'El estado Eclesiastico es el que mas daño nos hace, pues me consta que en el confesonario la primera pregunta que hacen es si el penitente es Patricio, o Sarraceno, nombre que se nos da a los verdaderos Españoles que reconocemos el congreso nacional [i.e. of Cádiz].' (No.97, d. Montevideo 12 April 1811, in A.G.I., Seville, B.A., legajo 156.) Also: '. . . hasta la gente mas infima ha tomado un tono de altivez, y soberbia insufrible, y su crasa ignorancia nada les dexa ver sino lo que les dicen sus curas, los quales por desgracia han sido los mas declarados enemigos de la buena causa sin eceptuar uno, y como ellos subsisten y han de subsistir siempre esta en pie el principal resorte, qe. la Junta pondra en movimiento quando le acomode sublebar la Campaña . . .' (No.239. d. Montevideo 18 October 1811.)

of entering an orchard and eating the fruit. He threatened to im-
prison Artigas, but Artigas was not the man to take such un-
reasonable treatment quietly, as he had shown before. He had no
undue awe of authority. Consequently, he thought his position
over, and on the 15th February he crossed the river into Buenos
Aires territory, intending to offer his services to the Junta to help in
freeing the Banda Oriental.[1] Salazar pointed out the extent of this
disaster for the loyalists: 'Artigas was the terror of the interior, the
white-haired boy of the authorities, because in any awkward
matter they called on him to take over, and success was certain
because he has an extraordinary knowledge of the interior, having
been born and bred in it' [this is not correct], 'and since he has been
constantly out on missions against robbers, Portuguese etcetera;
and besides he has many and influential relations; and in fine, when
one says Artigas in the interior, everybody trembles . . .'[2] The
Spaniards would soon tremble, too.

It is possible that Artigas had been approached by agents of
Buenos Aires before he changed sides. It was certainly part of
Buenos Aires' plan of action to win over influential leaders in the
Banda Oriental, and Artigas and Rondeau were the most likely
targets since they were the most active and respected creole
officers. In the 'Plan of operations' written by the Junta's secretary,
Mariano Moreno, as a scheme for the course the revolution should
take, these two are specifically mentioned as worthy of being won
over by making them every promise, 'as much for their knowledge of the interior, which we know is very extensive, as for their
own talents and the opinion, estimation and respect which people
have of them'.[3] Rondeau certainly had conferences with revolu-

[1] *A.A.*, t. III, pt. x, docs. 3 and 4.
[2] Letter of Salazar to Secretario, etc., no. 109, d. Montevideo 10 May 1811.
[3] *A.A.*, t. III, pt. x, doc. 1. The authenticity of the 'Plan de operaciones' has been questioned by Argentine historians, since it was thought to reflect too Jacobin a spirit to be respectable
for the Argentine founding fathers; but the findings of E. de Gandía, in *Las ideas políticas de
Mariano Moreno. Autenticidad del plan que le es atribuido*, uphold its authenticity. Contemporary copies of the plan are kept in the Archivo General de la Nación, Buenos Aires, and
the Archivo Histórico, Madrid. I have examined these, and incline to agree with Gandía.

tionary agents, and was believed in December 1810 to be ready to change sides. Not so much is known about Artigas, but it is known that when he crossed the river, he was accompanied by his lieutenant Hortiguera and his friend Peña, the priest of Colonia, and that Hortiguera had received revolutionary propaganda in the form of the Junta's news-sheet, the *Gazeta de Buenos Ayres*, which had been sent to him the previous December so as to seduce him. It seems likely that Artigas saw these papers too, and they were full of Moreno's revolutionary articles.[1] Others with Oriental sympathies were already in Buenos Aires or her dependent provinces, hoping and planning for an expedition to liberate the Banda Oriental. Among these were José's cousin Manuel Artigas and the officers Rondeau and Vedia, another regular soldier who had served for years in the Banda Oriental. Artigas offered his services to the Buenos Aires Junta, and his reputation and renown influenced the government, so that they made him a lieutenant-colonel and put one hundred and fifty men and two hundred pesos at his disposition for an attempt to rouse the Banda Oriental to rebellion. Rondeau became a lieutenant-colonel too, and chief of the operations in the Banda Oriental, while Artigas was made his second-in-command.[2] This assistance was not splendid, though it was not derisively small, since Buenos Aires was surrounded by enemies and had nothing to spare; but for Artigas it was enough.

Before the liberating expedition set out, however, the Banda Oriental was rising. The news of Artigas' flight to join the revolution, and the certainty that their natural leader would come back and free them made the men of the Banda Oriental begin their own liberation, in a surge of patriotic enthusiasm. Artigas encamped in Entre Ríos, the province across the river from the Banda Oriental, and stirred up the movement by means of correspondence with the leaders, at the same time as he was gathering resources for his own blow.

[1] Letter of Martín Rodríguez to Junta of Buenos Aires, d. headquarters, 28 December 1810, in *A.A.*, t. III, pt. IX, doc. 147. See also *ibid.* pt. X, doc. 7.

[2] *Ibid.* docs. 8, 10, 11, and 23.

In the Uruguayan river port of Paysandú an insurrection had been brewing for some months, with the encouragement of the local priests. Even before Artigas' flight, the revolutionaries here had prepared the first blow for the freedom of the Banda Oriental, but the Spanish troops who accidentally came through the town on the 11th of February broke up the conspiracy. The rising then started in the district of Soriano, favourably placed in the south-west of the country, so that it was in easy communication with the revolutionary headquarters in Buenos Aires and Entre Ríos. The local military chief, a *Blandengue* lieutenant, was faithful to Artigas, and joined a revolutionary group consisting of important and wealthy creole officials and landowners. Such men were typical of the revolutionaries of much of Spanish America; they were not men of the people, and they were interested not in democracy but in self-government. This group attracted to itself two useful helpers from the people: Benavídez, a militia corporal, and the Brazilian-born Viera, a ranch foreman. Both were strong, in-dependent men of the *campo*, outstanding in the gaucho qualities, and well fitted to become caudillos.

Benavídez and Viera were sure of a following of some two hundred faithful gaucho liberators. The conspirators gave the word for action after Artigas' flight, and the caudillos called their men to meet at dawn on the 26th of February on the banks of the Arroyo Asencio, in the Soriano district. The revolt against Spanish rule was proclaimed by this handful in that hidden corner of the country, and Uruguayans regard this so-called *Grito de Asencio* as the actual beginning of their struggle for liberty. The small army went to capture Mercedes, an important river port, on the 28th, and there it was joined by the town's garrison. There was some trouble about the command, but the forces grew in numbers with the adherence of some of the wealthier landowners, followed by the townsfolk.[1]

[1] *A.A.*, t. IV, pt. XI, docs. 1-20, especially no. 14, an account of the early movement in Mercedes and Soriano, February to 6 March 1811.

Soriano, the capital of the district, capitulated without a fight on the same day. More citizens joined the movement here, but the revolutionary army was still small, not much above three hundred in numbers, and the chief officers feared an attack by the superior Spanish forces when the news should reach Montevideo. Artigas was asked for reinforcements, and so was Belgrano, the Argentine commander at that moment attempting the liberation of Paraguay, and also the Junta of Buenos Aires itself. All were far away: Artigas, the nearest, was distant by some one hundred and thirty miles of bad roads crossed by dangerous rivers. But Artigas sent off eighty of his men as reinforcements, and Belgrano ordered a regiment stationed in Entre Ríos to cross the River Uruguay and help in the Banda Oriental campaign. Belgrano realised that the freedom of the Banda Oriental was more vital than that of Paraguay for the safety of Buenos Aires and of the whole emancipation of the Plate region; and besides, the people of the Banda Oriental were fighting for themselves, and only needed help, whereas the Paraguayans must first be conquered and then liberated. He wrote to convince the Junta of Buenos Aires of the wisdom of freeing the Banda Oriental, and especially of sending himself and his army there. He was beaten in Paraguay in any case. The Junta agreed to these plans and ordered Belgrano to march to the River Uruguay at Arroyo de la China (now Concepción del Uruguay) in Entre Ríos, ready to cross to the help of the Orientals.

All this took several weeks, during which time events in the Banda Oriental were decisive. Up to the end of March the revolution made great strides, as the villages joined with enthusiasm; and 'big gangs of gauchos met, well or badly armed, with lassos or bolas', and became revolutionary troops.[1] Elío at first paid little attention to the revolts, airily telling his worried subordinates that a sergeant and twelve men would quickly settle everything. When

[1] Letter Salazar to Secretario, etc., no. 268, d. Montevideo 19 November 1811, A.G.I., Seville, B.A., legajo 156.

it became obvious that the revolts were serious, he went in a corvette with a company of soldiers to Colonia, meaning to pacify the country. He found the situation much more alarming than he had allowed himself to think, and returned convinced that this was an important movement supported by the people. Yet he still committed his men in small expeditions instead of making one supreme effort.

Thus the insurgents were given time to unite and become strong, time to win victories they never should have had the chance of winning over Spanish troops – a factor as dangerous for Spanish morale and domination as it was encouraging for creole aspirations. But the Spaniards held the command of the rivers with their fleet based on Montevideo, and this was a considerable advantage since outside help was therefore difficult to gain for the revolutionaries. As the revolts spread the revolutionary troops advanced victoriously on Montevideo. All the Banda Oriental along the River Uruguay as far as the Brazilian frontier joined the patriots. The men were independent, tough backwoodsmen. The south and east of the country rose at the same time. A brother of the future General Rivera led the insurrection in the centre of the country, while a brother of Artigas himself roused the districts of Casupá and Santa Lucía, where the family lands were situated. Nearer still to Montevideo, Canelones rose, and even the district of El Pantanoso, led by a cousin of Artigas, the caudillo Otorgués. In the east, along the Atlantic seaboard, the country parts administered by Maldonado, Minas and Cerro Largo rose, with the future General Lavalleja as one of the leaders. All this took place within a month, with no bloodshed, so that it was obvious even to Elío that he was faced by a nation in arms. He accordingly had a gallows set up in the main square of Montevideo, and gave orders for the immediate execution without trial of anyone caught firing on his troops. As Salazar saw, the measure only made his opponents more bitter, and even turned many moderates inside Montevideo against the Spaniards. It had no repressive effect, because Elío could never catch the insurgents by his method of sending small expeditions, inevitably beaten, against them.[1] He never realised his own folly in underestimating his opponents.

Some help from outside had begun to reach the patriots. The Argentine officer Soler with twenty-five men, who came first, was able to lead the patriots early in April to the defeat of a Spanish water-borne attack on Soriano.[2] At the beginning of March Artigas, on his way across Entre Ríos with his small contingent, had been appointed commander of all the Uruguayan volunteers then fighting and any others he should enlist. Simultaneously Belgrano had been ordered to bring the remnants of his army into the Banda Oriental, taking supreme command of the patriot operations there. Rondeau, who had neither the will nor the attributes for becoming a caudillo, was made Belgrano's second-in-command. For some reason Rondeau received preferential treatment over Artigas from Buenos Aires, and this was the beginning of the personal friction which was to complicate future relations between the Oriental caudillo, Rondeau and the Buenos Aires government. Probably Rondeau was already less suspect than Artigas, who was clearly an Oriental patriot first, whereas Rondeau gave his loyalty first to the larger organisation of the whole Viceroyalty.

Early in April Belgrano reached Arroyo de la China with some twelve or thirteen hundred men, the remains of the army of Paraguay; and Rondeau came up from Buenos Aires with more troops, to bring the total up to fourteen or fifteen hundred. It was imperative to place more forces across the river to aid the Uruguayans, so Artigas, who presented himself to Belgrano when the general arrived, was sent at once into the Banda Oriental to train and organise troops at Mercedes.[3]

As soon as Artigas was established in Mercedes, he issued a

[1] *Ibid.*

[2] *A.A.*, t. IV, pt. XII, doc. 25, report of Soler to the Junta of Buenos Aires, d. Soriano 4-5 April 1811.

[3] *Ibid.* docs. 30 and 31, letters of Belgrano.

proclamation praising the conduct of the Junta of Buenos Aires and calling on his compatriots to join in 'fraternal union and blind obedience' to the revolutionary leaders.[1] The rivalry between the Banda Oriental and Buenos Aires was momentarily forgotten in the common need for action against the loyalists. Artigas was quickly surrounded by patriots of all classes who rushed to fight under him.

The campaign was rapid, thanks to Elío's mistakes. Belgrano set Artigas the task of organising the rising from Mercedes and directing the centre, while Artigas' cousin Manuel was put in charge of the north, and Benavídez was given the south-western sector, including Colonia, where a Spanish garrison held out. The patriot divisions, untrained and without discipline, but tough and warlike from their hard lives, and admirable fighters in their own land (all typically Spanish characteristics), pressed in on Montevideo, while Elío uselessly committed his troops in penny packets, hoping to last out until some longed-for relief should appear from Spain. San José was invested on the 25th of April, Minas had just fallen, and San Carlos and Maldonado fell on the 28th. The Artigas family lived up to its tradition, taking a full and foremost part in the country's affairs: Manuel Artigas received at San José a wound which proved to be fatal; while José's brother Manuel Francisco commanded successful forces in the east.[2]

In early May, Elío and his men were virtually confined to Colonia and Montevideo and the country up to four leagues north of the capital. Benavídez's men were facing Colonia, while Artigas, commanding the vanguard of the patriot forces, with about a thousand men, held a loose line round Montevideo, occupying the villages. Rondeau had been made commander-in-chief by the Buenos Aires government, which had recalled Belgrano ostensibly to answer for his defeat in Paraguay, but in reality because of political changes in Buenos Aires. It is a

[1] E. Loza, *La campaña de la Banda Oriental (1810-1813)*, H.N.A., vol. v, section 2, chap. xv, pp. 845-6. Proclamation of 11 April 1811, in *A.A.*, t. ív, pt. xII, doc. 37.

[2] *Ibid.* docs. 62-85.

commentary on Buenos Aires' need of officers that Rondeau had risen from captain to commander-in-chief within three months. Artigas began to advance towards Canelones, moving on the 17th of May to dislodge Spanish forces who had occupied his father's ranch. The next day a Spanish detachment of about a thousand men occupied a hill half-way between the village of Las Piedras and Artigas' camp, and Artigas moved forward to attack it. So began the celebrated battle of Las Piedras, in which Artigas completely broke the Spaniards after a six hours' fight, and which led directly to the disintegration of Elío's authority over the country. Elío had intended to keep open the road for supplies to enter Montevideo from the interior, but instead he had given the patriots the chance to wipe out all resistance in the immediate environs of Montevideo and to close in on the capital itself. He had never believed that the gauchos would dare to appear before his city;[1] now he had lost to them his only mobile forces. All he had left were the garrisons of Montevideo and Colonia, with about five hundred men in each.

The moral effect of Artigas' first important victory was out of all proportion to the material forces involved. Buenos Aires, discouraged by a series of reverses in Paraguay and the north of the Viceroyalty, was re-animated at the news, which also spread to Chile, encouraging the patriots there, and even to Peru, where the Spaniards and loyalists in their stronghold were proportionately dismayed. The thought that patriot troops were besieging 'the bulwark of this America' inspired the creoles as much as it depressed their enemies. In the Banda Oriental all the villages of the interior joined the patriot movement, so that the loyalists could obtain no fresh supplies even of food except by sea, where they still held command. Even his enemies attributed the great and sudden advance of the patriot cause directly to the revolt of Artigas, rather than to Elío's mistakes, which were by no means unimportant.[2] In the Banda Oriental Artigas' prestige over-

[1] Letter of Salazar, no, 268, *cit.* For the battle, see *A.A.*, t. IV, pt. XIII.
[2] *Ibid.* doc. 72, letter of a pro-Spanish Montevidean, d. 30 May 1811; also letter of Salazar no. 268.

shadowed that of any other individual. He was henceforth the only true *Jefe de los Orientales* (Chief of the Orientals), although he had not yet taken the title.[1]

The day after the battle, Artigas advanced towards the capital, now within three leagues, while Elío despairingly tried to halt him by offering an armistice pending the result of certain negotiations which had been suggested by Strangford, horrified as he watched the outbreak of hostilities from his vantage point at the Court in Rio de Janeiro.[2] Refusing this bait, intent as he was on capturing the citadel of the River Plate, Artigas advanced to the Cerrito, the hill just outside the city, whence he summoned the Viceroy to surrender. Elío in his turn refused, although he was in any case forced to order the evacuation of his other foothold in his Vice-royalty, Colonia, closely pressed now by Benavídez. The garrison of Colonia sailed down the estuary of the River Plate to join the defenders of Montevideo on the 29th of May. Artigas had already written to his chief Rondeau, urging him to rush forward the whole patriot army to make an early assault on Montevideo while its garrison was weakened by the blow of Las Piedras; but Rondeau, in his ignorance of the exact circumstances doubting the wisdom of attacking the fortress city, had not complied. Now it was too late: the defences, manned afresh, were too strong for the under-equipped patriot army, and it would be three more years before another such chance would present itself.

This check increased Artigas' dislike for Rondeau, and probably, too, began to re-awaken his Uruguayan's distrust of Buenos Aires, whose government had put Rondeau in command. Buenos Aires had also left Artigas in a comparatively junior position as chief of the patriot volunteers in the Banda Oriental, and even after Las Piedras made him no more than colonel of his own regiment, the *Blandengues*, although, strangely enough, the Buenos Aires *Gazeta* wrote of him after this as 'General' Artigas. Yet Artigas refused

---

[1] Anon., *Apuntes históricos*, p. 35.
[2] See Chapter IV, section 2 below.

honours offered him at this time by Elío as a bribe to gain his adherence to the Spanish cause, while he gratefully thanked Buenos Aires for its rewards: the present of a new carbine, one of the first made in Buenos Aires, accompanied by the gift of a sword, not from the government, but as a personal token from the captain of that port.[1]

The end of this glorious campaign, 'la campaña admirable', as it was called, was therefore the anticlimax of a siege of Montevideo, maintained by Rondeau's army, which included Artigas and his men. Elío soon recovered his aplomb as he discovered that he could keep up hostilities by means of his victorious naval forces, with which he even bombarded Buenos Aires on one occasion. Buenos Aires was made to feel the repercussions of Rondeau's mistake in other more vital but less spectacular ways, since Elío was allowed by his command of the sea to receive food and re-inforcements with which to withstand the siege, and to make damaging raids. And Elío was by no means beaten: he had other irons in the fire.

2. THE PORTUGUESE THREAT REVIVED

Elío hoped that Spain's ally Portugal could be persuaded to send troops from Brazil into the Banda Oriental to protect the Spanish authorities from the patriot attack. This was playing with fire, since the Portuguese had long craved just such an opportunity, and were by now dangerously attuned to the circumstances of the Plate region; but in those circumstances the Spaniards had to take the risk of the Portuguese simply occupying the Banda Oriental and incorporating it into Brazil. Elío hoped, too, that Princess Carlota Joaquina would help him to maintain Spanish power in the Plate, either by sending aid herself or by helping to persuade her husband the Prince Regent to send it.

In fact, when in 1810 Montevideo had refused to follow the

---

[1] *A.A.*, t. IV, pt. XIII, no. 6, letter of Artigas to the Junta of Buenos Aires, 10 May 1811; nos. 25 and 26, letter of the Junta to Artigas, 22 June, and Artigas to the Junta, 23 July.

lead of the Buenos Aires Junta, Carlota had sent to Montevideo offering to help to support the 'just cause' of her brother Ferdinand VII, but Montevideo had skilfully kept her from coming to the Banda Oriental while at the same time requesting her help. In reply Carlota had sent a printing press to combat the propaganda of the patriots, and with it her jewels, worth fifty thousand pesos, in a gesture full of meaning for Spaniards, reminiscent of the actions of Isabella the Catholic and of Isabel de Borbón, consort of Philip IV. Montevideo had been too gallant to sell the jewels, but had returned them with profound thanks.[1] Still, the connection with Carlota was not lost.

For the Junta of Buenos Aires, the Portuguese threat was very perturbing, and it was the reason for the approach made by the Junta to Strangford and Britain, asking for protection on the grounds that Portugal, Spain and Britain were allies, that Buenos Aires counted therefore as being within the alliance, and that she should be left in peace. For Britain, there was more than a grain of truth in this, and a great deal of common sense; and moreover Britain needed peace in the Plate for the sake of trade. So the question of Portuguese intervention became a four-sided contest: the Portuguese desiring to extend Brazil to the River Plate, using what they termed the 'Jacobin' unrest in the Plate provinces as their pretext; the Spaniards of Montevideo, helped by the Spanish diplomatists at Rio de Janeiro, trying to gain Portuguese help to subdue the 'insurgents', and hoping to be able to call the Portuguese off when this was accomplished; the patriots of Buenos Aires warding off Portuguese aggression by winning Britain's protective friendship; and Britain, represented by Strangford, protecting Spanish interests in the region by keeping the Portuguese firmly in check over the Banda Oriental. It was Strangford, who had the greatest power behind him, who eventually won the match; but it was Artigas and his Orientals who picked up the stakes, the

---

[1] See *acuerdos* of the Cabildo of Montevideo d. 13 August, 14 and 24 September 1810, in Maeso, *op. cit.* pp. 88–94.

possession of the Banda Oriental, although this turned out to be only temporary as the contest became merely the first round in a longer series.[1]

To begin with it appeared as if anyone but Artigas might profit. Dom João and his ministers, especially Linhares, the predatory and anti-British chief minister, merely awaited some opportunity of sending troops over the frontier, while the Montevideo authorities temporised without accepting the offered 'help' so long as they saw any hope of fending for themselves. Strangford kept the Portuguese well under control during 1810, as part of his policy, which fitted the British Government's aim (only expressed later), of bringing about a general pacification in the Plate region so as to allow British mediation between Spain and her insurgent colonies. In Rio de Janeiro, Princess Carlota's idea of taking over the government of Spanish America in the absence of Ferdinand VII received some encouragement from the ever-hopeful Portuguese, but besides the check her plan met in Montevideo, she made no headway in Buenos Aires, where her party had disintegrated and joined the patriots.

In Buenos Aires, in June 1810, fear of Portuguese aggression made the creoles believe that Rio de Janeiro had already sent troops into the Banda Oriental, evidently with British consent, and the British merchants established in the capital were made to tremble for their lives and property. They wrote begging Strangford to stop the Portuguese and prove Britain's innocence. The Junta itself, in August, warned Strangford that the country would rather be ruled by Joseph Bonaparte than by Carlota or the Portuguese, hinting at desertion from the allied ranks facing Napoleon. Strangford, however, had already heard the rumour of the invasion of the Banda Oriental, and had warned the Portuguese of Britain's displeasure if such a move were made. He had the whip hand, since Dom João was entirely dependent on British support for the protection of Brazil's coast and the eventual recovery of

[1] Street, *Strangford*.

Portugal from the French. The Portuguese minister Linhares denied that his troops had entered the Banda Oriental, which was probably true; and in any case the incident closed and the danger passed. But it had allowed Strangford to state his views with force: that Britain would not allow Portuguese aggression against Spanish America, and that she could not allow Carlota to impose a new government on the colonies.[1]

In August, too, Strangford sent an envoy to the Junta of Buenos Aires to advise it not to provoke Rio de Janeiro by any means, and specifically not to declare independence, but to continue to support Ferdinand VII. British trade, too, was to be favoured so as to win Britain's friendship. This politic advice made the Junta believe for the future that Strangford was supporting and protecting the patriots for their own sake (which was not true), and inclined them to accept his counsel. This confidence in Strangford was increased before the end of the year, when the minister refused to have British ships stopped by the blockade instituted by the Montevidean naval forces.

When Elío returned from Spain as Viceroy, and pugnaciously caused open war between Montevideo and Buenos Aires in February 1811 as well as precipitating the rising of the Banda Oriental, he was brought to think seriously of the help the Portuguese could give him. Princess Carlota answered an appeal he made to her with a promise that Dom João would order his forces in Rio Grande do Sul, the border province, to be ready to help the Spaniards of Montevideo against the insurgents. The Spanish ambassador in Rio de Janeiro, Casa Irujo, was unconvinced, however, of the need for Portuguese help in view of the danger to Spanish dominion of allowing the old enemy to send an army into the Banda Oriental. Furthermore, as he knew, the

---

[1] *Ibid.* pp. 493-4; also letter of the Committee of British Merchants in Buenos Aires to Strangford, 27 June 1810, Strangford to Wellesley no. 57, 23 July, nos. 61 and 63, 12 August, in P.R.O., F.O. 63/85; Junta of Buenos Aires to Strangford 10 August 1810, in AGN, B.A. *Correspondencia de Lord Strangford y de la estación naval británica en el Río de la Plata con el gobierno de Buenos Aires 1810-22*, pp. 23-8.

Spanish Regency had instructed Elío to avoid Portuguese aid, and had even urged Carlota not to trouble herself over Montevideo.[1]

In March, however, Elío knew that he was faced with a decisive situation in the patriot rising, and he tried to intimidate the Orientals by ordering them to return peacefully to their homes and submit, with the alternative threat of inviting his allies the Portuguese to send in the army they had waiting to 'pacify' the Banda Oriental. Buenos Aires remain d impervious to this threat, which she believed to be empty bluff, since she had both Linhares' and Strangford's assurances that Portuguese troops would not enter Spanish territory. Besides, a member of the Buenos Aires ruling clique, the rich merchant and expert intriguer Sarratea, had been sent to Rio in February to help Strangford in his lone effort to hold the Portuguese in check.[2]

Finally, in April Strangford, on his own initiative, offered British mediation between Buenos Aires and Montevideo so as to leave the Portuguese no excuse for invading the Banda Oriental, and at the same time to stop hostilities in the Plate, so damaging to British commercial interests there. Also, since Strangford's real interest was in preventing changes likely to cause trouble within the Anglo-Spanish-Portuguese alliance, he wanted to ensure that Buenos Aires did not throw off altogether her loyalty to Spain, as she certainly would if too hard pressed.[3] The object was to arrange an armistice as soon as possible, and then mediate in negotiations for a reconciliation between the Junta of Buenos Aires and Elío, the Viceroy.

Elío was sure that Buenos Aires would refuse the mediation, and so he tried to gain merit and time by accepting it himself. In any case, his situation was weak, for the patriots swept up to the walls of Montevideo. Buenos Aires did in fact refuse, on the grounds

[1] M. Blanca París y Q. Cabrera Piñón, *Estudios en torno al origen del Estado Oriental*: año II, pp. 189-304.

[2] Street, *Strangford*, p. 498.

[3] *Ibid.* Letters of Strangford to Wellesley no. 16, 7 April 1811 and 30, 1 May, in P.R.O., F.O. 63/102.

that the armistice was impossible since it would leave the part of the Banda Oriental which had always been Montevideo's district to Elío's tender mercies. It must be stressed, in view of later quarrels between Orientals and Argentines, that Buenos Aires was at this time gravely concerned for the safety of the Banda Oriental and her people. Buenos Aires considered the whole Banda Oriental as part of the national territory; it was always the Orientals who considered themselves as distinct from the others. But even Sarratea, who returned bearing Strangford's arguments, could not persuade Buenos Aires to relinquish defence of the unity and integrity of the old Plate Viceroyalty, including the Banda Oriental.[1]

Elío was at last forced to invite the Portuguese army in Rio Grande to come to his aid; but this was only when the patriots closed in on Montevideo, and he found that he could not buy off Artigas. Inside the city food and ammunition were scarce, though occasional sallies and more regular expeditions by sea prevented the appearance of the worst extremes. The defenders were by no means united: Elío had managed to alienate all the naval personnel under Salazar; and the city's Governor, Vigodet, and the Cabildo found the Viceroy stubborn and overbearing. The Viceroy was not even sure of the loyalty of the inhabitants.[2]

Elío had written several times since the latter part of April to Souza, Captain-general of Rio Grande do Sul, accepting the military help offered by the Portuguese. Then after Las Piedras he sent his secretary, Lieutenant-colonel Esteller, to Souza to urge him to advance with all speed, and offering to combine some plan for beating the patriot troops now surrounding the city. Even Casa Irujo, who before had solidly opposed any Portuguese intervention and had seconded Strangford's efforts, came round to the

---

[1] Letters of Junta to Strangford 18 May 1811, of Strangford to Junta 12 June, and Junta to Strangford n.d., AGN, B.A., *Correspondencia de Strangford, cit.*, pp. 76–80, 83–5, 44–8.

[2] Blanca París and Cabrera Piñón, *op. cit.* pp. 70–83. Also letter of Elío to Ministro de Estado, Spain, d. Montevideo 30 May 1811, published in *Correspondencia del Virrey Francisco Xavier de Elío.*

view in June that only Portuguese aid was likely to save Montevideo, the last Spanish foothold on the coast of the Plate Viceroyalty, and he changed his tactics. He now urged the Portuguese intervention, while trying to win promises that the troops would be withdrawn once the insurgents had been cleared out of the Banda Oriental.[1]

In June Dom João offered his own mediation between Montevideo and Buenos Aires, and when the latter refused rather than let the Banda Oriental go under Elío's rule, he allowed his troops to enter the territory, ostensibly to help his Spanish allies. Once inside, General de Souza issued a proclamation stating that the army came only to help; not to conquer, but to pacify. His further actions throughout the campaign belied his words. He had answered none of Elío's messages, and had not even allowed Esteller to report back to his chief; consequently the Viceroy was completely ignorant of Souza's movements and intentions, and naturally became suspicious, though he still needed his aid. Further enquiries brought no enlightenment, so that it was a dubious Elío who awaited the result of the Portuguese invasion in the southern spring of 1811. Many inside Montevideo showed their fear that it meant permanent occupation.[2]

Strangford, who was certain that the Portuguese meant simply to annex the Banda Oriental for themselves, intensified his campaign for an armistice between Buenos Aires and Montevideo. Linhares replied to his protests pointing out that the invasion was for Spain's sake, as it was indeed made to appear, and that in any case the British Government had given no clear indication of their wishes.[3] Buenos Aires, warned by Strangford and traditionally suspicious of the Portuguese, was equally sure of the probable outcome of the Portuguese invasions, and came to the decision that the only way out was to negotiate for some sort of peace

---

[1] Blanca París and Cabrera Piñón, *op. cit.* pp. 90-4.

[2] *Ibid.* pp. 95-9. Also letters of Elío to the Ministro de Estado, 16 September 1811, and Elío to the Ministro de Guerra, 22 September, in *Correspondencia de Elío*.

[3] Street, *Strangford* pp. 499-500.

with the Spanish authorities in Montevideo, so as to get the invaders out before they were really established.

On his own responsibility, Rondeau tried to persuade Elío to make peace and join him in throwing back Souza's slowly advancing army; but Elío still preferred the Portuguese risk to the insurgent risk, and made impossible conditions which the patriots could not accept. The Junta of Buenos Aires, harassed by the blockade and by the war in the north against the Peruvian pro-Spanish forces (a war which at this time was becoming more costly and unsuccessful), asked Elío to begin negotiations on two separate occasions in August. The talks broke down, the first time owing to Elío's impossible demands, and the second time, when agreement had almost been reached, because Buenos Aires could not in all sincerity allow Elío to govern all the Banda Oriental, which had fought so ardently for the patriot cause.[1]

It was the Cabildo of Buenos Aires, consulted by the Junta over the terms under negotiation, which stood out for limiting Elío's authority to the city of Montevideo and the surroundings within cannon-shot, so as to avoid handing over the patriot Orientals. But when the proposed terms became known to the Orientals serving with Artigas in Rondeau's army besieging Montevideo, the opposition among them was fierce. Led by Artigas, at a meeting on the 10th of September held in the General's headquarters at the Panadería de Vidal, a decrepit bakery in the besieging lines, the Orientals protested against the proposed sacrifice of their country for Buenos Aires' benefit, and affirmed Buenos Aires' obligation to defend the Banda Oriental for the sake of the liberty for which all the patriots were fighting. They even offered to maintain the siege themselves if the *Porteño* army could be turned about to face the Portuguese. From the point of view of Buenos Aires, however, it was folly to leave a useful army, consisting of the only good troops near home just then, in a position to be trapped and overwhelmed between the superior forces of the

[1] Blanca París and Cabrera Piñón, 2nd part, pp. 189-231.

143

Portuguese invaders and the Spanish defenders of Montevideo.[1]

The negotiations ended because of this intransigence of the Orientals. Here can be seen the first open signs of dissension between the patriot Orientals led by their caudillo Artigas, and the patriot government of Buenos Aires. It was being borne in on Artigas that the Banda Oriental was only a pawn to the government, likely to be sacrificed to the Portuguese; and therefore, so as to be sure of liberty and self-government, his country might be forced to fend for herself altogether – a prospect which was welcome to many Orientals. This was the beginning of a type of state organisation which became eventually a confederation of autonomous provinces, and whose rapid development was Artigas' greatest achievement.

Hostilities continued till the end of September, with the Portuguese slowly occupying all the length of the River Uruguay as far as the district of Soriano, and in the east taking the Atlantic seaboard and pressing close to Maldonado. The Orientals defended their homes with ferocity, but even so could only slow down the advance of superior numbers of regular troops.

In Buenos Aires, hopes had sunk so low with the disasters in the north and the Portuguese advance that almost any solution became acceptable. A new administration, a triumvirate, was set up on the 23rd of September so that the more concentrated form of government replacing the old unwieldy Junta could bring some decision to the dismal situation. One of the Triumvirate's decisive acts was to open negotiations again with Elío, at the beginning of October. Artigas, recognised leader of the Orientals and of their opposition to what amounted to surrender, was pushed aside: an envoy from Buenos Aires persuaded him to withdraw from the siege of Montevideo and concentrate his men at San José in the belief that a force was to be collected there with which to beat the Portuguese.[2]

By now both Buenos Aires and Montevideo were so frightened

[1] Letter of Artigas to the government of Paraguay, 7 December 1811, published in C. L. Fregeiro, *Artigas. Estudios históricos. Documentos justificativos*, pp.42-52.

[2] Loza, *op. cit.* p. 856.

of the Portuguese that the preliminaries of a treaty and an armistice were agreed upon on the 7th of October, and the treaty itself was signed on the 20th. By it, both sides recognised the sovereignty of Ferdinand VII and the unity of the Spanish nation; Buenos Aires was to make certain gestures of submission to Spain (which she never did, nor even intended to do); the Buenos Aires troops were to withdraw to the territory under her jurisdiction; Buenos Aires and Montevideo were to revert to the old conditions of trade, travel and other relations with each other; there was to be a complete amnesty and exchange of prisoners; and Elío was to try to persuade the Portuguese to withdraw, while both Buenos Aires and Montevideo agreed to unite in defending the Plate region against any foreign attack. All this was plain sailing, but the clause which handed over all the Banda Oriental and half of Entre Ríos to Elío was bound to create trouble within the patriot army.[1] It was not a happy solution for any of the patriots, but if the Portuguese had been ejected as a result, it would perhaps have been excusable and tolerable.

The various interests reacted differently. To Strangford, the treaty seemed to represent the attainment of the object of over a year's activity: it ought to keep the peace in the Plate and allow the projected British mediation between Spain and the insurgents to become acceptable to both sides. For Elío, the treaty seemed to be a step towards the complete reconquest, or rather 'pacification', of the Viceroyalty. For Buenos Aires, it was an opportunity to rest and prepare for further efforts against the Spanish authorities. Neither of these two latter parties meant the treaty to be permanent.[2] But for the Orientals and the Portuguese, the treaty was a profound disappointment. Hence both ignored it as far as they could and caused its rupture within a few weeks.

---

[1] Blanca París and Cabrera Piñón, *op. cit.* pp. 233-53. Letters of Strangford to Wellesley nos. 75, 22 November 1811, and 12, 13 February 1812, in P.R.O., F.O. 63/103, 123; Elío to Ministro de Estado, 3 November 1811, *Correspondencia de Elío.*

[2] Letter of Salazar to Secretario de Estado etc., no. 239, 18 October 1811, in A.G.I., Seville, B.A., legajo 156.

K

Artigas was the soul of Oriental independence. Even the Spaniards realised that only he could pacify the Banda Oriental, as only he was able to lead the people;[1] and Artigas could not be won over to the Spanish side, try as the Spaniards might. When Rondeau called the Orientals together at the army headquarters at the Quinta de la Paraguaya, a farm in the besieging lines, to discuss the treaty terms on the 10th of October, it was Artigas who persuaded them to accept, out of loyalty to the larger patriot cause. He had gone against the opinions of his people led by his own cousin and secretary Barreiro, and he carried them by sheer personal authority, as he stood to declare that since the Buenos Aires government ordered it, it must be necessary.[2] But he could not hide his disillusionment, although he obeyed the order to evacuate the Banda Oriental. Even the Spaniards heard that he considered himself deceived by the men of Buenos Aires, and that he repented having thrown in his lot with them. Yet Artigas duly began his withdrawal at the same time as Rondeau.

The Portuguese army did not withdraw. Souza, refusing to respect Elío's authority, was supported in his attitude by his government, who tried every way of keeping the army in the Banda Oriental, with the double object of occupying the province and of preventing any attack on Brazil by the patriots.[3] In December the Buenos Aires Triumvirate, one of whose members was Sarratea, who claimed to be a friend of Strangford's, appealed to the British minister to help them, on the grounds that they were loyal to the Spanish monarchy, and had a 'particular adherence to the British nation'. Strangford's efforts to get the Portuguese to withdraw were not, however, immediately successful.[4]

[1] *Ibid.*: Artigas 'tiene un tan extraordinario influxo y ascendiente con todos los naturales de ella [i.e., the country] que creo que se quitarían la vida pa. complacerlo . . . y juzgo qe si quisiera llamarse Rey dela Vanda Oriental, en el momento lo proclamarian.'

[2] Blanca París and Cabrera Piñón, *op. cit.* pp. 237-8.

[3] *Ibid.* pp. 269-76.

[4] Letters of Strangford to Wellesley nos. 12 and 13, 13 February 1812, in P.R.O., F.O. 63/123.

3. THE BIRTH OF URUGUAYAN INDEPENDENCE

The measure of Artigas' disappointment when the news of the ratification of the Treaty of October reached the Oriental camp at San José, on the 23rd, is contained in his own words:

'compare the glorious 28th of February [the date on which the Oriental patriots made their first important step, at Mercedes] with the 23rd of October, the day on which we received news of the ratification. What a singular contrast does the prospect of the one and the other present! On the 28th, heroic citizens shattering their chains and assuming the character granted them by nature, and which no-one had the authority to wrest from them; on the 23rd these same citizens united to those chains by a popular government...'[1]

As a result, he began to work not for the government of Buenos Aires, but wholly for his own people. Now there took place one of the most touching and admirable episodes of the whole emancipation movement in Spanish America: the Exodus of the Oriental People, as later writers have called it, or the *Redota* a rustic transposition of *derrota*, defeat), as those who took part in it said. But because of the defeat and the grimly purposeful reaction it brought about, Artigas was able, after years of struggle, to free his native province from dependence on both Spaniards and *Porteños*)

It had already been decided at the Congress in the Quinta de la. Paraguaya on the 10th of October that, at the ratification, Rondeau with the troops from Buenos Aires should withdraw to the Colonia district and there embark for home while Artigas with his loyal Orientals should retreat across the south-west of the Banda Oriental, cross the River Uruguay, and camp in Entre Ríos. As they retreated they were to watch the Portuguese, to ensure that the invaders behaved peacefully and did not ravage the country.[2] The movement began soon after the receipt of the news, and within

---

[1] Letter of Artigas to the *Junta del Paraguay*, d. Cuartel General en el Dayman, 7 December 1811, published in Fregeiro, *op. cit.* pp. 42-52.

[2] Col. R. de Cáceres, *Reseña histórica e imparcial* ..., in Museo Mitre, *Contribución documental para la historia del Río de la Plata*, t. v.

a few days the Triumvirate sent Artigas the appointment to the post of 'Lieutenant Governor, Superior Judge and Captain of War' of the district of Yapeyú, that remote village in the Misiones territory where the Argentine hero San Martín was born. It is significant that Artigas accepted the appointment not as a simple act of government conferring a post upon a citizen, but as the ratification of his position as *Jefe de los Orientales*. Artigas had in fact been elected or acclaimed *Jefe* by the Orientals probably at the Congress of the Quinta de la Paraguaya, and certainly before the end of October 1811.[1] Therefore he thanked the Triumvirate for ratifying 'the election of myself by these worthy sons of liberty', the Orientals; and so he opened the great question of whether the Orientals could use their liberty to set up their own organs of government, of which this was the first, or whether they formed part of a nation which could only have one superior government, that in Buenos Aires. The implications were to be worked out in the next two years.

As the patriot armies withdrew, four-fifths of the entire population of the country districts of the Banda Oriental left their houses, ranches and other possessions, and these families, piling their few moveable goods onto ox-carts, joined Artigas' retreating soldiers. Rather than give up their new and painful liberty and fall again under the Spaniards (which meant the fanatical Elío), or the Portuguese (which they believed, with some cause, might mean anything bad), the men, women and children, slaves and all, went into what could only be an uncomfortable and possibly a dangerous exile. 'They are resolved to lay down their precious lives before they will survive to feel the shame and ignominy to which they were destined', as Artigas wrote.[2] And so a total of over four thousand civilians joined Artigas' four thousand Oriental militia on the long and hazardous trek to Entre Ríos.[3]

[1] E. M. Narancio, *El origen del Estado Oriental*, pp. 276-7.

[2] Letter of Artigas to the *Junta del Paraguay*, 7 December 1811.

[3] Census signed by Artigas at Salto, 16 December 1811, sent to the Buenos Aires government, facsimile published by A. Fernández, (ed.), Museo Histórico Nacional, *Exodo del pueblo oriental.*

The Birth of Uruguayan Independence

Well-founded fears of Spanish reprisals and the depredations of Portuguese soldiery added to the anxiety of the Oriental people to go somewhere where they could be free. Rich and poor alike went. One rancher who trusted that the parties would adhere rigidly to the Treaty had to flee for his life, while the Portuguese, who had just failed to kill him, sacked the property he had stayed to supervise.[1] The Portuguese advance had been marked by similar incidents, from the frontier down. But not all was fear: the confidence felt by the Orientals in their leader Artigas, and their own desire for freedom, gave the exiles hope and courage in their sadness and defeat. And Artigas kept military discipline admirably among his men, so that in spite of all sorts of material shortages he had an army of cheerful, trained, enthusiastic patriots with him all the way.[2] The reason lay in Artigas' attitude: 'I do not wish anyone to come under duress. All must voluntarily undertake the enterprise of their liberty.'[3]

During this exile the Oriental poet Bartolomé Hidalgo, a partisan of Artigas, wrote the words of his *Marcha Oriental*, calling on his countrymen to unite in this act of resistance to tyranny and affirm their liberty:

> 'Orientales, la Patria peligra,
> reunidos al Salto volad,
> LIBERTAD entonad en la marcha,
> y al regreso decid LIBERTAD.'

The descriptions which the *Marcha* contains of the Orientals' hardships form an impressive background to the virile resolve to die with the honour of free men rather than live in chains:

> 'Ni el cansancio, la sed, la fatiga
> a la virgen pueden arredrar,
> ni a la esposa que a su tierno infante
> por instantes lo mira expirar.

---

[1] Letter of F. J. Martínez de Haedo to Buenos Aires government, January 1812, *cit. ibid*
[2] See Cáceres in Museo Mitre, *op. cit.*
[3] Letter of Artigas to M. Vega, 3 November 1811, Fernández, *op. cit.*

The Rise of Artigas

El anciano, con voz balbuciente,
a sus hijos procura animar,
y el ardiente clamor de la Patria
de sus pechos ahuyenta el pesar.'[1]

Artigas' detractors later asserted that the Exodus was forced on the people by Artigas, who thought that in this way he could keep his importance as leader of a people and avoid coming down to the level of a colonel in a defeated army. But even apart from Artigas' character and his correspondence, the evidence shows that the Exodus was spontaneous. Rondeau, the commander-in-chief, reported to Buenos Aires that he could find no way of persuading the Orientals to stay at home, and that they would follow Artigas.[2] Even the government of Buenos Aires, at the time of the Exodus, recognised that the Orientals were seeking Artigas' protection and leadership of their own accord.[3]

Although Artigas frequently referred with admiration and pity to the loyalty and trustfulness of the Orientals who joined the Exodus, he as well as Rondeau tried to persuade them to stay at home in the interests of their families and possessions, so that the people might be spared the arduous march while their goods might be saved from pillage. Also, Artigas was fully aware of the hindrance to his freedom and rapidity of movement represented by these thousands of weak and defenceless civilians moving at the speed of their ox-carts and requiring to be guided, guarded and provisioned by his troops.[4] He felt obliged to explain to the government of Buenos Aires, under whose military command he still held himself, how much he had tried to persuade the people to stay, how much they had suffered to be with him, and how little he would allow them to impede his activity in any necessary military operation. Yet he could not resist showing his paternal

[1] N. Fusco Sansone (ed.), *Vida y obras de Bartolomé Hidalgo*, pp. 45-8.
[2] Letters of Rondeau to the Buenos Aires government, 29 October and 3 November 1811, Fernández, *op. cit.*
[3] Documents *cit.* in C. A. Maggi, 'La Redota' (*el Exodo*).
[4] Documents *cit. ibid.*, and in Fernández, *op. cit.*

interest and pride in this people which had adopted him as their
leader: 'I will not hide from Your Excellency that by a singular
contrast of circumstances, I looked with secret pleasure on the
magnanimous resolve of my countrymen at the very same time as
I feared that they might be an obstacle to military movements.'[1]
The responsibility thrown on Artigas by the Exodus raised him
from a revolutionary hero to a father of his people. He grew to his
full stature as he defended his trusting Orientals from the dangers
around them.

The Banda Oriental was left almost entirely depopulated, so
that production of any sort ceased, and food, even meat, became
scarce. Artigas tried to win merit for his poor flock in the eyes of
the government of Buenos Aires by pointing out that the depopu-
lation meant that the Spaniards of Montevideo could draw no
resources of any sort from the land the patriots had been obliged
to leave.[2] What they could not take with them the Orientals
burned. It was a scorched-earth withdrawal, though that was not
its first aim. Materially the exiles suffered greatly too, sleeping in
the open or under a cart, eating meat and only meat, clothed very
soon in rags. A priest who accompanied his flock was hard put to
it to keep moral order among such a mixed company. Portuguese
parties dogged their steps, trying to provoke skirmishes which
would give their general a pretext for staying in the country; and
they succeeded at Belén, near Salto, in December, though they got
more than they bargained for and were well beaten.[3]

Safe from Portuguese harassing, Artigas then passed his people
over the River Uruguay into Entre Ríos, looking for a favourable
place to settle them as comfortably as possible despite their
poverty. By the first days of January 1812, in high summer, all
were across and encamped on the western bank of the river. Their

[1] Maggi, *op. cit.* p. 63.
[2] Letter of Artigas to the government of Buenos Aires, d. Río Negro 13 November 1812; in Fernández, *op. cit.*
[3] Letter of Artigas to the government of Buenos Aires, 14 February, *ibid.*; letter of Salazar to Secretario de Estado etc., 18 January 1812, A.G.I., Seville, B.A. legajo 156.

exile was to last until the following spring, in September, and in that period they were to pass through severe trials of their physical and moral constancy, trials which were the birth-pangs of their nation.

Buenos Aires could not let the Orientals settle where they desired, in Arroys de la China, a fertile place and a convenient centre, but which was unfortunately included within the Spanish limits set by the Treaty of October. The existing camp on the Uruguay was certainly useful for the vigilance of the Portuguese troops' movements, but it had none of the amenities needed for a large civilian settlement. The Oriental families suffered greatly in spite of the help sent for them from Buenos Aires. Artigas was at his wits' end, since he had nothing left with which to alleviate the shortages of every necessity but meat: 'A thousand times I have turned my eyes away from such a distressing picture', he wrote.[1] Even the hospital had only water and wild herbs to combat every ailment. Yet, observers remarked, both civilians and soldiers in the great camp bore everything cheerfully, and looked up to Artigas almost as if he were a god.[2] It was clear that Artigas would not be deposed from his leadership of the Orientals by any outside agency.

After some months of inactivity the Buenos Aires government awoke from its lethargy, and decided that since the Portuguese were apparently not retiring from the Banda Oriental, and in fact had become more hostile since the brushes with Artigas, the campaign might as well be opened again. Artigas was to be allowed to make an attack on the Misiones, which always fascinated him. In April, Artigas duly crossed the Uruguay with his men, and found that the civilians followed him. They would not be left behind by their *Jefe*, even on a dangerous campaign. But the Portuguese reacted quickly, concentrating to throw back the invasion, so that the Orientals, unsupported as they were, had to

[1] Letter of Artigas to the government of Buenos Aires, Fernández, *op. cit.*
[2] Letter of Laguardia to the Junta of Paraguay, and Vedia, *Memoria, ibid.*

reurn to exile over the Uruguay. For fear of Portuguese reprisals, Artigas made his camp further inside the interior of Entre Ríos, on the banks of the Ayuí stream. Here the Orientals remained for the rest of their exile.

Meanwhile the inevitable political crisis was approaching. In May 1810, the Junta of Buenos Aires had been set up as a provisional government to replace the Viceregal authorities within the limits of the Viceroyalty. The establishment of a permanent form of government was to be discussed and organised by a body to be composed of deputies from all the provinces.[1] It has been pointed out that these changes were founded on the idea of popular sovereignty: that is, the people of the Viceroyalty were to decide their own government since Spain had been left without a legitimate one. These notions had quickly been modified, however. In December 1810 an authoritarian faction of influential and powerful natives of Buenos Aires itself had cunningly perpetuated its own rule by admitting the provincial deputies into the Junta, instead of forming them into a congress to lay down the permanent form of government. Thus the deputies entered the provisional government, which began to seem permanent, while this enlarged Junta remained under the influence of the leaders of the *Porteño* ruling clique. Mariano Moreno, the most brilliant member of the first Junta, who had opposed this jettisoning of the original principles of May, was forced out of the government for his pains, and died soon afterwards while on a voyage into honourable exile as an emissary to Britain.

With this most clear-sighted of their opponents out of the way, and as the wars against the loyalists, both Spanish and creole, brought discouraging defeats, the government of the United Provinces of the River Plate suffered various more or less violent changes. All the changes, however, led to a further strengthening of the influence of Buenos Aires, the capital city together with its dependent province, by far the richest, most populous and most

---

[1] E. Ravignani, *Historia constitucional de la República Argentina*, t. I, chaps. VIII-XII.

advanced area in the whole Viceroyalty. A Triumvirate was set up as the government in September 1811, for the sake of strengthening the executive, and the tendency towards dictatorship, inevitably strong in such circumstances, led by 1814 to its replacement by a Supreme Directorate of one man – a *Porteño*, naturally.

In this desperate search for strength and stability based on the interests and wills of the most important men in what was undoubtedly the most vital and powerful province, Buenos Aires lost sight and memory of the original foundation of the new government of the Viceroyalty on popular sovereignty, and of the original invitation to the subordinate provinces to express their opinions concerning the form of government to be established. All was centralism for the sake of strength.

These subordinate, or rather 'interior' provinces, as they were called, had, however, traditions of independence of their own; and none more than the Banda Oriental, in spite of its never having been an Intendancy. So it is not surprising that the first and strongest reaction against Buenos Aires came from the Banda Oriental. Perhaps it is surprising that the reaction was not merely a blind affirmation of primitive love of independence, but a reasoned argument in favour of the idea of a confederation of the provinces of the Viceroyalty, allowing each a large measure of autonomy, and basing the whole on the concept of popular sovereignty applied within each province. It was Artigas who worked out this plan, following the notions of Moreno. The tragedy of Argentina, until the final settlement in 1880 of the problems brought on by this so-called 'capitaline' tendency, is that Buenos Aires was just powerful and lucky enough in the decade from 1810 to 1820 to crush Artigas and his aspirations.

Artigas had read some if not all of the articles which Moreno had published in the *Gazeta de Buenos Ayres* in the latter half of 1810. The *Gazeta*, established by the Junta of Buenos Aires, spread through the Viceroyalty, even into the Banda Oriental, still under Spanish rule, and it will be recalled that some copies came into the hands of Hortiguera, Artigas' lieutenant and partisan. In the *Gazeta* of the 6th December 1810,[1] Moreno wrote an article on the re-assumption of popular sovereignty by the people since the rightful King of Spain was captive. He added that because the King ruled each region as a separate kingdom (as the Spanish monarch did), once the monarchy disappeared the links between the kingdoms went too, since the 'social pact' was not between the various peoples, but between each individual people and the King; therefore he implied that each separate kingdom or province had the right to set up for itself, making a new social pact of its own. Indeed, Moreno saw that the formation of Spanish America into a single state was impossible owing to the diversity of the peoples and circumstances. He did not believe that even a federal system would work there, but described it rapidly before confessing that he thought a system of close alliances between the new American states would answer best, with each province setting up its own constitution and government, as best suited it. True federation could then come into being when circumstances were more favourable.

Clearly, from his other remarks and his work in general, Moreno was thinking of the Viceroyalties and Captaincies-general in advocating the formation of separate states later to become a federation. It is possible, however, that Artigas adopted Moreno's idea and applied them to the situation within the Viceroyalty of the River Plate.[1] Certainly, Artigas took up the idea of self-determination of the individual provinces within the Viceroyalty, and developed a plan of loose confederation between them, leading eventually to true federation. These notions were in the air at the time, and it is also possible that Artigas' plans grew up in response to the stimulus of the general atmosphere of political experiment: an atmosphere best reflected in Moreno's thought. In any case, the ideas of provincial autonomy based on popular sovereignty and leading to a confederation in which Buenos Aires

[1] See N. Piñeiro, (ed.), *Mariano Moreno, escritos políticos y económicos*, for articles in the *Gazeta*.
[2] Ardao and Castellanos, *op. cit.* p. 21.

would not be overwhelmingly powerful perfectly suited the opinions and temperament of Artigas, and those of the people he led. Spanish populism,[1] expressed in Juntas in Spain and Montevideo in 1808 and in Buenos Aires in 1810, besides other parts of Spanish America, was a common heritage, while Moreno's edition of a translation of Rousseau's *Contrat Social*, printed in Buenos Aires in 1810, was widely read too.

Artigas had joined the patriots and opened the campaign in the Banda Oriental believing in the principles of May 1810, and understanding that the Junta of Buenos Aires was protecting the Orientals who had declared themselves free, by sending troops and munitions to their aid.[2] This supposedly auxiliary nature of the Buenos Aires effort in the Banda Oriental was always upheld by Artigas, so as to prove the complete independence of the Banda Oriental. Besides the fact that the Junta of Buenos Aires had asked the provinces to confirm its establishment and to send deputies to form a congress, Artigas' belief was corroborated by a slight gesture to provincial autonomy made by the Junta in February 1811. This was the act of creation of popular Juntas to rule the provinces instead of the old Intendants, and it was a response to a deep-rooted desire in the provinces for a large measure of autonomy.[3] But in fact the Buenos Aires government became more 'capitaline' and centralist as the months passed, until Artigas realised, when Buenos Aires prepared to evacuate the Banda Oriental for the sake of the armistice with Montevideo and the Portuguese, that the Junta did not intend to consult the will of the Orientals or therefore to respect their autonomy.

Therefore Artigas ensured that the 'sovereign will' of the Orientals should be consulted in the two congresses already mentioned, that of the Panadería de Vidal and that of the Quinta de la Paraguaya; and he finally persuaded the Orientals to respect

---

[1] See Giménez Fernández, *op. cit.* and also above p. 105.

[2] Letter of Artigas to the *Junta del Paraguay*, 7 December 1811, *cit.*

[3] R. Levene, *Los primeros documentos de nuestro federalismo político.*

the military necessity for the Treaty of October, but with the reservation that they would make every effort to free their country with the help of Buenos Aires if possible, but not as dependants of Buenos Aires. From this time the presumed link with Buenos Aires, tacitly admitted by the Orientals on accepting the patriot cause and help of Buenos Aires, was broken. For these reasons the Orientals affirmed their 'primitive rights' of sovereignty and 'constituted themselves' by electing Artigas their *Jefe*.[1] It was the case of Buenos Aires and Spain in May 1810 applied now by the Banda Oriental to Buenos Aires, and founded on the same argument that a people left to fend for itself has the right to organise itself.

The arguments were formulated some months after the event by Artigas and his followers, and they have something of the air of a rationalisation of a process which was very confused at the time; but nevertheless they represent in synthesis the flood of ideas and emotions which swept the Oriental people into the Exodus, into suffering and into affirmation of their autonomy in the teeth of incomprehension, indifference or even the later opposition of the men of Buenos Aires, the second great enemy of the Banda Oriental, after the Portuguese.

Once in this situation Artigas acted as though he were the head of an independent state, although he still considered himself a military officer under the direct orders of the government of Buenos Aires. He and the Orientals were still willing to accept *Porteño* generals, men, money and munitions as aid, and even to serve under the generals, so long as their political independence were not questioned. As head of a separate state, Artigas sent an envoy and letters to the government of Paraguay, the remote province which had resisted incorporation into the *Porteño* system, and which had lately overthrown the Spanish rulers. He explained his position of independence of the Buenos Aires government and the reasons for it, declaring that 'the Orientals had sworn in the

[1] Letters of Artigas to Sarratea, 6 and 10 August 1812, and letter of the *Jefes Orientales* to the Cabildo of Buenos Aires, 27 August 1812, Narancio, *Origen . . .* , pp. 294-5.

157

depths of their hearts their irreconcilable hatred, an eternal hatred, for all sorts of tyranny'.[1] Here it is that Artigas' idea of confederation first appears in a document, for he gave an invitation to Paraguay to act jointly with the Banda Oriental in a form of alliance against the invading Portuguese. Paraguay accepted the idea of mutual help in defence, sending Artigas some bales of *hierba* and tobacco, but nothing more came of this suggestion. In 1812 Artigas sent other emissaries offering an effective alliance to found a bloc of provinces resisting both Buenos Aires and Brazil, but Paraguay remained, as always, shy of entanglements.[2]

The complete split between Buenos Aires and Artigas that was bound to come in these circumstances was delayed for a few months. Artigas' brushes with the Portuguese as he withdrew in the Exodus had been taken as a pretext to end the Treaty of October, and Souza insisted on staying in the Banda Oriental. Buenos Aires' decision to make a supreme effort to clear her enemies out of the Banda Oriental, even at the cost of neglecting the only less vital war in the north, took many months to be implemented. There were difficulties, first of raising and equipping troops, and secondly of the distance involved in sending armies with adequate supplies into the Banda Oriental by way of Entre Ríos. Reinforcements for Artigas, for instance, had to make a journey of ten weeks. The premature attack by Artigas recoiled; and in any case by May 1812 Buenos Aires had become more confident of her ability to eject the Portuguese by diplomacy. So there was an uneasy period of quiet.

Sarratea's appeal to Strangford, in December 1811, to use his influence to secure the withdrawal of the Portuguese troops in accordance with the Treaty of October, stirred the British minister to further efforts, which resulted in Dom João's promising to order his army to retire. But it stayed, alleging that it must do so in

[1] Letter of Artigas to the *Junta del Paraguay*, 7 December 1811, *cit.*

[2] Museo Mitre, *Contribución documental*, pp. 169-372, correspondence with Paraguay; also J. E. Pivel Devoto and R. Fonseca Muñoz, (eds.) Ministerio de Relaciones Exteriores, *Archivo histórico diplomático del Uruguay*, t. III, pp. 3-18.

order to protect Rio Grande do Sul from patriot reprisals, although in fact Souza was hanging on hoping to turn his invasion into a permanent occupation of the Banda Oriental. Vigodet, now Captaingeneral of Montevideo, and chief Spanish official in the region, joined with Souza in open fighting against the patriots, which continued in desultory fashion. Soon this skirmishing began to appear ruinous to the Rio de Janeiro government, but they would not ask for an armistice as this would be derogatory to the Prince Regent's dignity: the patriots were regarded as little better than bandits. In any case, such a gesture would probably have been scorned by the patriots, who would have been encouraged to resist more fiercely by such a sign of weakness. At length Strangford soothed Dom João by suggesting an altruistic motive for the armistice: the British mediation between Spain and the insurgents, still under discussion at Cádiz, must not be prejudiced by hostilities between Britain's ally, Portugal, and the patriots. The Portuguese condescended to see the justice of this, and in April 1812 sent an envoy, Rademaker, with Strangford's support, to open negotiations with Buenos Aires.[1]

It is clear from Strangford's explanation of the mission in a letter to the Buenos Aires Triumvirate that his aims were peace and protection of Spain's interests. He wanted the proposed treaty to stipulate the withdrawal of both Portuguese and Argentines from the Banda Oriental, and he also wanted Montevideo to be included in the cessation of hostilities.[2] He meant the Banda Oriental to return to Montevideo's administration, as under the Treaty of October; but if things had gone as he had planned it is more likely that Artigas' Orientals, breaking Buenos Aires' restraints, would have taken over the Banda Oriental as their right and continued the war against Montevideo themselves.

However, the terms of the armistice which was eagerly signed by Rademaker and the Triumvirate's representatives on the very

[1] Letters of Strangford to Wellesley nos. 12 and 13, 13 February 1812, nos. 15 and 16, 11 March, and no 30, 2 May P.R.O., F.O. 63/123.
[2] Letter of Strangford to the Buenos Aires government, 19 April 1812, in *Correspondencia de Strangford*.

night of his arrival, the 26th of May, bore little relation to the wishes of Strangford or the Portuguese. The troops of both sides in the Banda Oriental were to withdraw into their own territories, but what these were was not specified. Nor was Montevideo mentioned at all. Rio de Janeiro and Strangford were glad to have the terms re-negotiated, Rio because she wanted the patriots to retire west of the River Paraná, and Strangford because he wanted peace for Montevideo.[1] At this time, too, Strangford received the orders from London for which he had waited two years. Castlereagh, who had replaced Wellesley as Foreign Secretary, gave him clear instructions on British policy, so that he was able to inform Dom João that the Portuguese must keep out of Spanish territory. Consequently, when the new armistice terms arrived, Strangford forced the Rio government to accept them and take her forces out of the Banda Oriental.[2] Montevideo was still not included in the armistice, however. It was a great, though unintentional, victory for the patriot cause. Montevideo naturally desired anything but the withdrawal of the friendly Portuguese troops, and Vigodet treated Souza as 'General in Chief of the Allied Army' and sent him a gift of a hundred hens.[3]

Souza caused a flutter of excitement by announcing in August that he disapproved of the armistice. The Triumvirate became alarmed, especially when Rademaker suddenly fled. But Rademaker's loss of nerve and Souza's coat-trailing did not break the armistice, for Strangford was able to obtain reassurances for Buenos Aires from the government in Rio de Janeiro, and Souza was in fact made to retreat.[4] The Portuguese menace was removed

[1] Letter of Strangford to Castlereagh, no. 52, 16 August 1812, in P.R.O., F.O. 63/123.

[2] Letters of Castlereagh to Strangford no. 2, 10 April 1812, no. 13, 29 May, and Strangford to Castlereagh no. 43, 7 July, published as documents 54-56 in vol. I of C. K. Webster, (ed.) *Britain and the independence of Latin-America, 1812-1830*. Also Strangford to Castlereagh no. 66, 30 September, P.R.O., F.O. 63/124.

[3] Arch. Adm., caja 371, *oficio* of Vigodet to Ministro de Real Hacienda de la Colonia, 3 June 1812.

[4] Letters of Strangford to Castlereagh no. 66, *cit.*; and Herrera to Strangford, 26 August 1812, and Strangford to the Triumvirate, 6 October, in *Correspondencia de Strangford*, pp. 95-6, 104-5.

until Strangford's recall to England in 1815. Strangford's hopes of complete peace were not fulfilled, however, for the Portuguese withdrawal merely left the way open for the Oriental exiles to invade the Banda Oriental with the firm intention of ending all Spanish resistance, and without the interference of third parties.

CHAPTER V

FROM INDEPENDENCE TO CIVIL WAR

I. ARTIGAS AND SARRATEA, 1812-13

IN the Banda Oriental the patriots continued their operations against the loyalists. Strangford's 'friend' Manuel de Sarratea, who was president of the Buenos Aires Triumvirate in early 1812, took over the chief command of the *Porteño* troops who had been sent over to reinforce Artigas, and also of all the patriot operations to liberate the country. This in fact meant that on Sarratea's arrival in June 1812, Artigas was deposed from his command and that the Oriental claims to separate existence were denied. The Buenos Aires forces ceased to be 'auxiliary' and became the main part of an army, called 'of the North', which included the Orientals.[1] Sarratea was a centralist, an astute diplomat who had seconded Strangford's armistice efforts in Rio de Janeiro, and not a soldier. He can only have taken over in person in order to be at hand to decide any political problem brought about by the opening of a new Banda Oriental campaign in this way, particularly since it was now obvious that Artigas was not going to accept domination from Buenos Aires. The result was a clash of wills and ideas which made true reconciliation between Artigas and the Buenos Aires government impossible.

Sarratea was received with due honour on his courtesy visit to the Oriental camp on the Ayuí, but his own headquarters, established a short distance away, became a centre of attraction for faint-hearted Orientals. Sarratea could offer help to needy families, which Artigas could not, so that forty-two families left the Ayuí for the *Porteño* camp. Some officers and soldiers were seduced

---

[1] Letters of the *Jefes del Ejército Oriental* to the *Gobierno de las Provincias Unidas*, d. Barra del Ayuí, 27 August 1812 and *id.* to Buenos Aires Cabildo, same date, in Pivel Devoto and Fonseca Muñoz, *op. cit.* pp. 22-6.

too, although the great majority stayed with their *Jefe*, Artigas. Within two days of his arrival, Sarratea had taken over the command and had made another *Porteño*, Viana, chief of staff, while Artigas had presented his resignation. Artigas saw that it was time to be rid of his military subordination to Buenos Aires, so as to be in a position to act freely as leader of the Orientals. Sarratea saw the point too, and besides twice refusing to accept Artigas' repeated offer of resignation, he expressly forbade him to lead his Orientals back over the Uruguay.[1] Artigas and his loyal lieutenants protested to Buenos Aires against the denial of Oriental claims to autonomy which all Sarratea's actions implied; but Buenos Aires had intended to douse the spark of independence, and no redress was given. The situation was embittered when Colonel Ventura Vásquez, a young Montevidean officer who had joined the *Porteño* forces in 1810 and had in 1811 been seconded to aid Artigas in the training of his army, obeyed an order from Sarratea to leave Artigas and join his camp with what troops he could suborn. The blow was the harder because Vásquez had been put in command of the *Blandengues*, and he took them with him.[2]

The operations planned against Montevideo brought a complete split between the two leaders. At the end of July 1812 the Oriental troops were ordered to place themselves under the command of the *Porteño* vanguard, and the combined force was destined to escort the Oriental families back across the River Uruguay and to their homes. Artigas disobeyed the order so as to keep his troops unified under his own command, proudly telling the *Porteño* staff that his own troops would see to the escorting of their fellow-countrymen.[3] At the same time Artigas and Sarratea disagreed over the point of attack, so that Artigas on the 5th of August informed Sarratea that owing to his 'obligations' to the Orientals he could not allow his troops to take part in Sarratea's plan. As he

---

[1] Correspondence in Narancio, *Origen* . . . , pp. 277-8.

[2] 'See Apuntes biográficos sobre el coronel D. Ventura Vasquez, escrito por su hermano D. Santiago Vasquez', in Lamas, *op. cit.*

[3] González, *Las primeras fórmulas constitucionales* . . . , p. 8.

said: 'Your Excellency, so as to fulfil your worthy projects, should not have counted on citizens who carried on the war on their own account.' It was a declaration of independence, and Sarratea knew it, but he pressed Artigas to consider that such 'obligations' seemed to threaten the unity of the United Provinces of the River Plate, as the old Viceroyalty of the River Plate was called by the Triumvirate in November 1811.[1]

The veiled threat of Sarratea's rejoinder did not impress Artigas, who replied by making his own hints into clear statements. He pointed out the Oriental view that the Banda Oriental had been deserted by the *Porteños* at the Treaty of October, and that therefore the Orientals had considered themselves 'a free people with the consequent sovereignty', and had elected Artigas as their leader. Furthermore, this had been done in the presence of the *Porteño* envoy Pérez, so that Buenos Aires ought not to be ignorant of the situation of the Orientals. Sarratea's protest that the Buenos Aires government had received no notification of the Banda Oriental's independence merely gained the retort that that was Pérez's fault, that the Banda Oriental had followed the same principles as had Buenos Aires in her Revolution of May 1810, and that the Oriental troops were the Oriental people in arms and therefore were not bound to obey any other but their elected chief, Artigas.[2] These views were fully shared by a majority of the Orientals.[3]

Consequently the Oriental army of some three thousand men stayed in the camp of the Ayuí when, towards the middle of August, Sarratea sent the vanguard over the Uruguay to open the campaign. The Portuguese had gone, and at the same time Vigodet had drawn his Spanish troops back inside Montevideo, ready for the expected patriot attack. Some Oriental families began to return to their deserted homes as the Buenos Aires army

[1] Narancio, *Origen* . . ., pp. 279–80.

[2] *Ibid.* pp. 280–2.

[3] See note 1, p. 162.

under Rondeau marched to besiege the city. In mid-September Artigas independently crossed the river with his men, slowly following in the wake of the *Porteños* as he escorted the thousands of civilians on the homeward trek. It was the late summer of 1813 before the people from the southern and eastern districts reached their goals. This tame return in the wake of a foreign army was in no way a defeat of the Oriental hopes of 1811 and 1812. On the contrary, it was the return of a spirited and united people resolved to affirm their possession of their own land and to support their own leader.

Meanwhile, relations between Artigas and the Buenos Aires government deteriorated further, after a revolution on the 8th of October 1812 in Buenos Aires, which strengthened the centralist spirit of the government. Men of radical views in Buenos Aires had been dissatisfied with the progress of the revolution, slow in all matters, economic, political and military. A clique of *Porteño* enthusiasts now ruled, and provincial autonomy became even less respected than before. Yet Artigas hoped for a renewal of the early tendency to respect the wishes of the provinces; and he approached the new government in an optimistic frame of mind offering to forget bygones and to unite with the *Porteños* for the sake of winning the war against the royalists, provided that the 'system of confederation' were followed.[1]

These hopes were quickly dashed, as the *Porteño* government, already inclined to be hostile towards Artigas because of his federal notions, was turned openly against him by the intrigues of the young, influential and ambitious *Porteño* Alvear, one of the leading centralists and a natural enemy of Artigas. Carlos Antonio José de Alvear was born in 1789 in a village on the frontier of Misiones with Brazil, and died in honourable exile as Argentine minister in the United States of America in 1852.[2] San Martín, the great Argentine hero and liberator of half a continent, had also been

[1] Letter of Artigas to D. Tomás García de Zúñiga, 13 October 1812, in Pivel Devoto and Fonseca Muñoz, *op. cit.* pp. 73-5.

[2] See T. B. Davis, Jr., *Carlos de Alvear, man of revolution.*

born in Misiones, eleven years before Alvear, and was likewise to die in exile, but in France and with no honourable post. Both were the sons of Spanish officers serving on that remote frontier; both became officers in the Spanish regular army; both imbibed liberal and revolutionary notions, as had Rondeau, while on service in Spain fighting the French; and both came back to Buenos Aires, even in the same ship, the *George Canning*, from London in 1812 to offer their lives and talents to the new government of the old Plate Viceroyalty. Together they helped to found a revolutionary secret society, the *Logia Lautaro*, pledged to make the revolution a success; both benefited by the activities of this society and became generals in the Argentine army; but with these superficial matters the resemblance ends.

San Martín, the senior officer of the two (when he arrived he was already a Spanish lieutenant-colonel), the trained soldier of experience, the mature, reserved man, went on to bring military success to the movement with his brilliant liberation of Chile and most of Peru, before going into voluntary exile so as to avoid implication in the civil wars which tore Argentina at the time of his great successes.[1] Alvear, on the other hand, was only twenty-three in 1812, and had already spent some years as a prisoner of war on parole in England, since he had had the misfortune to be with his whole family in the flotilla of frigates set upon off El Ferrol by the British in 1804 before any declaration of war. Alvear had lost his mother and brothers and sisters then, and had been taken with his father to London, where he had had some schooling. In Buenos Aires he became the acknowledged leader of the radical party through the *Logia Lautaro*, and so the leader of an extremist opposition to the government of the day. It was Alvear's faction which brought about the change of government in October 1812, and set up a régime committed to implement an active, revolutionary policy, and founded on the principle of centralism for the sake of winning the fight against the royalists. Alvear brought his

---

[1] See the description of San Martín in Humphreys, *op. cit.* pp. 58-9.

own ambition and ungovernable self-will to this struggle, with results disastrous for the Banda Oriental, for Argentina and ultimately for himself. He turned more to politics than to soldiering, aided by his good looks, his excellent connections and his liberal fortune.

This man, an ensign in the Spanish army, became a brigadier (the highest rank in the patriot army) in 1814 at the age of twenty-five; and perhaps the rank was not altogether undeserved in view of his political talents. As early as 1815 he became Supreme Director of the United Provinces on the resignation from that office of his uncle, Posadas, whom he had helped to place there; but within a few months an anti-extremist and anti-Alvear revolution ended his career and forced him into exile in Brazil. He was not reconciled to eclipse, and returned to take a leading part as a general in the war against Brazil, from 1825 to 1828; but he ended, after a brief period of plotting against Rosas, as a pensioner of the tyrant, happy to save his own skin.

This Alvear, then, in 1812 was sent to try to placate the *Jefe de los Orientales*, but instead he conceived a yearning to be the hero of a campaign to liberate the Banda Oriental and capture Montevideo; so he never even visited Artigas. He supported Sarratea without troubling to investigate Artigas' point of view, and returned to Buenos Aires full of complaints about the *Jefe's* insubordination. So unity was not assured, and while Montevideo was again besieged by the patriots, a bitter struggle took place between Artigas and Sarratea, involving the Buenos Aires government, the loyal Orientals under Artigas, and the *Porteño* army in the Banda Oriental.

After Alvear's return to Buenos Aires the Triumvirate tried to damn Artigas in the eyes of the people, who tended to favour him as a successful patriot and democratic chief, by publishing forged documents in which the *Jefe* and his chief lieutenants were made to declare that they would accept no orders from Buenos Aires and have nothing to do with her. Some influential *Porteños*, however, recognised the truth and the justice of Artigas' grievances against Sarratea, and they tried to persuade the government to re-call Sarratea and his henchman Viana, and to make Artigas commander-in-chief of the joint army. But the Triumvirate was so set in its dislike of Artigas' ideas that no good came of the move. In fact, an emissary of Artigas' was so persecuted in Buenos Aires that he had to flee in fear of his liberty.

At this Artigas lost his remaining patience, dropping all idea of compromise, and deciding to take every possible step for the liberty of his own people and to waste no more time working for the despots of Buenos Aires. He would take over the Banda Oriental himself; and thereupon he issued orders to call up all the men left there, and to impound all arms for the use of the citizen army. Now that the liberty which had cost so much suffering was within grasp, there must be no weakening: 'Let us not cover our-selves with shame after working so hard, by bending the neck be-fore despots born in our midst, who wish to raise up thrones for themselves, sacrilegiously proclaiming against the adorable system of the peoples . . . Constancy and energy will fill us with glory.'[1]

This was a declaration of war against *Porteño* centralism on be-half of the peoples of all the provinces: it was a fully justified de-claration, but it had the unfortunate effect of being the remote cause of Artigas' downfall. Artigas in this way added to the already powerful enemies of Oriental liberty, Portugal and Spain, another open enemy, Buenos Aires, which never forgave Artigas and the Banda Oriental for this apparent desertion, and which from 1816 to 1820 stood by and allowed them to be overwhelmed by invasion from Brazil. Artigas took on too many enemies at once, considering the weakness of the Banda Oriental in numbers of fighting men, in economic strength, and in her position as a buffer province. But he was not merely foolhardy: he had no

[1] Letter of Artigas to Tomás García de Zúñiga, d. Costa del Yi, 20 December 1812, in Pivel Devoto and Fonseca Muñoz, *op. cit.* pp. 75-7.

alternative if he were to stand by his principles, and his position was stronger than it appears since by 1813 he had gained powerful backing in the other interior provinces of Argentina. The importance of the Federal League, as Artigas' system of provincial friendships became, was great, not only for the Banda Oriental, but for the future of Argentina too.

Since August 1812 the Portuguese had retreated, and in September the vanguard of the patriot army, largely composed of Oriental regiments seduced by Sarratea and commanded by Artigas' rival Rondeau, began moving up towards Montevideo from the River Uruguay. The Banda Oriental was in a state of chaos, since the royalists were not strong enough to keep garrisons anywhere but in Montevideo, and therefore tried to keep a semblance of order in the country by sending out 'Tranquillising Parties', punitive expeditions in fact. Creole bands of irregulars, almost bandits, kept the country in ferment. Some of these bands pressed back the Spaniards until by the beginning of October one of them, led by José Culta, a former corporal of *Blandengues* who had deserted because of the discomforts of the Ayuí, established a loose siege of the capital. On the 20th Rondeau's army arrived and the siege became formal.[1] It was to last, with varying success, until the fall of the city in June 1814. The royalists were numerous, strongly placed, and at this time well supplied, while the patriots were disunited and weak. But for the disunion Montevideo might have fallen considerably earlier, with proportionately good results for the creoles living there and for the whole Banda Oriental, ravaged as it was by the war.

This was the situation when the trouble between Artigas and Sarratea came to a head. The patriots rushed up troops as fast as they could to join the vanguard, suffering daily attacks by sorties of the besieged garrison. On the 25th of December Sarratea urgently ordered Artigas to march to the siege with all his men, and on the same day Artigas wrote to Sarratea making a clean

[1] Bauzá, *op. cit.* vol. III, pp. 108-34.

break with him because of the hostility shown by the Buenos Aires government. Artigas point-blank accused Sarratea of disloyal conduct towards him, and then justified himself and his compatriot Orientals in defending their own liberty. He ended on a note of indignation: 'Cease, Your Excellency, to give me orders; . . . do not count any more on any of us . . . The people of Buenos Aires is and always will be our brother, but never its present government. The troops under Your Excellency's orders will always be the object of our consideration, but in no way you yourself . . . I am not the aggressor, nor the one responsible.' If Sarratea wished to see Montevideo reduced, he must go back to the Argentine side of the Paraná, leaving Artigas in command with all the army's resources.[1]

To reinforce his written protests Artigas advanced to the ford on the River Yí at Durazno which formed part of the long line of communication between the army before Montevideo and Argentine territory, and there he cut off the supply train of Sarratea, who had just passed through to hurry to join the siege. Sarratea, in Santa Lucía, made an effort to stave off disaster by rounding up four influential Orientals and persuading them to undertake a mission to pacify Artigas. He verbally expressed his willingness to accept anything, and even to retire if nothing else would satisfy the *Jefe*, but he only meant to play for time to get into a safe position. The commissioners, headed by Artigas' rich friend the great landowner García de Zúñiga, found the Oriental army on the Yí, and at a meeting of the higher officers they were given Artigas' terms. Sarratea was to resign the chief command to Rondeau, and was to retire to Buenos Aires together with certain Oriental officers who had deserted Artigas and joined him. Artigas himself was to be in immediate command of all the Oriental troops, and all orders to them were to pass through him. The Buenos Aires troops were to be known as auxiliaries, so as to point out that the Banda Oriental was autonomous, although allied.

[1] Fregeiro, *op. cit.* pp. 119-25.

The document ended: 'Eternal glory to the constancy of the brave Orientals.'[1]

But Sarratea was by this time encamped on the Cerrito outside Montevideo, with his troops safely united, so he no longer feared Artigas, and simply refused to accept the terms he had promised before to respect. Artigas continued to advance, till by the middle of January 1813 he had established his army on the Santa Lucía river, at Paso de la Arena. Here he had upwards of five thousand men, many of whom had joined his army as he passed through the country. Among his officers at this time were the ferocious Otorgués, Rivera the future general and President of the country, and, as a lieutenant, Lavalleja, the future leader in the liberation from Brazil.[2] Nervous again at this proximity, Sarratea wrote to Artigas diplomatically explaining that he had resigned his command, but could not allow that to be made a formal condition, since both he and Artigas were subjects of the Buenos Aires government and could not make pacts. The emissaries had had no powers to make a treaty, he wrote, and it was null; but he had resigned, and that was the most important fact, although he could not agree to the other clauses. Meanwhile, until Buenos Aires gave its decision, he asked Artigas to help by ordering the Orientals not to molest the *Porteño* troops.[3]

Artigas rejected Sarratea's lame explanation, pointing out that both himself and the emissaries had believed in Sarratea's good faith and had made an agreement which was not intended to be a public treaty. In view of the need for action to save the country, and since Buenos Aires was delaying too long in deciding whether to accept Sarratea's resignation, Artigas expressed his intention of pursuing the course on which he had decided on the previous 25th of December: that is, hostility to Sarratea. As Artigas wrote,

[1] *Acta* of meeting in Artigas' camp, d. 8 January 1813, Pivel Devoto and Fonseca Muñoz, *op. cit.* pp. 77-8.

[2] Bauzá, *op. cit.* vol. III, pp. 142-3.

[3] Letter of Sarratea to Artigas, d. Cerrito 14 January 1813, Pivel Devoto and Fonseca Muñoz, *op. cit.* pp. 79-82.

tongue in cheek: 'Deeds alone can serve as a guarantee to promises. I am fully aware of the sincerity with which Your Excellency gives me his promises.'[1]

Even before this letter was sent Artigas' men were capturing the remounts of Sarratea's army and carrying off the draught oxen and food cattle, so that the siege was paralysed for lack of provisions, while a retreat was made impossible for lack of transport. So Sarratea made another feint, and sent Colonels Rondeau and French, both interested in the Banda Oriental, and both men whose honour Artigas respected, to try to come to an agreement with the *Jefe*.[2] Sarratea still protested his innocence and his willingness to retire personally, and explained that he was still merely waiting for the government's decision. It is likely, however, that by this date (17th January 1813), Sarratea had already received the government's answers to his letter written over a fortnight before in which he sketched the situation between himself and Artigas and presumably offered his resignation, or at least told the government that Artigas expected his removal. The Triumvirate's answer was written on the 14th of January and should have reached Sarratea at the Cerrito within three days, having been brought by boat, the most direct means, from Buenos Aires.

In any case, Sarratea's actions from this time were in perfect accordance with the Triumvirate's instructions (as indeed they had been before), for these advised Sarratea to treat Artigas with cold-blooded perfidy: 'Lastly, without openly attacking Colonel Artigas, nor leaving the command of your army, Your Excellency can act in the way which you think most suited to the importance and delicacy of the circumstances; and this government is confident in the cleverly thought-out combination of means which will assure us a happy result, such as we expect from the proven talent and determined zeal with which Your Excellency consecrates

[1] Letter of Artigas to Sarratea, d. Paso de la Arena, 17 January 1813, *ibid.* pp. 82-3.
[2] Letter of Sarratea to Artigas, d. Cerrito 17 January 1813, *ibid.* pp. 84-5.

his labours on behalf of the Fatherland.'[1] Open fighting would
be weakening and must be avoided for the sake of taking
Montevideo; but by any other means Artigas could be prostrated.
Intrigue was Sarratea's strong point, and he now betook himself to
his favourite work and pastime. Even if the missions of Rondeau
and French were not the result of these instructions, it was part of
Sarratea's general intrigue to get rid of Artigas, and the instructions kept him on the same line of action.

In three days Artigas was mollified, and he agreed to suspend
hostilities pending the government's decision. He was, in fact,
taken in as he had been before.[2] Sarratea's lines of communication
were opened again. But at the same time Artigas sent his trusted
friend García de Zúñiga on a mission to Buenos Aires offering
the terms he had offered to Sarratea on the 8th of January, with
the additional clause: 'The individual sovereignty of the peoples
will be declared and proclaimed indispensably as the sole object
of our revolution.'[3] This was precisely what the centralists of
Buenos Aires would never do, and it was the real apple of discord
between Artigas and Buenos Aires, as both sides well knew.
Nothing came of the mission, and relations between Sarratea and
Artigas quickly deteriorated again as Sarratea's duplicity became
evident.

Safe once again, Sarratea at once began destroying the caudillo's
power, trying to seduce his troops; and he even on the 2nd of
February proclaimed Artigas 'traitor to the Fatherland' and
offered amnesty to all of his men who would join the *Porteño* army
or desert under Otorgués. At the same time he wrote inviting
Otorgués to fill himself with glory by leading the desertion.[4]

[1] Letter of the Triumvirate to Sarratea, 14 January 1813, in E. Ravignani (ed.), *Asambleas
constituyentes argentinas . . .* , vol. VI, pp. 48-9.

[2] Letter of Artigas to Sarratea, d. Paso de la Arena, 20 January 1813, Pivel Devoto and
Fonseca Muñoz, *op. cit.* pp. 85-6.

[3] Terms signed by Artigas at Paso de la Arena, January 1813, and letter of Artigas to
García de Zúñiga, 21 January, *ibid.* pp. 89-91.

[4] *Bando* of Sarratea, 2 February 1813, and letter of Sarratea to Otorgués, 2 February, in
Ravignani, *Asambleas*, vol. VI, pp. 49-50.

Otorgués' answer was to put this letter at once before Artigas, who was naturally infuriated at Sarratea's double-dealing. Other evidence came to light, and Artigas could do nothing but write to Sarratea ordering him to leave the country and accusing him of treachery. Sarratea returned the charge, purposely attributing Artigas' complaints to jealousy for personal glory, and not to zeal for principles as was in fact the case.[1] Artigas then put the whole quarrel before Rondeau and French. These officers, considering their own honour involved, at last by a show of force persuaded Sarratea to retire in the interests of concord between the Orientals and *Porteños* in the Banda Oriental. Sarratea went, on the 21st of February, with as good a grace as he could muster, leaving Rondeau as commander-in-chief in his place.[2]

Vigodet, commander of Montevideo, had tried to win over Artigas to the Spanish side by promises of rewards, knowing Artigas' difficulties with the centralists; but the *Jefe* refused to listen to his proposals made at the time of these manoeuvres, and as soon as Rondeau took over the patriot army he showed his loyalty to the cause by joining in the siege with all his troops. But the important question, that of the liberty of the provinces, was not settled, and the amity amongst the besiegers soon showed signs of wearing thin since this very question at once became urgent.

2. THE FEDERAL CRISIS, 1813

One more result of the revolution of the 8th of October in Buenos Aires, which increased both the militant revolutionary element in the government and its centralist leanings, was the convocation of a General Constituent Assembly of the United Provinces for the 30th of January 1813, with the objects of settling the future form of government of the Provinces, affirming the new régime which

---

[1] Letters of Artigas to French and Rondeau, 13 February 1813; Artigas to French 14 February; French to Artigas 18 February; and Sarratea to Artigas 14 February, *ibid.*, pp. 50–4.

[2] Correspondence of French, Rondeau, Artigas and Sarratea, *ibid.*, pp. 54–6, and notes of Viana, Sarratea, French and Rondeau, *ibid.*, p.56.

had come into being in 1810, and expressing the 'general will' of the people.[1] As the President of the Assembly said in his opening speech, it was obvious that a constitution was needed in order to keep the confidence of the people, especially that of the interior provinces.[2] Consequently the question raised by Artigas, whether to have a centralist or a federalist form of government, was in the forefront of the minds of all the deputies who met in Buenos Aires. But such was the influence of the *Logia Lautaro* in Argentine politics that the Assembly elected as its own President that of this secret society, who was none other than Alvear; and the Assembly's general character was therefore centralist and extremist.

One of the Assembly's early steps was to try to persuade Artigas and the Banda Oriental to recognise its centralist authority by means of a commissioner, Vidal, appointed on the 17th of February. But neither Vidal nor the army commander, Rondeau, could make the *Jefe* commit himself. Artigas explained to Rondeau that he thought it necessary to call his own Congress of the Banda Oriental, and he must leave such a vital decision to a representative body. This idea was soon to form the basis of the Federal League, and Artigas believed that the other Argentine provinces, and even Paraguay, would adopt a similar system of local congresses which would be autonomous within the framework of the United Provinces.[3]

Artigas on the 21st of March sent out a circular calling for elections, and on the 5th of April a Congress of deputies of the Banda Oriental met at his headquarters outside Montevideo, under the aegis of the *Jefe* himself. Deputies came representing all the

[1] Proclamation of the Triumvirate, 24 October 1812, in Ravignani, *Asambleas*, vol. I, pp. 3-4, note 2.

[2] 31 January 1813, *ibid.* p. 5.

[3] Decree of the Asamblea General Constituyente 17 February *1813*, *ibid.* vol. VI, pp. 57-8; Bauzá, *op. cit.* t. III, pp. 147-8; Junta of Paraguay to Artigas, 19 January 1813, in Museo Mitre, *Contribución documental*, pp. 313-16; Comisión Nacional de Homenaje a Artigas, *El Congreso de abril de 1813 a traves de los documentos*, letter of Artigas to Rondeau, 28 March 1813, pp. 27-8.

regions, including Montevideo, even though the city was still in Spanish hands. They were well-known citizens, ranchers and merchants, and were joined by the leading representatives of learning in that poor district, Larrañaga, the priest and scientist, and Barreiro, a student of political theory.[1]

The *Jefe* addressed the Congress, telling it of the object for which it had beeen called, and in a few words tracing his own policy for the province and its particular problems. It was a business-like speech, appealing to common sense as well as to patriotism, and it was the first public expression, as far as we know, of Artigas' ideas on provincial liberty and democracy. Artigas began by underlining the elective nature of his own position, stressing the fact that he was reporting to a sovereign assembly of his people for the second time: the first time being the Congress of the Quinta de la Paraguaya, over a year before, where the decision to make the Exodus had been taken. As he said: 'My authority springs from you, and it ceases in virtue of your sovereign presence'; it was now up to the Congress to decide for the future. After referring to the sacrifices and heroic efforts of the Orientals in the war, he pointed out that they were a free people, and that the Constituent Assembly had met in Buenos Aires and had ordered them to recognise its sovereignty. Artigas had called the Congress to decide on this point, since it was a matter for the people to decide, not for him. Also, in case the Assembly were recognised, the number of deputies to be sent should be decided upon, and the deputies themselves elected. Finally, as a separate matter, some authority should be set up with the duty of repairing the economic health of the country. Artigas then went on to explain his troubles with Sarratea, elucidating the ideas behind his refusal to obey orders from Buenos Aires.

The basis of Artigas' political thought is here set out in a few lines: 'Citizens, the Peoples must be free. That state must be their

[1] H. Miranda, *Las instrucciones del año XIII*, p. 7, note 1, for list of members; *El Congreso de abril de 1813*, circular, p. 26. See also E. Favaro, *El Congreso de las Tres Cruces*.

only aim, and must be the motive of their zeal. Unfortunately it will soon be three years since our revolution, and we still lack a general safeguard for the people's rights. We are still trusting in men's faith, and the security of a contract has not yet appeared . . . The probity of men is very fickle; only the brake of a constitution can make it firm.' In Artigas' notions can be found one of the main currents of Latin American politics up to this time: a desire for, and a touching faith in constitutions, which appear to many statesmen to have the nature of a sheet-anchor amid the storms of politics. Men cannot be trusted, especially men seeking power; and this profound (and justified) pessimism in their outlook under-lies the apparent faith in externals of many Latin Americans. Artigas went on to advise the deputies that the province should not promise obedience without exacting certain conditions. They should remember how Buenos Aires and her men had failed the province in past campaigns; therefore 'Examine', he exhorted them, 'whether you should recognise the Assembly as an act of obedience or through some pact.' The *Jefe* was con-vinced that they should not merely obey, and moreover that to guarantee the results of recognition was not by any means the same as splitting off completely from the nation, as might be objected. In sum, 'making ourselves respected is the indestruc-tible guarantee of your continuing efforts to conserve the nation intact'.[1]

It is obvious from this speech that Artigas had given some thought to the problem of federalism, and that he had also applied to it the ideas of the 'social pact' or 'contract', the 'general will', 'popular sovereignty': all phrases of Rousseauesque origin, well established by then as part of the political jargon of the River Plate in speeches, newspaper articles and in conversations. It may be thought unlikely that a caudillo such as Artigas should have read Mariano Moreno's edition of the *Contrat Social* in Spanish translation, but he had enough education to do so, and in any case

---

[1] Congreso . . . 1813, pp. 29-32.

M

he had friends and advisers who could do it for him and discuss the thought with him, such as García de Zúñiga, Larrañaga, Barreiro and Monterroso.[1] He certainly had, as we have seen, the opportunity of reading or discussing Moreno's articles in the *Gazeta de Buenos Ayres*. By April 1813 Artigas' political notions were founded on a coherent theory of democracy as it was then understood, a theory justifying provincial autonomy and federation, and which included the ideas of complete independence from Spain and a republican form of government. It is a commentary on the variations of meaning of political jargon that on all these points he came into conflict with the *Porteños*, who at any rate pretended to uphold similar ideals, although some of them favoured constitutional monarchy and centralism.

The Congress discussed the problem put before it, and in the end agreed to recognise the Constituent Assembly and to be ruled by the constitution it should eventually promulgate, though on conditions safeguarding the Banda Oriental's liberty, as Artigas suggested. Under these conditions the war was to be continued against Montevideo; but the main provisos were that the Banda Oriental should be recognised as enjoying complete liberty, and as being in an offensive and defensive confederation with the rest of the United Provinces, while all of the provinces were to renounce submission such as they had given to the previous government of Buenos Aires. The Banda Oriental, reckoned to consist of five Cabildo districts including twenty-three settlements in all, was to send five deputies to the Constituent Assembly, and these deputies were at once elected. They were Larrañaga and Vidal for Montevideo, Gómez de Fonseca for Maldonado, Cardoso for Canelones, Salcedo for San Juan Bautista and San José, and Bruno de Rivarola for Soriano.[2] This act was submitted to the constitutencies for

---

[1] See E. Favaro, *Dámaso Antonio Larrañaga;* and E. de Salterain y Herrera, *Monterroso*.

[2] *Congreso* . . . 1813, *Acta* of session of the 5 April 1813, pp. 33-5. Why six deputies are named and not five is not clear. Miranda, *op. cit.* pp. 15-16, suggests that it might be a copying error, or possibly five were elected on the spot and added to Gómez Fonseca, already elected by Maldonado and already in Buenos Aires.

approval, which it duly received,[1] while Artigas informed Rondeau of the recognition and the conditions, and offered to have his army swear obedience to the Assembly now that this matter was settled.[2] The Congress remained in session for the other objects for which it had been called.

The deputies elected were as distinguished and educated a body of men as could be found, and they certainly bore comparison with the deputies from other provinces who went to Buenos Aires. Larrañaga, at the age of forty-two, was an agreeable priest, a native of Montevideo, who had studied with the Franciscans there, then in the ancient University of Córdoba in Argentina, and later in Rio de Janeiro. He produced original work in the fields of geology, geography and natural history, and was in correspondence with some European authorities on these studies. Bruno de Rivarola was also a priest, a native of Buenos Aires, but a friend, a valued adviser and an informant of Artigas. Vidal, too, was a priest, a native of Montevideo and a former candidate for the Spanish Cortes. Cardoso, an Oriental, had been a captain of *Blandengues* under the Spaniards and was now another valuable informant of Artigas' on affairs in Buenos Aires. Salcedo was an Argentine priest, living in Buenos Aires.[3]

On the 13th of April the Congress produced a document which is considered by Uruguayans to be one of the bases of their country's existence. It was called the 'Instructions which were given to the Representatives of the Oriental People for the fulfilment of their mandate in the Constituent Assembly sitting in the city of Buenos Aires'. Artigas as President of the Congress signed the Instructions, though exactly what part he played in their

[1] An example of Artigas' insistence on democratic forms is his letter to Soriano, d. 13 April 1813, in Arch. Adm., *libro.* 206, p. 1 and v., informing the township that its deputy to the Congress had arrived too late, and so someone else present had been nominated and had elected Rivarola as Soriano's deputy to the Assembly. Artigas asked the village to ratify this choice and his Instructions; but 'Todo esto es bajo la condicion de qᵉ. sea la voluntad de ese pueblo, qᵉ. de lo contrario, nada hay en el caso.'

[2] Letter of Artigas to Rondeau 5 April 1813, in *Congreso . . . 1813,* pp. 35–6.

[3] Miranda, *op. cit.* pp. 16–20.

production, and what part the other members, are matters of conjecture. At any rate, he approved of them and took the responsibility for their principles, and so these Instructions of 1813 are important as a statement of Artigas' thought and aims. His position, clear to himself since 1811, was now defined before the nation, and it did not change during the rest of his career.[1] In giving the Oriental deputies instructions on the kind of constitution he expected, Artigas was acting legally in accordance with a clause of the circular of the 24th of October 1812 calling for elections to the proposed Assembly.[2] Other provinces acted in the same manner towards their deputations.

The Instructions embraced three main topics: questions concerning the Banda Oriental alone; those affecting both the Banda Oriental and the other provinces; and those concerned with all the provinces seen as a single nation.[3] Although one or two of the clauses show signs of hasty writing (articles 19 and 20 for example), the whole is unmistakably coherent, the result of study and experience.

In the first group were articles 8, 9, 12 and 13. Article 8 stated that the people of the Banda Oriental formed a province to be called the Provincia Oriental. This was the first public statement that such an entity existed, although in fact it had done so, with its own government under Artigas, since 1811. Article 9 laid claim to the Seven Mission Villages and four others also east of the River Uruguay, all of which were in the 'unjust possession' of the Portuguese. Thus there recurs in what may be called the original constitutional document of the Uruguayan Republic one of the oldest themes of Uruguayan history, the struggle against the Portuguese; and also one of Artigas' favourite hobby-horses makes its appearance: the reconquest of the Eastern Misiones territory, which obsessed him to the point of causing him to make important

---

[1] Instructions of April 1813 published in *Congreso... 1813*, pp. 37-40.

[2] Ravignani, *Asambleas*, vol. I, pp. 3-4, note 2.

[3] See Miranda, *op. cit.* for a full discussion of all the articles.

strategic mistakes in his epically disastrous campaigns against the Portuguese from 1816 to 1820.

In fact, as the Uruguayan historian Miranda pointed out,[1] the Seven Mission Villages never had any connection with the Banda Oriental, although the new province had some claim upon the other four villages situated south of the Brazilian frontier on the River Ibicuy. The Seven Mission Villages had originally been part of the Jesuit Missions of Paraguay, and then later had fallen directly under Buenos Aires.

In articles 12 and 13 Artigas demanded the full opening of the ports of Maldonado and Colonia to all trade, and invited the British naval commander in the River Plate to protect any British ships which might take advantage of the new freedom. In this claim, the Orientals were following the traditional policy of freeing themselves from dependence on the port and trade of Buenos Aires: a policy which was in fact largely responsible for the feeling in favour of autonomy in the Banda Oriental. Also, Montevideo was the only real port, and it was still Spanish, so that other ports were needed for the economic survival of the province. But the hostility of Buenos Aires to these clauses can easily be imagined.[2]

The articles concerned with the Banda Oriental and its relationship with the other individual provinces contained the federal system in a nutshell. They held that all the provinces should have their own separate governments, for the sake of liberty, equality and security (article 4); that the Provincia Oriental entered into an alliance with each province separately for the sake of mutual defence (article 10); that the Provincia Oriental retained all its own sovereignty and powers except such as might be expressly delegated to the future federal authority (article 11); that provinces should not tax mutual trade or give preference by taxes or other means to any port (article 14); that the Provincia Oriental should be left to make its own laws about the goods of foreigners who

---

[1] Miranda, *op. cit.* pp. 231-42.
[2] *Ibid.* pp. 243-9.

died intestate (article 15); that the Provincia Oriental had its own constitution and had the right to accept or reject that to be produced by the Constituent Assembly (article 16); and that the Provincia Oriental had the right to raise regiments, militia, etcetera, affirming its own liberty and the right of the people to keep and bear arms (article 17).

These articles were aimed at the assertion of the independence of all the provinces, and particularly of the Provincia Oriental, with regard to Buenos Aires, in both the political and the economic spheres. Indeed, insufficient attention has been paid to economic factors in the history of the growth of federalism.[1] The fact that Buenos Aires and Buenos Aires province gained everything by the revolution of 1810, while the other provinces lost in varying degrees, helps to explain the growth of the federal movement, aimed at the retention of local government in local hands and not in those of the supposedly grasping *Porteños*. Therefore articles 14 and 15 were excogitated, for the purpose of putting Montevideo (when freed) and the other Oriental ports on an equal footing with Buenos Aires, and keeping the new province's resources for her own benefit. These ideas were popular in the other provinces, where they helped to spread the influence of the Federal League shortly to be founded.

The articles dealing with the nation as a whole included the first one of all, which was a plea for a declaration of complete independence from Spain and the Bourbons. This certainly chimed in with the thought of the *Logia Lautaro* at the time of the convocation of the Constituent Assembly, but for reasons of policy the *Porteño* view changed as the Allies won the Peninsular War, Ferdinand VII regained his throne, and Spain appeared to be about to crush the insurgents in America with her veteran troops. Artigas and the Orientals, however, did not falter in their faith.

Article 2 stated that the form of national government must be

---

[1] But see M. Burgin, *The economic aspects of Argentine federalism, 1820–1852*, where the question is treated for a later period and with emphasis on Argentina without Uruguay.

the 'system of Confederation' as a basis for the 'pact' binding the provinces together, and with this clause Artigas put himself at the head of a large and growing number of Argentines, including *Porteños*, who thought in the same way. Civil and religious liberty was demanded in article 3; separation of the three powers of government, dear to the eighteenth-century theorists, was required in articles 5 and 6 for both national and provincial constitutions.

Article 7 insisted that the national government must deal only with general affairs of the state, while other matters were to be purely provincial affairs. Military dictatorship was to be avoided by means of appropriate clauses in the constitution (as if this were possible), and linked with this demand was one that Buenos Aires should not be the seat of the national government (articles 18 and 19). These claims were all directed against the *Porteño* oligarchy, and they were popular with the other provinces. The question of the location of the national government, however, even outlasted the controversy between centralists and federalists, and a civil war was fought over it in Argentina before its settlement in 1880.

The last article (20) was a general request for good and republican government, and for a guarantee of the provinces against internal or external violence, and attacks on their liberty and sovereignty by any of the provinces, meaning, of course, Buenos Aires.

It was no wonder that the centralist-inspired Constituent Assembly in Buenos Aires refused to admit deputies armed with such instructions when they presented themselves in June; nor was it surprising, either, that Artigas found himself supported not only by the Provincia Oriental but by other provinces feeling the pinch of Buenos Aires' autocratic rule, notably the Littoral Provinces situated along the great rivers (Entre Ríos, Corrientes and Santa Fe), although Córdoba too showed sympathy.

The question of the origin of the ideas behind the Instructions has been very fully discussed by Uruguayan historians, among whom the consensus of opinion is that the Constitution of the United States of America and certain of the individual State constitutions and declarations (such as the Declaration of Rights of Massachusetts, and the Constitutions of New York, New Jersey, Pennsylvania, Vermont, and others) were used as models for the actual form of government.[1] The political thought was based on the ideas of the eighteenth-century Enlightenment, so much a part of the revolutionary thought of Spanish America. The Instructions did not fall out of the blue without preparation, and even in the River Plate area itself there had been recent manifestations of similar ideas, some of which have already been mentioned. The Buenos Aires government, indeed, had in November 1812 asked the *Sociedad Patriótica* to produce a project for a constitution and had appointed a commission to produce another, both to be submitted to the Constituent Assembly. Both of these turned out to be centralist in conception, as did a third project dated the 27th of January 1813, just before the Assembly met, and which was a perfected version of the second.[2] The origins of these documents can be traced to various French and North American charters.[3]

But another project, also of 1813, was of a federalist conception. It is likely that it was written by F. S. Cardoso, one of the Oriental deputies elected at the Congress of April, and so it is probably later than the Instructions; indeed some of its clauses copy the Instructions word for word. But its painstaking imitation of the North American Act of Confederation of 1777, Federal Constitution of 1787 and the Constitution of Massachusetts proves that these particular examples were both available and studied in the

---

[1] See Miranda, *op. cit.*, who gives a table comparing the Instructions with clauses of various North American constitutional documents, pp.303-8. The similarity is in many cases striking. See also P. Blanco Acevedo, *El federalismo de Artigas y la independencia nacional*, A. D. González, *Las primeras fórmulas constitucionales en los países del Plata (1810-1813)*; and A. Demicheli, *Formación constitucional rioplatense*, for a full account of federalism.

[2] Texts in Ravignani, *Asambleas*, vol. VI, pp. 607-16, 616-23, 623-33.

[3] González, *Las primeras fórmulas*, pp. 41-57.

Plate.[1] Besides the better-known French and North American documents, it is likely that others brought out before 1813 were known in the region, including among those with federal tendencies, for example, the 1811 Constitution of Venezuela, and that of Caracas of 1812, which were circulated in great numbers. The North American Federal Constitution itself had appeared in four different Spanish translations in 1810 and 1811: twenty-three years before it was published in French, though many other North American texts could be read in French before 1813: indeed, all the State constitutions appeared in translation in 1778, and even *The Federalist* appeared in French translation in 1792. Thomas Paine's work was known in Spanish by 1811, and with it a whole series of democratic ideas and examples.[2]

Indeed it is probably through the Spanish translation of Paine by the Venezuelan Manuel García de Sena, published in Philadelphia in 1811, that Artigas and his followers came to know so much about North American constitutional ideas. This book, called *La independencia de la Costa Firme justificada por Thomas Paine treinta años ha. Extracto de sus obras . . .* , circulated widely and was a favourite text-book in South America. Besides Paine's comments on government, the English constitution, monarchy and finance, the book contains translations of the American Declaration of Independence, the Articles of Confederation, the Constitution of the United States and those of Massachusetts, Connecticut, New Jersey, Pennsylvania and Virginia.[3] The likelihood that García de Sena's translation was the source of the Instructions is strengthened by the coincidence, in many places complete, between most articles of the Instructions and articles of various of the documents in the book; articles of the Instructions without direct coincidence

[1] For details see *ibid.* pp. 57-59. Text of project also in Ravignani, *loc. cit.*, pp. 633-8. The concordance of the various articles of this project with those of the Instructions deserves notice. Project art. 2 - Instr. art. 11; project art. 3 - Instr. art. 10; project art.37 - Instr. art. 14; project art. 46 last part - Instr. art. 17 last part; project art. 61 - Instr. art. 20 first part.

[2] González, *Las primeras fórmulas*, pp. 59-73.

[3] *Ibid.* pp. 62-73.

are either purely local in character (such as those dealing with the ports and taxes), or else follow from the spirit of these texts.[1]

The Instructions make quite clear, if clarification is necessary considering Artigas' pronouncements from 1811 onwards, what was Artigas' ideal of political organisation for the United Provinces: it was a very loose confederation, in which the provinces should have great power and full guarantees of liberty, including the raising of their own armies, while the national government should be weak, and should not exercise any control, let alone despotism, over the provinces. This was not what North American federalism meant in spirit, and in this sense the federalism of Artigas was a poor copy.[2] But Artigas was seeking to ward off the great danger of a *Porteño* centralised despotism, a danger which for historical reasons was especially great for the Provincia Oriental; and, as the other provinces realised, this was the way to do it.

The other extreme, chaotic lack of organisation due to the personal caprice of local caudillos lording it over their own provinces, might have become a fact through the acceptance of the principles of the Instructions as the basis of a national constitution.[3] But this case never arose, although chaos did ensue in 1819 and 1820 owing to the unresolved constitutional problem, when a completely unrealistic centralist constitution met the opposition of realistic caudillos. A federal form of government was the only possible one for the United Provinces simply because the provinces

[1] *Ibid.* pp. 143-52. Here is an example of this coincidence:

Instructions, art. 1

Primeramente pedirá la declaracion de la independencia absoluta de estas colonias, que ellas estan absueltas de toda obligacion de fidelidad á la Corona delos Borbones y que toda conexcion politica entre ellas y el Estado dela España es y debe ser totalmente disuelta.

U.S. Declaration of Independence, 1776, in García de Sena's translation.

... solemnemente publicamos, y declaramos, que estas Colonias Unidas son, y por derecho deben ser Estados libres e independientes; que ellas están absueltas de toda obligacion de fidelidad a la Corona Británica, y que toda conexión política entre ellas y el Estado de la Gran Bretaña es, y debe ser totalmente disuelta ...

[2] *Ibid.* p. 155.

[3] *Ibid.* p. 158.

themselves wanted it, fearing Buenos Aires as they did. It was not only undemocratic of the Buenos Aires minority to attempt to force the provinces into their mould, it was also short-sighted and foolish.

The Oriental Congress of April 1813 remained in session a few days more with the object of setting up a provisional government of the province, and then it was dissolved. On the 20th of April the Congress, with the addition of exiled citizens of Montevideo and people from the near vicinity heard Artigas speak of the need for some form of authority to look after the peace and well-being of the shattered country. The meeting decided to set up a 'Cuerpo Municipal' a Municipal Body, to administer the province for the time being. Members were elected: 'The citizen Josép Artigas', was made military governor and 'president without precedent' of the Municipal Body. Tomás García de Zúñiga and León Pérez became 'general judges'; Santiago Sierra was elected treasurer of the province, J. J. Durán 'judge concerned with economy', J. Revuelta 'judge concerned with vigilance', J. Méndez and Francisco Pla 'protectors of the poor', and Miguel Barreiro secretary and José Gallegos notary. This government proved to be capable, and in its short administration it brought some relief to the province.[1]

With the election, on the 5th of April, of the deputies to the Assembly at Buenos Aires, Artigas believed it possible to live in some degree of harmony with Rondeau and the *Porteños*. Consequently he swore his allegiance to the Buenos Aires government, and on the 8th Rondeau, his commander-in-chief, witnessed the public act of allegiance of the Oriental army, so that all seemed plain sailing at last. As a consequence of García de Zúñiga's mission Buenos Aires offered some minor concessions to Artigas, which Rondeau passed on to him, and Artigas accepted them pending the result of the deliberations of the Constituent Assembly.[2] Buenos

---

[1] *Acta* d. 21 April 1813, in *Congreso ... 1813*, pp. 41-3.

[2] Ravignani, *Asambleas*, vol. VI, pp. 59-62, documents on Rondeau's commission to come to an agreement with Artigas; Pivel Devoto and Fonseca Muñoz, *op. cit.* pp. 95-106, documents on the same subject.

Aires in fact did not accept the idea of confederation, but Rondeau made a written agreement with Artigas on the 19th of April stating that the Provincia Oriental formed part of the United Provinces in 'close and indissoluble confederation', and that the six Oriental deputies should join the Constituent Assembly, and presumably put forward their case there.[1] At the same time Artigas asked in the name of the Provincia Oriental and the Oriental army that the siege of Montevideo might be continued, with all possible aid from Buenos Aires and with Rondeau still in command, so long as the Oriental troops were left under Artigas. Some petty claims were made too, for the sake of soothing the pride of Artigas and his province, wounded by Sarratea and the slights of the Buenos Aires government.

It was not to be all plain sailing, however, for Buenos Aires had not been sincere in its offer to come to terms with Artigas. The government had only wanted internal peace without having to make any real concessions, and early in May 1813 it advised the Constituent Assembly that it certainly could not accept Artigas' federalist terms. At the end of the month the deputies of the Provincia Oriental crossed to Buenos Aires and presented their credentials to the Assembly, seeking admission as members, only to be rejected on the 1st of June on the grounds that their papers were not in order. In response to an appeal which the Oriental deputies lodged on the 11th, the Assembly discussed the questions, but again rejected the credentials as being insufficient and the deputies as having been illegally elected by a form of election not provided for in the circular of convocation of the previous October. These were pretexts, although there was some truth in the legal quibble. But the true reason for the rejection was political: the *Porteño* centralists did not wish to allow a hostile deputation to enter the Assembly and possibly align itself with the opposition, voting down the centralist proposals for a constitution and voting in their own project.[2]

[1] Convention signed by Rondeau and Artigas, 19 April 1813, *ibid.* pp. 102–3.
[2] González, *Las primeras fórmulas*, pp. 171–9.

3. THE PROVINCIA ORIENTAL, 1813-14

The rejection of the Oriental deputies was the rejection of Artigas' federalism. At the same time Argentine troops began disbanding the Oriental militia units along the River Uruguay. The snub was made the more insulting by the Buenos Aires government's failure to acknowledge a communication from the new Oriental administration, which took the name of *Gobierno Económico*, in which the latter gave notice of its existence. But Artigas dutifully arranged for the elections of the Oriental deputies to be ratified in the constituencies, hoping that this proof of the genuinely representative nature of the deputies would convince the Constituent Assembly. To Larrañaga, the outstanding figure among the deputies, he wrote a letter seething with indignation asking him to do anything he could to persuade the Buenos Aires government to stop this squabbling and help on the union of the patriots, and setting a time limit of three days for the government's reply. To the government he sent a strong protest against the provocations, and warned Buenos Aires that the Provincia Oriental was resolved to maintain its principles and would not be forced to conform. 'It is a raving delirium to form the project of subjugating the Provincia Oriental, after her absolute desolation has already sealed the august decree of her liberty', he wrote. He was ready for war with Buenos Aires if it was forced upon him, but he preferred peace and confederation.[1]

The result of this communication and of Larrañaga's conferences in Buenos Aires was that at the end of July the government angrily replied to the Oriental claims, defying Artigas and putting him in his place. Luckily the answer went to Larrañaga, who softened the language of the proposals it contained for obtaining the desired unity before passing the letter on. Both sides had lost

[1] Instructions and information, d. 29 June 1813, Pivel Devoto and Fonseca Muñoz, *op. cit.* pp. 109-11. Letter of Artigas to the Buenos Aires government, 29 June 1813, *ibid.* pp. 112-15.

their tempers and were in need of diplomatic intermediaries such as this priest.

The new terms offered by Buenos Aires were to the effect that the Provincia Oriental should send four deputies to the Constituent Assembly, including the one from Maldonado who had joined it separately in April. These members, in conjunction with their colleagues from the rest of the country, should decide on the future government of the whole nation. The Oriental deputies should speak for themselves and their province: that is, Artigas should not instruct them, as 'the general will of the Peoples and their representatives will decide, and all will obey'. But meanwhile the present government would remain authorised to keep order and make war.

These conditions were aimed at reducing Artigas' influence in the Constituent Assembly, over the Oriental deputies, and in the Provincia Oriental, but a distinct series of proposals had that province in view more especially. Rondeau was authorised to form a provincial government by calling the landowners together to settle the matter, and in this way Artigas' *Gobierno Económico* would be set aside. The provincial militia, who were under Artigas' own command, were to be paid and treated in the same way as Argentine troops, providing that they allowed the government to fix their numbers and that they kept their military discipline. In other words, they must obey unquestioningly Buenos Aires' commands even though their nominal leader, Artigas, might disagree. Finally, Buenos Aires tried to assuage Artigas' suspicions that they intended to use force to make the Provincia Oriental conform, by declaring that all their military dispositions were directed against the common enemy, Spain.[1]

This policy was calculated to make Artigas furious. He was touchy, and had often shown himself to be so, particularly since 1811, admittedly under considerable provocation. Buenos Aires

[1] Letters of the Buenos Aires government to Larrañaga, 26 July 1813; Larrañaga to Artigas, 29 July; Buenos Aires government to Rondeau, 14 August, *ibid.* pp. 115–19.

was determined to get rid of him, as he was well aware. The letters to Larrañaga and Rondeau made the intention perfectly clear. At Artigas' side, too, there was a handful of men encouraging him to come to an open break with Buenos Aires, but at this juncture Artigas' better nature was brought to the fore by the calm counsels of his *Gobierno Económico*, especially of García de Zúñiga, and by Rondeau's diplomacy; so that although even his own colleagues feared an explosion, Artigas brought himself to accept the new terms. By the end of August Artigas and Rondeau agreed on the convocation of a new provincial Congress before Rondeau so as to establish a new provincial government and decide on the new deputies to be sent to the Constituent Assembly.[1]

Artigas, Rondeau and the *Gobierno Económico* simultaneously sent circulars on the 15th of November to the Cabildos calling for the election of members for a provincial Congress. By previous agreement with Rondeau Artigas notified the Cabildos that the members should meet at his quarters first, then pass to Rondeau's headquarters. But Rondeau, suspicious of Artigas, sent out another circular ordering the members to congregate instead at the Capilla de Maciel, on the pretext that there must be no suspicion of force in their deliberations and therefore the Congress must not meet at his headquarters. But in this way the Congress was in fact removed from Artigas' influence by means of a broken agreement, and put entirely under Rondeau's own influence, since Rondeau would be in sole charge of it.[2]

Therefore the Congress of the Capilla de Maciel met on the 8th of December, under Rondeau's presidency. The Artigas supporters, who included García de Zúñiga, put forward a motion that the commander-in-chief should not preside, but it was lost and Rondeau took charge. The man in power usually has a majority in Latin American assemblies. Some members' credentials stated categorically that they must consult Artigas before

[1] Letter of Bruno Méndez to Larrañaga, 28 August 1813, *ibid.* pp. 119-21.
[2] González, *Las primeras fórmulas*, pp. 179-86; Bauzá, *op. cit.* vol. III, pp. 178-82.

joining the Congress, and so García de Zúñiga and Manuel Francisco Artigas, the *Jefe's* brother, were sent to smooth over the difficulty by inviting Artigas himself to appear at the Congress and explain, as had been his intention, what had resulted from the Congress of April. But Artigas, feeling himself scorned, refused to go, and said that the wishes of the people were being ignored. In its turn the Congress, which did not contain a majority of close supporters of Artigas, felt itself slighted, and voted that it should carry on without the nettled *Jefe* and in its present location.

The three new deputies to go to Buenos Aires were elected on the 9th, and a provincial government was set up, avoiding for the sake of peace similarities of name with any previous authority. Artigas' friend García de Zúñiga, J. J. Durán and Remigio Castellanos were the members. Such was the hostility to Artigas in the Congress dominated by Rondeau that the new government was given powers of *residencia* (full judicial investigation of the actions of a public officer) in the Spanish style over the members of the previous *Gobierno Económico*, and a complete break was made with the *Jefe*.

The rupture came when, on the 10th, Artigas sent a strong protest to the Congress for not coming to consult him, the elected *Jefe de los Orientales*, and coolly suggested that the Congress should dissolve itself and allow the people to confirm or reject its acts by electing a fresh one.[1] The Congress rejected the note, and closed its session of its own accord the same day, leaving in existence the things which had angered Artigas, and adding to the incendiary material a resolution that the Constituent Assembly was recognised as sovereign over the Provincia Oriental, which from that day was one of the United Provinces. This was exactly what Artigas had been fighting against, so it is no wonder that he broke with Rondeau soon afterwards; but it should be borne in mind, too, that Artigas' own irascibility was partly to blame: he was

---

[1] Letter of Artigas to the *Ciudadanos Electores*, 10 December 1813, Arch. Adm., book 206, ff. 24 and 25.

offered a chance by the Congress to go and put his point of view, which he refused to do from motives of pride.[1] Artigas showed great clumsiness as a politician in refusing to accept the Congress of the Capilla de Maciel, in which he had good friends, and in antagonising it instead. With tact he might have won the Congress over to his side and ended in a better position than he began.[2] Acting as he did, he left no alternative but a break with some of his best supporters, including his brother.

Artigas and Rondeau now both circularised the townships of the Provincia Oriental putting forward their respective points of view, and Rondeau added the threat of raising the siege of Montevideo if 'union' were not maintained. This led to protest and counter-protest from the two leaders, in which Rondeau, the career officer upholding discipline, insulted Artigas as a trouble-maker who hit out at the central government without which his people could not survive. Artigas suggested calling a new Congress, but neither could trust the other any more, and none was called.[3] But the work of the Congress of the Capilla de Maciel was annulled since the three deputies never entered the Constituent Assembly, and the Provincia Oriental was eventually, in March 1814, put under the administration of an Intendant Governor appointed by Buenos Aires.

Realising that the time had come for him to cut loose and fend for himself again, and wanting perhaps to avoid a threatened attack on his life, Artigas quietly on the 20th of January 1814 retired from the lines round Montevideo. He went with a small personal escort, and after him marched most of the Oriental troops there, over a thousand men, to encamp at the Paso de la Cabra on the Río Santa Lucía. A considerable gap was left in the besieging army, a gap which was not filled for some months, and which left Rondeau in a very uncomfortable situation.[4]

[1] See Bauzá, *op. cit.* vol. III, p. 181.

[2] *Ibid.*

[3] Letters of Artigas to Rondeau 10 January 1814, 14 January; Rondeau to Artigas 10, 12 and 14 January, Fregeiro, *op. cit.* pp. 204-16.

[4] 'Autobiografía del Brigadier General Don José Rondeau', in Lamas, *Colección*; letter of Rondeau to the Buenos Aires government, 25 January 1814, Fregeiro, *op. cit.* pp. 216-17.

N

From Independence to Civil War

Since the end of 1812 Montevideo had been closely besieged on
land, although at sea the Spanish Montevideo flotilla was usually
able to beat the embryo navy of Buenos Aires, so that some provisions had been able to enter through the port. The Spanish
bombardment of Buenos Aires in 1811 had not been a wasted
blow, either. Yet morale in the city of Montevideo was not high
by early 1814, because the provisions were barely sufficient and
disease was becoming a serious threat. Water had to be imported
at some risk in barrels. Land sorties, often undertaken, never met
with success. Some help had come from Lima, but it stopped in
1813, while from Spain a long-promised reinforcement of troops
came in August only to add to the number of mouths to feed, and
in such a ravaged state that disease brought by them spread
through the city.

Twice the Spanish commander, Vigodet, had tried to win over
Artigas by promises of great rewards, but the *Jefe* had refused even
though his relations with Buenos Aires had been bad. Artigas
stuck to the siege throughout 1813, and Montevideo's plight became serious as the patriots organised a flotilla which made the
entrance to the port dangerous. Yet Buenos Aires, in May 1813,
ordered Rondeau to raise the siege and leave the Provincia
Oriental to its fate, since Spanish reinforcements were expected.
Rondeau refused, sure that victory must soon come. He knew the
state of things in the city, having good sources of information
among the creoles there, who kept him posted by such picturesque
means as messages floated out of the port in bottles.[1]

Artigas must have been unaware of certain negotiations for an
armistice between Montevideo and Buenos Aires which had been
going on in Rio de Janeiro since December 1813, one of whose
results would be the desertion by Buenos Aires of the Provincia
Oriental. By the end of 1813 the United Provinces seemed to be
falling apart rapidly as Artigas' federal ideas gained ground; and at
the same time royalist troops from Peru inflicted heavy defeats on

[1] 'Autobiografía de Rondeau', in Lamas, *Colección*.

the patriot army in the north of Argentina which was fighting a defensive campaign in which in fact neither side could strike a decisive blow.[1] In Europe the Peninsular War was coming to an end and fresh Spanish armies seemed likely to be sent out to quell the revolution in Spanish America. Since the outlook was so black, the centralists of Buenos Aires decided to make use once again of Strangford's helpfulness, and sent to Rio the minister's old 'friend' Sarratea, Artigas' treacherous enemy. Sarratea had orders to enlist Strangford's aid for a mission to London to negotiate for a reasonable peace with Spain, under Britain's guarantee. Spain was to be wheedled into granting self-govern-ment to the Viceroyalty of the Plate, and Britain was to be tempted into making a secret engagement with Buenos Aires and later a commercial treaty which should guarantee support against any possible recrudescence of Spanish tyranny. In fact, as Sarratea admitted to Strangford, Buenos Aires would accept anything for peace 'short of unqualified submission to Spain'.[2]

Together with the Spanish minister in Rio de Janeiro, Strang-ford in December took the first step, which was to open negotia-tions for an armistice between Montevideo and Buenos Aires. The armistice was to be on the basis of Buenos Aires' withdrawal from the Provincia Oriental, in return for which the royalists were to make concessions where the war was apparently in stalemate, in Upper Peru (now Bolivia). The withdrawal from the Banda Oriental was the only solution in the circumstances, no doubt, but it must have given Sarratea and possibly the Buenos Aires oligarchy not a little satisfaction to know that Artigas would be left to face the music alone.

Envoys from Montevideo willingly joined in the negotiations, and in January 1814 the only point still at issue, the vital one of the

---

[1] See R. A. Humphreys, *op. cit.* pp. 55–8 for this campaign.

[2] Instructions and credentials of Sarratea, 19 November, 1813, AGN, B.A. Div. Nac., Sec. Gob., legajo 2-1-1 ; letters of Strangford to Castlereagh no. 103, 1 August 1813, P.R.O., F.O. 63/147, and no. 150, 18 December 1813, with letter of Sarratea to Strangford 10 December 1813 enclosed, F.O. 63/148.

lines to be occupied at the cease fire, was settled. But then news of
the defeats suffered by the United Provinces in the north arrived,
so the royalists refused after all to accept an armistice for that
theatre of war, hoping for definite victory there at last. The negotiations came to an end, and the terms as they stood then were sent
to Buenos Aires and Montevideo for their governments to settle
the question of peace among themselves, with Strangford's encouragement.[1]

The negotiations in the Plate area began, but Buenos Aires'
position was greatly weakened when Artigas withdrew from the
siege of Montevideo. Buenos Aires was almost in a panic because
of the various dangers pressing in on her, and the result was a
further concentration of power in the government. It was a
logical step, meant to increase efficiency in confronting the present
troubles, and perfectly in consonance with the *Porteño* centralists'
outlook. A Supreme Directorate was set up, in fact a dictatorship,
and Gervasio Antonio de Posadas was elected to the office of
Supreme Director on the 22nd of January 1814. He had been one
of the Triumvirs, and was a keen follower of the ideas of the
Logia Lautaro and of his nephew Alvear, and a member of the
Sociedad Patriótica a less secret club with notions similar to those
of the *Logia*. The armistice negotiations proved fruitless, although
they were continued for some months. Vigodet was too stubborn
a man to deal with.

Montevideo felt an immediate relief when Artigas left the siege,
and Vigodet determined at once to try to win Artigas and the
Orientals over to the royalist camp. He offered rewards to

---

[1] Letters of Strangford to Castlereagh, Separate, 4 January 1814, and no. 6, 20 February,
P.R.O., F.O. 631/67; Sarratea to Buenos Aires government, 11 and 12 January 1814,
AGN, B. A., Div. Nac., Sec. Gob., legajo 2-1-1; Sarratea to the Buenos Aires government, 12 February, *Correspondencia de Strangford*, pp. 132-4; MS. by Magariños, 'Resumen
de los sucesos mas notables que han preparado la re... de la America meridional, y
marcha que ha llevado hasta el 30... to de 1820', in AGN, Montevideo, Fondo ex-
Archivo y Museo Histórico Nacional, caja 178, Archivo Magariños. Mateo Magariños and
Manuel Durán were in Rio de Janeiro at this time as deputies of the Cabildo of Montevideo
asking for help in victuals and money for their city. Magariños acted as agent for the besieged city in the armistice negotiations, working with the Spanish minister, Castilla.

Orientals who would serve under him, and sent written proposals to Artigas and his lieutenant Otorgués offering great
advantages if they would come over for the sake of the peace and
prosperity of the Banda Oriental, which they would have, he
reminded them, the personal glory of attaining. The Cabildo
seconded Vigodet's efforts.[1] But although Artigas was solemnly
declared by Buenos Aires an outlaw with a high price on his head,
he refused the Spanish proposition, retorting with dignity that the
Provincia Oriental's troubles with Buenos Aires should have
shown Vigodet how sensitive the Orientals were about their
liberty.[2] To his friend Larrobla, who brought the letters from
Montevideo, Artigas wrote in noble words about his own desire
for peace in his country: 'I desire peace, and so much that I consider it the prime necessity, so that the few resources which yet
remain with which to provide for the country's re-establishment
should not be annihilated.' Artigas certainly did not want war, but
he insisted that peace could only be gained if Spain offered liberty
to the Provincia Oriental, and he was not prepared to compromise
on that.[3] Indeed, he ordered Otorgués and another lieutenant,
Hereñú, to attack Spanish boats on the River Uruguay which had
appealed to him for succour and provisions.[4]

The decree outlawing Artigas was the logical outcome of the
entire political and economic situation in the region, with im-
movable centralists in Buenos Aires facing stubborn autonomists
in the Provincia Oriental and other provinces led by Artigas.[5] In
the decree can be seen the result of all the years of antagonism
between the capital and the exploited territories, and of the

[1] Letters of Vigodet to Artigas, and the Cabildo to Artigas, 3 February 1814, in Pivel
Devoto and Fonseca Muñoz, *op. cit.* pp. 125-28.

[2] Letter of Artigas to Vigodet, and Artigas to the Cabildo, 25 February 1814, *ibid.* pp.
128-30.

[3] Letters of Artigas to Larrobla, and Artigas to Otorgués, 25 February 1814, *ibid.* pp.
131-3.

[4] Letters of Romarate (Spanish naval commander) to Otorgués, 13 March 1814, Artigas
to Otorgués 20 and 24 March, and Artigas to Hereñú, 8 March, *ibid.* pp. 134-6.

[5] Decree in Ravignani, *Asambleas*, vol. VI, 2, pp. 71-2.

bitterness of both sides, both sure that they were in the right. It was inevitable that the old Banda Oriental, finding a strong leader, should rebel against Buenos Aires, and equally inevitable that Buenos Aires should seek to retain and even extend her domination, especially in the heat of the revolution, which had proved economically beneficial to the capital. The decree was levelled against the Provincia Oriental as well as against Artigas, for any troops who continued serving under the *Jefe* were given forty days in which to desert, or else they would be shot when captured.

After this, Artigas became really hostile. He moved to the Río Negro with over three thousand men, then on to Belén in the Misiones, leaving Rivera with a division to intercept Rondeau's communications and sending Otorgués to cover the River Uruguay and prevent the entry of reinforcements. Artigas intended to rouse all the federalist feeling of the Littoral Provinces and raise a full-scale war against Buenos Aires, since he could count on the sympathy and support of a large proportion, perhaps the larger part, of the Argentine people. His prestige and power were greatly increased by the opportune victory of Otorgués in early March over a reinforcement of five hundred men under the *Porteño* officer Quintana, who were caught soon after crossing the River Uruguay and forced to surrender.

Buenos Aires' situation was rapidly worsening, as the Littoral Provinces began to stir. It is a measure of the government's complete bankruptcy of policy that within a month of outlawing Artigas in the most insulting and apparently irrevocable way, they sent two commissioners to parley with him and 're-establish harmony' in face of the common enemy, while almost at the same time commissioners were sent to Montevideo to open negotiations for peace on the basis of those begun the previous December in Rio de Janeiro.[1] Both these *démarches* failed, the latter because of

[1] Documents on the mission of Francisco Mariano Amaro and Lieut.-col. Francisco A. Candioti to Artigas, in Pivel Devoto and Fonseca Muñoz, *op. cit.* pp. 141-59. Letters of Strangford to Castlereagh no. 38, 20 April 1814, and no. 46, 21 May 1814, P.R.O., F.O. 63/167.

Vigodet's obstinacy, and the former because neither side had changed its views, already fully known to each other; nor would either come to a compromise.

In this extremity Buenos Aires determined to throw everything into the fight against Montevideo, in the hope of finishing it once and for all. First command of the sea had to be won, and it was accomplished by the *Porteño* flotilla under the Irish sailor Brown, with a staff almost completely of British officers. The Montevidean ships were beaten back into port in a long action which ended with the establishment of a blockade of Montevideo by the *Porteños*. Then Alvear, at the age of twenty-five one of the most influential men in the government ranks and, indeed, in the United Provinces, was sent over with fresh troops to take command of the siege of Montevideo in place of Rondeau. He landed with one thousand five hundred fresh men, and on the 17th of May took over from the general who had, in almost two years of siege, prepared the victory that Alvear's uncle Posadas was presenting to his ambitious nephew.

Montevideo was in a pitiful state. From early May there was only enough wheat to give bread to the sick, and all consumer goods were inventoried and their sale strictly regulated. There was no fuel, so the citizens' stocks of charcoal were confiscated for the use of the armouries, working feverishly to repair and make weapons.[1] Yet the Cabildo nobly supported the royalist effort to hold out, and was indeed partly responsible for sending out the fleet to do battle with Brown's ships rather than see the Spanish boats skulking in harbour with their crews' morale draining away. The Spanish fleet was beaten on the 16th and 17th of May, but even then the Cabildo called in the small boats used in the harbour and their crews to form some sort of flotilla.[2]

Vigodet was at last forced to send emissaries to Buenos Aires to sue for peace: the peace he had refused to discuss a few weeks

[1] *Borradores* of Cabildo edicts of 10 and 11 May 1814, Arch. Adm., caja 434.

[2] *Borradores* of the letter of the Cabildo to Vigodet, 22 April 1814, and of the Cabildo edict of 28 May, *ibid.*

before. But he was refused in his turn, and the city had to go through the terrors of a siege to the bitter end.[1] Alvear was given full powers to negotiate on the spot with the Spanish authorities, and on the 5th of June he offered to listen to Vigodet's proposals. Vigodet was willing to open negotiations so long as Artigas and Otorgués had representatives there: he was probably trying to win time and sow further dissension among the patriots, although it is true that he had been negotiating with the Orientals separately and unsuccessfully. Still, Otorgués had shown some sympathy in allowing fresh meat to Spanish ships for the use of women and children aboard until Artigas had stopped him, and perhaps Vigodet was hoping for some help in the conferences.

But Alvear was keenly alive to the danger of allowing any connection to grow up between the Orientals and the royalists, and he simply cut off the negotiations at once. He tricked Artigas and Otorgués, isolated Vigodet, and then on the 19th of June received new proposals, unaccountably, from Montevideo.[2] He freely agreed to honourable terms for the royalists, including a general avowal that the United Provinces recognised the authority of Ferdinand VII and would send agents to Spain to negotiate some satisfactory agreement. Also, among other matters, all the interests of the people of Montevideo would be respected, the Spanish troops would be sent back to Spain, and the city would be left with arms, munitions and warlike stores intact.

The treaty was ratified on the 20th of June, and on the 23rd the city was handed over. The day before, provisions had been allowed into Montevideo for the starving people. As soon as he was safely in possession Alvear repudiated the treaty, on the pretext that it had not been ratified; and in fact none of the terms was kept.[3]

---

[1] Magariños, 'Resumen . . .', MS., *cit.* p. 196 note 1.

[2] Alvear offered Otorgués the occupation of Montevideo on 7 June, in order to stop any communication between him and Vigodet. See letter of Alvear to Otorgués, in Bauzá, *op. cit.* vol. III, pp. 194-9.

[3] 'Y era natural, porque, no hallandose Montevideo en estado de defenderse ¿ con cual derecho pudiera pactar, como si en efecto fuera defendible?' commented a Montevidean. (*Anon., Apuntes históricos*, p. 46).

He had done what he did simply to gain possession of the city quickly and without loss. Montevideo became an enemy city occupied by an army bent on repressing any possible reaction. Posadas forthwith promoted Alvear brigadier and struck a medal commemorating the 'glorious' victory. This was the end of Spanish power in the Banda Oriental, and with it one obstacle was cleared from Artigas' path; but the country was still dominated by the old, familiar bugbear, Buenos Aires.[1]

[1] Bauzá, *op. cit.* vol. III, pp. 194-9.

CHAPTER VI

THE *PATRIA VIEJA*

1. THE PROVINCIA ORIENTAL, 1814-15

THE patriot occupation of Montevideo did not, as might have been expected, result in the unification of the Provincia Oriental and the spreading of peace and prosperity, but merely in the continuation of the split between the city and the rest of the province. Now the power of Buenos Aires was entrenched in the fortress city, while the Orientals held the country. For some months it was not clear whether this state of affairs would lead to open war, or whether some pacific solution would be found. The suspicions of both sides were always alert, and Alvear acted with the coldest treachery. One of his earliest acts after gaining possession of Montevideo was to attack and disperse the division of Otorgués at Las Piedras on the 26th of June, having previously offered him the occupation of Montevideo and so lulled his watchfulness. He assembled all the arms in the city and sent off to Buenos Aires a magnificent collection of over eight thousand rifles and three hundred and thirty-five guns, together with the royalist flotilla and other war material. Even the press, Princess Carlota Joaquina's gift, was packed up and sent to Buenos Aires. Montevideo was completely despoiled.

Buenos Aires quickly replaced the local authorities, sending the president of her Council of State, Nicolás Rodríguez Peña, to govern Montevideo as Delegate General Extraordinary of the central government. He took over on the 14th July, and on the 19th dismissed the members of the Cabildo and ordered the election of new officers whose names he stipulated. The whole Provincia Oriental was to be treated, if possible, as captured enemy territory.

It cannot be proved that this was a conscious movement specifically directed against the Oriental patriots, but certainly the result of the continuance of this new régime would have been to dispossess the inhabitants of the province, creoles as well as Spaniards, of many of their possessions and to affirm the dominance of Buenos Aires over the life of the province more strongly than ever before. For instance, a prize court set up in Buenos Aires on the 20th of June was installed just in time to seize all Montevidean ships and cargoes in harbour at the time of the occupation of that city; while a new court which was set up to judge questions of property sequestrated much of the land and many of the houses of Orientals, alleging faulty deeds, though this was usually a mere pretext. The property of men serving under Artigas was almost automatically seized, without any defence on the part of the absent owners, and that of Spaniards was confiscated. The Montevideans suffered also the exaction of heavy ordinary and extraordinary taxes. The rapacity of the centralists knew no bounds: Herrera, formerly the envoy of Montevideo to the Court of Spain and now *Secretario de Gobierno* (Secretary for Internal Affairs) of Buenos Aires, claimed and was awarded twenty-two thousand pesos for expenses during his stay in Spain, which he had already been paid before the Revolution of May 1810.[1]

Artigas saw all this going on, and as the Buenos Aires régime rapidly became more unpopular he regained his full prestige, some of which had evaporated as a result of the Congress of the Capilla de Maciel. His brother Manuel Francisco and his friend García de Zúñiga returned to the fold, and he became again the one great figure in the country. But he tried to live at peace with the régime at first.

As soon as Alvear had occupied the city and shown his hand, Artigas approached him, through the envoys Barreiro, García de Zúñiga and Calleros, hoping for some peaceful settlement. Terms

---

[1] Bauzá, *op. cit.* vol. III, pp. 203-7.

were agreed on the 5th of July, Posadas, the Supreme Director, approved them, and a pact was signed on the 9th by Alvear and the commissioners.[1] The conditions were, first, that the Supreme Director should publish 'a declaration re-establishing the honour and reputation' of Artigas, wounded by the decree outlawing him. Then Artigas was to be appointed commandant-general of the frontiers and country districts of the Provincia Oriental, in which he would have full authority. Oriental deputies would be elected for the Constituent Assembly, and, pending the promulgation of a constitution, a yearly provincial assembly should meet to discuss and advise the government of the province's needs. The central government should be recognised and obeyed by the Provincia Oriental, which was a constituent part of the state formed by the United Provinces. Finally, the territory of Entre Ríos and Corrientes, which had declared its adherence to Artigas, was not to be the object of any further pretension of the *Jefe*'s, and was not to be punished by Buenos Aires for following his lead.

Buenos Aires was of course willing to come to terms because of all the difficulties of the revolution and the wars, which had not lessened since the appointment of Posadas, but had rather increased with the spread of Artigas' federalism to other provinces and with the liberation of Spain and Ferdinand VII. Once again, it was a case of anything for peace, although in fact Buenos Aires was insincere in her concessions, and only meant to win time to gather fresh strength to crush Artigas. She was so desperate that at this time offers of submission to Spain on reasonable terms were put forward, favoured by both Posadas and Alvear, spokesmen of the ruling clique, and sponsored by Strangford. Alvear even issued an indirect invitation to Britain to take over all Spanish South America, while Posadas avowed that it did not matter whether their ruler were called 'king, emperor, bench or stool'. 'What we need is to live in order and enjoy peace, and we shall never gain this object while we are governed by persons with

[2] Documents published in Pivel Devoto and Fonseca Muñoz, *op. cit.* pp. 163-82.

whom we become familiar', he wrote.[1] It was an argument for monarchy, and from the middle of 1814 to 1819 a strong monarchist tendency became apparent in the policy of the Buenos Aires centralists. Against this tendency Artigas fought as against treason, following his aim for a federal and republican state.

In this atmosphere it was impossible for Alvear to receive Artigas' offers with sincerity. Rodríguez Peña, when he took over the administration of Montevideo in July, could not avoid suspecting every move of the caudillo, especially since bands of armed men, of whom there were many in the province who did not in fact owe allegiance to any government, attacked Maldonado, which was held by Buenos Aires, and committed outrages on the roads. He blamed Artigas for either having ordered the attacks or having permitted them and left them unpunished.[2] The Delegate General sent troops to protect other places, an action contrary to the terms of the pact of the 9th of July, which left the country districts in Artigas' hands. In his turn, therefore, the *Jefe* lost confidence in the *Porteños*, particularly since Buenos Aires had not by the middle of August shown any signs of fulfilling the other terms of the pact either.

Probably rendered nervous by Artigas' warlike preparations and the simultaneous spread of his influence in the Littoral, Buenos Aires on the 17th of August issued a decree at last reinstating the *Jefe*, making him an Argentine colonel again, and appointing him commandant-general of the rural part of the Provincia Oriental. But the pact of the 9th of July was not mentioned, nor were its other terms fulfilled; indeed it was never ratified by Buenos Aires.[3] Artigas was indignant enough to return his colonel's commission

---

[1] Letters of Staples (unofficial British consul at Buenos Aires) to the Foreign Office, 8 May and 10 August 1814, P.R.O., F.O. 72 (Spain)/171; Posadas to Strangford, 12 September 1814, *Correspondencia de Strangford*, pp. 168-70; Posadas to Sarratea, 14 September 1814, AGN, B. A., Div. Nac., Sec. Gob., legajo 2-1-1; letter of Posadas published in B. Mitre, *Historia de Belgrano y de la independencia argentina*, vol. II, p. 233.

[2] Letter of Rodríguez Peña to Posadas, Pivel Devoto and Fonseca Muñoz, *op. cit.* pp. 168-9.

[3] Decree, *ibid.* p. 176.

with the statement 'the fact of being useful to my country is reward enough', and demanded the publication of the pact.[1] He took action without delay to support his claims, and cut off all land communications between Montevideo and Buenos Aires, with the result that both he and the centralists prepared for the inevitable open war.[2]

Fighting broke out in the Littoral Provinces between the federalists, supported by the arch-federalist Artigas, and the *Porteños*, directed by Alvear. Colonel Soler, who became Governor-Intendant of the Provincia Oriental in August, began an advance from Montevideo into the interior, joining the forces of Alvear, who landed with an army at Colonia, intent on crushing the federal opposition at its source. Artigas' lieutenants Otorgués, Rivera and Lavalleja[3] opposed the invaders with their militia cavalry in a loose guerilla warfare, while Artigas himself directed the federal campaign in the Littoral and in the Provincia Oriental from his camp on the banks of the River Uruguay.

In September Rivera gained a small victory on the River Yí, but the campaign in general went badly for Artigas' forces. In Entre Ríos the *Porteños* beat the federalists under Blas Basualdo; in the Provincia Oriental Artigas was driven back from the Río Negro to the Arerunguá, close to the northern border. The Argentine Colonel Dorrego, who was in the future to become a federalist leader himself, defeated Otorgués in October in the east of the Provincia Oriental, capturing his artillery and the families of his troops, including his own, and forced him to take refuge in Rio Grande do Sul. Dorrego next marched against Rivera, who retreated to the River Uruguay, then, with reinforcements from Artigas, turned and chased Dorrego back to the shelter of the town of Colonia. It was a cruel campaign, and Dorrego in particular

---

[1] Letter of Artigas to Rodríguez Peña, 25 August 1814, *ibid.* pp. 179–80.

[2] Letter of Rodríguez Peña to Artigas, 29 August 1814, *ibid.* p.182.

[3] Juan Antonio de Lavalleja was still at this time a captain in Rivera's division, but was known for his courage and success in battle, and was clearly marked as a future great leader. See E. de Salterain y Herrera, *Lavalleja. La redención patria.* This is an important work on a leader who has not before received sufficient attention.

was harsh with the local people: civil wars, as this was in fact, are always the cruellest.[1]

Hard-pressed, both Artigas and Otorgués in September opened negotiations in Brazil with the Portuguese government, the Spanish chargé d' affaires, Villalba, and Princess Carlota for help in the struggle with the *Porteños*. Otorgués went so far as to claim that the Provincia Oriental recognised Ferdinand VII, now on his throne in Spain, and therefore deserved help from the Portuguese allies of the King, while Artigas offered to win the Provincia Oriental and hand it over to Portugal. Artigas had been driven to desperation by Buenos Aires' consistent treachery, and this was a ruse to gain aid quickly. It is the only instance of Artigas' using such an appeal, putting on the 'mask of Ferdinand VII' (as Monteagudo called it, in another context), and it is illuminating to compare this act with Buenos Aires' appeals to Spain for terms, and even for a Spanish prince to make a new kingdom in the Plate region. If some of the *Porteño* centralists believed in monarchy, Artigas did not.[2] In the end there was no result from these Oriental wiles except that Otorgués was allowed refuge in Rio Grande do Sul, and Villalba gave some two hundred rifles so as to keep Artigas and his men dangling, hoping for more aid. No-one had been taken in by Otorgués' appeal.[3]

---

[1] Perhaps the story is apocryphal that Dorrego, when in Colonia, organised a ball for his officers at which he personally served cantharides to the ladies, wives and daughters of the town's élite; but it is a contemporary story told by competent observers (Larrañaga y Guerra, *cit.* in Acevedo, *Alegato*, vol. II, p. 450), and it may well be an echo of some orgy of the Argentine officers. The ill-treatment of Otorgués' family by Dorrego is vouched for in Otorgués' moving words: 'Mi hija, digno objeto de mis delicias, ha sido víctima de la lascivia de un hombre desmoralizado y la violencia se opuso a su inocencia. ¡Qué cuadro tan lisonjero para un padre honrado y amante de su familia! ¡Y qué bases para fundamentar un gobierno liberal y virtuoso!...' (*ibid.* p. 451). Otorgués también mentions the 'desolaciones, muertes y violencias' caused by the Argentine army.

[2] Documents on the mission of Redruello and Caravaca to Rio Grande and Rio de Janeiro January 1814, in Pivel Devoto and Fonseca Muñoz, *op. cit.* pp. 185-92; Documents of the negotiations of Artigas with Rio Grande 1814, *ibid.* pp. 195-200; documents on missions of Barreiro to Rio Grande 1814, *ibid.* pp. 203-5.

[3] Letters of Villalba to the Duque de San Carlos, in Seville, d. Rio de Janeiro 27 November and 29 November 1814, giving details and enclosing Otorgués' credentials and instructions to Redruello and Caravaca, in A.G.I., Seville, Estado leg. 69.

But from these negotiations something can be learned of the size and condition of the Oriental army in 1814, since Otorgués' envoys gave details when asking for munitions and provisions. The details were probably falsified for the sake of hiding Artigas' true strength, but they give us the scale of the forces at least. The total strength was given as five thousand men, all cavalry, but able to fight as infantry as well. There were two regiments, the *Blandengues*, or light horse, whose colonel was Artigas, and the Oriental Dragoons, whose colonel was Otorgués. They needed one thousand five hundred rifles and the corresponding equipment, and also a 'considerable number' of pistols and sabres. Two medical chests complete with two competent surgeons were requested. As for provisions, the army simply took whatever fresh meat it wanted from estancias wherever it happened to be, and so it needed only tobacco, paper for cigarettes, and *hierba mate*, what they called their 'vices'.[1]

With affairs in this state the Governor Intendant, Soler, gave orders for the election of new deputies for the Provincia Oriental to the Constituent Assembly, and so the Cabildo of Montevideo circularised the country districts; but only those close to the city sent electors as requested. These had no choice but to obey, and their electors met together with those for Montevideo on the 24th of October and elected Pedro Feliciano Sáenz de Cavia and P. F. Pérez their deputies, with instructions to plead for the passing of measures which would bring protection and prosperity to the distracted province.

The Provincia Oriental seemed to be pacified, or at least Otorgués and Artigas were not active, and so Alvear returned to Buenos Aires to forward his schemes of self-aggrandisement, taking over the command of the campaign in the north against the royalists from Peru. But the resistance in the Provincia Oriental continued and grew stronger, until in December the

---

[1] Redruello and Caravaca to Villalba, 28 November 1814, Pivel Devoto and Fonseca Muñoz, *op. cit.* pp. 188–90.

Supreme Director ordered Soler, now commanding all the *Porteño* troops in the campaign, to complete the pacification within three months by a new and most conciliatory method: all officers, non-commissioned officers and partisan leaders caught under arms were to be shot, while the privates and unattached men in the province should be impressed into the Argentine army 'so that terror shall produce the effects which reason and interests of society cannot'.[1] Terrorism is the resort of those who feel their grasp slipping. Taxation, already heavy, was made crushing so as to pay for the fight against Artigas, and even Montevideo complained to the Supreme Director himself: with what result may be imagined.[2]

Under these auspices opened the campaign of Guayabos, which led to the final expulsion of the troops of Buenos Aires from the Provincia Oriental. Soler collected all the horses and mules available, and sent Dorrego north by forced marches to surprise Rivera, who was unsuspectingly encamped with inferior forces north of the Río Negro.[3] Rivera was beaten and pursued in a day-long running fight which covered nearly forty miles, but at the end of the day he was able to make a sudden volte-face and beat back the Argentines. Both sides rested for two days, then Rivera, on the River Queguay, received from Artigas a reinforcement of eight hundred *Blandengues* under Bauzá, who took command of all the Orientals.

Bauzá pushed Dorrego south again to the town of Mercedes, then further back to Colonia. Soler was forced to take his headquarters back to La Florida. Artigas at this juncture ordered Bauzá to retreat in order to guard the unprotected people of the interior from possible attacks by wild Indians, and Bauzá made his camp near Mercedes. Here the *Blandengues* suddenly mutinied because Rivera had punished one of them in an illegal manner, by striking

---

[1] 23 December 1814, Bauzá, *op. cit.* vol. III, p. 215.

[2] *Borradores* of the Cabildo of Montevideo to Supreme Director, 4 November 1814, Arch. Adm., libro 436; and *ibid.* libro 484, ff. 56 and 57. Heads of families were languishing in gaol since they could not pay taxes.

[3] *Borrador* of the Cabildo of Montevideo to Soler, 9 December 1814, *ibid.* libro 436.

him. Rivera was insulted, stripped and forced to hide to save himself, while Bauzá, to prevent complete disaster, raised an emergency alarm calling the army to battle positions, pretending that the enemy were attacking. The ruse succeeded, since discipline held firm when it was a question of battle. Artigas received reports of these happenings, and made some show of sternness by calling all the divisions back north of the Río Negro for consultation, but he studiously avoided apportioning any blame, and instead reorganised the divisions. It was the wisest thing to do with those men.

Dorrego took the opportunity to advance again into the interior, and Artigas sent Bauzá with a thousand men to stop him. The Argentine marched north, beyond the River Queguay, until he came to the confluence of the Arroyo Guayabos with the River Arerunguá. There the two armies encamped close to each other on the 10th of January 1815, and Bauzá on reconnoitring found that his opponents numbered one thousand seven hundred, and were well equipped and mounted. But by drawing the Argentines into an ambush, Bauzá was able to break their discipline and disperse them with a *Blandengue* charge, so that Dorrego had to flee over the River Uruguay into Entre Ríos with only a small escort. Rivera and Lavalleja played outstanding parts in this important victory.

When the news spread, Soler swiftly withdrew to Montevideo, leaving the Orientals in command of the interior. The *Porteño* domination was nearing its end, and the process was hastened by almost simultaneous victories of the federalists in Entre Ríos and Corrientes. The Buenos Aires oligarchy was tottering as the provinces successfully threw off the heavy centralist yoke. In almost all the United Provinces there was a reaction against the government, brought on by the centralists' own excessive stubbornness. The Army of the North, which Alvear had gone to take over, revolted against the command of a man they considered an upstart, while everywhere rumours went round that

Buenos Aires was selling out to Spain, as something leaked out about the monarch-seeking missions of Sarratea to Rio de Janeiro and of Belgrano and Rivadavia to Europe: these were the centralists' last resort in those years of uncertainty and threatened disaster. By 1814 the Plate region was the only area of Spanish America not altogether beaten and back under Spanish rule, so that it was natural for the leaders to look round for safeguards.

Alvear returned to Buenos Aires, and, ambitious as ever despite the warning he had received, he replaced his uncle as Supreme Director on the 9th of January, with the support of the *Porteño* secret societies. With everything crumbling about him in the provinces, and with the further threat of an expected Spanish expedition, Alvear was determined to avoid what he saw as the federalist anarchy by handing over the country to some foreign prince. Therefore at the end of January 1815 he sent M. J. García to Strangford in Rio de Janeiro with letters offering the United Provinces to Britain for the sake of peace, order and stability. Nothing concrete resulted from this scheme, nor indeed from any other monarchical plan, although the hope of a British protectorate was kept alive in the government, and even in newspapers, for months.[1]

Trying to diminish his troubles, Alvear sent the Secretary Herrera, a Montevidean himself, to the Provincia Oriental with full powers to come to terms with Artigas so as to present a united front to the external threats. The mission was begun in February, and the Montevideo Cabildo too tried to persuade Artigas to help to 'hoist over the pale wall of enmity the magnificent standard of union'; but it was in vain, since Artigas knew very well that he only needed to continue in his present course for Montevideo to be evacuated by the Argentines and fall into his lap. Indeed, Artigas simply demanded the evacuation of Montevideo and

---

[1] Letters of García to Strangford, 3 March 1815; Strangford to Castlereagh, 14 March. in Webster, *op. cit.* docs. 12 and 13; Staples to Castlereagh, 24 March, P.R.O., F.O. 72/178,

Entre Ríos by Buenos Aires, and Herrera was in fact forced to order the evacuation of the city on the 24th of February, remaining with the fond hope that this gesture would encourage the *Jefe* to continue negotiations and eventually deign to come to terms with Buenos Aires.[1]

Even in this extremity Herrera tried to give the impression that the *Porteños* were evacuating the city as a friendly move, whereas the truth was that they could not hold it against Otorgués, who was drawing a siege tighter round it. In fact Soler had wanted to evacuate without further ado as soon as Herrera came, while Alvear himself had ordered the preparations to be made on the 10th of February.[2] The people of Montevideo, after four years of almost constant war and siege, were unable to keep up with the taxes and unwilling to co-operate with the *Porteños*; and they became active supporters of Artigas, sheltering spies, aiding deserters, and doing what they could to help the Oriental cause. Desertion from the *Porteño* troops became serious as they realised that they could not hold out.[3]

On the 25th of February the Buenos Aires army sailed from Montevideo, taking with it every moveable gun and piece of warlike stores, and throwing into the sea what could not be taken. On the 23rd one hundred and twenty people had been killed in an explosion when troops carelessly or in panic shovelling gunpowder to be taken away struck a spark which blew up the magazine, and the next day the government archives were left open and were sacked by the mob.[4] This was the termination of an occupation more tyrannical than the Spanish domination.

There was heartfelt rejoicing in Montevideo when the Oriental

---

[1] Documents concerning mission of Herrera 1815 in Pivel Devoto and Fonseca Muñoz, *op. cit.* pp. 209-25, especially letters of Herrera to the Cabildo of Montevideo 24 February, pp. 223-5. *Oficio* of the Cabildo of Montevideo to Artigas, 8 February, Arch. Adm., libro 484, f. 58.

[2] Letter of Alvear to Herrera, 10 February 1815, *cit.* Acevedo, *Alegato*, vol. II, p. 458.

[3] Letters of the Cabildo of Montevideo to Herrera 10 February 1815 in Pivel Devoto and Fonseca Muñoz, *op. cit.* p. 215; and Herrera to the Cabildo, 24 February, *cit.* note 1.

[4] Anon., *Apuntes históricos*, pp. 48-9.

troops of Otorgués' division entered the city on the 27th. Otorgués became military governor by order of Artigas, although he was at first unwilling to take on the task, which he realised was outside his experience and feared to be beyond his capacity.[1] Balls and celebrations lasted until the 1st of March, and then on the 4th a new Cabildo was elected by petition of the citizens to replace the pro-*Porteño* one which had held office during the occupation. The new members were staunch Oriental patriots, many of whom had sided with Artigas throughout these struggles. García de Zúñiga became Senior Alcalde and political governor of the city. A wise, moderate man, well respected and liked by the citizens, his choice was a happy omen.[2] A new era, the first one of complete independence for the whole country, began in the Provincia Oriental.

2. THE GOVERNMENT OF ARTIGAS' 'PATRIA VIEJA'

Even in the comparative peace of the *Patria Vieja* of 1815,[3] Artigas was still at war. His interests in the Federal League increased until he became the most important figure in the United Provinces, with a proportional increase in the demands on his time and energy, as he advised, planned, ruled and fought at the head of his loose confederation. But notwithstanding this and the fact that his fifty years were beginning to tell on him under this enormous strain, he found time to improve the internal condition of his native province, always seeking to increase its happiness and prosperity.

[1] Letter of Otorgués to the Cabildo of Montevideo 21 March 1815, Archivo General de la Nación, Montevideo, *Correspondencia del Gen. José Artigas al Cabildo de Montevideo (1814-1816) y correspondencia oficial en copia*, p. 197. Other reasons or excuses Otorgués produced for not taking over the government were that he must stay in camp outside the city (1) so as to be in the country to organise its resources, and (2) so as to be with his troops, since only he could keep them disciplined and stop desertion (Otorgués to the Cabildo 13 March *ibid*, p. 196); and (3) he was badly dressed while on campaign and needed a complete outfit to appear decently dressed as governor. (Otorgués to the Cabildo 17 March, *ibid*. p. 197).

[2] Anon., *Apuntes históricos*, p. 49.

[3] This is the name given by Uruguayans to Artigas' Provincia Oriental, to distinguish it from the modern state of Uruguay which arose after the province's liberation from Brazilian control in 1828.

The *Jefe* rarely visited Montevideo, but made his headquarters usually on the banks of the River Uruguay, where he was more centrally placed to supervise all his protectorate; and his interests tended to make him concentrate more on improving the lot of the country people than that of the Montevideans, which was at any rate a refreshing change from the outlook of the Spanish government. But he did ensure that Montevideo was governed, and he did his best to find good men for the task. Montevideo certainly needed help by this time, as the *Porteños* left her defenceless and with the government archives sacked, so that eventually the new administration had to appeal to the public to return any of the papers which they had kept, in order to renew the continuity of affairs.[1]

The Provincia Oriental was in a disastrous state after four years of almost incessant fighting, of being overrun by armies which, friendly or otherwise, lived off the country. The herds of cattle and horses which were the country's main wealth, its true capital, were being hunted more fiercely than ever before; the country townships and isolated ranches were occupied and often sacked and all but destroyed; the flourishing little nucleus of agriculture which had grown up round Montevideo was turned into a wilderness even as early as 1811. Trade had almost disappeared, since Montevideo had been cut off from the interior, and the interior in any case was producing little.[2]

Some idea of the extent of the economic disaster is gained from the correspondence of the Consulado of Montevideo, set up at length in 1812. In that year the Consulado of Montevideo appealed to that of Havana, in Cuba, asking it to discourage importations of dried meat from other sources, and especially from Brazil, since the Brazilians had killed the previously important trade of the Montevideans by means of driving great herds of cattle from the Banda Oriental into Rio Grande do Sul, where they slaughtered

---

[1] *Bando* of the Cabildo of Montevideo, 29 January 1817, Arch. Adm. libro 482, f. 4.

[2] Letter of Artigas to the government of Paraguay, 7 December 1811, in Fregeiro, *op. cit.*

them and prepared the meat for export. Montevideo was unable to stop the rustling because of the war and the unsettled conditions it produced. The dried meat trade to Cuba was, of course, important since the slave population of the island was largely fed on this poor-quality food, which it was said to prefer. Havana refused to do anything for various reasons, but mainly because she must be sure that Montevideo could supply all that was needed, and at competitive prices, before she cut off a certain source. In all probability Montevideo could not have supplied the meat at that time.[1] Again, the state of the revenue from customs dues collected in Montevideo in May 1814, a time of strict siege and a blockade of increasing effectiveness, shows how small trade was then. The total revenue from customs was 106 pesos 2 reales, representing goods worth 9,062½ pesos, or about £1,510. The exports amounted to goods worth only 300 pesos, or £50, to Spain and Spanish possessions, and 291 pesos 6 reales, or about £48/10/0, to foreign ports.[2]

The state of the country parts is clearly brought out in a diary written by Father Larrañaga in 1815 when he was on a journey between Montevideo and Paysandú. Larrañaga, as an observant scientist, noted the bad roads, poor river crossings which could easily be improved, the taste for liquor of the country people, the sad, damp villages and roofless houses, the mosquitoes even in winter, and the mad dogs. But he also noted the spirit with which the people faced difficulties and dangers, their expert handling of their mounts, and the many partridges. He noticed the song birds, which is rare among people of Iberian culture. Cattle were scarce because of the wars, and comforts were almost non-existent, but there was a delicious variety of vegetables and, for him at any rate, enough to eat. Everything possible was made of leather, and

[1] Letters of the Consulado of Montevideo to the Consulado of Havana, 18 August 1812; and Consulado of Havana to the Consulado of Montevideo, 29 March 1813, in M.H.N., vol. v.

[2] M.H.N. customs statement in vol. x. The pound sterling/peso rate is that of 1812, as nearly as can be calculated.

tallow was the commonest medicine, either used as an ointment or taken in hot water as a cure for coughs and colds. The skulls of cattle were seats, and their bones were fuel for the fires. Therefore a shortage of cattle was the most hurtful deprivation for the country-dweller.[1]

It was obvious that the key to the prosperity of the Orientals was the improvement of the economic condition of their country, and Artigas was no less alive to this than to the political needs of his people. If federalism and political freedom from Buenos Aires meant the immediate survival of the province, a healthy and productive economy meant its future survival; and it was in fact the object which the Orientals had been seeking since before the revolution, in their quarrels with Buenos Aires. Consequently, Artigas' Instructions of April 1813 had contained clauses aiming at the opening of the ports of Maldonado and Colonia, alternatives to Montevideo, and the establishment of free trade between the United Provinces and equality of treatment for their ports and ships; and another clause contained an implicit declaration of economic independence for Artigas' province. Fulfilling this last aim, Artigas set up in April 1813 the Municipal Body known as the *Gobierno Económico*, so as to restore the province to its productivity.

This short-lived body, ignored by Buenos Aires, intended to make the creation and maintenance of an army possible by organising behind-the-line services, as well as to encourage the inhabitants to settle in the country and take up agriculture, not merely ranching. In fact the *Gobierno Económico* encouraged the local authorities in the province to become active again after the troubles of the war, although Artigas would not at that juncture create new authorities. The middle of a war was not the time for experiments, but for some date in the peaceful future a complete general reorganisation was promised. However, in a case of conflict of authority between a civil magistrate and a military commander, Artigas ruled that the magistrate was supreme in civil

---

[1] D. A. Larrañaga, *Viaje de Montevideo a Paysandú.*

matters and particularly in justice, while the commander could only fulfil the magistrate's wishes. Artigas had the right principles at heart, and was not the bloody despot he was painted by the Argentines.

In purely economic affairs the *Gobierno Económico* took steps to encourage agriculture in all districts, no easy task where the traditional form of exploitation was pastoral; and it even invited a local priest who had spent forty years studying the best methods of agriculture for that country to produce a long report on his work for distribution to farmers. The priest, one Pérez Castellanos, complied, but as in the case of the other enterprises of this government, later struggles intervened before any positive result had been obtained. However, rustlers and illegal hide-hunters were repressed by stronger police measures, which were put into force especially on the coast to stop the clandestine shipments. Taxes were collected again, and a provincial treasury was started.

But it was not until the *Porteño* evacuation of Montevideo in February 1815 brought peace to the Provincia Oriental that this work of organisation could continue. Even then, because of Artigas' frequent preoccupation with the affairs of the Federal League the progress was spasmodic. A provincial congress called in March to elect a government for the province had to be cancelled, probably because of Artigas' fight against the Buenos Aires Directorate, which was at its climax in the Littoral. Therefore the effective government of the province remained in the hands of the Military Governor of Montevideo, Otorgués, advised and assisted by the city Cabildo. Artigas himself was the real head of authority, having been declared *Jefe de los Orientales* in 1811 and having exercised this authority ever since; so that now in his absence his deputy took over automatically, although Artigas felt himself obliged to explain to the Cabildo the reasons for his journeys and to authorise it to keep order.[1]

[1] Letter of Artigas to the Cabildo of Montevideo, 25 March 1815, in *Correspondencia de Artigas*, pp. 200-1.

The 'Patria Vieja'

With the fall of the Director Alvear on the 16th of April 1815 as a result of the success of Artigas' Federal League, and with his replacement in Buenos Aires by a régime apparently more friendly towards Artigas, the *Jefe* felt that it was time to hold the promised congress. Therefore at the end of April he called for the election by all the townships of deputies to be sent to a meeting to be held at Mercedes. Artigas has been criticised as a completely self-willed caudillo, yet the care with which he organised several provincial congresses from 1813 onwards shows that his intention was to act with a mandate from his people. As he wrote in this instance: 'To consecrate the first step is the prerogative of the people'; and he issued a careful instruction on the manner of conducting the elections so as to make them as democratic as any of that period. All citizens were to vote in primary elections, and the Cabildos as such were not to take part.[1]

Once again, however, the Congress had to be postponed, and again Artigas had to make do with the organs of government which existed, pending the complete reorganisation he still hoped to effect when times were more apt. This time a reconquering expedition of ten thousand men from Spain had been announced, and preparations had to be made to repel it.[2] Before a provincial Congress could meet, indeed, there came the Portuguese invasion of 1816, which ended all hope of such an assembly, and ended the *Patria Vieja* itself.

Consequently the Provincia Oriental remained during the *Patria Vieja* period under the Military Governor of Montevideo, supervised and directed as occasion permitted by Artigas from his main headquarters at Purificación, near Salto on the River Uruguay. In Montevideo the government was wielded first by Otorgués, from March to June 1815, then by the Cabildo with the title of *Cabildo Gobernador*, and with the collaboration of Miguel

[1] Letter of Artigas to the Cabildo of Montevideo, 29 April 1815, *ibid.* pp. 219-20. By citizen was meant a person with certain residential and property qualifications, as under the Spanish law, or the contemporary English law; so that the gaucho militia and probably the majority of town and ranch workers would have no vote, though this was not shocking at that time. Democracy as we preach it was not then the aim.

[2] Letters of Artigas to the Cabildo of Montevideo, 24 May (2) and 13 June 1815, *ibid.* pp. 8-9; note of Zufriátegui, 1 March 1815, Arch. Adm., libro 199, f. 1.

Government

Barreiro, Artigas' active secretary, who was sent to replace Otorgués as the *Jefe*'s representative in Montevideo. Otorgués had not been anxious to take over the government in the first place, and during his short reign had shown himself to be incompetent; so that it was with relief that he obeyed Artigas' orders to take his troops and cover the eastern seaboard and frontier when the Spanish threat came. He would rather face ten thousand Spaniards than a handful of town councillors.

Yet the Cabildo was loath to see Otorgués leave the city, for he was to take away all the garrison, leaving Montevideo undefended and in fear of the expected attack. Consequently it disobeyed Artigas, and did not allow Otorgués to go for some weeks while it appealed to the *Jefe* to defend the capital. This brought Artigas' irascible temper to white heat, with a result fairly common in Latin American politics. He resigned at once as *Jefe*, and told the Cabildo to get on with defending and organising the province, since they did not obey his orders and seemed to believe that they knew better than he what was required. He naturally had organised an alternative defence, based on keeping his troops mobile and available outside cities, and not cooped up inside, like rats in traps, and no doubt his strategic instinct was right.

Artigas was not *Jefe* for nothing. He could lose his equanimity in the face of this meddling with his military plans in such critical circumstances, and he was always capable of reprimanding his subordinates, among them individuals such as Otorgués, Barreiro and Rivera, besides a body such as the Cabildo. It is partly from this human characteristic that the legend of Artigas as an uncouth caudillo springs. But as was his habit, he calmed down quickly and went on with his business as soon as the Cabildo sent him an abject deputation asking him to continue and not to resign. Otorgués took up his new post in the middle of June, and the Cabildo took over the government as ordered.[1]

[1] Letters of Artigas to the Cabildo of Montevideo, 1 and 24 May, and 13 June 1815. *ibid.* pp. 5, 8-9.

Otorgués was not a wicked man, but 'simple and inclined towards good, generous and a good friend'. He was born poor, and his education was not equal to his talents, which were uncommon: he had foresight and a quick grasp of situations. But he was too simple, possibly too humble before educated city men, and was easily led for good or ill.[1] A witness of Otorgués' rule in Montevideo blamed the unrest on the malcontents, still secretly in sympathy with the Buenos Aires government, who pretended to support him and under pretext of helping him spread 'fear and terror'. The previously well-disciplined troops inexplicably got out of hand once among Montevideo's meagre flesh-pots. A *Tribunal de Vigilancia*, security tribunal, which was itself secretly in support of Buenos Aires, was given the task of bringing order, and instead spread alarm by a series of arbitrary measures violating personal security; and indeed it brought Artigas and Otorgués to the verge of hostilities since the *Jefe* would not tolerate such a government and blamed his lieutenant. Luckily the trouble was cleared up and soothed by correspondence.

Porteño accounts show Otorgués' period of government as a reign of terror, with anecdotes of his spurred troops saddling and riding Spaniards in the streets, and other horrors. But what happened was that Otorgués began by treating the city as occupied enemy territory, and continued by treating the local Spaniards, of whom there were many, harshly but not brutally.[2] Otorgués had to take steps against sedition in this city which contained partisans of both Spain and Buenos Aires, especially since the threat of the new expedition from Spain was acute. Artigas himself had ordered measures to be taken against Spaniards, which was not an uncommon thing in all the areas of Spanish America where royalists and patriots were fighting, as Bolívar's war to the

---

[1] Anon., *Apuntes históricos*, p. 50.

[2] See Acevedo, *Alegato*, t. II, pp. 464-79. *Bandos* of Otorgués, 21 March 1815: '. . . no hagais qᵉ. vuestra imprudencia, me ponga en el doloroso caso de presentar nuevas aflicciones à este Pueblo desgraciado . . .', and 25 March: anyone caught hiding arms and munitions would be pilloried for three days in the main square bearing the notice 'Traydor à la defensa comun'. (Arch. Adm., libro 484).

death in Venezuela bears witness; although in Bolívar's case that measure had been forced on him by atrocities committed in the name of Spain by such men as Monteverde and Boves, who had no direct counterpart in the Plate region.

At the end of Otorgués' term Artigas began the famous concentration of Spaniards at his own headquarters, Purificación: so called because these enemies of American liberty would be purified there of their crime. This sinister-sounding place was not, however, a concentration camp as we have known them, but Artigas' own permanent headquarters, where the Spaniards with their families were made to stay and work on the land to support themselves. It was no more comfortable for Artigas' troops than for the Spaniards. Since it was distant from any possible point of Spanish attack and any centre of population, this potential 'fifth column' was kept harmless.[1] In fact, few were concentrated, for the Cabildo of Montevideo, whose members were in close contact with the local Spaniards, hesitated to exile or ruin men who were their neighbours, possibly their friends, and their associates in business, and they braved Artigas' anger by sending few and finding all sorts of excuses. Artigas expected thirty-two Spaniards from Montevideo, which was a small number considering the importance of the city as a Spanish stronghold, and in fact only nine had arrived by October 1815; and for months the Cabildo was scourged in the *Jefe's* letters because of its evasion of his orders.[2] Artigas did not reserve this treatment only for Spaniards. He ordered two of the three members of the discredited and dissolved *Tribunal de Vigilancia* to be sent to him for correction, although they gained a reprieve by writing verses to him on his saint's day and paying a moderate fine.[3] It must be realised that the *Jefe's*

[1] Acevedo, *Alegato*, t. II, pp. 479-86, and J. A. Rebella, '*Purificación*'. *Sede del protectorado de 'Los Pueblos Libres'* (1815-18).

[2] *Ibid*. Also, letters of Artigas to the Cabildo of Montevideo, 28 June, 4 and 28 August, 9, 16, 27 and 29 October, 12 November, 25 December 1815, and 18 June 1816, *Correspondencia de Artigas*, pp. 11-12, 27, 28, 34-5, 38, 41, 42-3, 46-7, 104; *Borrador* of the Cabildo to the Governor of Montevideo, 23 May 1815, Arch. Adm. libro 486, f. 261.

[3] Anon., *Apuntes históricos*, p. 51.

policy towards Spaniards, including his confiscation of their property for the benefit of the treasury, was in line with that of other revolutionary leaders. But at least his countrymen could pride themselves that he never declared war to the death: there was no need for it in the Provincia Oriental.

The *Cabildo Gobernador* of Montevideo carried on without change till the end of 1815. In August Barreiro was appointed as adviser especially concerning 'the way to set our commerce going; economy in all branches of public administration; the opening of foreign relations'. The order shows what was uppermost in Artigas' mind.[1] But when the time came for the annual renewal of Cabildo members, Artigas introduced an important innovation. He had been forced to postpone the reorganisation of the country, but he would improve what existed; and he decided to make the Cabildo a more representative body. For the future, each town in the province would send an elector to choose the new members of the *Cabildo Gobernador*, together with representatives of Montevideo, the suburb outside the city walls, and the retiring Cabildo members. The other Cabildos were also made partly elective in January 1816. It was still not modern democracy, but it was a workable and sensible reform. It was not dictatorship, and Artigas meant to educate his people for representative government.[2]

It was this *Cabildo Gobernador*, prodded on by Barreiro, in his turn receiving orders from Artigas, which reorganised Montevideo and its district so as to give it an active role in the independent province and in the wider sphere of the Federal League. The Cabildo formed a citizen militia, and punished the indifferent and the backsliders, native or foreign, with fines and physical castigation. A census of all arms and munitions, privately or publicly

---

[1] Letter of Artigas to the Cabildo of Montevideo, 13 August 1815, *Correspondencia de Artigas*, p. 24.

[2] Letters of Artigas to the Cabildo of Montevideo, 10 December 1815, 9 January 1816 (2), *ibid.* pp. 56-7, 66-7, 68-9; and Artigas to the Cabildo of Colonia, 10 December 1815, Arch. Adm., libro 206, ff. 32-3.

owned, was quickly taken.[1] The Cabildo encouraged citizens to seek justice through it (a Cabildo always had certain judicial powers), and to open businesses and shops, and to help on the prosperity of the country in any way. In return the Cabildo promised that guards and patrols would come to the aid of any citizen in trouble and needing protection in the streets or in his business, particularly the owners of *pulperías* (drink and provision shops), who were allowed to keep their establishments open until ten o'clock at night. Citizens were allowed to keep offensive and defensive arms with which to defend themselves and their property from disturbers of the peace and destroyers of liberty, so long as they notified the government of the arms which they held. Finally, the Cabildo issued a stern order forbidding people to give anything to any public servant, political or military, on his own asking alone and without express orders from the government. Evidently extortion had been a plague.

These orders, in their unemotional terms, give only a glimpse of the frightened life of the city which had just changed loyalties twice and now found itself helpless in the hands of an army of rough gauchos, at the whim of a remote warrior whose overwhelming desire just then was to win freedom for friendly provinces beyond the city's horizon. They bring a notion of the fear of the dark, muddy streets at night, patrolled very occasionally by an outlandish band of horsemen, perhaps ready to defend a citizen and his property against the assaults of their comrades off duty and inflamed with drink and gambling in the *pulperías*, or perhaps ready to join in a riot themselves. No wonder the Montevideans had to be encouraged to open businesses or that some of them secretly hoped for the return of the good old days of the Spanish peace, or even the comparative calm of the *Porteño* occupation.[2]

The property of creoles or foreigners who had fled from Montevideo when the Orientals occupied it and had not returned within

[1] *Bando* of the *Cabildo Gobernador* of Montevideo, 3 July 1815, Arch. Adm., libro 488, f. 1.
[2] *Bando* of the *Cabildo Gobernador*, 8 July 1815, Arch. Adm., libro 488, ff. 3-4.

a few weeks was confiscated by the *Cabildo Gobernador* and applied to the public benefit.[1] The *Cabildo Gobernador* also, on Artigas' instructions, wrote to the commanders of posts on the frontier with Brazil ordering them to be most vigilant and to stamp out both smuggling and cattle-rustling by the Portuguese, since these activities hindered the development of the country and were responsible for the lack of public funds with which to pay the troops.[2] Economy and strict administration were the need throughout the country, as they were for many decades afterwards, and this first government tried to lay the foundations of future progress by establishing them.

Connected with this concern was an attempt to stop vagabondage in the country. It was recognised that people, usually men, who lived off the country without working were parasites who hindered recovery, and that they ought to be made to do something useful. No poor-law system existed: nature and the Church, and private open-handedness, had so far taken its place. But now all available men must help the country with their work, or at least not harm it by living freely off it. In accordance with Artigas' ideas, therefore, the *Cabildo Gobernador* gave orders to the subordinate Cabildos to use all their zeal to exterminate idleness, the 'fertile mother of all sorts of crimes and excesses'. All men with no known work must be sent to Montevideo unless they could produce an employment certificate from some landowner within three days. Employers who gave certificates to unemployed men out of compassion and without employing them would be punished too.[3] *Vagos*, as these tramps were called, were commonly recruited into the army by press-gang methods either because they were idle or because they were suspected of being deserters, as many of them in fact were.

Without doubt the most important part of the work of the

[1] *Idem* 14 July 1815, *ibid.* f. 5.

[2] *Borrador* of the *Cabildo Gobernador* to the Commander of the Fortress of Santa Teresa, 25 August 1815, Arch. Adm., libro 489, f. 107.

[3] Circular of the *Cabildo Gobernador*, 17 July 1815, Arch. Adm., libro 713, f. 76.

Government

Cabildo Gobernador, under Artigas' direction, was the organisation of government in the country districts, and the attempted propagation of order and settlement there. This was Artigas' first care in the Provincia Oriental, and it was the vital part of his work for it. He had been keenly interested in this problem since his earlier campaigns as a *Blandengue*, and his interest had gained the necessary experience and examples for his future actions during his service under Azara at the foundation of Batoví. Indeed, Artigas' most constant aim and fundamental idea was the settlement and population of the country which he had seen so neglected under the Spanish authorities and the leaders of colonial Buenos Aires, and in this he did not belie the preoccupations of his family or his class. This urgent desire to make the Banda Oriental and its people prosperous was at the root of Artigas' actions, of his fight against Spaniards, Portuguese and *Porteños*. But the situation was a vicious circle, for it was necessary for the country to be well populated and prosperous for a successful defence against these enemies to be possible. Here is the reason for his failure: he could not create prosperity and defend it at the same time, yet that was the feat that the circumstances demanded.

As soon as he was able, after Alvear's fall had brought some relief, Artigas turned his attention to the economic state of the Provincia Oriental, and especially the settlement of the country. In his first orders to the Cabildo of Montevideo when it became the government Artigas stressed the urgency of bringing peace and security to the interior as well as to the city, and gave instructions on what to do.[1] A few weeks later Artigas, writing now as if his formulation of a plan for the settlement of the country were well known, ordered the Cabildo to take certain measures pending the implementation of the plan: the Cabildo was to direct all ranchers to put their ranches in order, repairing wrecked buildings, rounding up and branding the neglected stock, and in general to tidy up

[1] Letter of Artigas to the Cabildo of Montevideo, 28 June 1615, *Correspondencia de Artigas*, pp. 237-8.

the mess left behind by the chaos of the war years. If within two months ranchers had not obeyed, their land would be confiscated and given to 'useful hands, which with their labour will advance the settlement and with it the prosperity of the country'.[1]

The tone of social morality, reminiscent of the Spanish reformers of the eighteenth century, which is here evident, is always present in Artigas' social and economic measures. The settlement of the land was seen as a way of rewarding and encouraging the industrious as well as a benefit in itself. Only a few days later this second idea was stressed in another of Artigas' general instructions to the *Cabildo Gobernador*, which among other matters urged a zealous protection of the country districts, for 'if this is not done we risk starvation'. The remaining cattle must be preserved, for if they were allowed to be wasted 'we shall see the complete disappearance of our country's most precious treasure'.[2]

Within three days of this there took place in Montevideo a meeting of the ranchers of the province, presided over by Juan de León, the *Alcalde Provincial* (chief magistrate of the country districts), and attended by Fructuoso Rivera, military commander of the city since mid-July.[3] León and León Pérez had been commissioned by the Cabildo to make a pilgrimage to see Artigas and describe to him the disorder of the interior and suggest some method of remedying it; and accordingly the meeting had been called to ask the opinions of the ranchers themselves first.

Two ranchers, Manuel Pérez and Francisco Muñoz, presented proposals in writing, which the meeting decided to send to the *Jefe*. Rivera made a speech which gives us a curious insight. He inveighed against the depredations practised on the herds by commanders of troops stationed in the interior, who openly set up as purveyors of hides, using their soldiers as cowboys. This helped to

---

[1] Letter of Artigas to the Cabildo of Montevideo, 4 August 1815, *ibid.* pp. 28-9.

[2] Letter of Artigas to the Cabildo of Montevideo, 8 August 1815, *ibid.* pp. 246-8; *Bando* of the *Cabildo Gobernador* publishing the new orders, 7 September, Arch. Adm. libro 490, ff. 3-4.

[3] *Acta* of the Cuerpo de Hacendados, 11 August 1815, *ibid.* libro 212, ff. 125-7.

Government

ruin the cattle industry, and any individual rancher who opposed it ran the risk of death, so that until this abuse was stopped no advance was possible. Artigas should be asked to assemble all the troops in one place and let the local militia garrison the rest of the country. The meeting agreed to pass on this suggestion too.

León and León Pérez therefore went to discuss these matters with the *Jefe* at Purificación, and the result of their deliberations was the 'Reglamento Provisorio de la Provincia Oriental para el Fomento de su Campaña, y Seguridad de sus Hacendados' (Provisional Ordinance of the Provincia Oriental for the advancement of its country districts and the security of its ranchers), with which the two commissioners left again for Montevideo on the 10th of September 1815.[1] Meanwhile Otorgués received orders to begin a provisional settlement of the interior.[2]

Artigas' fundamental charter for the interior was like the previous efforts of Azara in 1800 and 1801 and of Sobremonte in 1805 in that poor settlers were to be encouraged to take a stake in the country by grants of frontier land; but it differed entirely from these in its aim. Whereas the earlier plans had envisaged the building up a settled population to withstand the infiltration of Portuguese pioneers into the empty lands, Artigas' plan was primarily for the good of the province, and the settlers were to be chosen from those who needed land most: 'the most unfortunate shall be the most privileged. Consequently free negroes, *Sambos* in the same condition,[3] Indians, and poor creoles, all may be granted *estancia* lots, if with their work and their probity they are inclined towards their own happiness and that of the Province.' (Article 6 of the Reglamento.) This noble sentence proves Artigas' right to a place in the first rank of the liberators of Spanish America, and is the best retort to his detractors.

[1] MSS. of the Museo Histórico Nacional, Montevideo, Biblioteca Pablo Blanco Acevedo, vol. xxiii, *Correspondencia de Artigas*. Also contemporary copy in Arch. Adm., libro 490, ff. 6–9. See Appendix I.
[2] Letter of Artigas to the Cabildo of Montevideo, 18 August 1815, *Correspondencia de Artigas*, p. 26.
[3] *Sambos*, or *Zambos*, were people of mixed Indian and negro blood.

The Reglamento was a complete scheme for organising the interior. The *Alcalde Provincial* was charged with its execution, although he was subordinate to the provincial government in Montevideo, and he was to be assisted by three *Subtenientes de Provincia* (Sub-lieutenants of the province) who were subordinate to him. These four officers were each to have direct charge of one of the four districts into which the province was now divided, and if they needed help they could appoint subordinate magistrates, *Jueces Pedáneos*, within their districts. (Articles 1 to 5.) For the time being these officers were to concentrate on settling the interior with 'useful' people, granting plots of empty land to active and needy folk of any colour. Preference was to be given to the poor, to poor widows with families, then to single creoles, and lastly to foreigners. (Articles 6 and 7.)

Rules for claiming and giving the lands were strictly laid down, and also conditions under which the lands could be kept, once claimed. The settler had to build some sort of house and two stockyards within two months, and he might be given another month's grace, but after that if this condition were not fulfilled the land was to be given to some other claimant 'more industrious and beneficial for the Province'. (Articles 8 to 11.)

The lands available for distribution were those of émigrés, 'bad Spaniards and worse Americans', that is royalists, whether Spanish or American born, and any lands which between 1810 and the Oriental occupation of Montevideo in 1815 had been sold or given by the government of the city, unless the recipients were patriots, in which unlikely case they could keep all, or unless they were Orientals, in which case they would be permitted to keep one estancia lot. 'Enemies' who were married might be allowed to retain enough land to maintain their families, but single men lost all. (Articles 12 to 15.)

Then came the technical details. The plots were to be one and a half leagues long by two leagues wide, though they might vary according to the quality of the land, and they should be provided with a reasonable water supply and have fixed boundary marks, so as to avoid future litigation. The officers were to make sure that no settler was in possession of more than one plot, so that men already rich could not benefit under the scheme. A man who only possessed the standard-sized farm plot, which was much smaller, might be granted an estancia. Certain lands were to be reserved for breeding and grazing army horses. The settlers could not sell or mortgage their lots pending further legislation. Artigas was to be informed of the number of lots granted and their situation. Previous grants were to be ratified under this scheme on petition of the beneficiaries. (Articles 16 to 21.)

Concerning the stock itself, it was laid down that the officers were to give permission for the settlers to hold rodeos and drive off to stock their ranches any cattle and horses on the ranches of enemies of the country; but these rodeos must be supervised to prevent waste of the resources by excessive chasing or simply killing the animals for their hides. All killing of cattle by ranchers was to be forbidden unless the animals already bore the killer's own brand. No cattle must be exported to Brazil, nor must any females be killed until the province's stock was replenished. (Articles 22 to 24.)

The *Alcalde Provincial* was to have a sergeant and eight men, and the *Subtenientes* a corporal and four men each with whom to supervise these regulations and keep order generally in the province: that is, a police force of one sergeant, three corporals and twenty men for a country nearly as big as Great Britain. The *Subtenientes* were not judges, but the *Alcalde Provincial* was. The former were police officers, and one of their duties was to send any unattached wandering men to Montevideo for enlistment in the army, so that all ranchers were to provide their hands with certificates of employment lest they should meet this fate. Any deserters found were to go the same way, and common criminals such as murderers, or suspects, were to be sent to the capital too to stand trial. (Articles 25 to 29.)

In this way Artigas organised for the province a form of settlement, complete though rough and ready. The plan itself gives a fair idea of the social conditions of 1815 and the enormous difficulties before Artigas, and it enhances the stature of its author as the father of his country. The notion of taking from enemies to give to poor friends was the kind of rough justice best appreciated by the men of the interior, whom Artigas knew so well, and who had made him their *Jefe*.

The Cabildo of Montevideo published the new regulations towards the end of September 1815, but the *Alcalde Provincial* found the chaos of the interior too great for his energy, and progress was slow and slight. Artigas tried to speed things up with fresh orders in November, since he saw how the country people, completely lacking in public spirit, were quickly destroying the cattle in the absence of the police force for which he had provided.[1] But not until the 14th of January 1816 did the *Alcalde Provincial* publish the names of his *Subtenientes* and issue the invitation to claim grants under the Reglamento; and even then few applied because life was still too easy on the open plains where any man could live by killing and eating any animal he found, and because prospective settlers were afraid to go far from towns before law and order were well established. It cannot be denied that they were wise. Besides, the *Alcalde Provincial* acted slowly and often what he did was foolish: he was once accused of killing cattle for no apparent reason or purpose. The danger to men of being picked up by some recruiting squad was so great that even the meagre harvests were in danger of being lost for lack of labour.[2] But before any real or permanent good came of the *Jefe*'s plans the Portuguese invasion overwhelmed the province.[3]

[1] Letter of Artigas to the Cabildo of Montevideo, 12 November 1815, *Correspondencia de Artigas*, pp. 47-8.

[2] Letter of Pedro Josef Zavala to Governor Pablo Perez, d. Partido de Sn. Ramon y Begija, 2 January 1816, Arch. Adm., libro 602, f. 1.

[3] E. M. Narancio, *El reglamento de 1815*, letter of Artigas to the Cabildo of Montevideo 22 June 1816, *Correspondencia de Artigas*, pp. 105-6.

The settlement plan was criticised at the time not for its principles but for its slack application. It was felt that the *Cabildo Gobernador* had always regarded it with coolness and only affected to approve of it. Also, the officers in charge were left too independent and tended to take lands from their owners without any hearing merely because they were Spanish or sympathised with Spain. The new ranches were often given away without being accurately measured, which meant a waste of land; and in any case a new and poor rancher obviously could do very little with his land unless he were given a herd of cattle and a loan of money with which to organise its protection and keep it from running loose. And finally, there still remained the problem of providing for the sons of the new ranchers: at the death of the father the ranch would inevitably be split into units too small to be economically useful, unless fresh lands were made available for each new generation. The result was likely to be that the lands would be put up for sale, and bought back again by the wealthy ranchers, who would thus build up large estates and squeeze out of existence the small men who might become a yeoman class. All previous schemes had foundered on the rock of royal meanness in granting too few cattle or not granting lands to the sons of the first recipients, and therefore the country had remained in its underpopulated state.[1]

Agriculture, in Artigas' view, had to take second place in these desperate circumstances, with cattle-ranching first since cattle could immediately make the province solvent and partly settled, whereas agriculture was much slower in its effects, and at first could only supply internal needs, not external trade. As a long-term process, undoubtedly the encouragement of agriculture would have been better, with its tendency to form a rooted and prolific peasantry, but Artigas had not the time to spare, with the country in ruins and his enemies all around. Therefore when the Cabildo of Guadalupe (sometimes called Canelones), encouraged

[1] Anon., *Apuntes históricos*, pp. 51-3.

by the Reglamento, produced in October 1815 a plan for establishing agriculture, Artigas felt obliged to have it postponed in
favour of concentrating on ranching, since 'undertaking everything at this moment will mean accomplishing nothing'.[1] It is a
pity he took this line, but he could hardly do otherwise at that
juncture. He certainly had weighed the arguments (Guadalupe had
ensured that) and realised all that agriculture had to offer, but he
was not stirred even by the obvious truth that it seemed just to
encourage the increase of men after eighty years dedicated to the
increase of cattle since the foundation of Montevideo. One small
experiment in town planning was undertaken when the *Jefe* permitted the inhabitants of Las Víboras to move the village lock,
stock and barrel to a better situation and laid down the organisation of the new place, rather in the manner of his other, large-
scale plans.[2]

A further step was taken towards the definite organisation of the
province with the creation of Departments in January 1816. With
Artigas' approval the Cabildo of Montevideo divided the province
to the south and east of the Río Negro (the more settled parts)
into six Departments, with the existing Cabildos in towns as the
departmental authorities. The Departments were Montevideo,
Maldonado, Santo Domingo Soriano, Guadalupe, San José and
Colonia. North of the Río Negro Artigas decided not to set up
Departments, but to leave the sparse population under the existing
administrators, the Alcaldes and military commanders. At their
creation Artigas made the Departments the basis of a new militia,
almost on the lines of the modern Territorial Army in Britain.[3]

---

[1] Letter of the Cabildo of Guadalupe to the *Gobernador Intendente* of the Provincia
Oriental, 30 October 1815; Proyecto de Agricultura pa la Villa de Guadalupe, same date,
Arch. Adm. libro 207, ff. 37-41; letter of Artigas to the Cabildo of Canelones, *Correspon-
dencia de Artigas*, p. 55.

[2] Letter of Artigas to the Alcalde and *Vecindario* of Las Víboras, d. Quartel Gral, 12
February 1816, Arch. adm. libro 713, f. 5.

[3] Letters of Artigas to the Cabildo of Montevideo, 20 and 26 January, 3 and 10 February
1816, *Correspondencia de Artigas*, pp. 72, 74, 75, 76-7; Artigas to the Cabildo of Soriano, 7
February 1816, Arch. Adm. libro 206, ff. 39-40.

The *Jefe* was in fact an active and watchful head of this rough system, taking a special interest in economic affairs and even making small economies in government expenditure. None of his subordinates dared establish new taxes without consulting him, and permission was always refused since he knew that the province was in ruins. When Montevideo first came into the hands of the Orientals the Cabildo attempted to curry favour with Artigas by offering to place new taxes on native and foreign merchants; but he not only refused, he even threatened to resign, darkly hinting:

The People are sovereign, and they will be capable of investigating the operations of their representatives. [He explained:] I am not blind to the need in which we are of funds to attend to a thousand urgent matters, and setting aside all the other shortages, it would be enough for me to see that which is shown in the poverty which accompanies the glory of the brave army which I have the honour to command, and which has been clothed only in its laurels for the long period of five years, abandoned always to need for the longest imaginable period, and without any other succour but the hope of finding it one day; but the very word *Tax* makes me tremble.

The war and the *Porteño* occupation had ruined everything, and more taxation would only hinder recovery; what Artigas wanted was help for industry and commerce to revive before all else.[1] This was a complete reaction from previous régimes, and deserved to form a precedent for future ones.

To provide money for his army, so as not to have to raise taxes or use the already nearly exhausted treasury of Montevideo, Artigas, no less than *Jefe de los Orientales y Protector de los Pueblos Libres*, frequently sent from his headquarters boatloads of local produce, such as hides and tallow, for sale on the open market at Montevideo. With the money gained, the Cabildo would buy provisions, arms and munitions, which would then be sent back in the same boats up-river to Purificación. The confiscated goods of

---

[1] Letters of the Cabildo of Montevideo to Artigas, 17 April 1815, *ibid.* libro 484, ff. 104-105; *id.* to *id.*, ? April, *ibid.* f. 106; Artigas to the Cabildo of Montevideo, 1 and 2 May 1815, *Correspondencia de Artigas*, pp. 220-1, 6; and Museo Histórico Nacional, Montevideo, Biblioteca Pablo Blanco Acevedo, vol. XXIII, *Correspondencia de Artigas*.

Spaniards were sent the same way, for the good of the province.[1] When Artigas had to call on the treasury to pay for shipments of arms and munitions which unexpectedly became available, he was careful to arrange for the exact amount to be paid. There was no corruption under his eyes.[2]

Artigas made his soldiers produce the hides and tallow he exported from Purificación, as any rancher would employ his men. He meant even soldiers to be productive. And like a rancher, he kept his eye on the state of the market, ordering the Cabildo to store his goods if prices were low, and ensuring also that the products were of high quality so as to get the best prices.[3] He even set his soldiers to making beds, cutting timber, collecting horsehair and horns, all to send to market in Montevideo.[4] Once Artigas paid on the nail with the fruits of his own industry for two hundred rifles brought to him at Purificación.[5] In August 1816, owing to the Portuguese invasion, Artigas could no longer spare his men nor be sure of remaining static at Purificación, and so he was obliged to stop large-scale production; but for over a year until then he had made his army almost self-sufficient, given an example to his people, and helped his country onto her feet again.[6]

The *Jefe* was rightly strict in his inspection of the use of public funds. Absolutely incorruptible himself, he insisted on the same standard in civil servants. He would not even give a grant of state-owned cattle to his own father, a large rancher ruined by the wars, but asked the Cabildo of Montevideo it if could see its way to making the grant; although of course the Cabildo would naturally

[1] Letters of Artigas to the Cabildo of Montevideo, 1 July, 30 October, 4 November, 30 December 1815, 23 February, 26 February, 2 March, 30 May, 9 August 1816, *Correspondencia de Artigas*, pp. 13, 43, 226-8, 61-2, 81, 84, 86, 101, 114-15.

[2] Letter of Artigas to the Cabildo of Montevideo, 15 August 1815, *ibid.* p. 25.

[3] Letters of Artigas to the Cabildo of Montevideo, 26 January, 23 February, 6 May, 9 August 1816, *ibid.* pp. 73-4, 81, 97, 114-15.

[4] Letter of Artigas to the Cabildo of Montevideo, 26 February 1816, no. 2, *ibid.* pp. 86-7, gives a list of one shipment, which consisted of 80 beds, 28 wheel-spokes, 14 axles, 2,350 horns and 600 horn-tips.

[5] Letter of Artigas to the Cabildo of Montevideo, 3 April 1816, *ibid.* pp. 92-3.

[6] Letter *id.* to *id..*, 9 August 1816, *ibid.* pp. 114-15.

humour the *Jefe's* whims.[1] Civil servants must be native Orientals, prepared to serve, not to make a living,[2] and even if they were not adherents of Artigas they could serve in high positions so long as they were honest and competent.[3] But there must not be many, because they were merely a burden on the province, which could only become prosperous through productive work.[4] He himself would scold the Cabildo for letting ships slip out of the port of Montevideo without paying duties,[5] or personally gave orders about a single grant of land as a gift.[6] He himself appointed an agent extraordinary to help to suppress smuggling throughout the province,[7] and he refused to grant Soriano public money to build a new Town Hall because there were greater needs for the province than that.[8] Artigas gave the Inspector of Revenue his orders, and made it clear that local tax and customs offices in provincial towns were dependent on the central treasury, which was a normal organisation whose existence had been lost sight of during the fighting.[9]

In this work the co-operation of Barreiro as Artigas' delegate in Montevideo from August 1815 was invaluable. He began by dissolving the suspect *Tribunal de Vigilancia* and obeyed Artigas' instructions to cut government spending to the bone. One of his actions was to prune expenditure going through the hands of dishonest contractors; and by keeping the expenses generally within the revenue he made government without extortion possible. This young man quickly showed himself to be a first-rate administrator, even a statesman, and he won the admiration of the

[1] Letter *id.* to *id.*, 18 June 1816, *ibid.* pp. 103-4.
[2] Letter *id.* to *id.*, 28 June 1816, *ibid.* pp. 11-12.
[3] Letter *id.* to *id.*, 3 August 1815, *ibid.* p. 20.
[4] Letter *id.* to, 12 August 1815, *ibid.* pp. 22-3.
[5] Letter *id.* to, 20 August 1815, *ibid.* pp. 26-7.
[6] Letter *id.* to *id.*, 4 September 1815, *ibid.* pp. 30-1.
[7] Letter *id.* to *id.*., 16 February 1816, *ibid.* p. 79.
[8] Letter *id.* to Cabildo of Soriano, 13 May 1816, Arch. Adm. libro 206, f. 49.
[9] Letter of Artigas to the Cabildo of Montevideo, 17 March 1816, *Correspondencia de Artigas*, pp. 90-1.

Montevideans. As one of them wrote: 'In sum, this austerely disinterested young man showed himself to the admiration of all to be most versed and expert in the most arduous business. His more than moderate education, his vast mental power, his tender heart, and a fortunate conjunction of moral attributes, made him be regarded as an Iris of concord. Some held him to be of fickle and inconstant tendency, but they did not remember that in the statesman one should not study the private man. He found some way of executing everything in his charge with speed and without affectation, at the same time maintaining the city on a good defensive footing.'[1] He was one of Artigas' successes in government.

External trade was another of the *Jefe*'s preoccupations. He hoped to help it to recover and so to increase the province's prosperity, but he closed the port of Montevideo at one stage to prevent an outflow of capital and goods to Buenos Aires.[2] However, in July 1815 he was asked by the commander of the British naval squadron, Captain William Bowles, how British merchants might trade with his protectorate, and he decided to open the ports of Montevideo, Colonia and Maldonado to all but *Porteño* ships, so long as the visiting foreigners maintained no relations with Buenos Aires during the hostilities between the federal provinces and the *Porteños*. It was natural for him to impose the traditional restrictions on consignees of cargoes, who must be natives: as in 1809 at the official opening of the Plate to British ships, and as in Buenos Aires since then, the handling of the goods imported must be carried on only by local merchants, so that they should be assured of their share of the profits. The restriction was intended to bring prosperity to the natives. A British protest concerning the cutting off of trade with Buenos Aires brought a haughty reply from Artigas: 'If he [the British commander] is not satisfied, you [the Cabildo of Montevideo] make all their ships leave our coasts, for I will open trade with whomsoever it suits us . . . The English must

[1] Anon., *Apuntes históricos*, pp. 50-1.
[2] Letter of Artigas to the Cabildo of Montevideo, 8 July 1815, *Correspondencia de Artigas*, pp. 14-15.

realise that they are the ones who are given favours, and therefore must never constrain us: on the contrary, they must submit to the laws of the country as all nations demand, even the English in their own ports.'¹ This reflection of the Spanish attitude towards trade is still present in much of the commercial organisation of the Latin American countries.

British goods flowed into the Provincia Oriental, whether by direct importation or clandestinely through Buenos Aires. In June 1815 the treasury officer at Colonia found so many that he enquired from his chief in Montevideo whether he should tour the businesses dealing with them and tax them, since they had paid no customs dues.² Some of the British were little better than pirates. One of their practices was to land on the Isla de Lobos, off the port of Maldonado, and kill and skin the seals from which the island took its name. Maldonado considered those seals its own perquisite, and normally drew a large income from the herds; so that when British ships took the skins without so much as asking permission of the authorities, much less paying for them or even paying export duties, those authorities tried, without much success, to capture the offenders or at least to get the skins back from them.³ Some British sailors added insult to injury by accepting the hospitality of Maldonado to load fresh fuel, water and food, and then sailing to the island and calmly taking on board all the prepared skins, salt and any other articles which they found there. Nothing could be done to stop them but send out a privately hired boat from the port, but big seas turned it back three times, and by the time it reached the island the British had gone; and then the boat was forced to wait there for three days for the weather to abate before making the return voyage to the

¹ Letter of Artigas to the Cabildo of Montevideo, 31 July 1815, 3 and 12 August, *ibid.* pp. 17-18, 19-20, 22-3.

² Letter of T. F. Guerra to J. Guerra, Ministro Principal de Hacienda de Montevideo, d. Colonia 17 June 1815, Arch. Adm. libro 212, ff. 207-8.

³ Letters of Bianqui to Otorgués, d. Maldonado 12 May 1815, Arch. Adm., libro 486, f. 21; and *id.* to *Cabildo Gobernador*, 21 July, *ibid.* libro 488, f. 22.

port. Again, Father Larrañaga found near Colonia a British merchant spreading terrible rumours of the arrival within a few days of a reconquering Spanish expedition. The merchant wished to strike the people with panic so that they would sell their hides and other products cheaply in order to be able to gather some cash before fleeing.[1]

Smuggling remained one of the chief problems of the new government, and as always the Brazilian border was the main danger point. The treasury officer at Maldonado, who was in charge of the finances and taxes of the Atlantic seaboard and its hinterland as far as the frontier, tried to investigate the extent of smuggling and to tax the goods. He wanted to send a secret agent to check the sources of supply of the country *pulperías*, and he attempted to terminate the smuggling condoned by certain frontier guard commanders, but to no avail. Indeed, the commanders, far from helping the treasury in any way, defrauded it further by collecting taxes on the *pulperías* in their own districts for their own use in maintaining their troops.[2]

The heart-breaking difficulties of trying to improve matters in that country are well illustrated by the problems faced by the treasury officer in Maldonado. Apart from his troubles with pirates, smugglers and high-handed soldiers, he found other problems of administration. A hospital which had at one time existed in Maldonado had been derelict since the English Invasions, and he begged for supplies from the two hospitals in Montevideo.[3] He had to find the means from his scanty funds to clothe the squadron of Dragoons which was garrisoning Maldonado, and then to provide the standard rations besides, consisting of bread, meat, and if possible *hierba* and tobacco, for a troop of militia in Maldonado and the garrison of San Carlos, up towards the Brazilian frontier. He finally made a bargain with the purveyor of bread whereby the latter's debts to the tithe fund were

[1] Larrañaga, *Viaje*, pp. 88-9.
[2] Letters of Bianqui to Otorgués, 12 May 1815, Arch. Adm., libro 486, f. 20; and *id.* to *Cabildo Gobernador*, 4 July, *ibid.* libro 488, ff. 9-10.
[3] Letter of Bianqui to Otorgués. 31 May 1815, *ibid.* libro 486, ff. 31-32.

cancelled in return for the cancellation of the bill for bread. There was no ready money.[1] Besides these day-to-day affairs, this officer was in charge of the establishment of a new state remount depot on an estancia in his district at Rincón de Pan de Azúcar, which was a stretch of three square leagues of good, well-watered pasture which he had to survey and then staff and fill with stock, turning off it the stock of local squatters.[2]

In order to increase the volume of trade, 'which constitutes the sinews of the State', the *Cabildo Gobernador* issued orders in September 1815 for the conservation of cattle and the opening of the ports of Maldonado, Montevideo and Colonia to the commerce of all nations on the payment of due taxes, and providing that the consignees were creoles. To discourage smuggling, it was announced that foreign goods landed elsewhere would be liable to seizure. But further, there was another step towards a nationalistic policy in certain orders which provided that all establishments for producing tallow, hides and any other product of the country must be under the charge of natives; the buying of products of the country anywhere in the province outside the capital was to be in the hands of creoles only; foreigners might buy in Montevideo through official agents appointed by the Consulado, but in no case directly themselves. As a general principle, only creoles were allowed to buy products of the country and sell foreign goods.[3] Artigas' aim clearly was to permit and even encourage international trade, so long as the creoles kept internal trade in their own hands, so that the state and the people should benefit directly. These aims have a long history since his day in the Plate countries and others of that continent, so that the modern economic nationalism there is no new growth fostered only by a

[1] Letters of *id.* to the *Cabildo Gobernador*, 22 July 1815, *ibid.* libro 488, f. 22; *id.* to Ministro Principal de Hacienda de Montevideo, 4 July and 1 July (2) 1815, *ibid*, libro 212, ff. 197, 198 and 199.

[2] Letters *id.* to *Cabildo Gobernador*, n.d., and *id.* to *id.* 26 December 1815, *ibid.* libro 492, ff. 24 and 25.

[3] *Bandos* of the *Cabildo Gobernador*, 7 and 16 September 1815, *ibid.* libro 490, ff. 3-4, 1.

reaction against 'foreign exploitation' in the nineteenth century.

Yet Artigas was strict about maintaining standards of honesty in business: these regulations were not merely a trap for the foreigner. He ordered the Cabildo of Montevideo to be sure to keep internal trade in the hands of creoles, but he also wrote: 'Punish severely any who undertake illegal business, or who by bad dealing degrade American honour. Let us teach our countrymen to be virtuous in the presence of Foreigners, and if their own honour does not contain them within the limits of their duty, at least let the punishment which they shall receive do so.'[1]

Artigas' very close watch on the smallest details of administration, his orders cloaked as requests for popular support, his offers of resignation when his orders were dilatorily obeyed, his energetic reprimands in the name of the people, and his requests for authorities to swear oaths of allegiance to the country and in effect to himself,[2] show him as a popular caudillo. But his sincerity in believing in his own representation of the popular will, and his democratic intentions, cannot be doubted. Besides, his government had to be strong in the treacherous atmosphere of the Plate region in 1815 and 1816. Perhaps nothing shows Artigas' strange mixture of idealism, strength of will chafing at self-imposed curbs, and real goodness so well as his entirely patriarchal manner of granting boons to deserving citizens and his swift and terrible justice. For instance, he gave a gift of a confiscated ship to one man, money to another, liberty to a slave on a small payment, a free house to the widow of his brother killed in action;[3] and on the other side of the medal, he can be found giving a sentence of

[1] Letter of Artigas to the Cabildo of Montevideo 8 August 1815. *Correspondencia de Artigas*, pp. 246-8.

[2] Eg. '... jurando p^r. el nombre sagrado de la Patria cumplir y desempeñar fiel, y legalm^{te}. los empleos q^e. seles han confiado, o q^e. en adelante se les confirman, y se conservan ilesos los dr̄os dela Banda Oriental q^e. tan dignam^{te}. representa el Gefe de los Orientales Ciudadano Jose Artigas.'(Artigas to the Cabildo de Montevideo, 9 January 1816, *ibid.* pp. 66-7.)

[3] Letters of Artigas to the Cabildo of Montevideo, 12 August 1815, 18 and 30 November, 3 February 1816, etc., etc., *Correspondencia de Artigas*, pp. 22-3, 49, 51-3, 75, etc.

death at once and on the spot for a murder, without need for formality, or having terrible personal interviews with dishonest or suspect civil servants, and all the time thrusting forward his representative character by appealing to popular feeling in such cases, and despoiling hostile Spaniards to give to upright patriots.

But what shows Artigas in the best light is his concern for spiritual and intellectual things in the midst of his multifarious worries and activities. He wanted the press to be used as a means of education as well as of propaganda, and therefore he spread Montevideo-printed almanacs, exercise books and text-books, besides government decrees, throughout his protectorate. His concern for education was echoed by humble people in his country, in a touching way which brings us closer to those men who, we may think, were scarcely half-civilised, but who by their preoccupation with more than purely material things in the midst of their hardships and wants remind us of our common ideals no less than of our common humanity. As some of them wrote when thanking the *Cabildo Gobernador* for a consignment of thirty-three children's first reading books, thirty-three almanacs and twenty-four multiplication tables to give to the poorest children of their district: 'since you are caring for the pauper families, cast a glance also at the spectacle of all our children. What can we expect of these at a later age?' There was need of a school, of a teacher for all the children, and indeed the many wandering families who gave no education to their children should be forced, for the sake of the children and of the country in the future, to settle on the lands offered by the government.[1]

Artigas cordially approved Father Larrañaga's plan to set up a public library in Montevideo, and ordered the Cabildo to help the enterprise, while at the same time providing that any books found among confiscated enemy property should be given to the new

[1] Letters of Artigas to the Cabildo of Montevideo, 3 August 1815, 23 October and 25 November, *ibid.* pp. 19-20, 38-9, 51; Cabildo of Corrientes to the Cabildo of Montevideo, 3 January 1816, Arch. Adm. libro 202, f. 312; Cabildo of San José to the Cabildo of Montevideo, 12 March and 16 of the 'Mes de America' [May] 1816, *ibid.* ff. 77-78 and 102-3.

library.[1] He founded a school at Purificación, and encouraged education wherever he could, so long as it was not Spanish propaganda under the guise of elementary instruction.[2] Artigas encouraged the Church, and though he stepped in to prevent the hierarchy in his province from being subservient to that in Buenos Aires, he took great trouble to spread the influence of religion, even building a rustic chapel at Purificación, with ornaments sent by the Cabildo of Montevideo.[3] Another benefit, though not directly a spiritual one, was the active help Artigas gave to an Englishman who came to spread vaccination among the peoples of the Federal League. Smallpox was a scourge especially terrible among the Indians of the Misiones, to whom Artigas gave the greatest consideration in this matter.[4]

At this climax of his life, Artigas seemed to have a prophet's talent for writing unforgettable things. His greatness appears in sentences of proverbial force, some of which have been quoted. But every letter contains some noble phrase: 'Among free men the weak can have no place'; 'He who will not enter into the order of society through hope of receiving some benefit must be terrified by the dread of punishment'; after giving all the help he could to poor Indians in the Misiones: 'I can pride myself on having been more than generous, and therefore believe me that there is nothing for which we should grieve more than our own indigence'; a government is needed which 'being just in its principles must be equally just in its results'. 'Wishing to be free, the multiplicity of enemies will only serve to redouble our glory.'[5] Artigas spoke as a father of his country should speak.

[1] Letter of Artigas to the Cabildo of Montevideo, 12 August 1815, *Correspondencia de Artigas*, pp. 23-4.

[2] Letters of Artigas to the Cabildo of Montevideo, 10 September 1815, 16 October, 17 March 1816, 27 April, *ibid.* pp. 29, 37-8, 89-90, 96.

[3] Letters of Artigas to the Cabildo of Montevideo, 12 October 1815, 25 and 12 November, 13 January 1816, *ibid.* pp. 36, 40-1, 46-7, 70-1.

[4] Letters *id.* to *id.* 17 March 1816, 11 and 27 April, *ibid.* pp. 89-90, 93-4, 95; Cabildo of Colonia to *Cabildo Gobernador*, Arch. Adm., libro 202, f. 167.

[5] Letters of Artigas to the Cabildo of Montevideo, 9 and 17 March 1816, 27 April, 24 May, 6 July, *Correspondencia de Artigas*, pp. 88-9, 89-90, 95, 100, 108-9.

CHAPTER VII

THE FEDERAL LEAGUE

I. THE SPREAD OF FEDERALISM

ARTIGAS' ideas on federation probably influenced Argentina more than they did Uruguay; but the Federal League which grew up in response to them was itself of importance in determining the future course of Uruguayan history because of the reactions it produced in Buenos Aires. Some sort of federal organisation of the Plate provinces was in Artigas' mind as early as 1811, when he began to set up the Banda Oriental as an autonomous state. In December of that year he suggested to Paraguay the formation of a loose union to oppose Portuguese aggression, and although the offer was neither taken up nor rejected, Artigas did not lose hope,[1] and continued to correspond with the government of that remote province. In 1813, at the time of the federal crisis symbolised by Buenos Aires' rejection of the Oriental deputies to the Constituent Assembly, Artigas strongly urged the Paraguayans to unite with him.[2] His idea was for those provinces which had decided to resist *Porteño* centralism to send deputies to form an opposition bloc in the Constituent Assembly, and he believed that he could count on six deputies from the Provincia Oriental, probably seven from Paraguay, and two from Tucumán, which was independently taking the same line as the Provincia Oriental. Moreover, his cry of 'Liberty, equality, security' was echoed by men in all the provinces, where a strong current of discontent with the *Porteño* régime had been spreading ever since the centralists had captured the government in 1811 by ignoring the first Junta's half-promise to respect provincial wishes.

---

[1] Letter of Artigas to the government of Paraguay, 7 December 1811, in Fregeiro, *op. cit.*

[2] Letters of Artigas to the government of Paraguay, 8 February 1813, 17 April, 29 May, 30 June, 3 July, 26 August; and government of Paraguay to Artigas, 19 January 1813, 15 March, 29 July, 26 August, in Fregeiro, *Artigas*, pp. 185–204.

Paraguay soon decided to go her own way, and under the enigmatical rule of Doctor Francia became a land of mystery to the outside world, into which travellers such as the scientists Bonpland, Rengger and Longchamp disappeared to return unexpectedly only after years of negotiation with the authorities, and into which Artigas himself finally withdrew to find hospitable asylum at the moment of his catastrophe in 1820. The Littoral districts, Entre Ríos, Santa Fe and Corrientes, however, went the way of federalism. They saw from close at hand the struggle of the Provincia Oriental against *Porteño* centralism, since they were the neighbouring lands along the Rivers Uruguay and Paraná. They would be the scene of the military triumph of federalism in 1815, since after the *Porteño* expulsion from the Provincia Oriental in that year they formed the cockpit where the forces of Buenos Aires and those of Artigas could clash: they were on the land road from the Provincia Oriental to Buenos Aires, so that both sides attempted to bring them within their respective systems.

The struggle was decided between 1812 and 1815 in favour of Artigas and federalism, since the Littoral and its people found themselves under an uncongenial centralist rule and witnessed the Provincia Oriental's successful break away from it. During the Oriental Exodus, which took Artigas into Entre Ríos, the Littoral learned to respect the *Jefe*'s ideas and fraternised with his people, so that gradually the ideal of provincial autonomy as expressed in Artigas' Instructions of 1813 spread there. Entre Ríos became Artigas' first ally, under the lead of the local militia commander, Eusebio Hereñú, who accepted the *Jefe*'s plans and his help in resisting the *Porteños*[1]

Early in 1814 the countryside of Entre Ríos and Corrientes rose against the *Porteño* governors and garrisons, and turned to Artigas for help and support, military and political. Other provinces joined Artigas' movement and thereby turned it into a league,

[1] See Ardao and Castellanos, *Artigas*, pp. 55-71; F. A. Arce, *La formación de la Liga Federal*; F. A. Arce and M. Demonte Vitali, *Artigas, heraldo del federalismo rioplatense*; P. Blanco Acevedo, *El federalismo de Artigas y la independencia nacional*, p. 68.

even a loose confederation, during the succeeding year: Santa Fe and Córdoba cast in their lot in March 1815, and Montevideo was freed in April. In this year Artigas was nominated their Protector by the Cabildos of the capital cities of the provinces which accepted his lead, and he took the title of Protector of the Free Peoples. His headquarters remained at Purificación, whose utility as a centre from which to supervise his interests increased with the accession of more provinces. From here he directed the war against the *Porteños* and that against the Portuguese who invaded the Provincia Oriental in 1816. The signal for the rising of the Littoral in 1814 was Artigas' withdrawal from the patriot siege of Montevideo and opening of hostilities against Buenos Aires. At this, Artigas communicated with the network of agents and sympathisers he had built up in Entre Ríos, Corrientes, Santa Fe and Córdoba, and sent out the call to arms against the oppressive centralists. The peoples were encouraged by the success of Artigas' audacity, which was symbolised by a victory in Entre Ríos over a *Porteño* expedition led by Holmberg: Holmberg, the professional German mercenary who had been sent by the Supreme Director, Posadas, to crush Artigas and autonomy, and to put into effect the orders issued in February 1814 outlawing the *Jefe* and putting a price of six thousand pesos on his head.

Holmberg met his defeat at the hands of the caudillo of Entre Ríos, Hereñú, in February 1814. At the same time, in the Provincia Oriental, Otorgués won his victory over the *Porteño* force commanded by Quintana, so that by March *artiguismo*, as the ideas and system of Artigas were called, had spread far in the Littoral. Arroyo de la China was soon freed, and then on the 10th of March Bautista Méndez led a popular movement in Corrientes and won self-rule for the people of the province. Artigas had naturally already informed Corrientes of his activities in the Littoral, and had asked the province to join him in fraternal union against the tyrants of Buenos Aires. Within a few days of the revolt he wrote to the Cabildo of Corrientes offering to protect the province 'with all the resources of the league', encouraging it to call a congress of the people to establish a popular government, and declaring that all the peoples along the Uruguay and the Paraná were now placing themselves under the same reformed system.[1] Once all the provinces were safe a general organisation would be arranged, 'each one of the provinces considering its own especial and respective advantage, and all shall remain in perfect union with each other; not in that niggardly union which obliges each people to deprive itself of a part of its confidence in exchange for servile obedience, but in that union which springs from mutual interest itself, without prejudice to the rights of the peoples and to their free and entire exercise'. This showed that a federal league was to be formed on the basis of Artigas' consistent ideas of popular sovereignty and provincial autonomy. Artigas offered at this time to be protector of these free peoples if they should choose him, and there could hardly be any doubt at this stage that they would, since his power and prestige had spread far beyond his own province. He was the most powerful and respected man in all the provinces of the Plate. On the 29th of April the Cabildo of Corrientes declared the independence of the province 'under the system of federation, with General Artigas as Protector'.

Some idea of the Protectorate and of the scale of Artigas' operations is gained on considering that the town of Corrientes, on the confluence of the Rivers Paraná and Paraguay, is about seven hundred and fifty miles from Buenos Aires by river, the quickest and most direct route then. It is close to the frontier of Paraguay, and by an indirect and difficult route involving the crossing of very large tracts of open country, sailing down part of the Paraná and crossing the Uruguay, it is about four hundred miles from the site of Artigas' headquarters at Purificación. The Robertson brothers, who were active merchants in this region about the time of Artigas, provide much information on the lands of the Federal

---

[1] Letters of Artigas to the Cabildo of Corrientes, 5 and 29 March 1814, in L. M. Torterolo (ed.), *Artigas y el Cabildo de Corrientes*.

League in their accounts of their travels. Of Corrientes, J. P. Robertson wrote that the land was fertile and the River Paraná beautiful and salubrious, but the country had a very sparse population: he saw not above five small towns during a ride of two hundred and eighty leagues, and only a miserable hut every fifteen miles or so in between. He found the heat in the middle of the day 'all but insupportable. Not a soul was to be seen in the streets of loose and burning sand.' The cows, which normally wandered in the streets, sheltered from the sun under the shade of trees or of the tall prickly-pear hedges.[1]

Robertson found the houses lofty and airy, built on the court-yard plan with open galleries on to the patios, for the sake of coolness. The people, once indoors, surprised him by taking off their 'upper garments' and walking about, 'the women in a chemise and petticoat, with a loose kerchief about the neck; the men in an open-breasted shirt and trousers, the sleeves of the former rolled up to the elbows. They either swing in their ham-mocks, walk in listlessness, or flap themselves with fans made of straw.' The living rooms were simply furnished, and usually cluttered up with horse gear. The language used in the home was Guaraní, the local Indian tongue, spoken also in Paraguay; and in fact the women normally spoke Spanish badly. All, men and women, enjoyed smoking cigars, another custom which shocked Robertson. But he was pleased to note that 'the female mulatto slaves are particularly handsome in Corrientes', and that the hos-pitality given him there was as generous and simple as elsewhere on his journeyings in the interior.

At this juncture Buenos Aires opened what is now called a 'peace offensive', since the situation in the Littoral was clearly be-yond her power to resolve favourably by force, threatened as she still was by royalists in the north and in Montevideo. While Artigas consolidated his hold on the Littoral by sending his brother Manuel Francisco as his representative in Entre Ríos and Corrientes

[1] J. P. and W. P. Robertson, *Letters on Paraguay*, vol. I, pp. 247-57.

to help to stave off any *Porteño* attack, and encouraged Corrientes especially by sending there his lieutenant Genaro Perugorría with orders to aid the congress which the Correntines were about to call, Buenos Aires attempted to ensnare the *Jefe* by means of diplomacy. But the mission of the Santa Fe notables Fray Mariano Amaro and Francisco Antonio Candioti to Artigas in March and April 1814, trying to gain peace and union on behalf of the Directory in Buenos Aires, only succeeded in causing more defections from the centralist cause.[1]

At Belén on the 23rd of April these envoys and Artigas signed a plan for the re-establishment of fraternity and harmony between the *Jefe* and the Director, but Posadas rejected it when it was sent to him. He could not accept, as his envoys had done with enthusiasm, a plan including articles which insisted on autonomy for Entre Ríos and the Provincia Oriental on the grounds that their peoples had proclaimed independence under their Protector, Artigas. The latter was willing to join the siege of Montevideo again in an 'offensive and defensive league' with Buenos Aires, until at the end of the war against the Spaniards some general organisation should 'constitutionally unite and bring into a league among themselves all the provinces'. Therefore the main result of the negotiation was that Candioti and Amaro returned to Santa Fe convinced of Artigas' good intentions and the justness of his views. They spread their impressions among their friends, and thus prepared for Santa Fe's incorporation into the Federal League a few months later.

Artigas' willingness to make sacrifices in order to gain peace is further proved by his approach to Alvear in July, after the fall of Montevideo to the Argentine leader, when he offered to forego claims to the adherence of Entre Ríos and Corrientes so long as they kept their autonomy and their people were not persecuted for their political views.[2] The *Porteño* centralists were still

---

[1] See the documents concerning this mission in Pivel Devoto and Fonseca Muñoz, *op. cit.*, pp. 141-59.

[2] See documents in *ibid.* pp. 163-82; and see above, pp. 203-4.

frightened by the spread of *artiguismo*, and so Posadas accepted the treaty this time, hoping to lessen his difficulties and if possible turn the renouncement of control into propaganda showing Artigas as a traitor to his responsibilities towards his protectorate. Artigas staved off this trouble by telling his brother Manuel Francisco to inform all the *Entrerrianos* of his reasons for this action and to assure them that in case Buenos Aires should choose to ignore the wishes of the people, the *Jefe* promised his full protection.[1] But mutual suspicion effectively prevented the implementation of the pact of July 1815, which was, in fact, never ratified by Buenos Aires. Artigas, indignantly refusing to accept his reinstatement as a colonel in the Argentine army, opened hostilities before the end of August by cutting off communications between Montevideo and Buenos Aires. It was the beginning of the campaign which culminated in the Oriental victory of Guayabos, and led to the Oriental occupation of a liberated Montevideo in February 1815.[2]

Campaigns against the centralists were fought at the same time in the Provincia Oriental and in Entre Ríos, and they served to consolidate the Federal League at the end of 1814 and beginning of 1815. While the Provincia Oriental was in flames, Posadas attempted once again, in September 1814, to subdue Entre Ríos and Corrientes, organising them as separate provinces of the United Provinces of the River Plate and trying to impose a centralist governor, Colonel Blas José Pico. The people refused to accept this vice-dictator, and remained in arms against the Directory even when in the spring and summer the war went badly for the federalists both in the Provincia Oriental and in Entre Ríos. The *artiguista* caudillo Blas Basualdo met defeat in Entre Ríos at the hands of the *Porteño* leaders Hortiguera, Melián and Baldenegro, and Artigas' trusted lieutenant in Corrientes, Perugorría, turned traitor and joined the centralists, dissolving the local congress, of which he was president. But by the time that the *Porteños* had been

[1] Letter of M. F. Artigas to the Cabildo of Corrientes, 29 July 1814, in Torterolo, *op. cit.* pp. 174-175.
[2] See above, pp. 204-13.

forced to retire from Entre Ríos, in February 1815, Perugorría had already been defeated and shot. This is in fact one of the few recorded instances of an execution ordered by Artigas. Almost simultaneously with the victories of February news reached Artigas of the decisions of Santa Fe and Córdoba to join his protectorate.

Just then the *Jefe* was advancing through the Littoral, passing through Arroyo de la China, Nogoyá and Paraná. His brother Manuel Francisco was firmly in charge there, and under him were trusty local *caudillos*, mostly small ranchers originally: Hereñú in Paraná, where the headquarters were, Correa in Gualeguay, Samaniego in Gualeguaychú, and Verdum, an Oriental, in Arroyo de la China. Hereñú had helped Santa Fe to depose the unpopular *Porteño* governor, Eustoquio Díaz Vélez. The province of Santa Fe had been well prepared beforehand by Artigas' friends there and the activities among the local people of Candioti and Amaro: indeed Candioti had become the most active *artiguista* leader in the province. River launches from Corrientes and forces from Entre Ríos had converged on Santa Fe, and on the 24th of March Díaz Vélez fled from his untenable situation. Candioti himself became interim Governor, and, in the Artigas manner, a provincial congress was convoked. It confirmed Candioti in the governorship. Artigas reached the city of Santa Fe on the 14th of April, and there he planned the last stages of his struggle against Alvear, before returning through Paraná to Paysandú in the Provincia Oriental to fulfil a promise he had given to the Cabildo of Montevideo that he would superintend his native province.[1]

J. P. Robertson provides much information on the importance of Santa Fe and of Candioti, and his evidence shows that the spread of federalism to this province was not a purely political matter, but a political reaction whose main cause was economic necessity,

[1] Letters of Artigas to the Cabildo of Montevideo, 3 and 12 April 1815, in *Correspondencia de Artigas*, pp. 3–4. See also Junta de Historia y Numismática Americana, Publicaciones de la Filial de Rosario no. 3, *Diario de Don Manuel Ignacio Diez de Andino, crónica santafecina, 1815–1822*, pp. 25–8.

as was the case with the growth of the federal idea in the Banda Oriental.[1] The town, containing in those days about four or five thousand souls, is about half-way between Corrientes and Buenos Aires, situated on a tributary of the Paraná. It is distant by about one hundred and fifty miles of hard going from the site of Purificación, which is due east, across the River Paraná, across all of Entre Ríos, and then across the River Uruguay. Santa Fe was of poor appearance, built on the Spanish colonial gridiron plan, with the usual single-storeyed houses built round a patio, showing plain, mean exteriors and simple interiors without luxury. The streets were of loose sand except for one, which was partially paved. The climate was hot in summer, and Robertson's Scottish prudery was shocked at the way the people opened their houses to the view of all and lounged about half-dressed, smoking, sipping *mate* and eating water-melons. This was the first time he had seen ladies smoking huge cigars and spitting when necessary. 'Oh! it was a terrible shock to my nerves', he wrote.

But here, as everywhere, he met true hospitality, at the hands of a family of complete strangers, who gave him their best: a simple room, a negress to attend him, and a place in all their doings. His nerves were in for a difficult time, for the first thing they did was go for a bathing party in the moonlight; and there the ladies and gentlemen could see and joke with each other, although it was true that they were all dressed, 'the ladies in white robes, and the gentlemen in white drawers; – but there was something that ran rather counter to my preconceived notions of propriety and decorum'. He was, it should be added, not yet twenty at the time.

One day, as young Robertson was sitting, quite the *Santafecino*, without jacket or waistcoat at the siesta hour, he saw Francisco Candioti, who was his host's uncle, riding up. Everyone who had ever been in that country knew of Candioti, 'lord of three hundred square leagues of territory, owner of two hundred and fifty thousand head of horned cattle, master of three hundred

---

[1] J. P. and W. P. Robertson, *Letters on Paraguay*, vol. I, pp. 197–223.

thousand horses and mules, and of more than half a million of dollars, laid up in his coffers, in ounces of gold imported from Peru'. He was just back from one of his periodical journeys to Peru, which had taken six months, and there he sat, talking, mounted on the finest horse Robertson had seen there and dressed in the height of gaucho fashion. He was a 'patriarchal potentate', a 'prince', yet simple, courteous and unostentatious with all his wealth and power.

His appearance is worth describing, since it gives some idea of that of many of the influential men of the interior who favoured Artigas and federalism, rich estancieros of the Provincia Oriental, Entre Ríos, Corrientes, Santa Fe and Córdoba. Apart from his dignified good looks and open-air health, his dress was magnificent.

His poncho had been made in Peru, and, beside being of the richest material, was embroidered on a white ground in superb style. Beneath it he wore a jacket of the finest India cloth, covering a white satin waistcoat, which, like his poncho, was beautifully embroidered, and adorned with small gold buttons, each depending from a little link of the same metal. He had no cravat, and the collar and front of his shirt displayed, upon fine French cambric, the richest specimens of tambouring which could be furnished in Paraguay. His lower vestment was of black velvet, open at the knees, and, like the waistcoat, adorned with gold buttons, depending also from little links of chain, evidently never intended for connexion with the button-holes. From under this part of his dress were to be seen the fringed and tamboured extremities of a pair of drawers, made of the fine Paraguay cloth. They were ample as a Turkoman's trousers; white as the driven snow, and hung down to the calf of the leg, just far enough to show under them a pair of brown stockings, manufactured in Peru from the best Vicuña wool. The potro boots of Señor Candioti fitted his feet and ankles, as a French glove fits the hand, and the tops of them were turned over, so as to give them the air of buskins. To these boots were attached a pair of unwieldy silver spurs, brightly polished. To complete his personal attire, the princely Gaucho wore a large Peruvian straw hat, with a black velvet band around it, while his waist was girded with a rich crimson sash of silk, serving the treble purpose of riding belt, braces, and girdle for a huge knife in a morocco sheath, from which protruded a massive silver handle.

His horse was, if anything, even more richly caparisoned, with ornaments of pure silver which must have weighed at least ten pounds on his harness.

The rise of Santa Fe to a certain importance was intimately connected with Candioti's own rise, and was even 'essentially owing to his spirit, industry, activity, and indefatigable perseverance'. Until the middle of the eighteenth century the district had been a backwater, but Candioti, as a poor young man, had taken a few mules for sale to Peru, where the silver mines were busy and the need for transport was great in that mountainous region. Candioti had realised the possibilities of that market, and of another market for mules in the carrying trade from Paraguay to all the towns of the Viceroyalty of the River Plate. He therefore put all his meagre resources into buying an estancia in Entre Ríos for the purpose of breeding mules, and from that time made a yearly journey to Peru with a train of five or six thousand mules for sale. His sales were successful, and he invested the profits in ever more land and stock, which were both cheap then, until he became the great patriarch that he was in Artigas' time. Others in Santa Fe followed his example until there was a very important trade in mules to Peru and the town also became a commercial cross-roads for the trade from Paraguay for Chile and Peru. 'It extended its influence and increased its wealth by the acquisition of many estates on the Banda Oriental and Entrerios, where most of the mules for exportation were bred.'[1]

This fact goes far to explain the friendship between Artigas and Candioti, which is evident from their letters and their actions; and it also supplies a strong economic motive for the unification in the Federal League of the Littoral and the Provincia Oriental. Buenos Aires' intervention was neither needed nor wanted in that simple but adequate system.

To complete the portrait of Candioti the patriarch, it is necessary to add that he only had one child, a daughter, by his wife, but

---

[1] *Ibid.* and also vol. II, p. 194.

he had so many illegitimate children, for all of whom he provided with due pride, that most of his many estancias were managed by one or more of his sons. He had uncounted possessions,
yet his horse-gear was kept on a rack in the sparsely-furnished
drawing-room; and he never, 'even by chance, looked into a
book'.

Artigas' idea was that the Federal League should eventually
include all of the United Provinces, but in fact the League reached
its greatest extent with the adherence of Córdoba. In February a
Cordobese delegation asked Artigas to intervene in their province
to help to free it from *Porteño* domination; and therefore as soon
as Santa Fe had come into the fold Artigas made plans to send
auxiliary forces across that province to the aid of the Cordobese
people, and warned both the Cabildo and Ocampo, the Governor
of Córdoba, of his intentions and of their obligation to banish
Porteño influence and troops from their province. At a *Cabildo
Abierto* on the 29th of March 1815 Ocampo accordingly resigned,
and Colonel José Xavier Díaz, a federal sympathiser, was elected in
his place. Luckily, although Ocampo was the governor imposed
by Buenos Aires, he was himself a Cordobese and only desired
peace for his people, so that no resistance to the change was permitted to develop.[1]

A new Cordobese delegation held conferences with Artigas at
Bajada del Paraná between the 12th and 14th of April, when
doubtless the federal system was discussed, and Córdoba was invited to send deputies to the League's Congress, which Artigas
planned to hold at Arroyo de la China. Díaz governed according
to Artigas' notions in Córdoba.

Artigas' protectorate was now at its apogee. It was popular,
founded on public approval and private conviction in all the
provinces it embraced. Artigas' own interest for the welfare of the
people was shown by two typical foundations erected by his
order: those of two schools, one in Santa Fe and the other in

[1] Letter of Ocampo to Artigas, 29 March 1815, in Arch. Adm., caja 461; 2.

Arroyo de la China. This latter was the first school in Entre Ríos. Desertion from the forces of Buenos Aires testified that even among them discontent was spreading, and respect for Artigas and the ideas he represented existed.[1] A contemporary diarist remarked on the wisdom and expert diplomacy shown by Artigas in forming his Federal League, since from small resources he increased his power until it overweighed that of Buenos Aires itself. In spite of all the horrors attributed to him by Buenos Aires, 'one cannot doubt that this caudillo, economical in the use of paper [in fact he used quantities in his administration], and isolated in the private counsel of his own mind, is extraordinary and original in all respects. At least this much must be said in honour of the arms [that is, those of Buenos Aires and of Portugal] which did not scorn to measure themselves against his.'[2]

Yet the centralists' view of the federal rising against Buenos Aires was dark, and unfortunately it was this view which the historians of Argentina, *Porteños* themselves, such as V. Fidel López and Bartolomé Mitre repeated and reinforced during the rest of the century, thus obscuring for generations the true nature of the movement.[3] Mitre called it a dissolution, and condemned it as an ignorant, selfish and half-baked schism in the greater movement of revolution against Spain. 'At the head of this element there placed themselves obscure caudillos, virile characters, fortified in the tasks of the range, inured to disorder and blood, without notions of morality, rebels to the discipline of civil life, and they became the leaders of those energetic and brutal instincts [of the rural population], which bordered on fanaticism. Artigas was their incarnation: the image and semblance of semi-barbarous democracy, in him the people admired their own figure, and many minds

[1] Letter of Quinta, López and Carranza to Colonel Manuel Artigas, d. Rosario 30 March 1815, in Arch. Adm., caja 461; 2. These three offered to change sides followed by 250 men, and promised to persuade others to come, because of their conviction that Buenos Aires was wrong to encourage civil war.

[2] Anon., *Apuntes históricos*, p. 53.

[3] V. F. López, *Historia de la República Argentina, su origen, su revolución y su desarrollo político;* B. Mitre, *Historia de Belgrano.*

prostituted themselves to it. Such was the progenitor of federation in the River Plate.'[1]

This is an exaggeration, of centralist tendency. Artigas based his government on principles, which is more than did his adversary at this moment, Alvear, who was imposed by the centralists as the new Supreme Director in January 1815. Artigas' rule was desired by the provincial peoples, which was not the case with that of the *Porteños*. He loved peace, and even in March 1815 was prepared to receive the envoys of Alvear, Colonel Galván and Brown, the Irish commander of the Buenos Aires fleet, and listen to their proposals for a termination of hostilities.[2] Alvear was reduced to offering autonomy to the federalist provinces pending a general congress of the United Provinces which would decide on the form of government, in return for peace and an alliance against the threatened Spanish expedition.

But the situation was too tense for a settlement. Inside Buenos Aires discontent with Alvear grew strong among the people and the troops, and even spread to the Cabildo. Outside, the federal forces, the famous *montoneras*, bands of irregular cavalry, were advancing towards the Buenos Aires provincial boundary from Santa Fe. Alvear was cornered, but in a fury he tried a last fling in early March, when he sent out a force of one thousand six hundred men under the command of his War Minister, Viana, with Colonel Álvarez Thomas as leader of the vanguard, to stop the federal advance on the line of the River Paraná. At Fontezuelas on the 13th of April the whole vanguard rose against Alvear and was followed by the rest of the expedition. Alvear's resignation was then demanded. Artigas had encouraged the rising, and had sent Hereñú to help it with his forces; and Álvarez Thomas had been cunning enough to see the way things were going in the province and among his own troops, and had taken the lead in the desertion to the federal ranks. His intention in fact was to keep the

[1] Mitre, *op. cit.* vol. II, p. 232.
[2] Documents in Pivel Devoto and Fonseca Muñoz, *op. cit.* 229–33.

true federal troops out of Buenos Aires by himself forcing Alvear's fall, and later he meant to set up a centralist régime again under his own lead.

So a federal movement inside Buenos Aires was forestalled, but the people rose on the 15th of April to depose Alvear. The young Supreme Director had the sense not to try to resist, which would have led to useless bloodshed, and resigned on the 17th, to sail aboard an English ship to an ignominious exile. By the 21st of April a new form of assembly named a Junta of Observation and intended to act as a moderating force on the executive had already been called, had met, and had elected Rondeau Supreme Director; and in his absence in command of the army fighting the royalists in the north of the United Provinces, the Junta had appointed Colonel Álvarez Thomas his interim substitute. Álvarez Thomas had won the round. He was virtually dictator of the whole country by reason of the nomination of an assembly representing only the province of Buenos Aires. Centralism had not taken long to subvert the designs of the Federal League, though it was as yet a disguised centralism. On the 5th of May the Junta of Observation produced a 'Provisional Statute' giving a temporary constitution to the United Provinces, and at the same time promising a General Congress of the whole nation to decide on the permanent constitution to be adopted. The Congress was to be held in Tucumán and not in Buenos Aires, so as to avoid the appearance of its being under pressure from the *Porteños*.[1]

Montevideo's pleasure at the apparent settlement and at the fall of Alvear was extreme. At the news of the federal triumph in Santa Fe and Córdoba, the Cabildo sent an extravagantly worded letter of congratulation to Artigas, praising him, his activity, his liberal ideas, and his sacred cause, the rights of the provinces. Alvear was called 'the Tyrant who with hypocritical mask in fact oppresses the People, tramples on their rights and on their very liberty, taking pleasure in the slaughter of his fellow-

[1] See E. M. Narancio (ed), *Contribución documental para la historia de Artigas y del movimiento de 1815.*

citizens'.[1] When Alvear fell, the Cabildo of Montevideo wrote congratulating the Cabildo of Buenos Aires on the appearance at last of 'Liberty, that Deity which until now has been an unknown being and whose name has been sacrilegiously profaned in order to oppress and bring horror to the Provinces'.[2] A sisterly remark. Artigas was treated to another list of epithets for Alvear: 'that miscreant man', 'that monster', whose 'colossal fall' had pleased everyone in Montevideo.[3] Finally, the Cabildo of Montevideo invested Artigas with the title of 'Patron and Protector of the Liberty of the Peoples',[4] a title well earned and freely granted.

Two actions typical of Artigas occurred at this period of triumph. In May the caudillo Blas Basualdo, a warlike and successful lieutenant of Artigas' for five years past, died after a long illness. Artigas mourned in him a faithful comrade and patriot, and ordered a funeral feast to be held in the Montevideo Town Hall after a service in the main church of the city. The feast was to be served with 'the greatest frugality', although the Cabildo was to attend in full ceremonial dress. At the end, the only cup of wine at the feast was to be poured as a libation over a palm tree which was to stand in the centre of the table. Romantic honours for the patriot dead, and Spartan economy for the living: this sums up Artigas' attitude. The second action took place in July, when the Cabildo of Montevideo voted to reward the Protector by giving his poor mad wife a completely furnished house and a pension of one hundred pesos a month, and educating his son José María free of expense. Artigas refused this gift, saying that it was too generous in view of the financial situation: 'I could never consent to this extravagance', he wrote; and he ordered his family to live in their own house and to accept the free education and only fifty

[1] Letter of the Cabildo of Montevideo to Artigas, 14 April 1815, Arch. Adm., libro 485; ff. 101a and 101b.
[2] Letter of the Cabildo of Montevideo to the Cabildo of Buenos Aires, 24 April 1815, *ibid.*, f. 115.
[3] Letter of *id.* to Artigas, 25 April 1815, *ibid.* f. 116.
[4] Letter of *id.* to the governor of Montevideo, 25 April 1815, *ibid.* f. 117.

pesos a month. He was himself too poor to be able to refuse the chance of some help for his family.[1]

After the exile of Alvear, his most faithful lieutenants were imprisoned and then tried by a military court set up by the Cabildo of Buenos Aires and Soler, now commander-in-chief. One of the most compromised of the officers, Paillardelle, was executed, but public opinion in Buenos Aires would stand no more, so the court decided to get rid of the most obnoxious of the others at the same time as ingratiating themselves with their chief enemy by choosing the six who had offended Artigas the most and sending them to him at Purificación as a present to do what he liked with. Such a gesture shows the cruelty and moral cowardice of the ruling clique of that time. Artigas returned the six to Buenos Aires with the remark that he would not be the *Porteños'* executioner, even though the six included the Oriental Colonel Ventura Vásquez who had deserted him for Sarratea at a critical moment in 1812 and had fought against him since.[2]

Still a true settlement between Buenos Aires and Artigas had not been reached, although on the surface the situation had eased. Álvarez Thomas sent two commissioners, Colonel Blas José Pico and Doctor Francisco Bruno de Rivarola, to Artigas on the 11th of May provided with the same instructions as Alvear had given Galván and Brown in March. Nothing had changed in Buenos Aires but the names. The main motive for the *démarche* was fear of the threatened Spanish expedition, which in fact never arrived in the Plate since it was diverted to cope with Bolívar in Venezuela when the Spanish foothold at Montevideo was lost in 1814.[3]

The deputies went first to Arroyo de la China, and then by boat to Artigas' headquarters of the moment at Paysandú, which they reached on the 26th of May. The talks were postponed by Artigas

[1] Letters of Artigas to the Cabildo of Montevideo, 21 May and 31 July 1815, in *Correspondencia de Artigas*, pp. 231-2, 243.

[2] See 'Apuntes biográficos sobre el coronel D. Ventura Vasquez', in Lamas, *Colección*.

[3] See documents on the mission of Pico and Rivarola in Pivel Devoto and Fonseca Muñoz, *op. cit.* pp. 237-49.

for a few weeks on the pretext that he was waiting for news from Montevideo, and they ended in disagreement after heated discussions. Pico and Rivarola in their report to their government complained that they had received 'a very good welcome, fine words and flattering proposals before our talks began, and much coldness, difficulties and distrust when we came to make the treaty'. They had been kept waiting until the 16th of June for the talks to begin, and they felt slighted.

The *Jefe* was at the crest of his wave in those days of June 1815, and we are fortunate to have this portrait of him just then:

In nothing did he seem a general: his dress was civilian, and very simple: trousers and jacket of blue without froggings or facings, shoes and white cotton stockings; a round hat with crown, and a cloak of thick cloth were his only finery, and even these were poor and old. He is a man of regular and robust formation, with a fairly pale complexion, with very good features, and a somewhat aquiline nose; black hair sprinkled with grey; he appears to be about forty-eight years old [in fact he was fifty-one]. His conversation is pleasant, he speaks quietly and slowly; it is not easy to take him in with long-winded arguments, since he reduces the difficulty to a few words, and, full of great experience, he possesses foresight and extraordinary judgment. He knows well the human heart, especially the hearts of our fellow-countrymen, and so there is none to equal him in the art of managing them. All surround him and all follow him with love, even though they live naked and full of poverty at his side, not for lack of resources but for the sake of not oppressing the people with taxes, since he prefers to resign his command rather than see that his orders are disobeyed on this point . . .

[Artigas' food was frugal:] a little roast beef, broth, a meat dish, ordinary bread, and wine served in a cup for want of glasses; four spoons of tinned iron, with no forks or knives but those that each man brought, two or three crockery plates, a pewter dish with the edges broken; for seats three chairs and a hide chest, the rest of the diners having to stand . . . the table covered with a cloth of cotton from the Misiones, but without napkins, and . . . much of this was borrowed.[1]

His visitor, the priest and scientist Larrañaga, was describing his establishment at Paysandú in June 1815. Artigas rose early, and

[1] Larrañaga, *Viaje*, pp. 116-19.

breakfast 'was not tea nor coffee nor milk nor eggs, because there was none of these . . . ; nor was there *mate*, but a *gloriado*, which is a sort of very hot punch made with two beaten-up eggs which were found with difficulty'. A great pot of it was made, and it was passed round from hand to hand, all sucking through the same *bombilla*, the tube used for drinking *mate*. The *Jefe* impressed his visitors with his Spartan life and his activity.

In Paysandú on the 16th of June Artigas opened the talks by presenting to the Argentine commissioners a project for a treaty of peace and friendship between himself and the government of Buenos Aires. It was based on the Instructions of April 1813, and provided for federal autonomy for the Provincia Oriental and the other provinces, with an added guarantee of freedom especially for the provinces of the Federal League. Also, Artigas claimed the return of the arms and munitions stripped from Montevideo at the withdrawal of the *Porteño* troops in February, including the cannon, muskets and swords, nine gun-boats, powder and shot, and the press originally sent by Princess Carlota Joaquina. Money, and tools for farmers, were to be sent as part of the reparations for the destruction caused by the *Porteño* occupation.

The next day Pico and Rivarola presented in their turn a draft treaty recognising the autonomy of the Provincia Oriental, cancelling debts on both sides, giving Corrientes and Santa Fe liberty to choose their own governments, and offering an alliance against the Spaniards. Clearly the two sides were far apart in their desires, except for the vague common wish to present a united front in case of a Spanish attack. Buenos Aires sincerely believed that she owed the Provincia Oriental nothing since she had expelled the Spaniards in 1814 at the expense of much financial and military effort. On the other hand, Artigas equally sincerely believed that Buenos Aires had robbed the Provincia Oriental of all her military resources and ought to restore them. Buenos Aires was attempting merely to skate over the federal question for the sake of present harmony, but that question was not settled and was indeed being left open for some future time when Buenos Aires might be in a stronger position.

Therefore on the 18th of June Artigas broke off the negotiations, since he was convinced that Buenos Aires would never agree to the conditions he offered, which truly guaranteed the security and, he thought, the happiness of the provinces. In a letter to the Supreme Director he showed that he was prepared to accept any reasonable terms himself, in view of the poverty in Buenos Aires caused by the wars, but he could not agree to forego the arms. He realised that the *Porteño* refusal to entertain this clause sprang from distrust of himself and the use to which the arms would be put, and he went on to accuse the present government of being no more liberal than that which had just fallen: 'All the conditions for peace come down to one thing: that *we* on our side shall make war no more.'

But Artigas, or at any rate some of his advisers in the League, did not entirely lose hope of coming to an agreement with Buenos Aires. Even before Alvear's fall, Artigas had thought of calling a congress of deputies of the provinces of his protectorate so as to discuss coming to terms with Buenos Aires and consider means of common defence. At the end of April and in May the invitations were sent out for the provinces to elect deputies and send them to form this Congress at Arroyo de la China. This meeting, sometimes called the *Congreso de Oriente*,[1] came together for the specific purpose of confirming the *Porteño* nominations of Rondeau as Supreme Director and Álvarez Thomas as his substitute, but it provided Artigas with a further opportunity of approaching Buenos Aires with proposals for peace. As Artigas wrote to the Cabildo of Montevideo: 'I am going to take the last steps dictated by reason and prudence for such a worthy object.'[2]

The Congress met on the 29th of June, and heard Artigas' exposition of the failure of the negotiations with Buenos Aires, and

[1] See J. M. Traibel, *El Congreso de Oriente.*
[2] Letter of Artigas to the Cabildo of Montevideo, 28 June 1815, in *Correspondencia de Artigas*, pp. 10-11.

his proposal to send four deputies of the Congress to Buenos Aires with the object of renewing the talks there, on the same bases of peace, with federation. At once the Congress chose the members to go: they were the representatives of Santa Fe and of Córdoba at the *Congreso de Oriente*, Pascual Diez de Andino and José Antonio Cabrera, with Miguel Barreiro to represent the Provincia Oriental, and the Correntino José S. García de Cossío to represent 'the Continent of Entre Ríos'. These deputies were chosen so that all the areas of the Federal League should be represented before the government of Buenos Aires, thus showing the unanimity of the peoples.[1]

The deputation boarded a sloop and sailed at once down the River Uruguay, reaching Buenos Aires on the 11th of July. On the 13th they presented a note of the 'Plan' they bore 'for the re-establishment of concord' to the Supreme Director's substitute, Álvarez Thomas, who submitted it to a special Junta of all the *Porteño* authorities for consideration, even though, as he wrote later, he himself had seen in it very little advance on Artigas' last proposals and was not inclined to accept it. The Plan was short and to the point: a defensive and offensive alliance between the League and Buenos Aires was offered, and most of the arms taken by the *Porteño* troops from the Provincia Oriental were to be returned, some were to be given to the provinces of Santa Fe and Córdoba, and the rest were to be kept as a central deposit in Buenos Aires. The deputies offered to appear before the Junta to explain the proposals. The small advance seen by Alvarez Thomas in the terms was the omission of any reference to monetary claims.

No answer was vouchsafed to the deputies, nor were they invited to explain their mission in any conference. Instead, they received a peremptory order to lodge themselves aboard the Buenos Aires warship *Neptuno*, under Brown's command, under

[1] See the documents on this mission in Pivel Devoto and Fonseca Muñoz, *op. cit.* pp. 253-81; for the deputies chosen see doc. no. 8. The 'Continent of Entre Ríos' included Corrientes and the Misiones besides Entre Ríos.

the specious excuse that this would 'avoid reciprocal embarrassments'. It was obvious that they were being imprisoned, and they demanded their passports but were not given them. The reasons for this extraordinary treatment of envoys, as Álvarez admitted in an insulting letter written to Artigas on the 1st of August, were that it was now known that the Spanish expedition was not coming, and the Director was taking advantage of this to prepare a little expedition of his own to win Santa Fe back to his side. He knew that Artigas' deputies had got wind of this, and therefore had detained them lest they should 'precipitate you into opposing the fulfilment of this measure in the peace which is best for us all'.[1] Álvarez Thomas had shown himself in his true colours, and open war must be the result of his cunning folly.

The mission failed without even an interview taking place, but as a last resort the deputies attempted to make a pact with one single article: 'There will be peace between the territories which are under the command and protection of the *Jefe de los Orientales*, and the Most Excellent Government of Buenos Aires.' But even to this, Buenos Aires replied offering peace, but appointing as the boundary between the two territories the line of the River Paraná; that is, cutting off Córdoba and Santa Fe from the Federal League without more ado.[2] This was unacceptable, of course. The fundamental trouble was always the same: the Federal League saw in the Buenos Aires government merely one more provincial government, whereas the Buenos Aires government considered itself to be the national government, though never elected or even proclaimed by the whole nation.

Finally the deputies were permitted to return to Artigas, bearing yet another letter from Álvarez Thomas preaching his 'principles of moderation', and boasting that he would 'keep all the harmony which may be compatible with the interests and the decorum of the Provinces which I have the honour to command'.[3] There

---

[1] *Ibid.* no. 25.
[2] *Ibid.* nos. 26 and 27.
[3] *Ibid.* no. 29.

could only be from now on war between Artigas and the centralists until one or the other was crushed and subdued.

Artigas thanked the deputies to the *Congreso de Oriente* and sent them home towards the middle of August to report to their provinces on the failure of the mission. There was no other business, for the Congress was not intended to go into legislative matters even though Santa Fe had presented her deputy, Diez de Andino, with instructions which sketched in some detail a federal system for the provinces similar to that envisaged by Artigas.[1] Sante Fe desired 'a perfect federal government' and the 'conservation of the rights of the Peoples', based on Artigas' Instructions of April 1813. Candioti, who never looked into a book, expounded his ideas on the precise amount of sovereign power that the province should think of handing over to the proposed central government: all had at least the federal terminology off by heart.

But at this moment of the climax of Artigas' power, the signs of its decay were present. There were Portuguese troops collecting on the Brazilian frontier, preparing to reopen the attack which had been stayed by Strangford three years before. Artigas pretended to think that these new movements were merely a nervous reaction to the movements of Otorgués covering the Oriental side of the frontier.[2] But more threatening just then was the *Porteño* advance towards Santa Fe. An 'Army of Observation' sent by Álvarez Thomas under the command of Viamonte ostensibly to protect the town from the attacks of wild Indians occupied Santa Fe on the 25th of August 1815, helped by internal dissension. Candioti, the stout federalist caudillo, had been ill for some days and died on the 27th, so that there was no strong figure to rouse an opposition to the *Porteños*. A Governor sympathetic to the centralists, Tarragona, was imposed over the protests of the Cabildo, and the province of Santa Fe was degraded to the rank

[1] *Ibid.* nos. 1–5.
[2] Letter of Artigas to the Cabildo of Montevideo, 8 August 1815, in *Correspondencia de Artigas*, pp. 246–8.

of a 'lieutenancy' of Buenos Aires. War between Artigas and
Buenos Aires had begun again.[1]

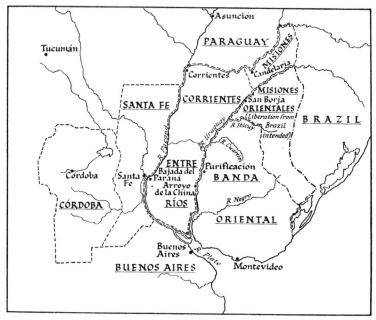

Artigas' *Liga Federal* in 1815

2. THE PROTECTORATE OF ARTIGAS

That society was rough and life at times precarious in the lands of
the Federal League was blamed on Artigas by the *Porteños*. But it
was the breakdown of government due to the pressure of external
and internal wars and the instability of the various régimes in
Buenos Aires which caused the normally unpolished life of remote
provinces to take on this element of insecurity from 1814 onwards.
Indians from the wild Chaco invaded the Santa Fe ranches, carry-
off cattle and women, and bands of outlaws made all travel
perilous.[2] This happened not because Artigas formed the Federal
League, but because there were no troops to spare for internal

[1] Junta de Historia y Numismática Americana, *op. cit.* pp. 28-9.

[2] Junta de Historia y Numismática Americana, *op. cit.* p. 26; also J. P. and W. P.
Robertson, *Letters on Paraguay*, vol. III, 66-7.

order. Artigas' own record of policing the interior of the Banda Oriental would be enough without further proof to show that this state of affairs existed against his will.

The Robertsons, who became involved in this disorder, blamed it on the caudillos under Artigas, who were insubordinate and uncouth, in their estimation. But the Scots merchants were biased against the Protector and his lieutenants since they themselves were friends of the *Porteño* clique, particularly of Posadas and Alvear, who had permitted them to undertake their considerable enterprises. The Robertsons repeat all the *Porteño* gibes about Artigas' complete ignorance and his turbulence, and in this way they helped to spread the view commonly held of Artigas in the nineteenth century. Yet they were honest enough to trust their own observations, and reported faithfully his sagacity, daring, popularity and his strictness.[1]

Just before Santa Fe joined the Federal League, W. P. Robertson was in the town and listened to the centralist gossip about the state of things across the River Paraná in Entre Ríos and the Provincia Oriental. 'The most frightful disorder and anarchy prevailed;' he reported, 'the name of Artigueño, in fact, was held to be equivalent to that of robber as well as of murderer.'[2] But he might have thought that his amiable and distinguished friend Candioti would not have joined such a band, as he was in fact plotting to do at this very time. He did see that the *Santafecinos* favoured Artigas, though he never really understood the principles behind the League, since he had little idea of the local politics, and in fact he blamed Santa Fe's adherence to federalism merely on the insolent manner of the *Porteño* officers of the garrison, who treated the provincials as inferiors.[3]

Robertson noted three facts, however, which help to explain Santa Fe's defection to the federal camp and the state of poverty

---

[1] *Ibid.* vol. ɪɪ, pp. 178–83 and vol. ɪɪɪ, pp. 66–7.
[2] *Ibid.* vol. ɪɪ, pp. 189.
[3] *Ibid.* vol. ɪɪ, p. 193.

into which the region appeared to fall as soon as Artigas took on the Protectorate.[1] The first was that Santa Fe's extensive trade in mules to Peru and her carrying trade to Paraguay were cut off, since Entre Ríos and the Provincia Oriental were the breeding grounds for the animals, and they were subject to Artigas; whilst Peru and Paraguay at that period were cut off by the accidents of war and politics. Therefore Santa Fe's prosperity, and especially that of Candioti, were ruined, and the best hope of even a partial recovery lay in joining the Federal League and regaining the supply of mules. Secondly, the ravages of the Chaco Indians were severe and could not be checked by force because there was none. The raids were so destructive that, it will be recalled, the pretext under which Álvarez Thomas was allowed to recapture Sante Fa in August from the federalists was that he intended to send an army to repress these Indians. The people of Santa Fe were desperate enough to fall into the trap. The third factor was the arrival of a plague of locusts at the same critical time, so that the region was stripped bare. A drought, added to the other calamities, destroyed many herds, with the result that there was nearly a famine in that land of plenty. No wonder the land looked ravaged under the Federal League, and no wonder there were bands of un-ruly gauchos turned bandits marauding in the province for a living.

At Corrientes, which was in the hands of the 'Artigueños', and which he entered by stealth and in fear, Robertson found that all was peace and quiet. There were no sentries posted, even at night, on the outskirts of the town.[2] His friends there laughed heartily at his fears and assured him that all was quiet in Artigas' hands, and that trade along the River Paraná was perfectly safe, although in remote country districts some federal troops were as bad as bandits. The federal Governor, Méndez, was most courteous and respectable, to Robertson's patent surprise.[3] The soldiery, even in

---

[1] *Ibid.* vol. II, pp. 194-8.

[2] *Ibid.* vol. II, p. 232.

[3] *Ibid.* vol. II, pp. 235-7.

the country, though rough and fierce-looking, respected Artigas' authority and aided Robertson in his journeyings. 'Their beards were black and bushy; their hair hung thick and matted from under old foraging-caps; and their small, dark eyes scowled from beneath very shaggy eyebrows. Their blue jackets, with red facings, were all the worse for wear; their shirts (which apparently had never been washed) were open at the collars, and showed each a rugged and bronzed neck beneath. Tawdry waistcoats, – a sort of kilt, called a chiripà – ample drawers under this, and botas de potro, from the feet of which their bare toes protruded, – completed their attire. Each carried a carbine in his hand, and each had a long knife stuck in his girdle; while his sabre kept dangling and clattering by his side.'[1]

The fact was that the whole Plate region was in a state of civil discord, and the Robertsons failed to allow for this, trusting in their status as British subjects to get them out of any trouble into which they might thrust themselves. Theirs was a typical attitude: that they were superior to the petty squabbles of the people among whom they travelled, traded and made their fortunes. They failed to understand that Artigas was attempting to weaken the *Porteños* by cutting off their trade, and this nearly brought J. P. Robertson to an untimely and unpleasant death. He insisted on taking a mixed cargo, including rifles and munitions specially desired by Francia, the dictator of Paraguay, from Buenos Aires up the rivers to Asunción, through the middle of Artigas' Protectorate, although not exactly in time of bitter conflict. Inevitably, he ran into trouble.[2]

Robertson had taken the precaution of procuring a passport from his friend Alvear, then Supreme Director, and Herrera, the Secretary of State, and nothing could have been more calculated to infuriate the federalists. Captain Percy, the officer in command of the British naval squadron stationed in the River Plate to protect British commerce, had given him a sailing licence. But at Santa

[1] *Ibid.* vol. II, pp. 241-2.
[2] *Ibid.* vol. III, pp. 66-94.

Fe Robertson's friend Candioti played the gentle pirate and with many apologies relieved him of his firearms, giving in return full recompense and a letter of explanation to the tyrannous Francia. Candioti needed the arms to beat back the Indians and to prepare to fight the threatening *Porteños*, and necessity knows no law.

Robertson sailed on under Candioti's licence, but fell into a trap prepared by Hereñú, the caudillo of Entre Ríos, who had also heard of the shipment of arms. The Scot was badly manhandled and his life was saved only by the intervention of an Indian soldier who took a fancy to him. His ship and cargo were seized, his personal effects appropriated by the drunken sergeant and men who had ambushed him, and he was finally taken to Paraná to await Hereñú's pleasure. On the voyage he was forced to play his flute to the gang who, dressed partly as gauchos and partly as Bond Street dandies in Robertson's clothes, drank his wine and danced on the deck.

At Paraná Robertson was gaoled, as decently as that rough country permitted, but he managed to smuggle a message down the river to Captain Percy begging for help. Percy sent a tough lieutenant to Artigas at Paysandú bearing a peremptory demand for Robertson's release and the restoration of his goods, and Artigas, who had heard of the matter only twelve hours before from Hereñú, sent an angry order to the latter to do as Percy asked. Percy had already sent a similar message to Hereñú, who realised that he had overstepped the mark and freed Robertson and his ship and restored what could be collected of his goods.

This incident shows that Artigas was not always responsible for the actions of his lieutenants, but that he was obeyed and feared when he gave orders. It also proves that Artigas was anxious to keep on goods terms with the British, for the sake of their commerce, which was important to his Protectorate, and possibly through awe of the threat of British displeasure represented by Percy's action. But it certainly also proves Robertson's foolhardiness.

There were two sequels to this event: the Robertsons were ordered out of Paraguay for ever by Francia when he heard of the loss of the rifles meant for him. Perhaps the Scotsmen were safer out of the power of that maniac; and in any case they found that they were able to do good business under Artigas in the Littoral. This was the second sequel. Artigas did his best to encourage foreign trade, and favoured these brothers, whose energy promised much.

Besides his own effects and some finery for Francia which the soldiers stole, J. P. Robertson lost to Hereñú a consignment of uniforms and sabres to the value of about £1,200. The troops were always in need of clothing and arms, and the treasury was always poor, so there was nothing extraordinary in this. In the Provincia Oriental in 1818 the soldiers then opposing the Portuguese only possessed a *chiripá*, and wore their equipment over their bare skin.[1] Robertson decided to go himself and protest to Artigas at his headquarters at Purificación, and it is to this chance that we owe a description of the *Jefe*, his usual headquarters and his surroundings at the height of his power.[2]

Armed with letters from Captain Percy, Robertson sailed up the River Uruguay to see Artigas. The site of Purificación is splendid, since it stands on a high bluff, called now the Meseta de Artigas, among rolling grassland on the eastern bank of the river. From the turf, dotted with low shrubs and enlivened by coveys of partridge, there is a fine view over the river, nearly a mile broad here, and westward over the flat, fertile plain of Entre Ríos to a distant horizon. Now there are the remains of a hut built of turf, and the uncertain lines of protective trenches, filled in and grassed over, to remind the visitor of Artigas' power and the hard life he and his men led there, remote from any town, but in the centre of vast lands of which he was the Protector.

Here, Robertson saw 'the most excellent Protector of half of the

---

[1] *Ibid.* vol. III, p. 98. See Arce, *La formación de la Liga Federal*, p. 96, quoting from the *Memorias* of Colonel Ramón Cáceres.

[2] J. P. and W. P. Robertson, *Letters on Paraguay*, vol. III, pp. 101-10.

New World, seated on a bullock's skull, at a fire kindled on the mud floor of his hut, eating beef off a spit, and drinking gin out of a cow-horn! He was surrounded by a dozen officers in weather-beaten attire, in similar positions, and similarly occupied with their chief. All were smoking, all gabbling. The Protector was dictating to two secretaries, who occupied, at one deal table, the only two dilapidated rush-bottom chairs in the hovel.' As Robertson wrote, it was just like his prison at Paraná, except that here there were no chains. The floor was littered with envelopes addressed to the Protector from all corners of his lands, and from as far as fifteen hundred miles away. Couriers dashed up on steaming horses every half hour and others galloped away again. 'Soldiers, aides-de-camp, scouts, came galloping in from all quarters. All was referred to "HIS EXCELLENCY THE PROTECTOR"; and His Excellency the Protector, seated on his bullock's skull, smoking, eating, drinking, dictating, talking, despatched in succession the various matters brought under his notice, with that calm, deliberate, but unintermitted nonchalance, which brought most practically home to me the truth of the axiom, "Stop a little, that we may get on faster". I believe if the business of the world had been on his shoulders he would have proceeded in no different manner. He seemed a man incapable of bustle, and was, in this single respect (if I may be permitted the allusion), like the greatest commander of the age.' By that Robertson meant Wellington, a very great compliment indeed.

Artigas surprised Robertson in his prejudice by receiving him with cordiality and more: with 'comparatively gentlemanlike manners, and really good breeding'. He joked about the discomfort of his headquarters, made Robertson sit on a bed and gave him meat, drink and a cigar. Robertson joined in the conversation and Artigas went on with his dictation, 'getting through a world of business, at the very time that he was condoling with me on my treatment at the Bajada [del Paraná], condemning the authors of it, and telling me how instantaneously, on the receipt of Captain

Percy's just remonstrance, he had given orders for my liberation'.

Everything was happening at once all the time in that single room, one long meal, chatter and continuous letter-writing. Towards evening Artigas took Robertson on an inspection of the camp. All the officers and men, including the Protector, had their horses ready saddled and bridled next to their huts, so that an advance or retreat could be started at once, 'at the rate of twelve miles an hour'. Seventy-five miles' forced march in a night was nothing to them, and this mobility was probably the federalists' best weapon. All the staff, about twenty in number, rode with Artigas, using no formality, but laughing, joking, shouting and using Christian names except to Artigas, whom they called, with evident respect and affection, 'mi General'.

There were about fifteen hundred troops in the camp, mostly Indians from the Eastern Misiones, and very tough cavalrymen. They were scantily clad, wanted only pasture for the horses and beef for themselves, and camped in rows of huts made of mud and hides. About a dozen better cottages stood about the camp.

Robertson now took the opportunity of asking for compensation for his property, and Artigas, who had obviously been showing him everything so as to impress him with his lack of resources, opened a chest and pointed to three hundred pesos in the bottom of it, explaining that this was his whole treasury, and that the compensation required, six thousand pesos, was as impossible to find as might be six hundred thousand. The Scot had no answer. He had seen and understood enough to realise that to press his claim was useless, and so he desisted. Instead of direct compensation, he obtained a useful licence to trade in Corrientes, which soon repaid his loss. He left thinking that he had at least retrieved something by his boldness; and doubtless Artigas was pleased because he had paid back nothing and had ensured that one of the things he most wanted, foreign trade, entered his Protectorate to bring with it prosperity and revenue.

Before leaving the subject of Artigas at Purificación, there is one more observation to make: Robertson gives no indication at all of having seen anything of cruelty, imprisonments, *enchalecamientos* (sewing up prisoners in a fresh bull's skin so that they were squeezed to death as it dried) and other tortures described by the *Porteños*. He can have seen nothing untoward, because if he had he would certainly have described it at his usual length, writing as he did with some prejudice against the federalists and safely back in Britain over thirty years afterwards.

Commercial development in the Federal League was allowed under the same general rules as in the Provincia Oriental. In May 1815 Artigas threw open the ports of the Protectorate along the rivers.[1] The Robertsons were inveigled into establishing their business at Corrientes, but unfortunately their bad impression of the federalists was reinforced there because they arrived just at the time of the revolt against Artigas inspired by the traitor Perugorría, and witnessed the federal reaction to it. Indeed, the federal cavalry which restored Artigas' protection of Corrientes impressed the populace with its errors by pillaging the town; although J. P. Robertson, who was there, was safe enough because he had Artigas' passport, and the federal Governor, Méndez, gave him a guard for his goods.[2]

Once order had been restored the cavalry were withdrawn, and business picked up again under the care of the Robertsons. They later prided themselves on having introduced the common use of money in commerce in Corrientes, in place of the traditional bartering of goods,[3] though it is likely that the shortage of cash had been rendered acute by the revolutionary wars which cut the Plate region off from the source of its silver, Peru. Corrientes normally exported the local products; hides, wool, and some cotton, sugar and timber to the value of about five hundred thousand pesos a year in time of peace, but during the civil wars

[1] *Borrador* of the government of Montevideo to the Administrador de Aduana, 26 May 1815, Arch. Adm., caja 461; 4.

[2] J. P. and W. P. Robertson, *Letters on Paraguay*, vol. III, pp. 136-9.

[3] J. P. and W. P. Robertson, *Letters on South America*, vol. I, pp. 51-4.

this trade had dropped off almost to nothing. The Robertsons blamed Artigas for this, but of course it could be argued that the *Porteños* were equally to blame, without assessing the effect on trade of the war against the royalists and the Portuguese threat. The estancias were denuded of cattle and men, and the whole country was a prey to Indians, bandits, vultures and wild dogs.[1]

The Robertsons naturally feared for their lives and property amidst this turmoil, and trusted at first to Artigas' licence and to occasional bribery with money and bottled porter to free them from the attentions of brigands, whom they named 'Artigueños'. Their worries were ended by the help of one of the lesser federalist leaders, a fierce, raw-boned, red-haired gaucho called Campbell: the Gaucho Pedro Campbell, an Irish deserter from Beresford's force during the English Invasions, who was more feared than any native gaucho, and was respected next to Artigas himself.[2] Campbell punctiliously administered what would now be called a 'protection racket' for the Robertson's benefit. His power was great, since he was an intimate of Artigas, the commander of a river squadron, as well as a great fighter; and so he was able to look after the Robertsons' business interests in that wild country for the year they stayed there, for the modest sum of twelve hundred pesos. He organised safe wagon-trains, using federal troops to drive and protect them.[3]

Smuggling was rife, although the Robertsons do not admit to having taken part in it. One local ship-owner, at least, used large quantities of that rare delicacy, porter, in winning the connivance of the officials, from the governor down. Stout, wine, stockings for the ladies, and other gifts eased the path for many a trader, and the treasury suffered considerable loss even though the people were more prosperous than before.[4]

The Robertsons' activities greatly helped to restore trade and

[1] *Ibid.* vol. I, pp. 22–6.
[2] *Ibid.* vol. I, pp. 27–30.
[3] *Ibid,* vol. I, pp. 59–67.
[4] *Ibid.* vol. I, pp. 105–10.

industry in the province. They used the accepted system of extending credits (*habilitaciones*) of money and goods to estancieros on the understanding that they would be repaid in hides and other local produce in due course. But they were successful in operating this risky system because they reversed the usual practice, and charged only low rates of interest on their advances, and therefore they got a large number of estancieros interested; and secondly they had the powerful assistance of Campbell in collecting the produce, and even in accompanying timid estancieros from the town to their deserted estancias, putting these into order again, and helping to get the hides ready for shipment. Artigas had not been mistaken in putting the trade into the hands of two Scotsmen and allowing his Irish lieutenant to support them. Campbell encouraged the cowboys to return to their jobs, and even policed the district efficiently, breaking up with his own knife dangerous fights in *pulperías*. In this way the province became active again, and long wagon-trains brought the produce in peace from the estancias to the Robertsons' warehouses.[1] Their success was such that the Robertsons exported over fifty thousand cow-hides and other things in proportion in one year.

Yet because these operations were so large, and because the Robertsons gave such favourable terms, the many small local merchants found themselves losing business, and protested bitterly. This was, of course, the case foreseen by Artigas with his regulations forbidding the entry of foreigners into the interior trade of the Provincia Oriental and the League.[2] The feeling ran so high that at one stage W. P. Robertson was on the point of being shipped off to Purificación as an *europeo*:[3] a deliberate mistake on the part of the mayor, since although it was true that *europeos* were to be concentrated, it was normal to use the word in the sense of European Spaniards, as opposed to American Spaniards. Other Europeans were simply foreigners.

[1] *Ibid.* vol. I, pp. 174-98.
[2] *Ibid.* vol. I, pp. 282-7.
[3] *Ibid.* vol. III, pp. 78-88.

However, by the end of 1816 the province's treasury was so flourishing that from bankruptcy in mid-1815 it had risen to show a surplus of £6,000, which, with Artigas' encouragement, the governor of Corrientes, Méndez, expended on arms and munitions with which to fight the Portuguese invaders of the Provincia Oriental. The firm of Robertsons provided the articles, and the government of Buenos Aires gave the necessary licence for their passage up the rivers.[1]

Artigas desired to attract British commerce above all, so that in 1817 it was natural for him to make an agreement regulating this trade with the commander of the British naval squadron, at that time Captain William Bowles. Since 1815 the British had known that they were welcome in the Protectorate, and now the matter was to be put on an official footing and the commerce itself intensified.[2] In July Artigas invited Bowles to send an officer to Purificación for this purpose, and accordingly Lieutenant Edward Frankland was sent, and a convention was signed by him and Artigas on the 2nd of August 1817. Under it, the ports of the Provincia Oriental were opened to British commerce on certain conditions and with certain advantages over other foreign traders. Artigas promised to protect in all his ports legitimate British merchants in possession of the British commander's passport, whilst the merchants were to pay all the legal import and export duties, but were not to pay any extraordinary tax, such as a forced loan. The British could only trade in the ports, and not in the interior, and they must not be given passports into Artigas' ports if they had been trading with his enemies, who were at that time Portugal, Spain and Brazil. The import duty was not light at twenty-five and a half per cent., and the export duty was in proportion, but this was not excessive for that time and place. Bowles himself and Staples, the British Consul in the Plate region, ratified

[1] *Ibid.* vol. III, pp. 70-8.

[2] See the documents in Pivel Devoto and Fonseca Muñoz, *op. cit.*, pp. 359-70, the majority of which are copies of originals existing in the P.R.O., Admiralty and Foreign Office archives. Copy of the convention in Webster, *op. cit.* doc. no. 70a.

this document with no qualms, presumably because they held that it only had a local significance, and did not realise that it was tantamount to a British recognition of the existence *de facto* of Artigas' government: a recognition which was not granted by Britain to any of Spain's former colonies until the next decade. Consequently, although Artigas circularised his ports on the 19th of September with the new regulations, the British Government learned with surprise of the convention and refused to authorise it;[1] but the commerce continued nevertheless, with all the ports of the Protectorate, and from it those lands drew revenue as well as supplies, both needed during the new campaigns which began in 1816.

[1] Letter of Castlereagh to Chamberlain, 22 January 1818, doc. no. 70 in Webster, *op. cit.* Webster notes that the despatch was signed and filed, but apparently never sent. However, the British Government gave no official approval to the convention.

CHAPTER VIII

CATASTROPHE

I. THE BACKGROUND TO THE PORTUGUESE INVASION
OF 1816

ÁLVAREZ THOMAS attempted to break up the Federal League by sending the 'Army of Observation' into Santa Fe in August 1815 and launching an attack from there on Hereñú in Entre Ríos in November.[1] Viamonte, whose troops garrisoned Santa Fe, was 'a blunt and honest soldier, but a great disciplinarian, who had long ruled the inhabitants rather despotically, [and] was anything but a forbearing sub-delegate from the metropolis.'[2] Therefore it is not surprising that Álvarez's attempt met only temporary success. On the 31st of March 1816 the advance of a relieving army commanded by José Francisco Rodríguez, sent from Entre Ríos by Artigas, coincided with the rising of the local caudillos Estanislao López and Mariano Vera, and Viamonte was forced to surrender Santa Fe once again to the federalists.[3]

In November 1815, also, the *Porteño* forces had met a severe defeat at the hands of the royalists at Sipe Sipe in Peru, and had been forced to retreat into the northern part of the United Provinces. The losses of arms and equipment and the need to form a new force with which to stem the royalist advance compelled the government to take harsh measures, such as imposing a forced loan, and to act in an arbitrary manner even worse than its previous high-handedness.[4] In the provinces near at hand dislike for

[1] Junta de Historia y Numismática Americana, *op. cit.* pp. 29-30.
[2] J. P. and W. P. Robertson, *Letters on South America*, vol. II, pp. 247-8.
[3] Junta de Historia y Numismática Americana, *op. cit.* pp. 38-46.
[4] J. P. and W. P. Robertson, *Letters on South America*, vol. II, pp. 238-45. Before Sipe Sipe one citizen fled from Buenos Aires to Montevideo, 'del despotismo mas absoluto, dela arbitrariedad mas remarcable, y delas injurias mas notorias, que marcaron las paginas dela Revolucion dela America del Sud.' Reply of Dr Vidal, in a letter of Zufriátegui to the *Cabildo Gobernador*, 7 September 1815, Arch. Adm., libro 199, ff. 105-106.

279

the *Porteño* rule increased, while others disregarded the capital as far as possible: in the north, Güemes, a local caudillo, led the men of the province of Salta in a guerilla war against the invading royalists, while in the west, Cuyo looked to San Martín for leadership.

General Belgrano was sent with a fresh army from Buenos Aires in an attempt to save Santa Fe for the centralists, but he halted his advance in April and came to terms with the victorious federalists. He sent Díaz Vélez as his agent, and the latter on the 9th of April signed the Pact of Santo Tomé with the Oriental commander Rodríguez. This was a cunning arrangement that Díaz Vélez would force Belgrano to resign his command and take over himself and that then Santa Fe and the Orientals would help Díaz Vélez to overthrow Álvarez Thomas in Buenos Aires. The first part of the plan was carried out by a *pronunciamiento* (a 'pronouncement' of aims, therefore a revolutionary uprising) at Rosario on the 11th of April, upon which Díaz Vélez duly issued a threat against Álvarez Thomas and praised the spirit of the *santafecinos* and the Orientals. As a result Álvarez resigned and was replaced as interim Director by Antonio González Balcarce, who was in favour of sending a mission to make a definite peace with the federalist provinces; but Balcarce was himself replaced on the 3rd of May, with the election of Juan Martín de Pueyrredón as Supreme Director by the national Congress which had now met at Tucumán, hundreds of miles away in the interior.

In Santa Fe, the local leader Vera was elected governor by a majority despite the disapproval of Artigas' representative. Nevertheless, Vera was allowed to take charge. He was a federalist, but one more interested in provincial autonomy than in co-operation within the Federal League, and therefore he favoured the proposals of a mission sent from Buenos Aires to make peace, as had been provided in the Pact of Santo Tomé. The result was that the so-called Treaties of May, signed on the 28th of May 1816 between Santa Fe and the *Porteños*, stipulated the province's independence but also arranged for her deputies to enter the Congress at Tucumán. However, the Treaties were not ratified, and an assembly in Santa Fe decided on the 10th of June to pass the *Porteño* envoys on to Artigas for a fresh treaty to be made, more in accordance with his ideas. The envoys preferred to return to Buenos Aires, and so another attempt to split Santa Fe from the Federal League failed. But it was ominous that Córdoba, the most far-flung of the federalist provinces, weakened and sent deputies to the Congress of Tucumán.

Pueyrredón, a great centralist, followed the same line of attempting to split off Santa Fe when he took over the government, and indeed he seized the city in August 1816 only to be compelled to relinquish it at the end of that month since the *Porteño* troops were besieged there and could obtain no provisions. In October Pueyrredón tried by sending envoys to win Santa Fe over peacefully, but again he was rebuffed, and was told that the province would make no settlement unless Artigas were a party. After this the centralists' efforts eased off for a time, since two things occupied the Directory's attention. The first was the imminent departure of San Martín from Mendoza with his expedition to free Chile from Spanish rule; and the second was the invasion of the Provincia Oriental by Portuguese troops led by General Lecór. Both events were products of *Porteño* policy: both were expected by the Buenos Aires government to free Argentina from the threats of troublesome neighbours. Pueyrredón would return to the attack on the federalist provinces once Artigas was fully committed in the Provincia Oriental and San Martín was safely ensconced in a liberated Chile.

The extent of the encouragement given by the *Porteño* leaders from Alvear onwards to a projected Portuguese invasion of the Provincia Oriental is still a matter for conjecture because of the secret nature of any negotiations which took place. At the least, however, there was connivance at this seizure of a part of the old Spanish Viceroyalty, and there are some indications that it was more. In any case, even a refusal to help Artigas to repel the invaders was a form of treachery in the *Porteños*, however incensed they might have been at Artigas' attitude towards the question of national organisation. From 1813 various missions had been sent from Buenos Aires, first to Rio de Janeiro to confer with the Portuguese government and Strangford, and then on to Europe to seek some method of coming to an agreement with Spain, or of gaining peace under some powerful foreign protection. Indeed, Buenos Aires offered a crown in South America to some unlikely European princes between 1814 and 1819.[1] Alvear in January 1815 sent Manuel José García as his special envoy, with orders to make what arrangements he could with Strangford and the Portuguese Court; and although the negotiations came to nothing, they prepared the way for fresh offers presented to the Portuguese by García later in the year. It had by then become clear that Britain would not abandon her position of neutrality friendly to all sides.

Therefore in November 1815 the interim Director Álvarez Thomas made García his plenipotentiary at the Court in Rio de Janeiro. It is possible that García may already, in conversation the previous January, have sounded the Portuguese on the subject of proclaiming the Prince Regent of Portugal Emperor of America, with possession of the Banda Oriental and dominion over Buenos Aires.[2] Then Herrera, the Montevidean who worked for the Buenos Aires government, an enemy of Artigas and a monarchist *faute de mieux*, like the others in the capital, fell from favour when Alvear was deposed, and went into exile in Rio de Janeiro. There he too encouraged the Portuguese government in its designs on the Provincia Oriental. García, who was a subtle diplomatist but without the determination to persevere for liberty, served Portuguese policy faithfully in the belief that he was saving his

[1] E. Ravignani (ed.), *Comisión de Bernardino Rivadavia ante España y otras potencias de Europa, 1814-20;* J. Street, *La influencia británica en la independencia,* chap. III, pp. 62-80, in *Revista Histórica,* Montevideo, t. XXII, 1954.
[2] P. Blanco Acevedo, *El federalismo de Artigas,* p. 99.

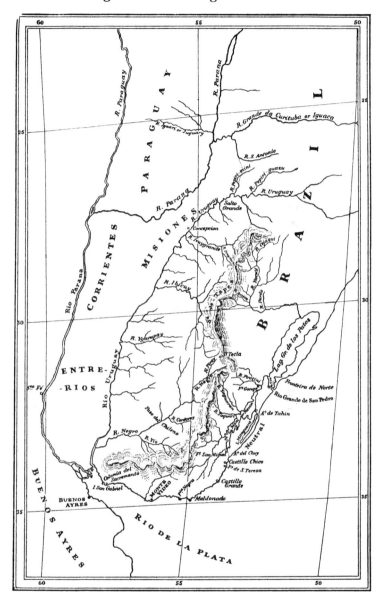

The Banda Oriental about 1825
(From Foreign Office Memorandum, February 1826, in P.R.O., F.O. 97/76)

country from anarchy or from reconquest by Spain.[1] Alvear himself had expressed to Britain in March 1815 his willingness to buy safety from Spain by putting any part of the Provinces into the hands of the Portuguese,[2] and García subscribed to the same idea, as it seems likely did others of the ruling clique.

The Prince Regent of Portugal, Dom João, and his government were as willing to stretch the frontiers of Brazil to the River Plate in 1815 as they had been in 1812, when Strangford had stopped them. Now their desires were supported by force, since the termination of the war in Europe left them with thirty thousand Portuguese troops unoccupied; and their appetite was sharpened since at the end of that war they had been forced to restore French Guiana, which had been seized as an act of revenge against France. Furthermore, Strangford returned to England early in 1815, leaving only a chargé d'affaires, Chamberlain, to look after Britain's interests in Rio de Janeiro and in the whole of South America, since no representatives were accredited to the insurgent colonies of Spain. At the same time the British influence over the Portuguese government faded when Portugal had been restored to the Prince Regent after the liberation of the Peninsula from the French invaders. No longer was British protection essential to the Portuguese Court, and Dom João felt free to act in the Plate region whenever an occasion should present itself.[3]

An excuse was at hand in the threat which the Portuguese pretended was represented by Artigas to the tranquillity of the provinces of Brazil nearest to his territory. The Portuguese claimed that they feared incursions by Otorgués into Rio Grande do Sul, although in fact it was the Brazilians who had pushed over the frontier into the Banda Oriental. There was more truth in the claim that since 1814 Artigas had occupied and 'liberated' those parts of the Eastern Misiones which he believed should belong to

---

[1] Mitre, *Historia de Belgrano*, chap. XXXIV.

[2] Letter of Staples to Castlereagh, 24 March 1815, P.R.O., F.O. 72/178.

[3] R. de Mendonça, *História da política exterior do Brasil*, pp. 81-94; M. de Oliveira Lima, *Dom João VI no Brasil 1808-1821*, vol. II, pp. 605-52.

the Provincia Oriental, and which had been handed over to the Portuguese in 1750 in exchange for Colonia. Therefore early in 1815 the Portuguese government arranged for the transfer from Portugal to Brazil of a part of the veteran army, under the command of Lieutenant-general Carlos Frederico Lecór. A division of crack troops, consisting of four battalions of light infantry, six squadrons of cavalry and two parks of artillery, a total of five thousand men, was sent from the mother country, and troops which could be spared from the other Brazilian provinces were concentrated in Rio Grande do Sul.[1] The British Government was warned of these movements in May 1815, and was told that they were deemed necessary to keep the frontier safe and to observe the actions of the Spanish expedition which was being prepared to be sent out to the River Plate. In November the first transports arrived in Brazil, and the troops were sent to Rio Grande to join the ten thousand men already there.[2]

Chamberlain watched the warlike preparations with frustration and anxiety, reporting to his Government that it was clear from his sources of information that the forces being concentrated were meant not for security but for an attack to win for Brazil her 'natural boundaries' of the river system in the south. He saw the last batch of troops arrive from Portugal on the 30th of March 1816, and go immediately to Rio Grande do Sul. He saw extensive naval preparations being made, and in May protested to the government in Rio de Janeiro that all these things must mean hostilities against the United Provinces.

The reply he received from the Portuguese ministry gave a hint of connivance with the Buenos Aires government. The Minister of State, Aguiar, urbanely informed Chamberlain that no attack on the territory governed by Buenos Aires was intended, but only on

---

[1] Rocha Pombo, *História do Brasil*, vol. III, pp. 346-7.

[2] Foreign Office Memorandum, February 1826, of what has passed respecting Monte Video, from the Period of its first occupation by the Portuguese in 1811, to that of its incorporation with the Brazilian Empire in 1824, with Extracts from the Treaties referred to, and a Map of the Territory in Dispute, P.R.O., F.O. 97/76. See map, p. 283.

Artigas' domain. Artigas, he wrote, was an enemy of Buenos Aires and a disagreeable neighbour to Brazil, and therefore the Portuguese intended to 'pacify' him. Chamberlain pointed out that he had heard nothing of the alleged attacks and depredations of Artigas on Portuguese territory and property, and he therefore made a formal protest against any Portuguese aggression against the provinces of the Plate. It was unavailing. The Portuguese fleet sailed from Rio de Janeiro for the south in June and landed troops at St Catharine's Bay, whence an attack was to be made on the Provincia Oriental.

On the 20th of July Chamberlain reported to London the death sentence of the *Patria Vieja*. He had learned that the government of Buenos Aires had lost all hope of defending the liberty of the United Provinces, and had secretly negotiated to hand over the whole territory to Portugal, to avoid what seemed an inevitable defeat by Spain, and to gain peace and trade at any price. This was to be the beginning of the 'Empire of South America'. Nicolás Herrera himself had accompanied Lecór to the south as his secretary, presumably to help in the government of the province to be conquered. Chamberlain had the evidence to support this fantastic story: he sent Castlereagh the details of the negotiations between García and the Portuguese which had taken place since 1815, and with increased intensity since March 1816; and he forwarded certain intercepted correspondence of García's about the secret understanding, including a draft treaty whereby Buenos Aires accepted Portuguese sovereignty and arranged for joint action with the Portuguese to suppress 'the dissatisfied', that is, Artigas and the federalists. In fact, as Chamberlain reported in August, the Portuguese had cleverly avoided signing this or any treaty with Buenos Aires, but, without committing themselves to any conditions, they 'were taking advantage of the offers made by the latter', so as to invade the Provincia Oriental. Portuguese governors for Maldonado, Montevideo and Colonia had already been appointed, and were merely awaiting the expected quick victory to convert the *Patria Vieja* into a Brazilian province.[1] It seemed that everyone knew about the secret understanding but Artigas. Many men in the United Provinces who were not federalists were patriotic enough to condemn the agreement, and their opposition made the Directory's rule uncomfortable from the middle of 1816 until its fall in 1820; and that fall was brought about in part by the efforts of men sickened by the cynical treachery of the régime.[2] Pueyrredón himself, who was Supreme Director from 1816 to 1819, was not responsible for the initiation of the policy which led to the agreement with the Portuguese Court; indeed he probably only heard of it from the Minister of Foreign Affairs in Buenos Aires, Tagle, in August 1816, when he arrived from Tucumán to take up the reins of government, and that month the Portuguese attack was launched. Tagle knew of and supported García's scheme,[3] but the details appear to be mainly García's own. Pueyrredón was naturally perplexed, played for time, and soon lost the confidence of many of his own people when the Portuguese invaded the Provincia Oriental without his taking any action. The Congress of Tucumán only added to the confusion by issuing the Declaration of Independence of the United Provinces on the 9th of July. A few days later the agreement with the Portuguese came to the Congress's notice, and it began discussing it in secret sessions.[4]

At first surprised and somewhat shocked, the Congress soon recovered itself and began to play the double game as well as García himself, so that on the 28th of August it advised the

[1] *Ibid.* where all the relevant documents are summarised. The documents in full are in P.R.O., F.O. 63, e.g. Letters of Chamberlain to Castlereagh, 22 May, 22 June, 20 July, separate 20 July and secret, 31 July 1816, 63/193.

[2] *Resumen de los sucesos mas notables que han preparado la revolucion de la America meridional . . . hasta 1820*, MS. *cit.*, AGN, Montevideo, Fondo ex-Archivo y Museo Histórico Nacional, Archivo Magariños, caja 178.

[3] Mitre, *Historia de Belgrano, loc. cit.*

[4] See *Actas secretas del Soberano Congreso de las Provincias Unidas en Sud América, de 1816-1819*, in Ravignani, *Asambleas Constituyentes*, t. I, pp. 481-582, especially sessions of 19, 23, 24 July, 25, 27, 28, 29 August, 4 September, 19, 23, 24, 25, 27 October, 3, 17, 23, 24 December 1816.

Supreme Director to send a secret agent, as García had suggested, to consult with the invading General Lecór, but at the same time to put the country into a state of defence. Artigas should be given some aid, 'without taking any risk or compromising the success of the negotiation'. In other words, for the sake of external appearances Buenos Aires was to give a minimum of support to Artigas, while at the same time arrangements were to be made with the Portuguese for them to occupy the Provincia Oriental. The Congress even appointed two envoys to be sent to Lecór and work in conjunction with Herrera: one envoy was given secret instructions to negotiate on the basis of 'the liberty and independence of the provinces represented in this Congress'; therefore it was implied that the Federal League was left for the Portuguese to do as they liked with, although in fact it was later made clear that only the Provincia Oriental was to be sacrificed. The military success and state of good order of the United Provinces were to be stressed so as to discourage the Portuguese from advancing too far; and the envoy must describe the desire for a constitutional monarchy on the English model which had been expressed by the government, the Congress and most respectable citizens. This was held to be a form of government which would ensure tranquillity and 'draw closer [the country's] relations and interests to those of Brazil, up to the point of identifying them in the best possible form'. Therefore Dom João was invited to declare himself the protector of the United Provinces and to 're-establish the House of the Incas' there, uniting it by marriage to the Braganzas; but actual submission to Portugal was out of the question. A prince of the House of Braganza, or another prince related by marriage, might be acceptable as a last resort, but in any case, never a Spanish prince. These ideas merely reflect the desperation of those days, however ridiculous they appear now.

The second envoy was issued with most secret instructions to spy on Herrera and the Portuguese forces and their progress in the campaign, and to gain more information by any means about

García, who was regarded as a little extreme even by the Congress. If the Portuguese would accept none of the choices of government offered them, the second envoy was to suggest that the United Provinces might possibly accept the ruler of Brazil as their king so long as they had a separate constitution and formed a separate state from Brazil. All this was reported to the Supreme Director for him to implement.

Pueyrredón paid lip service to democratic methods of government, but used despotic ones. He had been a good soldier, but in civil office he showed haughtiness and pride: 'He carried his respect for military discipline into the cabinet', and insisted on having supreme command as his title implied. A high hand might have been good for the country if the mind directing it had been intelligent and scrupulous, but Pueyrredón was not scrupulous. He used his power not to stamp out corruption and disorder and to fight foreign enemies, but to suppress open manifestations of discontent with his government's venality, apathy and downright treachery in the case of Artigas.

The Congress of Tucumán was at first over seven hundred miles from the true seat of government and counted for nothing; and then after its transfer to Buenos Aires in May 1817 it became entirely subservient to the administration. The banishment without trial of opponents of the policy of supineness in the face of the Portuguese advance exacerbated feeling against the government, though it kept men silent in public. Arbitrary arrests and imprisonments of opponents of the régime added to the discontent and made many regard Artigas' ideas with favour. Even a foreign observer noted that 'the remonstrances of the Buenos Ayres Government [to General Lecór on his advance into the Provincia Oriental] were so very polite, that, according to general opinion, Pueyrredón looked on the Brazilians as more legitimate occupants of the Banda Oriental than was his hated enemy, the Protector Artigas'.[1] This may have had more than a grain of truth in it.

[1] J. P. and W. P. Robertson, *Letters on South America*, vol. III, pp. 235-42.

Catastrophe

In the face of so much feeling in favour of opposing the Portuguese attack, Pueyrredón held his hand over the negotiation desired by the Congress, and played for time by consulting it several times on points raised by its instructions. And by the end of October the Congress was changing its mind again and hardening the terms to be offered to the Portuguese: it was feeling safer since by then the Spanish threat was known to have evaporated, and the royalists were being held in the north. Pueyrredón was still consulting the Congress about procedure in December, and had gone so far as to enquire whether he should delare war on the Portuguese, as a bluff, to satisfy the opponents of the policy of inactivity.[1] More consultations and secret sessions of the Congress delayed the issue, but the whole process resulted in June 1817 in Pueyrredón's being granted the free hand he had in fact taken all the time.[2]

By this time the Portuguese invasion of the Provincia Oriental was well advanced, and a bitter war was being waged there. In the latter half of 1815 Artigas had received disquieting news about the concentration of Portuguese troops on the frontier of the province, and he had taken some precautions, sending forces to watch his side of the border, but then had decided that the threat was not serious.[3] Early in 1816 he listened calmly to fresh rumours of a Portuguese or a Spanish invasion, and took further precautions, though he still affected to believe that the threats were merely *Porteño* propaganda.[4] But before the end of January 1816 he was seriously perturbed by more trustworthy information of the Portuguese preparations; yet he was confident in the strength of the Federal League and promised to make his enemies respect the liberty of his people.[5] He rapidly arranged for boats to be kept at

[1] Ravignani, *Asambleas, loc. cit.*

[2] *Ibid.* sessions of 7, 8, 9, 11, 24 January 1817, 28, 31 May, 7, 14, 25 June.

[3] Letters of Artigas to the Cabildo of Montevideo, 25 September 1815, and 2 October, *Correspondencia de Artigas*, pp. 32, 34.

[4] Letters of Artigas to the Cabildo of Montevideo, 8 and 9 January 1816, *ibid.* pp. 65-6, 67-8.

[5] Letter of 12 January 1816, *ibid.* p. 69.

PLATE 3

Soldiers of the Banda Oriental

important river crossings for the sake of speedy troop movements, and sent spies into Rio Grande do Sul to gain positive intelligence of the Portuguese forces.[1] As the months of waiting slowly passed, Artigas kept his head and his confidence, collecting his information and concentrating and organising his army of eight thousand men.[2]

While this was going on, Artigas was carefully watching the affairs of the Federal League, and particularly the centralist moves against Santa Fe. He had not yet connected the Portuguese threat with his centralist enemies, but he was prepared to face them both, if necessary, in open war.[3] In July 1816 he proudly declared: 'Wanting to be free, the multiplicity of enemies will only serve to redouble our glory.'[4] His people still hoped for union with Buenos Aires in the face of danger, and their mood was expressed in a patriotic drama produced by the poet Hidalgo in Montevideo at this period. There is an over-enthusiastic hopefulness in the hero's best speech:

> ¡Tiemblen los enemigos cuando sepan
> que la unión nos sostiene en lazo estrecho!
> ¡Cochabambinos fuertes, y Paceños,
> Cordobeses, Salteños, Tucumanos,
> Argentinos y hermanos los más tiernos
> del resto de Provincias que hoy defienden
> la LIBERTAD del Meridiano suelo,
> con la unión os convida vuestro hermano
> que ansia por estrecharos en su pecho!'[5]

Artigas planned his resistance with the double aims of rendering a Portuguese advance difficult and costly, and of making an attack

[1] Letter of 26 January 1816, *ibid.* p. 73; Texera to Artigas, 21 February 1816, Arch. Adm. libro 203, ff. 3-4.

[2] Letters of Artigas to the Cabildo of Montevideo, 15, 17 February, 11 April, 29 June, 1 July, *Correspondencia de Artigas*, pp. 78, 80, 93, 106-7, 107-8; *Acta* of the Cabildo of Maldonado, 18 June 1816, Arch. Adm. libro 202, f. 181.

[3] Letter of Artigas to the Cabildo of Montevideo, 2 August 1816, *Correspondencia de Artigas*, p. 113.

[4] Letter of 6 July 1816, *ibid.* pp. 108-9.

[5] 'Sentimientos de un patriota', in N. Fusco Sansone (ed.) *Vida y obras de Bartolomé Hidalgo*, pp. 48-56.

of his own on Brazil his main counter-stroke. Therefore local militia troops were raised throughout the Provincia Oriental, and commanders of merit appointed: Artigas' brother Manuel Francisco was put in charge of the militia cavalry for the zone between Santa Lucía and Montevideo, the Home Counties of Uruguay. Inside the capital a militia was raised separately. Between the rivers Santa Lucía and Yí, Tomás García de Zúñiga had command of the militia. The men of the eastern part of the country, Maldonado, San Carlos, Rocha, up to the border at Santa Teresa, were also formed into cavalry militia. This, the Atlantic seaboard, was clearly the danger point since the frontier here came down closest to Montevideo, and also sea-borne landings could easily be made. Colonia's militia was commanded by Fuentes, and Soriano's by Pedro Gadea. The regular troops were concentrated at strategic points. Divisions under Rivera and Otorgués were covering, at Cerro Largo and Melo, the most likely route across the frontier. Artigas himself would lead the counter-attack towards the Portuguese headquarters in Rio Grande, while the Indian caudillo Andresito (who had taken the surname of Artigas) would cross the River Uruguay from the region of Corrientes, invade the Portuguese Misiones, and get behind the enemy at São Borja. Two other columns, coming from Entre Ríos under the command of Sotelo and Verdum, would also cross the Uruguay into Portuguese territory at Yapeyú and north of the River Arapey.[1] In the early months of 1816, while the troops were moving, arms and munitions were collected and civilian morale was kept up by energetic pronouncements. Horses, without which war was impossible in that country, were brought together in a large remount depot safe in the centre of the country.

Artigas did not expect the Portuguese to march directly on

[1] Letter of Artigas to the Cabildo of Montevideo, 29 June 1186, in *Correspondencia de Artigas*, pp. 318–19; also O. Antúnez Olivera, *Artigas como militar*; and M. V. Martínez, *Andresito caudillo guaraní*, especially pp. 51–61, transcripts of Artigas' orders to Andresito on the invasion of the Misiones.

Montevideo, because that would expose their column to his attacks, and he felt confident of being able to cut it to pieces almost too easily. He underestimated the effect of the overwhelming numbers of the Portuguese and the consequent ease with which they attacked in various places. Rivera was put in charge of the general defence of the route to Montevideo, however, in case of need. The Cabildo of Montevideo, less confident than Artigas, wanted to dismantle the walls of the city, obviously to avoid another siege, but Artigas forbade it since, he held, the walls themselves imposed respect and counted as a passive force which the enemy must take into account. But he made his brother military commander of the city, to bolster the people's courage, and ordered the militia of the neighbouring Departments to protect the city in case the Portuguese were to advance too close.[1] By the end of July all was as ready as it could be made, and news trickled through daily from the frontier posts that the Portuguese were concentrated, and that minor skirmishes were taking place. Artigas boldly announced: 'I am sure that they will not advance with impunity, nor will they triumph except after having shed enough blood to seal our total extermination.'[2]

At this stage Pueyrredón made a typically niggardly gesture, in consonance with the Congress's instructions of a few weeks later to give Artigas some aid but not enough to cause trouble for Argentina with the Portuguese. He sent the *Jefe* a gift of one hundred quintals of gunpowder and three hundred sets of cavalry harness to help in the defence of the Provincia Oriental, together with the message: 'Your Excellency should firmly believe that this aid and any more needed by that beautiful Province would be immense if they could be measured by the will and desires with which they are offered by this Government.' A few days later Pueyrredón wrote to Artigas again in an unctuous tone, offering to do all in his power to end the discord between them by showing

[1] Letters of Artigas to the Cabildo of Montevideo, 1 and 14 July 1816, *Correspondencia de Artigas*, pp. 320, 324-5
[2] Letter 27 July, *ibid.* pp. 324-5.

every 'generosity' on his side and without asking for any reciprocation from Artigas: but he was sure, he went on, that Artigas would excel him in generosity, and that would heal the wounds without the need for diplomacy and negotiations. The Director

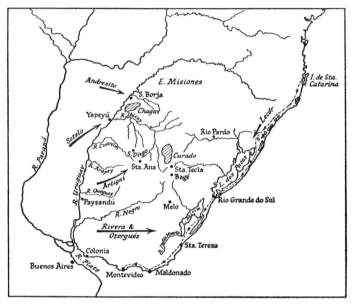

Portuguese Invasion, 1816: Original Disposition of Forces
Copied from Tasso Fragoso, *A batalha do Passo do Rosário*

was at pains to stress his 'frankness' and 'good faith', and ended by begging Artigas to return, out of his generosity, Colonel Viamonte and some *Porteño* troops held prisoner by the federalists.[1]

Yet in August the *Porteños* seized Santa Fe at Pueyrredón's command. Finally, too, on the 18th of August Artigas admitted to having received information which opened his eyes to the agreement between Buenos Aires and the Portuguese over the invasion of the Provincia Oriental. A letter intercepted at Santa Fe showed him that 'our political existence was undermined by the intrigue

[1] Letters of Pueyrredón to Artigas, 30 July and 3 August 1816, Arch. Adm., libro 203, ff. 19, 20-1.

with the Portuguese cabinet: and that it was not without foundation that we regarded with suspicion all the agents of Buenos
Aires'.[1] Artigas knew exactly what weight to give to Pueyrredón's
aid and his offers of peace, which reached him at the same time.[2] A
mission sent by Barreiro, civil governor of Montevideo, asking
Buenos Aires for arms and munitions in the urgency of the last
days of August met with fair promises, but no deeds.[3]

As August wore on, Portuguese troops crossed the frontier in
various places and retired when the Orientals attacked them.
Probably these were probing advances intended to make the
Orientals reveal their forces and dispositions. On the 28th came the
attack of the Portuguese vanguard under General Pinto de Araújo
Correa, with no previous declaration of war. The frontier was
crossed in the east, on the flat and lagoon-studded plains near the
fortress of Santa Teresa, and this time the Portuguese were in earnest.

2. THE PORTUGUESE INVASION

The Portuguese plan of campaign was adequately based on an un-
questionable superiority of numbers, equipment and training. The
Captain-general of Rio Grande do Sul, the Marquess of Alegrete,
with the forces of his province, which amounted to about six
thousand men similar in background and training to the Oriental
troops, was to cover the frontier. His tasks were to keep the
Orientals occupied all along the line, to see to the safety of
Brazilian territory in case of an Oriental invasion, and at the same
time to protect the flank of the main Portuguese thrust. His forces
were in two divisions, one in the Misiones, commanded by
Brigadier Chagas and with headquarters at São Borja, within
reach of the River Uruguay, and the other on the Río Pardo
frontier commanded by Lieutenant-general Curado. These forces

---

[1] Letter of Artigas to the Cabildo of Montevideo, 18 August 1816, in *Correspondencia de Artigas*, p. 328.

[2] Letter of 18 August 1816 (2), *ibid.* p. 328.

[3] Letters of Victorio García de Zúñiga to Barreiro, 26 and 31 August 1816, in Pivel Devoto and Fonseca Muñoz, *op. cit.* pp. 285-6.

might invade Corrientes and make for Santa Fe in order to draw Artigas away from the Provincia Oriental. It was planned to make the main thrust with an army under Lieutenant-general Lecór, who was to strike down the coast from the Laguna Merim, through the port of Maldonado and on to capture Montevideo. The Portuguese subscribed to the classic maxim that the possessor of the capital is master of the country.

The route along the Atlantic coast was to be followed by the veterans of the Peninsular War, strengthened by some of the Rio Grande cavalry, and totalling some six thousand of the best troops in South America. A sea-borne force was to link up at Maldonado with the marching column, and it would bring the numbers advancing on Montevideo up to about ten thousand. There were no mountains or other important natural obstacles once the army was past the causeway over the low-lying lagoon terrain commanded by the fortresses of Santa Teresa and San Miguel. The Brazilian plan is easily understood by a traveller going along the coastal plain from Santa Teresa to Montevideo, passing through the unfortified port of Maldonado, which could be no obstacle, but on the contrary a useful intermediary base. To face about sixteen thousand men Artigas had about eight thousand. Of these three thousand, mainly local militia, were destined for the defence of the Provincia Oriental, and the rest were a striking force for a deep penetration into the enemy's own territory.[1]

Lecór took his time on his approach march to the frontier, going through Santa Catarina to reach Rio Grande towards the end of September 1816. But Alegrete had received orders from Rio de Janeiro to attack in August, and so various points of the frontier were crossed and Artigas' troops were engaged. As the Orientals attacked the secondary forces of Alegrete, Lecór's army drove across the frontier and made straight for Maldonado, while

[1] On this campaign see J. S. Torres Homem, *Annaes das guerras do Brazil com os estados do Prata e Paraguay*, pp. 58-88; Tasso Fragoso, *A batalha do Passo do Rosario*, pp. 109-30; Antúnez Olivera, *op. cit.;* Rocha Pombo, *op. cit.* vol. III, pp. 347-56.

PLATE 4

(*a*) The border lands between Brazil and the Banda
Oriental seen from the fortress of San Miguel

(*b*) The *Salto* of the Exodus of 1811

Rivera opposed it with skirmishers, awaiting a favourable opportunity for a decisive blow.

On the other side of the country, Curado advanced along the River Uruguay into the region of the Cuareim, then turned east towards the central front and sent a column straight into the heart of the Provincia Oriental towards Santa Ana. Oriental forces attacked the column and turned it back, even though the battle itself was won by the Portuguese on the 22nd of September. Another Portuguese column had wheeled to face the threat from the west, where federalist forces under Sotelo were making to cross the Uruguay and to cut off the Portuguese rear along the River Ibicuy. On the 21st of September these federalists were surprised and defeated in the middle of their river crossing, but Sotelo raced north and attempted to cross elsewhere, only to meet the same skilful opponent. He marched further north, into the Misiones, intent now on joining forces with Andresito.

Andresito had himself attacked on the 21st of September at Itaquí, had gone on to defeat Chagas and had laid siege to him in his headquarters at São Borja. But the Portuguese column which had beaten Sotelo rushed up to relieve São Borja and threw Andresito back across the River Uruguay in October. Altogether, the prospects were bad for Artigas' plan of capturing the Misiones and causing havoc in the Portuguese rear. With the Misiones safe, Curado turned his attention to a federalist division under Verdum which had crossed the Uruguay and gone as far as the source of the Ibirocay, advancing towards Curado's own headquarters on the River Ibirapitay Chico. A column commanded by Brigadier Menna Barreto accordingly sought out Verdum and defeated him on the 19th of October. The Portuguese were winning all along the line, but Artigas himself had yet to come into action.

Curado detached a force under Brigadier Joaquim de Oliveira Alvarez to deal with the Oriental leader, and the clash between them took place near the Corumbé hills, on the headwaters of the River Cuareim. Artigas it was who attacked. He had no artillery, and Oliveira Alvarez had two guns, which had a moral effect. Artigas probably had less infantry but more cavalry than the Portuguese, and in fact was fighting with a typical federalist army against the more regular, European organisation of the Portuguese. The *Jefe* therefore depended on an enveloping cavalry charge in a semi-circular formation, keeping his few infrantry-men in the centre, spread out in a single line to make them appear more numerous than they were. He had about fifteen hundred men in all. The Portuguese, who were said by some to have only eight hundred men, though other accounts say more and none can be trusted, beat back Artigas' charges with their fire, and followed up the disorganised federalist cavalry, winning a complete victory. It probably represented the superiority of a balanced force employing regular tactics over a more primitive and un-disciplined horde. Within thirty-six days, therefore, all Artigas' invading columns had been defeated by a mobile, determined, skilful, intelligent and numerous enemy. Artigas' fine plan of counter-attack came to nothing even before the end of October 1816. But at any rate, his blows had been fierce enough to prevent Curado from invading the Provincia Oriental in the west, and the Portuguese leader was obliged to take refuge behind his own frontier.

Meanwhile Lecór's veteran army advanced, the vanguard commanded by General Sebastião Pinto, the rearguard by General Bernardo da Silveira, and the centre by Lecór himself. Marching south between Lagunas Merim and Mangueira, they passed through Santa Teresa and, skirmishing as they went, they slowly advanced along the plain until Rivera attacked Pinto at India Muerta on the 19th of November. His fourteen hundred gaucho militia charged with ferocity on the Portuguese vanguard, which had a solid core of an equal number of infantry besides five hundred cavalry. After four and a half hours of bloody fighting Rivera was forced to admit defeat, though both sides suffered heavy casualties.

At this stage Pueyrredón took a hand in the game again. He had tried to appease the anti-Portuguese opposition in Buenos Aires by announcing great preparations for war and by sending a derisory aid to Artigas with much publicity, though he did not close his ports to Portuguese ships or recall García. At the end of October he decided on another stroke of propaganda, having already determined to ignore the compromising policy recommended to him by the Congress of Tucumán. Instead of sending to Lecór the Congress's mission with its two sets of Machiavellian instructions, he sent in November Colonel Nicolás de Vedia with open instructions to demand Lecór's retreat from the Provincia Oriental on the basis of the armistice of 1812. It was all carefully publicised as a challenge to the Portuguese, but Lecór himself reported to his government that it was merely a gesture to impress the people of the United Provinces with Pueyrredón's zeal for the safety of the country. To prove his good will to the Orientals, Pueyrredón announced Vedia's mission to Barreiro, still in charge of Montevideo, to the Cabildo of that city and to Artigas, informing them all that he had just become aware of the Portuguese attack and was making this attempt to stop it.[1] Artigas for one was not taken in, and declared Buenos Aires' conduct criminal and reprehensible, and also closed his ports to her ships. The delay of three months since the Portuguese invasion began was too long to excuse in this way. Nevertheless Vedia returned to Buenos Aires in December bearing a reply from Lecór intimating that he would obey the orders of the Prince Regent in Rio de Janeiro and would continue his march. Still Pueyrredón did not declare war: still the agreement with the Portuguese held good.

Barreiro and the Cabildo of Montevideo grew increasingly alarmed as Lecór came on, until on the 6th of December they sent a mission to Buenos Aires begging for aid and armed with powers to make any necessary arrangement with Pueyrredón.[2] At the

---

[1] Documents in Pivel Devoto and Fonseca Muñoz, *op. cit.* pp. 286-91; also letter of Artigas to the Cabildo of Montevideo, 30 November 1816, *Correspondencia de Artigas*, pp. 330-1.

[2] Documents in Pivel Devoto and Fonseca Muñoz, *op. cit.* pp. 291-322.

Catastrophe

same time Barreiro wrote asking Artigas if the city should resist
the Portuguese advance to the bitter end, or be evacuated by the
troops and given up without a fight so as to avoid losses. Artigas
took a decision which had long been prepared by the circumstances of his life, by the Federal League, and by the establishment
years before of his headquarters at Purificación, when he replied
ordering Montevideo to be evacuated. He had decided that the
city was unnecessary to him and to his plans. He was denying the
theory of war followed by the Portuguese and the Europeans. The
city could not be helped easily, and the troops for its defence were
occupied on the frontier, where they were more useful. 'My plan
has always been to sustain the war in the open country in view of
the resources there', he wrote; and he was right, with his gaucho
army. He ordered the garrison of Montevideo to leave the city
and fight in the country, and gave instructions for the dismantling
of the fortifications so that they should be of no use to the enemy
if the city were occupied. He himself still hoped to strike a decisive blow across the frontier.[1]

When Barreiro's agents, Durán and Giró, reached Buenos Aires,
they were welcomed by Pueyrredón. The Supreme Director had
made up his mind to go one better than the Congress of Tucumán: instead of handing over the country to Portuguese rule or
protection at once, he would try first to persuade the Provincia
Oriental to join in union with the United Provinces, and therefore
he offered to go to war with the Portuguese on this condition.
Always a centralist, Pueyrredón could not understand the point of
view of the other side. He in fact succeeded in persuading Durán
and Giró on the very day of their arrival to accept a pact trading
their province's freedom for Argentine assistance. It was a pact
which their plenary powers and Barreiro's talk of union with
Buenos Aires (by which he meant presenting a united front to the
Portuguese) allowed them to accept without qualms, and which

[1] Letters of Artigas to the Cabildo of Montevideo, 9 and 19 December 1816, *Correspondencia de Artigas*, pp. 331-2, 332-3.

the state of nervous tension prevailing in Montevideo made them greet with enthusiasm.[1] The aid promised consisted of a first contingent of a thousand men, together with two hundred quintals of gunpowder, one thousand rifles, eight large bronze cannon and some lighter guns; and the first thing requested in return was that the government of Montevideo should be handed over to the Cabildo, no doubt so as to reduce Artigas' influence through his delegate, Barreiro. A wedge would be driven between Artigas and Montevideo, and some Montevideans, seeing that Artigas apparently could not stop the Portuguese advance, would probably invite Buenos Aires to take the city first.

Pueyrredón even now could not avoid the intricacies which were typical of the Directory and the Congress. He excused himself from delaring war on the Portuguese before he had sent another agent to warn Lecór of the latest developments and to summon him to retreat before it was too late. In reality, it is likely that Pueyrredón was attempting to use his pact with Montevideo as a lever with which to direct Lecór's movements. However, as an earnest of his good faith, the Supreme Director arranged to send off a part of the promised aid to Montevideo.[2]

Barreiro indignantly rejected the terms which Pueyrredón offered, and Pueyrredón at once cancelled the sailing of the ships carrying his aid. Durán and Giró, not surprisingly, received a most severe reprimand for their folly from Artigas himself. Yet Barreiro sent another mission seeking help from Buenos Aires, and in December the Supreme Director attempted again to gain the union he felt to be so close by sending two agents to place the whole situation before Artigas. At the same time he sent a gift of arms for Artigas' troops: three hundred rifles, the same number of cavalry harnesses, thirty thousand cartridges and two pieces of

[1] Letters of Durán and Giró to Barreiro 8 and 9 December 1816, Pivel Devoto and Fonseca Muñoz, *op. cit.* pp. 296-7, 298-9. Also Memorandum . . . respecting Monte Video, MS. *cit.*, P.R.O., F.O. 97/76, p. 44.

[2] Letter of Durán and Giró to Barreiro, ? December 1816, Pivel Devoto and Fonseca Muñoz, *op. cit.* p. 306.

field artillery.[1] The *douceur* was noticeably smaller than the aid
Pueyrredón had promised to Montevideo a few weeks before. Yet
the Director must have been sufficiently impressed by the strength
of the feeling growing against him amongst his own people to
make this gesture. It was, however, natural and probably wise of
Artigas to refuse to have any dealings with him.

The Orientals had begun the fight against the Portuguese in
high spirits, which are reflected in Hidalgo's *Cielito Oriental:*

> Cielito, cielo que sí,
> cielo hermoso y halagüeño,
> siempre ha sido el portugués
> enemigo muy pequeño.
>
> Enviadle pronto a dizer
> a vosso Principe Regente
> que todos vais a morrer,
> e que nau le fica yente. [2]

But 1816 had ended badly for Artigas' arms, and 1817 began in a
worse fashion. The local Cabildos had been rallied and resistance
groups built up in December, and Artigas, partly satisfied at having
made Curado retire into Brazil, planned to open the new year
with an attack on him. The *Jefe* intended to break up Curado's
army while it was resting and refitting, and then cut in behind
Lecór, who was still slowly consolidating his hold on the east
coast.[3] But the Portuguese, now under the command of Alegrete,
who faced Artigas, got in their blow first. Alegrete learned that
Artigas was concentrating his army on the River Arapey, and
opened his campaign towards the end of December 1816 by sending out a detachment under Brigadier da Costa to make a feint

[1] Letter of Durán and Giró to Cabildo of Montevideo, 30 December 1816, *ibid.* pp. 320-1.
See also documents *ibid.* pp. 325-34 on the mission to Buenos Aires of V. García de
Zúñiga; and Memorandum . . . respecting Monte Video, MS. *cit.*, P.R.O., F.O. 97/76,
p. 45, summary of a letter of Chamberlain, no. 16, 17 February 1817.

[2] N. Fusco Sansone, *op. cit.* pp. 21-2.

[3] Letter of Artigas to the Cabildo of Soriano, 7 December 1816, Arch. Adm., libro 206,
ff. 57-60.

toward Santa Ana so as to draw Artigas' attention, while he himself moved the bulk of his forces across the River Cuareim.

Artigas had sent the main party of his troops under Colonel Latorre to meet da Costa, and was caught by Alegrete, who on the 1st of January 1817 rapidly crossed the Cuareim and placed his army between Latorre and Artigas. The Portuguese took up their position on the banks of the Arroyo Catalán, tempting Latorre to attack, and on the 3rd of January Alegrete sent Abreu with a detachment to attack Artigas in his camp on the Arapey. This attack had such success that Abreu was able to seize all the supplies of Artigas' army, and it is inexplicable how Artigas let himself be surprised in such a way. The next day Latorre attacked Alegrete, who was ensconced in a strong position defended on three sides by natural obstacles. Even so, Latorre's impetuous charges on the flanks and across the Arroyo Catalán were being no more than held, and the fight was in the balance, when Abreu returned unexpectedly and charged Latorre's force in the left flank, with the inevitable result. But after these hard-won victories the Portuguese drew back to the other side of the Cuareim to recover.

The outnumbered and outmanoeuvred Orientals withdrew to Purificación, though not in despair. Artigas urged the people to redouble their efforts, promising that the enemy would extend his dominion only over the dead bodies of the Orientals. 'We have been unfortunate when we expected to be glorious', was the nearest he came to a complaint. Nor did he blame himself, as many men might, for his lack of success. Now he intended to hold the line of the Uruguay, which was vital for the support of his troops still fighting on the other side of the province, since their supplies came either along or across the River.[1] The towns along the western side of the Provincia Oriental, still awaiting the Portuguese advance, loyally sent their men to replenish the formations. Colonia conscripted every creole of sixteen years of age and over,

---

[1] Letter of Artigas to the Cabildo of Soriano, 14 January 1817, Arch. Adm., libro 206, ff. 61-2.

and all freed slaves and slaves owned by foreigners, and also tried to win back deserters by offering an amnesty to those who rejoined the colours.[1]

But on the Atlantic coast nothing could dislodge Lecór. He had tried ever since the start of his invasion to win the good will of the inhabitants by promising them peace under the protection of His Most Faithful Majesty the King of Portugual, who would treat them as his own children. As he himself announced, Lecór was therefore not so much a general as a friend of the Orientals. The only enemy he was fighting was Artigas and those who followed him.[2] In November 1816, when Maldonado was occupied by Vianna's landing from the Portuguese fleet, the people of the town were in fact happy to escape being too close witnesses of war and devastation, and to carry on with their business in peace.[3] Lecór's propaganda had a considerable effect, and he supported it with the solid benefits of protection and trade. He was in no hurry to conquer: what he wanted was to unite a contented Provincia Oriental to Brazil for ever, and therefore he preferred persuasion to killing.

Lecór's attitude and proclamations, together with their own inclinations towards peace, led many influential Montevideans to conceive feelings of sympathy for Portugal. They had had too much of war and privation since 1811. When Barreiro withdrew together with the garrison from Montevideo in January 1817, the Cabildo lost no time in sending a deputation to invite Lecór to occupy the city peacefully, as a friend and protector, since this was the desire of the citizens.[4] On the 20th of January Lecór fulfilled that desire, to the acclamation of the populace. At once he began to win sympathisers for union with Brazil, by governing the city according to its own laws, keeping officials in their posts, and

[1] *Bando* of the Cabildo of Colonia, 19 January 1817, Arch. Adm., libro 715, f. 6.
[2] *Edicto* of Sebastian Pinto de Araujo Corea, d. Quartel General del Campo de Santa Teresa, 31 August 1816, Arch. Adm. libro 604, f. 220.
[3] Oliveira Lima, *op. cit.* vol. II, p. 634.
[4] Rocha Pombo, *op. cit.* vol. III, p. 348; also Anon. *Apuntes históricos*, p. 56.

distributing rewards and favours to leaders of the party opposed to a return to Spanish rule. A deputation consisting of Larrañaga and the worthy administrator Bianqui was sent at once by the Cabildo to Rio de Janeiro in order to petition for the incorporation of the Provincia Oriental into Portugal's dominions and for the retention of Lecór as governor.[1]

Clearly, the Portuguese feared being forced either by warfare or by European opinion to return Montevideo to Spain, and indeed the question was brought before the representatives of the major European powers in Paris in January 1817, and Portugal's action was censured as an attack on Spain's rights.[2] The so-called Mediating Powers helped to persuade Portugal to promise to restore the Provincia Oriental to Spain, but Spain was never able to fulfil the main condition of sending troops over to replace those of Portugal, and meanwhile the Portuguese attempted to consolidate their hold. Another interested party, Buenos Aires, was obviously too much occupied with trouble in the federalist provinces and with the war against the royalists in Chile and in the north to have energy to spare for a war against the Portuguese, even if the Directory had wanted one. Indeed, as a Brazilian historian points out, 'the occupation of Montevideo at that moment was a great service to the Argentine revolutionaries', since Buenos Aires could not have fought even Artigas with such success herself.[3] At any rate, the Directory's agreement with the Portuguese government precluded all fear of interference from that quarter. As Chamberlain, the British chargé d'affaires in Rio de Janeiro, acutely observed when writing of the ill success of Artigas: 'the policy of Buenos Ayres, in involving Brazil in a War with that Chief, had without doubt been very successful. By creating a misunderstanding between Portugal and Spain, it was effectually

---

[1] Documents in Pivel Devoto and Fonseca Muñoz, *op. cit.* pp. 337–56.

[2] Proceedings of the Ministers of the Mediating Powers at Paris, and of the Congress at Aix la Chapelle, on the Subject of the Difference between Spain and Portugal. January 1817 to January 1820. P.R.O., F.O. 97/76.

[3] Rocha Pombo, *op. cit.* vol. III, pp. 349–50.

protected against any Attack from the latter', and 'would probably bring about the total destruction of the Person it considered as its most dangerous Enemy'.[1]

Yet in January 1817 Lecór found himself besieged inside Montevideo and a small district just outside the walls by a furious gaucho army led by Rivera and aided by Barreiro and the troops who had formerly been the garrison of the city.[2] Artigas and his lieutenants remained masters of the interior, apart from a narrow corridor along the coast, for two more years, during which the partial successes of Portuguese columns were constantly cancelled out by the resilience of the gauchos. An effective corsair force blockaded Montevideo and decimated Portuguese shipping, and blocked supply routes even as far away as European waters.[3]

The British Government viewed the Portuguese invasion as a violation of the armistice arranged under Strangford's aegis in 1812, which had been intended to protect Spain's possessions. Therefore Chamberlain continually protested to the Portuguese government, and Castlereagh accepted Spain's invitation in 1816 for Britain to be one of the Mediating Powers in the dispute between Spain, her insurgent colonies and Portugal. Also, Castlereagh instructed Chamberlain to press Dom João to withdraw his troops from the Provincia Oriental or risk losing Britain's friendship. In April 1817 the Portuguese replied refusing to relinquish their hold on the province, and alleged that its possession was essential for Brazil's safety because of the failure of Spain to pacify the area and because of what was called Artigas' attack on the Eastern Misiones.[4] Therefore the Portuguese 'pacification' continued, and so did the British protests.

In Buenos Aires, the fall of Montevideo aroused a patriotic out-

---

[1] Letter no. 74, 2 August 1817, summarised in Memorandum . . . respecting Monte Video, MS. *cit.* P.R.O., F.O. 97/76, p. 69.

[2] R. Grandsire, *Voyage*, *cit.* in H. D. Barbagelata, *Sobre la época de Artigas*, pp. 15-16.

[3] A. Beraza, *Los corsarios de Artigas*.

[4] Memorandum . . . respecting Monte Video, MS. *cit.*, P.R.O., F.O. 97/76, pp. 54-63 summaries of letters Castlereagh to Chamberlain no. 11, 19 December 1816 and Chamberlain to Castlereagh no.27, 5 April 1817.

cry, and Pueyrredón tried to silence his critics by exiling first Dorrego, who had some federalist views; and then, as a movement in favour of overthrowing him gained strength, the influential soldiers and politicians French, Pagola, Baldenegro, Agrelo, Manuel Moreno, Chiclana and Pazos Kanki were sent after Dorrego to find asylum in the United States of America. Still war was not declared on Portugal; but when in March 1817 news reached Pueyrredón of San Martín's successes against the Spaniards in Chile, the Director, possibly feeling some relief in the pressure on him, made some warlike gestures towards Lecór, but nothing more. He publicly proclaimed war on Portugal, but privately assured Lecór that nothing serious was intended,[1] and indeed he allowed the exportation of food from Buenos Aires for the Portuguese besieged in Montevideo. But the Director revealed his true feelings when he gladly helped in the desertion of Colonel Rufino Bauzá and six hundred black troops from Artigas' forces, with the connivance of Lecór, who gave them passage through Montevideo. Bauzá was not a friend of Artigas', and had decided that the type of partisan warfare being carried on in the Provincia Oriental after the fall of Montevideo was not the war for a gentleman. Further, in 1819 Pueyrredón persuaded Lecór to close all his ports to ships sailing up the River Uruguay, for those ships mostly carried supplies to Artigas, their common enemy.[2]

Yet Artigas' popularity in the Provincia Oriental did not dissolve with his defeats, nor did the peoples' enthusiasm for federalism. Even in October 1817, after over a year of losses, the people of Colonia, when offered the choice of electing a new *Jefe*, acclaimed Artigas with shouts of 'Long live Artigas. Long live our *Jefe* Artigas. No other General but Artigas – we named him to begin with, and he will be our Leader while he has life, and we are

[1] Memorandum . . . respecting Monte Video, MS. *cit.*, P.R.O., F.O. 97/76, pp. 51-52, summaries of letters of Chamberlain no.5, 6 March and no.26, 5 April 1817.

[2] Letter of the Barão da Laguna (Lecór) to Teniente Rey, d. Montevideo 12 February 1819, Arch. Adm., caja 529, Documentos Diversos.

very content with all he has done and all that he may do in the future.'[1]

Still the Portuguese continued to prevail, perhaps because of numbers more than for any other reason. The Misiones were devastated by Chagas so that they should not attract or harbour Artigas. At length, in 1818, the Portuguese made a serious attempt to cut the Provincia Oriental off from the federalist bases in Entre Ríos, so as to force the Oriental troops to evacuate their own province. The ports from Colonia up the River Uruguay had proved to be invaluable havens for Artigas' corsairs, whose depredations were so great that they must be stopped, and therefore those ports must be captured. A Portuguese naval squadron penetrated into the River Uruguay in May 1818, and Curado had begun his march down the river from inside Brazil in February. Curado pushed rapidly south, defeating Artigas' lieutenants as they opposed him, until he captured Purificación and linked up with the ships. Finally Lecór and Curado had sealed off the Provincia Oriental, helped by a reinforcement of a further three thousand men. One by one Artigas' officers were captured: in 1818, Lavalleja, Otorgués, Manuel Francisco Artigas and Bernabé Rivera were lost in this way. From then only the forces of Fructuoso Rivera and those of Artigas were left in the field.

Artigas fought on, using Entre Ríos as the platform from which to operate. He set up artillery at Arroyo de la China and other points on the west bank of the Uruguay in an attempt to disrupt Portuguese navigation. But Bento Manoel led a Portuguese detachment into Entre Ríos and silenced the guns, after which he retreated. The Portuguese in fact made no effort to gain a permanent foothold west of the Uruguay in case Buenos Aires should be provoked in earnest by such an incursion into territory she considered her own.

Even after this Artigas had the boldness to make an expedition, at the beginning of 1819, into the Misiones, linking up with

[1] *Acta of Cabildo Abierto* in Colonia, 22 October 1817, Arch. Adm., libro 751, ff. 11-12.

Andresito and penetrating far behind the Portuguese lines in the hope of forcing Curado to abandon the Provincia Oriental. It was a shrewd blow, but it was doomed to fail, just as Artigas' original plan of counter-invasion had been doomed, for lack of men and material. In spite of the initial Oriental successes, the bulk of the Portuguese army proved to be too great. Artigas was beaten back, and Andresito, his most faithful officer, was taken prisoner. Fructuoso Rivera was still fighting inside the Provincial Oriental, at the head of the sole *artiguista* force left there. Defeated at Arroyo Grande on the 25th of October, he took to the hills and continued the struggle as a guerilla chief.

In December 1819 Artigas threw everything he had left into another invasion, this time into the north of the Provincia Oriental with fresh forces from Corrientes and Entre Ríos. Again his object was to draw the Portuguese northwards from the rest of the province, but instead he drew onto himself an army which marched south from across the Brazilian frontier. Artigas won two partial engagements, and then put his army under the command of Latorre, who was met in a strong position on the River Tacuarembó Chico by the Portuguese on the 22nd of January. A bloody battle ended in Latorre's defeat and the failure of Artigas' last fling in his province. The *Jefe* succeeded in gathering together the remnants of his army and escaping with them across the Uruguay into Entre Ríos. No explanation has been found for Artigas' odd habit of putting his lieutenants in command of his forces in big battles. Perhaps he felt too old and cold-blooded to command himself, or perhaps he felt himself to be no tactician to measure up against the European-trained troops he was fighting. It is possible that he felt that he must not become too closely involved in a battle personally, for that would hazard the life or liberty of the Protector of the Free Peoples, not of a mere general. At all events, it is true to say that the only important battle he won himself was Las Piedras in 1811, although neither did the officers he put in command win many battles.

Even after this disaster, Artigas had grounds for hope. The federalist caudillos of the Littoral, who were still supposed to be under his hegemony, were in the process of winning a war against Buenos Aires, so that Artigas might yet turn the United Provinces into a confederation with their help and win back the Provincia Oriental. Therefore Artigas sent orders to Rivera to abandon the struggle in their province and join up with him in Entre Ríos, but Rivera refused to obey. He tried to fight on, and his army dwindled as men deserted or went off individually to join Artigas, until in March 1820 Rivera decided to accept an offer made to him by the Portuguese to retain him in his rank of colonel of an Oriental regiment if he submitted to King João VI.[1]

Rivera, at the age of about thirty-five or thirty-six at that time, was at the height of his powers and popularity among the Orientals. He was their only consistently successful soldier. Father Larrañaga describes a meeting with him in 1815, soon after the fine victory of Guayabos: 'He appeared to me about twenty-five years old, good-looking, round faced, with large and modest eyes, very attentive, and expressing himself with courtesy. His dress was simple: riding boots in the English style, trousers and jacket of fine blue cloth, round hat, with no other mark of rank but the sabre and sash of crimson silk, and his aide wore the same dress. In everything these officers maintain complete equality, and are only distinguished by the greatness of their actions, through which alone they make themselves respected by their juniors. They detest all luxury and anything which might unman them.'[2] A trusted and brilliant lieutenant of Artigas' ever since 1811, he had not allowed himself to be suborned, but was bending before superior force in order to spring upright again when the time came to lead his compatriots to freedom and the formation of a new nation. No doubt he refused to become an émigré because he was interested not in the fate of the Federal League, but in that of his

[1] Rocha Pombo, *op. cit.* vol. III, pp. 354-5; I. De-María, *Rasgos biográficos de hombres notables . . .* vol. I, pp. 85-97.
[2] Larrañaga, *op. cit.* pp. 91-2.

province; and possibly he realised how easily émigrés lose touch with their native countries and their problems. Rivera was the last of Artigas' lieutenants to sheathe his sword, and it was on him that the *Jefe*'s mantle fell in the years after Artigas' own defeat and exile in Paraguay, although it was the comparatively obscure Lavalleja who began the reconquest of the province in 1825 and organised the first independent government.

3. THE END OF THE FEDERAL LEAGUE

In contrast to what occurred in the Provincia Oriental, the policies and the arms of the federalists in the rest of the Federal League met with increasing success from 1816 to 1820, although the influence of Artigas was increasingly diminished by his defeats at the hands of the Portuguese. Pueyrredón and the centralists, after the failure of their efforts in 1816 to persuade Santa Fe to desert Artigas, stood aside for some months while the Portuguese invasion matured and San Martín's Chilean venture became successful.

To face the Portuguese threat Artigas called together the best troops in the Littoral and brought them across the Uruguay to take part in the ill-fated counter-invasion of Brazil led by Verdum. A sidelight on the movements involved is thrown by one of the Robertsons, who describes the departure of Colonel Méndez, the loyal *artiguista* governor of Corrientes, leading his forces to guard the frontier. All the revenue brought in by the Robertsons' trade was sunk in a consignment of arms imported by the same firm under a licence granted, curiously enough, by Buenos Aires.[1] At Arroyo de la China Artigas stationed Comandante Francisco Ramírez, the local caudillo, as organiser of the supplies and reinforcements from the Littoral, which were concentrated there prior to being ferried over the Uruguay to Artigas' headquarters.

This withdrawal of the troops restricted Artigas' hold on the Littoral to what his personal influence with the local caudillos was

---

[1] J. P. and W. P. Robertson, *Letters on South America*, vol. III, pp. 70-8.

worth. Pueyrredón about the middle of 1817 began to make friendly approaches to some minor caudillos in Entre Ríos, Hereñú, Correa, Carriego and Samaniego. It was an ideal moment for breaking Artigas' influence there and then persuading the Littoral provinces to leave the Federal League and join the United Provinces. Already on the 6th of September Chamberlain reported to London from Rio de Janeiro: 'In August a new Chieftain, named Irenu, had started up in the Province of Entre Ríos. He gave money to all deserters that joined him. He was supposed to have been set up by Buenos Ayres, for the purpose of opposing Artigas, should he cross the Uruguay, and so prevent the Portuguese from having a right to pass into that Territory . . .'[1] but there can be little doubt that hostility to Artigas was the main motive behind this stroke.

Artigas relied on a brother of the Governor of Santa Fe, José Ignacio Vera, and on Francisco Ramírez to outwit the *Porteños* and if necessary suppress any revolt by Hereñú and his friends. By September it was obvious that this group had embraced the alliance of Pueyrredón, in whose pay they were, but Vera and Ramírez stood firm at the key points, Paraná and Arroyo de la China. Pueyrredón sent his allies arms and other aid, with the result that they revolted openly in November.[2] A *Porteño* force of six hundred men led by Colonel Montes de Oca invaded Entre Ríos at the same time. At length Pueyrredón had come out into the open, and now Artigas had wars to fight against two superior enemies on widely separated fronts.

On the 13th of November, therefore, Artigas sent to Pueyrredón and the towns of the Federal League a note accusing the Supreme Director of denying the sacred rights of the peoples who had taken Artigas for their leader, and enumerating all the Director's acts against the League and its defenders. Pueyrredón's complicity with the Portuguese was censured in detail and his con-

[1] Memorandum . . . respecting Monte Video, MS. *cit.* P.R.O., F.O. 97/76, pp. 72-43, summary of letter of Chamberlain no. 86.
[2] J. Pérez, *Ramírez y Artigas*, p. 41.

duct labelled criminal, and finally Artigas challenged the Director: 'I shall speak this time and for all: Your Excellency is responsible before the altars of the Fatherland for your inaction or malice against our common interests. One day that grim Tribunal of the nation will rise and it will administer justice. Meanwhile I challenge your Excellency in the face of the enemy to fight with energy and to show the Virtues which ought to make glorious the name of American.'[1]

The Protector then arranged for Vera to be reinforced from Santa Fe and Ramírez from the Provincia Oriental, and these two decisively defeated Montes de Oca on the 25th of December. Pueyrredón had expected the *Entrerrianos* to follow Hereñú and his friends, but the majority were aware that their interests were not served by the *Porteño's* policies, and they stayed loyal to federalism. Even so, Pueyrredón sent another force into Entre Ríos in March 1818 and its leader, Marcos Balcarce, received the active assistance of Hereñú, Correa, Carriego and Samaniego. Ramírez waited for them on the Arroyo Saucesito, where he completely routed them on the 25th of March, killing Samaniego and taking many prisoners and much booty in the form of guns and equipment. Henceforth Ramírez was undisputed master of Entre Ríos, and even the ravages of the Portuguese foray led by Bento Manoel did not prevent him from throwing back another *Porteño* invasion later in the year led by Hereñú and Correa.

In 1817 Córdoba felt the pinch of centralist rule, and a weakened federalist party worked for reunion with the Federal League. But the *Porteño* general Belgrano sent Colonel Juan Bautista Bustos with a force to pacify the province. The attraction of Artigas' prestige was still strong there, and increased as the Directory continued to lose favour owing to its arbitrary centralism and its chicanery over the Portuguese attack on the Provincia Oriental. Even remote Santiago del Estero, in the north, was in communication

---

[1] Letter of Artigas to Pueyrredón, 13 November 1817, *cit.* in A. Capillas de Castellanos, *La lucha contra el centralismo y el Tratado de Pilar.*

with Artigas in 1817 over the question of confederation, and it seemed as if the United Provinces might throw off the centralist yoke and take the Protector as their chief.

But as before, the test case was in Santa Fe, the most important province for either side to hold since it commanded the communications between Buenos Aires and the provinces and armies in the north and north-west, particularly in Córdoba and Tucumán. Furthermore Artigas' system had opened to trade the rivers, also commanded by Santa Fe, and had therefore brought some prosperity to the Littoral, whereas the locking out of Buenos Aires from these channels and the blockade of that port harmed *Porteño* commerce and greatly diminished her influence throughout the interior. The governor of Santa Fe, Mariano Vera, was in an uneasy position between the two camps, and being in any case not a very convinced federalist, he was ready to listen to Pueyrredón. It is true that he gave assistance to his more federalist brother fighting in Entre Ríos, but he himself remained undecided, probably waiting for one side or the other to gain an advantage.[1] As a result, Vera aroused the opposition of loyal federalists in his province, and this precipitated a revolt against him in July 1818, so that he found it safest to resign from the governorship and leave Santa Fe. The Cabildo tried to regulate affairs and arranged elections for a new governor; but in the midst of this increasingly obscure situation, which showed signs of complete breakdown, Lieutenant-colonel Estanislao López, the commander of the local *Blandengues*, assumed the government of all Santa Fe, imposed order, and allied himself to Artigas. López thus rose to great power in a key position, and, realising this, held himself independent from any ruler, although he claimed to be a federalist and prepared to meet an imminent attack of the centralist troops.[2] Therefore two independent caudillos, López and Ramírez, became the arbiters of the Littoral as Artigas' power diminished.

[1] Junta de Historia y Numismática Americana, *op. cit.* p. 83.
[2] *Ibid.* pp. 93-100.

314

Pueyrredón's activities touched Corrientes in 1818. Galván was sent there in March to organise a centralist revolution, and he succeeded in encouraging Colonel Bedoya to rise and depose the Governor, Méndez, in May. Artigas therefore ordered Andresito to invade the province with his army of seven hundred Misiones Indians and restore it to federalist control. This was accomplished in July, and from then until October, when Méndez was reinstated, Andresito, assisted by Pedro Campbell, exercised a curious military government which occasioned many incidents which may have a comic side to them when seen from our distance in time but which were very disagreeable for the fearful *Correntinos*. They were forced to submit to the whims of an Indian chief who was extremely sensitive to any real or imagined slight to himself, his race, his army or his hero, Artigas.[1] In fact the Indians were well disciplined, although the people of Corrientes had been terrified by rumours about their cruelties. These men were warlike despite their shortages of food and clothing. One 'outrage' they committed shows the social strain of those days. Andresito invited the *Correntinos* to see his men perform native dances, but was insultingly told that white people did not want to watch a gang of Indians dancing. In revenge this fearsome chief went no further than to force all the men of the town to spend one day cleaning and weeding the main square, which was a great insult to those people used to the service of slaves, and meanwhile their ladies were made to dance all day with the Indians.

The war on other fronts against Artigas was not neglected by the Directory. At the end of 1817 the agreement with the Portuguese received fresh attention. Pueyrredón asked the Congress to approve a treaty negotiated by García in Rio de Janeiro, which gave the Portuguese a free hand with Artigas and guaranteed them the friendship, trade and intercourse of the United Provinces, and even their help in certain cases. The Argentines hoped that their allies

---

[1] J. P. and W. P. Robertson, *Letters on South America*, vol. III, pp. 159–78. The Robertsons wrongly date their descriptions of Corrientes under Andresito's rule as 1819.

would consent to evacuate the Provincia Oriental once Artigas was crushed, but no-one in touch with the situation could seriously believe that they would.[1] Chamberlain had reported the Portuguese view in September 1817, when he wrote that the possession of the Provincia Oriental meant that Portugal might command the whole South Atlantic. With no more than twenty-five warships, Brazil could control the route from Europe to India, and with Montevideo and Maldonado in her power she would have all the ports of the east of South America from Cayenne to Cape Horn. Two months later a Portuguese minister said in private conversation that 'if Europe leagued against Brazil it would throw itself into the arms of Buenos Ayres, and set Her at defiance'.[2] This was the importance to the Portuguese Court of the adventure and of the agreement with Buenos Aires.

The projected treaty was therefore submitted to Dom João's government by García, but no official acceptance was ever made.[3] By 1818 the Portuguese had realised that their plans were going very well without any need for a compromising commitment with the United Provinces, especially one which might limit their tenure of the Provincia Oriental or of other parts of Artigas' protectorate which they might occupy. In view of the state of opinion among the European powers, also, Dom João probably stopped short of signing a treaty which would give *de facto* recognition to the United Provinces and cause even more trouble with the Holy Alliance. There is no doubt that the lack of a treaty was dangerous for the United Provinces, whose politicians, it seemed, had been fooled into taking no action against the Portuguese attack.

Another blow, among the many lesser ones struck against Artigas, was the publication in 1818 of Sáenz de Cavia's notorious

---

[1] Ravignani, *Asambleas constituyentes*, vol. i, secret sessions of the Congress of Tucumán for 5, 8 and 10 December 1817.

[2] Memorandum . . . respecting Monte Video, MS. *cit.*, P.R.O., F.O. 97/76, pp. 73-75, summaries of letters of Chamberlain, no.88, 6 September 1817 and no.104, 11 November.

[3] Ravignani, *Asambleas constituyentes*, vol. i, secret sessions of 25 August, 8 and 17 October, 24 December 1818.

pamphlet condemning the Protector of the Free Peoples and all his men as savages. Pueyrredón knew the propaganda value of the printed word, and Sáenz de Cavia had a grievance against Artigas because he had lost a post in the Montevideo administration when the Orientals occupied the city in 1815 at the *Porteño* evacuation. Copies of the pamphlet were sent to officials and priests throughout the province of Buenos Aires so that they could spread the word among their charges. The *Classification of Don José Artigas* which sums up the accusations in the pamphlet is a list of the strongest epithets:

insubordinate, disobedient, a rebel. Traitor to the fate of America, a deserter from her colours ... Fanatic, turbulent, seducer of the peoples, anarchist. Apostle of lies, impostor, hypocrite. Propagator of the greatest errors, of false theories, of antisocial principles ... Breaker of the fifth, sixth and seventh Commandments of the Decalogue ... Immoral, corrupt, libertine ... A new Attila of the unhappy districts which he has protected. Devouring and bloody wolf in the skin of a lamb. Origin of all the disasters of the country. Scourge of his Fatherland. Opprobrium of the nineteenth century. Insult to the human race. Dishonour of America ... One of those terrible scourges which God visits on nations *when he wishes to punish them in his fury.* [1]

But it was in Santa Fe that the Directory fought hardest and longest, as Colonel Juan Ramón Balcarce camped near the provincial border between Buenos Aires and Santa Fe with his *Porteño* Army of Observation. He tried without success to persuade some minor caudillos to revolt against López, but when hostilities opened in September 1818, the Director stood alone facing the federalists after all. Balcarce concentrated his three thousand men at San Nicolás, on the provincial border, while on the River Paraná a flotilla with Hereñú and three hundred men was ready to support the land operation. At Frayle Muerto, on Santa Fe's border with Córdoba, Colonel Bustos had been waiting since the end of 1817 for fighting to begin. But the Director had no unified

[1] Anon. (P. F. Sáenz de Cavia), *El Protector nominal de los pueblos libres, D. José Artigas clasificado por El Amigo del Orden, cit.* See pp. 43–6 for the 'classification'.

317

plan of action, so that Estanislao López was able to take the initiative, attacking in November and immobilising Bustos where he waited, while allowing Balcarce to advance almost unmolested towards the undefended city of Santa Fe. Artigas sent a force from Entre Ríos, commanded by Ricardo López Jordán, to the aid of his ally. Balcarce got within a league of Santa Fe, but was so harassed by the federalist guerillas, who cut off his line of communications, that after three days of indecision he began to retreat, at the beginning of December, on the orders of Pueyrredón leaving the territory devastated and without resources.

As Balcarce retreated, Pedro Campbell attacked and pushed him uncomfortably fast. Hereñú was left without support and was defeated by Estanislao López and by Ramírez, the Entrerrian caudillo, who had joined in the fight. So the Federal League fought the war, although it was significant that the caudillos acted independently, and Artigas no longer controlled them. Balcarce fell back from Rosario to San Nicolás, beyond the provincial border, and there he resigned his command to Belgrano, from whom the government hoped to obtain better results.[1]

The Directory in fact lost its head at this failure, and even turned the Army of the North, which was covering the route of any possible royalist attack from Upper Peru, back towards Santa Fe. In early 1819 a total of seven thousand troops was therefore concentrating on the key province. But the federalists, with their wild *montonera* cavalry, held their own. Estanislao López attacked and beat Bustos again, before turning round and crushing another *Porteño* invasion led by Viamonte, who withdrew to Rosario. The federalist troops were about two thousand strong, besides an indefinite number of partisans. But although in March 1819 López seemed to be enjoying great success, he was astute enough to realise that his resources could not compare with those which the Directory could bring against him. Belgrano was advancing on

[1] Junta de Historia y Numismática Americana, *op. cit.* pp. 100-1, gives some details of the campaigns.

him from Córdoba with a large army, and San Martín had sent some troops back from Chile to Mendoza, and had received orders to return with all the Argentine forces in order to crush the Federal League. San Martín in fact refused to take part in civil war, and instead went forward to liberate Lima, but although López probably knew of this decision, he was sufficiently impressed by the size and quality of the forces closing in upon him. Also, López was experiencing difficulties with the indisciplined troops under Campbell and López Jordán.[1]

On the other hand, both Belgrano and Viamonte were profoundly discouraged by the fierce opposition of the guerillas, and so López was able to persuade the latter to negotiate an armistice on the 5th of April at Rosario, preliminary to a ratification signed at Rosario on the 12th, which arranged for a meeting on the 8th of May to 'seal for ever concord between sister peoples'.[2] Deputies were to be invited from the government of Santa Fe and 'the others on the other side of the Paraná', that is, the Federal League, as well as from the Directory. *Porteño* troops were to withdraw from Santa Fe and Entre Ríos, and in return Santa Fe was to allow free communications through her territory between the armies of the United Provinces, and all channels of intercourse and trade with Santa Fe, Entre Ríos and the upper Paraná were to be opened to Buenos Aires.[3] These provisions would, of course, have the effect of loosening the strangle-hold which Artigas was maintaining through the Federal League on Buenos Aires' trade with the interior. But when the *Porteño* deputies arrived on the 8th of May, they found only López's agent ready to discuss further union with them. The other provinces of the Federal League abstained from making peace with a government which they distrusted very deeply; and Artigas, who was piqued since the

[1] *Ibid.* p. 160. note 14 and p. 161 note 15.

[2] *Ibid.* pp. 131–40.

[3] Documents in Ravignani, *Asambleas constituyentes*, vol. VI, t. 2, pp. 120-1; and Memorandum .. respecting Monte Video, MS. *cit.* P.R.O., F.O. 97/76, p. 84, summary of letter of Chamberlain no.36, 29 May 1819.

Catastrophe

armistice had been entered into without any reference to him and since it contained no promise that Buenos Aires would declare war on the Portuguese, refused to countenance it, and instead issued another condemnation of Pueyrredón for his complicity with the Court at Rio de Janeiro.[1] The Oriental and Entrerrian troops aiding Estanislao López considered the armistice and the agreement with Buenos Aires as treason to the federalist cause, and therefore withdrew from Santa Fe into Entre Ríos.

Buenos Aires' situation changed slightly at this period, since in April 1819 the Congress produced the national constitution on which it had been working for some years. It was a centralist charter, admirably adapted for a monarchy, and the hunt for a suitable prince went on in Europe.[2] The Duke of Lucca was considered, since he was related to the Spanish Royal House, and would presumably be able to persuade the Spaniards to relinquish further attempts to recover the Plate provinces by force. It was known that an expedition for this object was indeed being prepared in Cádiz. Also, a monarchy ought to satisfy certain European powers which were suspicious of the rise of new republics. A marriage between the new king and a Braganza princess would solve the problem of Portuguese interference, which was beginning to be an embarrassment, and it might bring back the Provincia Oriental as the princess's dowry. Many castles in the air were built by the centralists in 1819.

In June Pueyrredón left the Directory, recommending the election of a more experienced military commander. Rondeau was chosen, a docile and disciplined soldier, but hardly the statesman that was needed. So Pueyrredón, who had governed dictatorially and had alienated public opinion even in Buenos Aires, departed leaving the whole region in a chaos which only years of wars and dictatorships and re-thinking of principles would resolve into order. Nothing was done to solve the immediate problem of

[1] Documents in Ravignani, *loc., cit.* pp. 123-7.
[2] Ravignani, *Comisión de Rivadavia.*

giving the country the federal and republican form of government which most of its people desired, and therefore the civil war dragged on to a bitter end in anarchy. Rondeau offered peace and union to Artigas in view of the Spanish threat, and Artigas made it a condition of his acceptance that Buenos Aires should declare war on Portugal. Rondeau refused, not wishing to add to his enemies, and decided that he must fight Artigas to a standstill.

Artigas still maintained his views on confederation, in which he saw the only hope of peace for the Plate territories as well as the salvation of the peoples' liberty. Therefore in September 1819, even though the war in the Provincia Oriental was going against him, he prepared to open a new campaign against Buenos Aires. To bring Santa Fe into line with the Federal League and break her uneasy neutrality he first cut off trade with her, and then produced sufficient proof of Buenos Aires' complicity with the Portuguese to bring the people of Santa Fe back onto his side. It now looked as though the Portuguese would not stop at the River Uruguay, but that they might continue their advance and occupy Entre Ríos and even Santa Fe.[1] At the end of September the doubtful province was once again federalist and *artiguista*.

There had not been real peace, even after the armistice of April. The *Porteño* armies had remained menacingly on the borders of Santa Fe, and in Entre Ríos Hereñú and Correa had continued to skirmish with the federalists. But fighting broke out on the 14th of October, when López interrupted the free passage of a *Porteño* convoy crossing Santa Fe with supplies for the army in Córdoba. Ramírez crossed into Santa Fe from Entre Ríos at Artigas' orders, and by the middle of the month he and López were advancing towards the frontier with the province of Buenos Aires. The Directory's prestige rapidly declined throughout the provinces. The exiled ex-Supreme Director Alvear paradoxically joined Ramírez, having come from Rio de Janeiro to Montevideo in the hope of reinstating himself; and at the same time a similar figure, Miguel

[1] Junta de Historia y Numismática Americana, *op. cit.* pp. 149, and 163-4 note 28.

X

Carrera, a revolutionary from Chile exiled by the patriot government of O'Higgins, came to fight on the federalist side.[1] Rondeau, aware of the weakness of his support, vainly tried to negotiate a settlement,[2] and as a last resort took the field in an attempt to stave off the federalists.

In December, Pedro Campbell, as admiral of the federalist river flotilla, swept the *Porteño* boats from the Paraná. Then early in January 1820, Colonel Bustos of Córdoba deserted the centralists and set himself up as caudillo of an independent province. Tucumán deposed its government and set up a new one hostile to Buenos Aires, while the Directory's forces in the north rejected the capital's authority. Thus the Federal League's enemies were greatly reduced, and Artigas must have hoped that the other provinces would join his confederation at last: Córdoba, Tucumán, and even remote San Juan, San Luis and Mendoza. The last three did become federalist and joined in a league with Córdoba, not with the original Federal League; but still a confederation of all drew nearer. La Rioja followed these examples, and it seemed as if a landslide in favour of federalism had started. Artigas' principles were sweeping the centralists out of power, but Artigas himself rapidly lost his influence as the Portuguese affirmed their hold on the Provincia Oriental.

Inside Buenos Aires confusion and fear reigned,[3] and the many federalist sympathisers won much support. The Directory's agreement with the Portuguese over the Provincia Oriental earned the centralist leaders increasing disgust, until the fallen Pueyrredón and his personal followers, especially Tagle, who had initiated the policy, became the targets of accusations from all sides of having brought the country into mortal danger. Sarratea moved the outcry, foreseeing a quick federalist victory and wishing to gain by it. Consequently Pueyrredón and Tagle were exiled at the

---

[1] *Ibid.* pp. 149–50. Also J. Pérez, *op. cit.* pp. 7–11.

[2] Documents in Ravignani, *Asambleas Constituyentes*, vol. VI, t. 2, pp. 129–31.

[3] J. P. and W. P. Robertson, *Letters on South America*, vol. III, pp. 299–301.

end of January 1820. Juan Pedro Aguirre was elected substitute Director in Rondeau's absence in the field, and at last it seemed possible for peace to be brought to the Argentine scene again, since peace was so ardently desired by Buenos Aires.

The federalist forces of about sixteen hundred men advanced, led by Ramírez as Artigas' lieutenant, crossed the Buenos Aires border and marched towards the capital. Rondeau went forward to meet them with all the troops he could muster, some two thousand irresolute *Porteños*, and the armies clashed on the 1st of February at Cepeda. The battle was a foregone conclusion since the *Porteños* were completely demoralised before it began. After it the road to Buenos Aires lay open to the federalists.

Ramírez reported his success to Artigas, who was at that time sorely in need of such news after his defeat at Tacuarembó and his flight from the Provincia Oriental. The federal leaders Ramírez and López then received a deputation from Buenos Aires offering peace between their government and the Protector of the Free Peoples.[1] So that Buenos Aires could take its place as just one province among all the others, the Congress was dissolved and the Directory brought to an end. Now a settlement on federalist lines could organise the future government of the United Provinces. The Cabildo of Buenos Aires became the temporary government of the province, and it called a *Cabildo Abierto*, which set up a commission which elected Sarratea governor. It was ominous that this enemy of Artigas should come to power at such a critical moment. He and Ramírez and López negotiated a treaty of peace which was signed on the 23rd of February at El Pilar.

Meanwhile Artigas, still full of fight and apparently unconscious of his imminent fall, was planning to protect the Littoral from what seemed like certain invasion by the Portuguese, and also to win back the Provincia Oriental. Encouraged by his lieutenants' success against Buenos Aires, he circularised all the provincial governments which had declared themselves independent, offering

[1] Documents in Ravignani, *Asambleas constituyentes*, vol. VI, t. 2, p. 131.

to form an alliance which would become the basis of a confederation.

But Ramírez and López and Sarratea were playing the Protector false, the first two because of their personal ambition and all three because they had no wish to become involved in a war with Portugal over the Provincia Oriental, which they considered to be not their affair. Sarratea was no federalist, but an intriguer who would view the ruin of Artigas with pleasure. The Pact of El Pilar worked that ruin. It provided for a federal form of national government and stipulated that deputies elected by all the provinces should meet and arrange it at San Lorenzo in the province of Santa Fe. The peace was limited to the hostilities between the provinces of Buenos Aires, Entre Ríos and Santa Fe, although Buenos Aires was asked to remember the plight of the Provincia Oriental and out of her 'generosity and patriotism' to give help against the Portuguese. The members of the previous government of Buenos Aires must be tried for their crimes against the nation, and certain other technical matters were settled.

A copy of the Pact was to be sent to 'the Captain General of the Banda Oriental', Artigas, who was no longer referred to as the Protector of the Free Peoples. The omission of the title was not accidental. Although Ramírez had received instructions about the pact from Artigas, the former had no powers to sign on behalf of the latter. It was to be left to Artigas, if the Pact suited him, to establish with the other federalist provinces those relations which he might consider to be to the interest of his province. In this way, Artigas was pushed off his pedestal, and was merely treated by courtesy as the leader of a province which was not even really in his possession.[1] And further, Artigas' wishes that a confederation should be established were ignored, but the actual organisation of the national government was left to another Congress which might well be as irresponsible as the previous ones. No true alliance had been established, but a pious hope had been expressed that Buenos

[1] Copy of the Pact of El Pilar, *ibid.* pp. 131-2.

Aires would help to fight the Portuguese. Artigas rejected the Pact on these grounds, and further objected that Corrientes, the Provincia Oriental and the Misiones had not taken part in the negotiations, as they ought to have done, and Corrientes and Misiones had not even been mentioned in the Pact.[1]

A secret agreement had been made at El Pilar that Buenos Aires should provide the two caudillos with considerable quantities of arms, munitions and military equipment with the main object of preventing the Portuguese from establishing themselves in Entre Ríos.[2] Probably it was already in the minds of the three negotiators that the arms might be useful to help to get rid of Artigas altogether.

Despite the objections to the Pact of El Pilar from the point of view of Artigas and the Provincia Oriental, it is nevertheless the starting point of Argentine reconstruction after the misrule of the Directory. Some feeling of Argentine nationality would save the United Provinces from breaking up altogether, although in that process Artigas was jettisoned and with him his plans. Perhaps if these had been accepted a peaceful federalist settlement of the Argentine problem of government might have been reached in the 1820s instead of sixty years later. But the civil war in Argentina between various *Porteño* and provincial leaders continued in June 1820, plunging the country deeper into chaos before a temporary equilibrium was found in 1821, after the death in action of Ramírez. At least the centralists did not win outright, and federalist ideas were not wiped out, thanks to the leadership of Artigas in the critical years from 1813 to 1820.

The extinction of Artigas' influence came quickly after the supposed federalist victory of Cepeda and the Pact of El Pilar. After Tacuarembó the Protector established a small headquarters at Ávalos, in the province of Corrientes. His circular to the independent provinces went out from here, and meanwhile he

[1] J. M. Traibel, *La Liga Federal*, pp. 156–7.
[2] Documents in Ravignani, *Asambleas Constituyentes*, vol. VI, t. 2, pp. 133–7.

attempted to take his rightful place in the defence of the Federal League; but aid which he sent to Entre Ríos to help to put down the troublesome caudillos Hereñú and Correa was rejected, and Ramírez chose to regard as invasions certain expeditions which Artigas sent down the River Uruguay to watch for Portuguese incursions. Of all the independent provinces, only Corrientes and Misiones joined Artigas, who represented the Provincia Oriental, in signing a treaty known as the Pact of Ávalos, on the 24th of April 1820. Governor Méndez of Corrientes and the Indians of the Misiones were the last faithful supporters of the defeated leader. The Pact of Ávalos was a last desperate attempt on the part of Artigas to attain his ideal of confederation. The three provinces bound themselves in the interests of their freedom, independence and federation to fight together with all their strength. Artigas was once again, and for the last time, recognised as the Protector of the peoples in the League, and he was given the authority to make war and peace with external and internal enemies, so long as he made no treaties except on the basis of the liberty and independence of the three provinces. These three provinces each had the independence 'according to the principles of federation' to elect their own governors and arrange their own economic affairs. Any other province which accepted these provisions might join the League, though it only existed pending a final settlement of all the affairs of the nation by some General Congress of representatives of all the provinces.[1] It can be seen that Artigas' principles remained constant to the end.

Sarratea encouraged Ramírez to oppose Artigas by force, and hostilities began in June 1820. The caudillo of Entre Ríos had been well armed by Buenos Aires, and was superior in numbers of soldiers and resources to the ageing and unfortunate *Jefe*. At first Artigas, helped by Corrientes, won some advantages, but *Porteño* infantry turned the scales at the end of the month. Successively Artigas' remaining lieutenants went under: López Chico at

[1] Documents in Pivel Devoto and Fonseca Muñoz, *op. cit.* pp. 373-4.

Gualeguay, Perú Cutí and his Indians at Yuquerí, Matías Barú at Mandisoví. Others made their peace separately with Ramírez. By the end of July, Artigas himself, defeated and cornered, was lucky to escape with his life while his headquarters and equipment were captured.

The *Porteño* river flotilla defeated Pedro Campbell on the River Corrientes, and soon Corrientes itself fell to a movement of sympathisers with the new power, Ramírez. It is an ironic commentary that if there had been fear and some brigandage in Corrientes under Artigas' rule, they were much worse after his fall, when the most shocking atrocities were committed.[1] Artigas continued to be driven deeper into the wild terrain of the north of the province, ever nearer to the Paraguayan border. Méndez, still faithful, supported him in the Misiones, but even there Ramírez's troops relentlessly hunted the remaining *artiguistas* down until the *Jefe* at last fled to the headwaters of the River Morocotá. On the 5th of September Artigas crossed the upper Paraná at Candelaria into Paraguay, never to return to the world outside or to take any more part in public affairs.

Probably Artigas had crossed into Paraguay hoping to gain an alliance which would help him to continue the struggle, but if so he reckoned without Francia's nature. It is unlikely that Artigas was thinking of giving up the fight without further blows.[2] But Francia refused to grant him an interview, and instead gave him a frugal asylum from which he was not allowed to depart.[3] Artigas disappeared after September 1820, but his work did not. The lands of the Plate eventually came round to his ideals, and Uruguay,

---

[1] J. P. and W. P. Robertson, *Letters on South America*, vol. III, pp. 188–90.

[2] D. Hammerly Dupuy, *Rasgos biográficos de Artigas en el Paraguay;* also E. de Salterain y Herrera, *Artigas en el Paraguay.*

[3] L. A. Demersay, *Histoire physique, économique et politique du Paraguay et des établissements des Jésuites*, vol. II, pp. 365–6: 'Francia, jugeant qu'il était au-dessous de sa dignité d'admettre en sa présence un homme perdu de crimes, refusa de le voir; mais voulant respecter, comme il le disait lui-même, les droits sacrés de l'hospitalité envers un ennemi, il l'interna dans le village de Curuguaty...' In fact, Francia simply did not want to embroil his country in the civil war in the United Provinces, and therefore quietly dropped his former tone of friendship with Artigas.

when she was eventually freed from the Brazilian yoke, owed her consciousness of nationhood largely to Artigas and his leadership. But because Artigas had been ruined by the *Porteños* and their dupes the caudillos of the Littoral, Argentina and Uruguay went their separate ways instead of combining in a strong federation which would have increased the power and importance of the Plate region. Artigas had been crushed between the two great forces grinding together on the Banda Oriental: Spain and Portugal, later the United Provinces and Portugal in America.

CHAPTER IX

THE BIRTH OF URUGUAY

I. THE ESTADO CISPLATINO

ARTIGAS and his lieutenants kept up the fight against the Portuguese from 1817 to 1820 in the country districts of the Provincia Oriental, but besides this the Portuguese hold was rendered precarious by other factors. Inside Montevideo and the other parts occupied, conspirators in favour of Spanish rule or *Porteño* rule or home rule by Artigas kept Lecór anxious; and also there was the wider question of a possible intervention by the European powers who were mediating between Portugal and Spain. In 1819 Spain was concentrating an army at Cádiz to send to the Provincia Oriental to take over from the Portuguese, as had been arranged as a result of this mediation. Indeed, at this point Portugal seemed determined to evacuate the Provincia Oriental and hand over the parts she held to the Spanish army. The Directory in Buenos Aires gained information of this decision and ordered the agent García to make strong representations in Rio de Janeiro against such an act of treachery to the agreement between the two governments. García was to make it clear that Buenos Aires was resolved to maintain her independence, and if Portugal handed over Montevideo to a Spanish expedition, the United Provinces would make an alliance with Artigas and fight both Spain and Portugal. On the other hand, if the Portuguese would assist Buenos Aires against Spain, Brazil would be given commercial and territorial rewards. It was time for Dom João to decide on his attitude toward Spain, for the good of his Empire and for the sake of his 'natural Friends and Allies, the New Governments of South America'.[1]

But Portugal dared not commit herself to an alliance with the

[1] Memorandum . . . respecting Monte Video, MS. *cit.* P.R.O., F.O. 97/76, pp. 87-102, especially letters of Chamberlain Secret 10 October 1819 and Most Secret 27 October.

United Provinces, nor dared she announce the annexation of the Provincia Oriental for fear of the European reaction. Lecór was left to his own devices, and attempted to bring the Provincia Oriental of its own accord into the Portuguese Empire. He was forced to deport some loyal Spaniards and to repress some manifestations in favour of ending Portuguese rule. Dom João in 1819 made his task no lighter by announcing to the Cabildo of Montevideo that he was preparing to evacuate the city in view of the imminent arrival of the Spanish expedition,[1] but in fact he never took this step, and Lecór continued to govern the territory as if it were already part of Brazil. The agreement with Buenos Aires seemed to hold good, even if it were only an unwritten understanding, so that Lecór had no real fears of intervention by the United Provinces. In fact, the war waged by Pueyrredón against the Federal League assisted Lecór by dividing Artigas' troops, resources and attention. Yet in order to add to the confusion of his putative allies in Buenos Aires, Lecór astutely supplied Alvear with money in 1819 and sent him into Entre Ríos to join the federalist forces fighting against the centralists.[2]

Lecór, a shrewd soldier endowed with a fine presence and agreeable manners, had been a successful general who had won Wellington's approval in the Peninsular War, and he was anything but attracted by the gaucho warfare he met in the Provincia Oriental.[3] But, probably in part because of this, he won the war by diplomacy from inside the walls of Montevideo, and seemed likely to win the peaceful and even friendly co-operation of the people of the province. He himself married an Oriental lady of the best Montevideo society, and encouraged his officers to do likewise for the sake of cementing a permanent union between the two nations. It was largely Lecór's doing that the Provincia Oriental became the Estado Cisplatino, a part of Brazil, and it was

[1] Oliveira Lima, *op. cit.* vol. II, pp. 645–6.

[2] *Ibid.* p. 649. On the agreement with Portugal, see Memorandum . . . respecting Monte Video, MS. *cit.* pp. 87–99.

[3] J. E. Pivel Devoto, *El Congreso Cisplatino (1821)*, especially pp. 111–13.

hardly his fault that the forces of tradition, the long-standing rivalry between Lusitanians and Spaniards in the Plate region, gave those Orientals who desired liberty their chance in 1825.

Therefore Lecór concentrated on winning the good will of the Orientals and left the fundamental question of the settlement between Spain and Portugal to the diplomats in Europe, where Palmella, the Portuguese ambassador in London, served his country well. In this he had the advantage that the people of the towns and the more productive ranchers were heartily sick of the seemingly never-ending campaigning over their territory. The towns had been ten years without peace and therefore without business by 1820, and the country had been ravaged by several waves of campaigners, not least by the latest one.[1] But Lecór was generous to the vanquished: he offered amnesties to all who would desert from the Oriental forces, and gave officers the option of serving in their former rank and with full pay in local regiments attached to the Portuguese army or, if they preferred, of being allowed to leave the Provincia Oriental for Buenos Aires or any other foreign port. This helps to show how sure he felt that Buenos Aires would never fight him. Impressed slaves who deserted from the Oriental forces would be freed.[2] He took particularly strong measures against Brazilian rustlers in the Provincia Oriental, and compensated ranchers who suffered from their depredations. His troops had orders to pay for victuals, which they did not always do, and to protect the inhabitants from all harm. The people were guaranteed all their previous rights and employments.[3] The establishment of schools on the Lancaster system was permitted.[4] But Lecór firmly dissolved the Cabildos of the towns which had held out the longest against the Portuguese, though he

[1] Report of Francisco Agustini, in A.G.I., Seville, B.A. 156, on the state of the Plate provinces, d. 21 December 1821.

[2] Decree of Lecór, 6 June 1817, Arch. Adm., caja 482; 4.

[3] Declaration of Lecór, 5 February 1818, Arch. Adm., caja 483; 1.

[4] Paper containing a description of a schoolroom for a Lancaster system school, Arch. Adm., caja 587; 2.

promised to encourage the prosperity of those towns and to re-establish the Cabildos when their revenues could bear the expense.[1] Lecór wore the velvet glove in the Provincia Oriental.

Lecór attempted to revive Montevideo as an emporium of trade, and one of the things he did fulfilled a desire of many years' standing among the merchants: he encouraged the building, at public cost, of a lighthouse on the Isla de Flores. Funds of the Montevideo Consulado were applied, with his blessing, to the improvement of the roads leading out of the city and in its vicinity.[2] It was only in a secret agreement that the *quid pro quo* for the lighthouse appeared: the advancing of the Rio Grande do Sul border some way into the territory of the Provincia Oriental. Partly by such means, but mainly by the act of bringing peace to the ports of the Provincia Oriental, Lecór assisted in the recovery of the country's trade, even though there were protests that when the old stocks of hides and tallow which had accumulated had been exported the province's trade would fall off. The reason put forward was that the laws tended to discourage the killing of cattle in the province and to encourage their exportation to Rio Grande do Sul, so that indeed some *saladeristas* were leaving the Provincia Oriental for the neighbouring Brazilian province, where their businesses would prosper more than at home.[3] In fact the amount of trade passing through Montevideo under Lecór's administration was higher than at any time between the English Invasions and the opening of the war of liberation from Brazil.[4] But it is clear that the old fear of the Brazilian competitor was so deeply rooted that it would not die out, whatever Lecór might do, and this was symptomatic of the whole problem of the ownership of the Banda Oriental. Orientals and Portuguese or Brazilians

---

[1] Letter of Lecór (now Barão da Laguna) to the Cabildo of Colonia, 3 June 1818, Arch. Adm., libro 713, f. 175; Libro de Acuerdos of Soriano, *ibid.* libro 68.

[2] Letter of Barão da Laguna to Consulado of Montevideo, 5 May 1819, in M.H.N., vol. XIII.

[3] Observations of the Síndico General del Comericio to the Consulado, *ibid.*

[4] See Appendix II, numbers of ships entering and leaving Montevideo.

were like Spaniards and Portuguese in Europe, or like oil and water: they would not mix.

The majority acquiesced in the Portuguese occupation, and many of the official class collaborated, whether won over by Lecór's rewards and decorations or by the prosperity promised by peace, or by their state of moral and physical exhaustion caused by the defeat following years of revolutionary strife. The Cabildo of Montevideo had hurried in 1817 to beg King João VI to annex the Provincia Oriental, and it had been the priest in charge of the main church of Montevideo, Larrañaga, and the official in charge of the treasury and customs, Bianqui, who had gone to Rio de Janeiro to press the claim. Other Cabildos in the province hastened to offer their services in the enlistment of a native militia to support the occupation.[1] Rivera in 1820 became the colonel of a regiment called Dragoons of the Union, and Lavalleja joined the same regiment with the rank of lieutenant-colonel as soon as he was released from imprisonment in Rio de Janeiro. Other Oriental officers joined: Sáenz, Delgado, Martínez, Ysas Calderón, Manuel Lavalleja, Bernabé Rivera and more.

A change in the situation of the Portuguese government occurred as a result of the liberal movements in the Peninsula which came to a head first in Spain. There, Colonel Riego led a revolt in January 1820 among the troops waiting at Cádiz to sail to Montevideo, and the threatened expedition was thus made impossible. Dom João could now consider the annexation of the Provincia Oriental to Brazil without serious thought of the repercussions in Europe. Also, it was clear that the province could not be left permanently under a costly military occupation, so that liberal Brazilian statesmen were able to persuade Dom João to permit the Orientals to elect a provincial Congress to decide freely on their own destiny. The fact was that the liberal movement in Spain had touched off a similar one in Portugal, which in turn

[1] Eg. *borrador* of Cabildo of Maldonado to the Colonel of the Militia and Chief of the Department of Maldonado, 2 February 1820, Arch. Adm., libro 290, f. 114.

encouraged the Brazilian liberals. Dom João reluctantly decided that he must return to Portugal in 1821 to look after his dynastic interests, leaving Brazil in the hands of native liberals and in a state of ferment.[1]

Lecór therefore received orders to call the *Congreso Cisplatino* in April 1821. Buenos Aires was surprised, puzzled and suspicious. Balcarce, the substitute Governor of Buenos Aires, made a suggestion that the Portuguese must be ejected from the Provincia Oriental so as to ensure the safety of Entre Ríos, on which Lecór had an acquisitive eye. But Lecór now began to consider how to maintain his own hold on the Provincia Oriental, since the Court's departure for Lisbon made the future of Brazil itself uncertain. The Portuguese troops in Brazil appeared to support a liberal Portuguese constitution, whereas the Brazilian troops seemed to reject it, not out of dislike for its principles so much as out of a desire to make Brazil a country in her own right. In Montevideo the Portuguese troops mutinied and demanded the settlement of their arrears of pay and their transport back to Portugal, and Lecór was obliged to agree. Buenos Aires at this felt that the time was ripe for her to encourage a revolt of the Provincia Oriental in favour of union with the United Provinces, and therefore the governor, Martín Rodríguez, sent agents to summon Lecór to abandon the province and also secretly to bring Rivera over to the Argentine way of thinking. The Orientals were, it was true, in a state of bewilderment, but these gestures had no effect. Buenos Aires was calmed when a Portuguese consul arrived and gave a reasonable explanation for the calling of the *Congreso Cisplatino*: it had met to decide on the fate of the province, not merely to vote incorporation into Brazil. But in July 1821 this Congress in fact determined to request the province's incorporation, so that Buenos Aires believed she had been duped by the Portuguese.

In fact what had happened was due to Lecór's intrigues. He had

---

[1] Homem, *op. cit.* pp. 88–99; Fragoso, *op. cit.* pp. 131–7; and especially Pivel Devoto, *El Congreso Cisplatino*; also *La misión de Juan Manuel de Figueiredo*

gathered a circle of Oriental collaborators, known as 'the Baron's Club', since he had been made Barão da Laguna for his services to Portugal. This group included at one time or another several Oriental notabilities such as Tomás García de Zúñiga, Juan José Durán, Herrera, Lucas José Obes, Father Larrañaga, Bianqui, José Raimundo Guerra, as well as lesser figures. In the main, they were men who stood to lose their lucrative posts,[1] their influence, their honours, perhaps their liberty or even their lives if the Provincia Oriental became independent or voted to join some state other than Portugal. Neither these men nor Lecór wished to see the Provincia Oriental give its vote freely: all of them wanted the province to remain under Portuguese rule and then quietly join Brazil when the inevitable movement of Brazilian independence should arise.

Consequently Lecór ordered Durán, the provisional Intendant Governor of the province, to convoke the Congress for the 15th of July; and the two arranged not to hold popular elections of deputies, as were the specific orders of Dom João, but themselves to choose certain government officials of the province as nine out of the eighteen deputies. They allowed the pro-Portuguese Cabildos to choose the other nine. In this way Lecór made certain of obtaining a servile Congress which would not reflect the aspirations of the majority of the Orientals. It was the antithesis of what Artigas had fought for: here government meant fraud and force. But it is also a fact that the Congress contained some notable men, who perhaps sincerely desired tranquillity above all else just then, such as Durán himself, who was the president of the Congress, and García de Zúñiga, the friend of Artigas, Larrañaga, Rivera, Bianqui and Llambí, a rising young lawyer. These men petitioned for the province to be incorporated into Portugal's dominions as the Estado Cisplatino, a name which came into use in September 1821.

[1] See R. D. Campos, *Brigadier General Dr. Thomás García de Zúñiga . . .*, pp. 133–50, which includes a list of some posts accepted by Orientals under the Portuguese administration.

The Birth of Uruguay

The Portuguese government was in fact itself surprised and embarrassed at this result, since it was trying to stand side by side with the liberal Spanish government in a Europe which desired to end such liberal experiments. Lecór was reprimanded and asked to explain his conduct, but he had realised his position, and instead of obeying his master in Lisbon, he put himself in February 1822 in the hands of the Prince Regent, Dom Pedro, whom Dom João had left in Brazil to care for the interests of the Braganzas there. Brazil's independence was obviously drawing close, and Lecór was showing which way the wind blew with him.

The Regency government in Rio de Janeiro accepted Lecór's gift with alacrity, and began to try to link the Estado Cisplatino to Brazil by ordering various improvements to be made there. In April 1822 Lecór received orders from the liberal Brazilian states-man José Bonifácio de Andrada to establish a high school in Montevideo, and to begin a new road between Montevideo and Maldonado, to repair other roads and to put the port of Maldonado in order. Other reforms were projected in response to the petitions of Lucas José Obes, the Oriental agent sent to Rio de Janeiro to assist in the business of the incorporation.[1] But the country people had good reason to remain suspicious of any régime connected with Brazil. Since the beginning of the invasion they had witnessed a large influx into the Provincia Oriental of Brazilian ranchers, who had been encouraged by orders given out by Lecór for the sale and even the free granting of empty lands. Indeed it had been one of the motives of Obes' visit to Rio de Janeiro to complain about this injustice as well as about the continual disorder, robbery and violence which afflicted the province owing to the lack of discipline of the occupying troops in country districts.[2]

[1] Museo Histórico Nacional, Montevideo, Biblioteca Pablo Blanco Acevedo, MS. vol. 132, no. 49, letter of Joaquín de Oliveira Alverez to L. J. Obes, 20 March 1822; no. 50, J. B. Andrada to Barão da Laguna, 3 April; no. 51, Andrada to Obes, 18 May; no. 52, Andrada to Laguna, 5 June; no. 54, 20 July.

[2] C. Carbajal, *La penetración luso-brasileña en el Uruguay*, pp. 71-5.

The Estado Cisplatino

On the 7th of September 1822 Dom Pedro himself, rather than lose Brazil for his dynasty, proclaimed the country independent of Portugal and became its head as the Emperor Pedro I. There were some objectors, mainly among the Portuguese troops, but the independence movement succeeded quickly and almost bloodlessly, since it had been prepared for by the transfer of the Portuguese monarchy to Brazil from 1807 to 1821. In the Estado Cisplatino, Lecór came out on the side of Brazil with the Brazilian troops, while the Portuguese troops held Montevideo. A minor campaign took place, but the Portuguese soon capitulated and gladly sailed for home in November 1823. It is significant of Lecór's methods that the Cabildo of Soriano, which had been in dissolution since his government took over, was re-created with his 'approval' on the 8th of November 1822, and on the 9th it recognised Dom Pedro I as Emperor of Brazil, including the Estado Cisplatino.[1]

Rivera had fought for Lecór, but some Orientals had declared for the Portuguese, and all hoped to gain something for their country. Inside Montevideo, some proclaimed a revolution and looked to Buenos Aires and Santa Fe for help before the now indifferent Portuguese left them. The British consul in Montevideo was at one time approached with a petition for Britain to aid the Oriental effort;[2] and the Cabildo, in December 1822, declared the Provincia Oriental's incorporation into Brazil null and invited Rio de Janeiro to withdraw the Brazilian troops and allow the Orientals to make a decision freely. The Cabildo was hoping to put the province under the protection of the United Provinces; but Buenos Aires was cautious. It was only in September 1823 that her government sent José Valentín Gómez to Rio de Janeiro to ask for the return of the Provincia Oriental. But Dom Pedro decided to

---

[1] Libro de Acuerdos del Cabildo de Soriano, Arch. Adm., libro 68. For a complete account of the Oriental movements for and against independence after 1822 see P. Blanco Acevedo, *Informe sobre la fecha de celebración del centenario de la independencia*, pp. 44 ff.

[2] Letter of T. S. Hood to Canning, d. Montevideo 22 April 1824, doc. no.22 in Webster, *op. cit.*

keep the Estado Cisplatino because of its 'well-known fidelity' to Brazil, of which he had been persuaded by Lecór; and in May 1824 the authorities of the province, including the Cabildo of Montevideo, swore their allegiance to the new Brazilian constitution.

At the time that the Cabildo of Montevideo had declared the nullity of the province's incorporation into Brazil, it had sent a mission asking Buenos Aires to give her aid to a project for a revolt in favour of the United Provinces. But Buenos Aires was led by the centralist ministers Rivadavia and García, who prevented any action for fear of a possible revival of federalism through the caudillos of the Provincia Oriental and also for fear of being drawn into a disastrous war with Brazil.[1] The Montevideo Cabildo held elections and so turned itself into a representative body, hoping to lead a revolt using weapons which the Portuguese troops had thoughtfully left behind when they sailed. But few would join in a rising at that time, certainly not Rivera, who stayed loyal for the moment to Lecór and even warned the Cabildo that the time was not ripe for 'complete independence', since in its weakness the province could only become a battlefield for the Argentine and Brazilian armies. Many of the estancieros supported Lecór and Brazil because they were tired of upheavals and wanted their cattle to be left in peace. Perhaps Rivera and García de Zúñiga, who also declared for Lecór and Brazil, hoped to be able to gain some sort of autonomy from Brazil once the new Empire had settled down.

But Lavalleja rose in revolt in the district of Tacuarembó, only to be forced by Rivera to flee into Entre Ríos and make his way from there through Santa Fe to Buenos Aires. Here Lavalleja found a club of Oriental revolutionaries, the *Caballeros Orientales*, working to gain for their province the sympathy and aid of the government. After the definite acceptance of the Estado Cisplatino into Brazil in 1824 these elements were supported by a

[1] For these events see De-María, *Hombres notables*, vol. I, pp. 85-187, *El general don Fructuoso Rivera*, pp. 98 ff.; E. de Gandía, *Los treinta y tres orientales y la independencia del Uruguay*, pp. 147 ff.; D. Carneiro, *História da Guerra Cisplatina*, pp. 33 ff.

stronger movement in favour of independence inside Montevideo and in the interior of the Estado. Even Rivera, perhaps urged by legitimate ambition, began to come round to the view that it was time to consider the liberation of the 'patria', and secretly sounded opinion in the country districts.[1]

By the end of 1824 and beginning of 1825 it was clear to Lecór that something was stirring in the Estado Cisplatino. He was safe in Montevideo, where the majority supported Brazilian rule and peace, and indeed were under the influence of that distrust of the country districts which so hampered the organisation of both Uruguay and Argentina. But in those districts it only needed a lead for the majority to rise against the foreign domination.[2] Patriot agents were everywhere, and in the United Provinces Orientals continued to try to persuade the governments of Buenos Aires, Sante Fe and Entre Ríos to undertake a liberating expedition.

Then in December 1824 occurred an event which heated the cool heads of the Buenos Aires government: it was Bolívar's victory at Ayacucho in Perú over the last Spanish army in South America. When the news of it reached Buenos Aires in January 1825 the city indulged in a burst of enthusiasm, since all Spanish South America was free except, as the people remembered, the Banda Oriental. The people, and opinion expressed in newspapers, infected the Buenos Aires government with an enthusiasm for the redemption of the Estado Cisplatino and its union with the United Provinces. Artigas' ideal of independence for the Banda Oriental was forgotten by Buenos Aires and shelved by the Orientals, who so much desired Argentine aid. The Oriental émigrés in Buenos Aires, led by Manuel Oribe and Juan Antonio Lavalleja, began to plan to make a landing on Uruguayan territory and proclaim the revolt against Brazil. Their schemes were passed secretly to friends over the River Plate and met with a patriotic response, which was only repressed on the surface when Lecór gained information

[1] De-María, *op. cit.* vol. I, pp. 106-7.
[2] This split is clearly shown by the documents published in *Documentos para servir al estudio de la independencia nacional*, especially vol. II.

about the illegal meetings and the patriot plans. Men in Buenos Aires and in Entre Ríos prepared to help their Oriental neighbours, and all that Lecór could do was to ask Rio de Janeiro to send reinforcements ready for the war he knew was coming. Rivera realised that he was becoming suspect to Lecór, and to throw him off the scent, he issued in February 1825 a manifesto in which he declared himself a fervent partisan of Brazil; yet he recruited good patriots into his regiment of Dragoons ready for what he too knew was inevitable.

The political scene in the United Provinces had gone through some changes since the federalist victories of 1820 and the disappearance of Artigas, but the policy of Buenos Aires with regard to the Banda Oriental was the same. 1820 was the year of anarchy in the Buenos Aires government, as Balcarce ousted Sarratea from power, then Alvear attempted a *coup*, followed by Soler. Dorrego, who had federalist sympathies, was elected governor of Buenos Aires province, and next the more centralist Martín Rodríguez. But confusion over the identity of the government actually in power was so great that on one day in 1820 there were at least three authorities with some claims to be the government of Buenos Aires. Rodríguez brought calm, helped by his ministers Rivadavia and García; and Buenos Aires province prospered under their centralist and Europeanised administration. A kind of confederation was created between the provinces of Buenos Aires, Entre Ríos, Santa Fe and Corrientes, and the other provinces were to be allowed to join when the projected national general congress should meet. General Las Heras succeeded Rodríguez in April 1824, and under him a national Constituent Congress met in Buenos Aires in December. By this time there was a general feeling in the United Provinces that there should at least be a minimum of union among them and, especially in view of the rapidly developing movement in the Banda Oriental, that there should be some sort of central government ready to face a possible war.

Therefore the Congress decided on the 23rd of January 1825 that, pending the definite constitution of the country, the government of Buenos Aires province should act as the national government for war and foreign affairs. This government, led by Las Heras, was at last permitted to form a national army consisting of contingents from all the provinces, up to a total of eight thousand men. When the Orientals revolted, this government took the precaution of creating an Army of Observation to watch the line of the Uruguay, under the command of Martín Rodríguez, and to be ready for any necessary action.

On the 19th of April 1825 the Oriental patriots struck the first blow. Thirty-three volunteers led by Lavalleja and known in the history of the Plate countries as the Thirty-three Orientals (although several were Argentines, one a French Basque and two negroes) landed from small boats at the shore of La Agraciada, near Colonia. There they found horses provided secretly by their friends, and rode to raise the people of the Estado Cisplatino in revolt. The Buenos Aires government had still not declared itself in favour of the revolt, as Lecór was aware, but influential citizens put pressure on the men in office and personally helped the expedition by subscribing considerable sums of money on loan to the active Oriental treasurer and organiser in Buenos Aires, Trápani. The wealthy Anchorena family, the first to subscribe, gave three thousand pesos, and also persuaded their friends to give generously, with the result that within a few months over sixteen thousand pesos had come from private citizens. The money was spent on arms, uniforms, munitions, medicaments, and on transport for all these things; but it would not have gone very far towards filling the Orientals' needs but for help given by the government from October onwards.

Impressed by the efforts of the Orientals and of their own citizens, and undoubtedly, like the latter, thinking of the advantages to be won by regaining the Banda Oriental as a 'beautiful estancia' for the province of Buenos Aires, as it had been in

The Birth of Uruguay

colonial times, the Buenos Aires government generously gave over one hundred and seventy-six thousand pesos in the first four months after its decision to give aid.[1] It was helped to make up its mind, no doubt, by the politic determination taken in August 1825 by a patriot provincial assembly of the Provincia Oriental to seek admission to the Constituent Congress. Trápani had urged on the new Oriental provisional government the need for such a gesture to allay the lingering suspicions of the *Porteño* government that the Provincia Oriental would take Argentine help only to become entirely independent after all.

By the end of October, then, the government of Buenos Aires had handsomely accepted the Oriental offer of union and had begun to send aid to the patriots. The instructions which the Oriental Congress of 1825 gave to the deputies it sent to the Constituent Assembly of the United Provinces were limited to four articles: the first contained a plea for the maintenance of the established religion of the country; the second a plea for the maintenance of liberty 'under the system of representative government' and no other; the third an order for the deputies to consult the provincial Congress in case of doubt on any point; and the last a request that the United Provinces should declare war on Brazil and send help to the Provincia Oriental.[2] The contrast with Artigas' instructions of 1813 could hardly be more striking: to gain such an abject surrender on the part of the Orientals the *Porteño* centralists had fought and intrigued hard; but it was to be an empty victory for their successors in the government of the United Provinces.

But to begin with, the thirty-three stood alone against Brazil on the beach of La Agraciada, though supported by true sympathy in Argentina.[3] On the 20th of April Lavalleja began to recruit

[1] See Razón de las cantidades administradas por don Pedro Trápani, *Documentos para servir al estudio de la independencia nacional*, vol. I, pp. 231-60.

[2] Documents on the reincorporation of the Provincia Oriental into the United Provinces, *ibid.* pp. 121-7.

[3] In addition to the works mentioned p. 338 note 1, see Fragoso, *op. cit.* pp. 139 ff. for this campaign.

342

patriots as he marched on Soriano. This town surrendered to him, and some men joined him, bringing the numbers of his force to a hundred. Lecór had decided that Rivera was trustworthy, and he sent him to put down the revolt. But Rivera moved out from his headquarters at Colonia into the open country, instead of marching straight for Lavalleja while his opponent was still weak. Probably Rivera intended to allow the Orientals to gather forces, and perhaps he hoped to find some excuse for throwing over his fidelity to Brazil without altogether losing his honour. At all events, on the 29th of April Rivera allowed himself with only a small escort to be 'surprised' by Lavalleja, and after a short private conference, the two former lieutenants of Artigas announced their union in a crusade against the Brazilians, and Rivera's escort went to swell the Oriental 'army' to about one hundred and fifty men.[1] The 'capture' of Rivera was of the greatest benefit to the Oriental cause, for it brought with it not only the prestige of Artigas' best lieutenant, but also the good will of a large number of cowboys and their bosses and of many waverers. But Rivera was more in favour of complete independence, perhaps in conjunction with the Brazilian state of Rio Grande do Sul, than of union with the United Provinces, and so he brought with him others who had similar aims. From the 29th of April it was certain that the revolt would not feebly flicker out, but that it would be at the least a serious military commitment for Brazil to face.[2]

Almost at once Rivera proved his value by surprising a Brazilian force of one hundred and eighty men and forcing it to surrender, and by gaining the adherence to the crusade of Major Calderón and a squadron of a hundred Oriental hussars. The advance went on in the direction of the capital, and the countryside rose to welcome the patriots. Canelones was occupied, and already on the 7th of May the army was on the Cerrito, in sight of Montevideo and threatening it; while at the same time Colonia was besieged.

[1] De-María, *op. cit.* vol. I, pp. 108-9.
[2] Salterain y Herrera, *Lavalleja*, t. XXV, pp. 114-16, 137-52.

Inside the capital there was panic among the Brazilians, and many troops deserted. At this point the Buenos Aires government took action, sending the Army of Observation into Entre Ríos to guard the River Uruguay and perhaps to render the Brazilians more nervous. Loads of arms and ammunition were sent across the River Plate by Trápani for the Oriental army, but still no official aid came from Buenos Aires.

Before the end of May, while Rivera set about the Brazilian forces, Lavalleja began to organise a provincial government. He sent circulars calling for the election of deputies for this, and sent a commission to Buenos Aires to organise the help coming from there. The provisional government of delegates from the Departments was established at the small town of La Florida on the 14th of June, and on the 17th it called for elections to a provincial Congress. On the 21st a mission was sent to Buenos Aires to proclaim the Provincia Oriental's union with the United Provinces and to ask for the government's help against the Brazilian usurpers.[1] Trápani worked behind the scenes, advising Lavalleja how he should act and attempting to persuade the *Porteño* leaders to commit their country to a war with Brazil.

The mission received a warm welcome from the people and the army, but the government of Buenos Aires hesitated still. Not even when the Provincia Oriental's House of Representatives, most of whose members were veterans of Artigas' army and keen patriots, voted the province's incorporation into the United Provinces in August, nor when the incorporation was accepted by the nation in October, did the Buenos Aires government make any official move. In November, however, the governor, Las Heras, reported to the government of Brazil the reincorporation of the Provincia Oriental in the United Provinces, and expressed his country's determination to defend its frontiers 'against force and seduction'. This was tantamount to a declaration of war against Brazil.

[1] Documents on the actions of this government in *Edición conmemorativa del centenario de 1825*.

What had taken place was not merely the political submission of the Provincia Oriental to the United Provinces, since the Oriental submission was probably only intended to be a temporary phase by most of those who engineered it; but it was essential to appear to submit in order to gain the United Provinces' military support. There had been a mass rising of the country districts of the Provincia Oriental, which practically confined the Brazilians to possession of the main towns, and also some important though small victories of the Orientals over the Brazilian army had taken place. After these, the enthusiasm of the *Porteños* knew no bounds, and war was inevitable. While Lavalleja, appointed Governor and Captain-general of the Provincia Oriental by the provisional government, dealt with the politics, hoisted the flag of the United Provinces and organised a formal administration, General Rivera became Inspector-general of the provincial forces and pushed the war on. The Orientals met some reverses outside Colonia and Montevideo, and in September Rivera was defeated while trying to stop the advance of twelve hundred fresh Brazilian troops under Abreu, now a baron and a general of the Brazilian Empire. But on the 24th of September Rivera won an important victory over them at Rincón de las Gallinas, near Soriano, and followed it up, together with Lavalleja, with a glorious victory on the 12th of October at Sarandí, in the centre of the province, between La Florida and Durazno.[1] Therefore on the 25th of October the Argentine Constituent Congress accepted, after a delay of two months, the reunion of the Provincia Oriental. This hesitancy strengthened a current of opinion which existed among the Orientals in favour of complete independence. In any case, the Orientals remained distrustful of Buenos Aires, and intended that their province should have autonomy within the very loose confederation called the United Provinces. They desired to avoid the hegemony which the *Porteños*, for their part, meant to impose on their estancia.

[1] Salterain y Herrera, *Lavalleja*, t. XXVI, pp. 1-46.

Lavalleja and Rivera were appointed brigadiers of the Argentine army to mark the union, and in response to Buenos Aires' challenge the Emperor of Brazil declared war on the United Provinces on the 10th of December 1825. The Argentine provinces welcomed the war and willingly sent their contingents to form a united army with which to crush the Brazilians. It was the continuation of the old struggle between Portuguese and Spaniards. On the 26th of December the Army of Observation was led by Rodríguez across the River Uruguay into the Provincia Oriental, amid the enthusiasm of Argentines and Orientals. The Brazilians seemed unable to co-ordinate their efforts, perhaps because Lecór, who was over sixty years of age, preferred intrigue to war. They found themselves hemmed in inside the coastal towns, whilst the patriots quickly took command of almost the whole of the interior. Some Orientals who lived in the towns under Brazilian domination, particularly Montevideo, tried to prove their loyalty to Brazil, but many became suspect and suffered imprisonment.

By the beginning of 1826 the Brazilians held only Colonia, Maldonado and Montevideo, and an Oriental force led by the caudillo of the east coast, Colonel Leonardo Olivera, had recaptured the frontier fortress of Santa Teresa, had passed the Chuy and had invaded Rio Grande do Sul.[1] In reply to the patriot successes, a Brazilian fleet under Admiral Rodrigo Lobo declared a blockade of the Argentine ports, and a sea war opened.

The loyalty of the Provincia Oriental to the national government had not been secured by the United Provinces' entry into the war against Brazil. The political situation was bound to remain complicated by the unsolved question of the permanent form of government to be adopted by Argentina. The Orientals had a traditional dislike of *Porteño* domination, and this was the reason for the success of Artigas and his ideas amongst them in former years. *Porteño* troops who came to fight for them were yet unpopular with the ordinary Oriental folk, although contingents

[1] C. Pintos Diago, *Leonardo Olivera.*

346

from other provinces were well received. Even in the 'national' war against Brazil, Lavalleja and his helpers were the effective government of the Provincia Oriental, although they paid lip-service to the 'national' government, which was merely the government of Buenos Aires. This tendency was strengthened when the Argentine Constituent Congress produced in 1826 a centralist constitution for the nation, and when the centralist, Europeanised Rivadavia was elected the first national president.

It should be realised that up to this time the vast majority of Orientals had not desired what would now be called independence, but rather autonomy under a system of loose confederation. This was the meaning of 'independence' to those people, led by no less a man than Artigas, who clearly had desired provincial autonomy for all the United Provinces and had practised it in his Federal League. Rivera and a few Orientals were at this period thinking of complete independence for the Banda Oriental, but the movement was not yet important. To the Orientals in general, all Argentines were brothers, not cousins. They were of the same name and blood, even though they might quarrel. Indeed, nearly every province had a more or less bitter quarrel with Buenos Aires at some stage in the period when national organisation was in the process of being worked out. However, the events from 1826 to 1828 completely changed the circumstances of the Banda Oriental and the attitude of its people, so that in the end Uruguay emerged as a separate republic.

Inside Argentina proper, the struggle between centralists and federalists continued, and it flared up again after the centralist political success of 1826. There were to be repercussions in the Provincia Oriental. The *Porteño* centralist statesmen were suspicious of the Orientals, whom they regarded as trouble-makers in the union of the provinces. It was significant that the Buenos Aires Foreign Minister was now M. J. García, who had been Pueyrredón's agent in Rio de Janeiro at the time of the agreement with the Portuguese over the invasion of the *Patria Vieja*, and who had always shown hostility to the Provincia Oriental. But at this time Rivera's more extreme ideas came into conflict with Lavalleja's moderation over the question of autonomy in the resurgent Provincia Oriental, and the coincidence of these mutually hostile movements on either side of the River Plate marks the beginning of the struggle for a truly independent Uruguay.

A serious mistake of the *Porteños* came just then and ended for ever any chance of union founded on trust. It was an obvious move against the Oriental army, made by General Rodríguez, the commander of the Argentine forces which entered the Provincia Oriental in January 1826 to carry on the national war against Brazil. Rodríguez suspected Lavalleja's good faith, and attempted to split up the Oriental forces among the various divisions of his army, so trying to remove their independence of action. It appears a reasonable step, since the army was a national one under Rodríguez's supreme command, and it was fighting a national war. The contingents from the other provinces were indeed incorporated in this way into the army. But it was an impolitic action in the critical state of Oriental opinion, and Lavalleja, as Governor of the province, refused to allow the Oriental forces to be broken into small divisions, although he still attempted to maintain cordial relations with Rivadavia's government. On the other hand, Rivera revolted with some of his troops and became a rebel against the national government, receiving asylum and help from the caudillo Estanislao López of Santa Fe. Rivera was to reappear shortly, to win great popularity among the Oriental people and lay the foundations of his leadership of one of the parties into which they soon split.

As a result of this evidence of the unreliability of the Orientals and of Rodríguez's inability to control them, Rivadavia dismissed the commander-in-chief and replaced him by sending Alvear to command the national army in the Provincia Oriental. Alvear, the former centralist dictator, was back in favour with the government of Buenos Aires. Also, the arrival of an English mediator in

the war was expected soon, and Rivadavia wished to be able to
impress him with the sight of a unified and active army in the
field led by this brilliant general. In fact, Alvear had had little
experience in the field and hardly any in high command, being
more of a politician and intriguer than a soldier. But he was
determined both to beat the Brazilians and make the Provincia
Oriental obey the constitution of 1826. The Oriental government
had accepted this centralist constitution because of the need for
help in the war, but almost all the Argentine provinces, with their
autonomous leanings, had rejected it. At all events, under great pressure from Alvear and the government of Buenos Aires, Lavalleja,
for the sake of unity in the war, accepted a military post under
Alvear's command and left the government of the Provincia
Oriental in the hands of a substitute. At least by this he ensured
that the provincial government survived whatever the *Porteños*
might do with him.[1]

The war was stagnant while these political moves took place,
but the Brazilians slowly gathered forces in the frontier town of
Santa Ana, while the Argentine and Oriental army reorganised
and settled these differences. If the Brazilians had struck early in
1826 with their armies in Montevideo and on the frontier the war
might have been quickly won; but it was only in December 1826
that they gave signs of activity. Amid a great show of bellicosity
the young Emperor, Pedro I, took command of his forces in
person, with the intention of winning what was becoming a
shameful and losing fight. Apart from small land skirmishes, 1826
was a year of sea war, during which the Irish sailor Brown,
Admiral of the Argentine fleet, took the offensive. Although he
was outnumbered and often defeated, by the decisive month of
February 1827 Brown gained the important advantage of command of the River Plate and was able to harass successfully the
Brazilian fleet along the Atlantic coast of the theatre of war. It was
perhaps unfortunate for the Brazilians that Dom Pedro was

[1] See Salterain y Herrera, *Lavalleja*, t. XXVI, pp. 75-129.

obliged by the death of his consort to return to his capital without commanding a campaign. Instead of Pedro, the Marquess of Barbacena became the commander-in-chief, a poor soldier, although he tried to reorganise his heterogeneous army and infuse some spirit into it.

At the beginning of 1827 Barbacena had an army of nearly four thousand three hundred men on the Rio Grande frontier, though many of the troops were unfit to fight owing to sickness. In Rio Grande there was a force of seventeen hundred men in reserve. Opposing him was Alvear, who had taken over command of the united patriot army on the 1st of September 1826 and had at first spent his energies attempting to force the *riveristas* to submit. His troops were as badly prepared as were Barbacena's: the greatest difference was that the Argentines received their pay nearly on time, whereas the Brazilians' pay was at least three months in arrear. This shows an important distinction between the resources and warlike possibilities of the two countries. By the end of 1826, the patriots had over eight thousand men in the field, with Lavalleja and Soler as Alvear's chief lieutenants.

Alvear's plan was to carry the war into Brazil, and accordingly he concentrated his forces in December and marched across the frontier towards Bagé, intending to keep the Brazilian forces divided and beat them piecemeal on their own soil. But here Alvear's inexperience played him false, and his movements in that virgin country were so slow that he gave the enemy the time to concentrate. Yet the Brazilians felt themselves too weak to attack, and contented themselves with making a long and arduous retreat, attempting to stop Alvear's advance by leaving no provisions behind for him. Finally, however, the armies clashed on the 20th of February at Ituzaingó, on ground chosen by the Argentines, and the Brazilians, few in number and not so well armed as their opponents, and even worse led, were beaten after a confused battle. Lavalleja, commander of the patriot van, distinguished himself by disobeying Alvear's dispositions for the battle, with the result that the two generals, already on bad terms, almost came to blows. It seemed inevitable that *Porteños* and Orientals could not serve together.[1] The losses were not overwhelming on either side, but the Argentines were unable to follow up their advantage beyond an ineffectual pursuit of the retreating army for a few hours. The main result of the battle, however, was that it left both sides exhausted after the long preliminary marches. Alvear was soon forced to limp back into the Provincia Oriental, all the time apprehensive of the appearance of a reorganised Brazilian army. But both sides were without fresh horses, so that no serious action was possible, and the military operations ended in a stalemate.

In Argentina, a civil war was beginning as the federalist caudillos in the interior rose against Rivadavia's centralist régime. The President therefore decided to use the forces left at his disposal in an attempt to stop the federalist movement from spreading. Accordingly no more reinforcements could be sent to Alvear, so that a renewal of the war could not be undertaken. At the same time the *riverista* opposition in the Provincia Oriental grew stronger. Brazil, too, was without resources, so that after the battle of Ituzaingó the only end to the war must be one brought by diplomacy. Skirmishes continued to take place, and even another pathetically lame 'invasion' of Rio Grande by Alvear, but it was a guerilla war which could go on indefinitely without major hurt to either side.

2. DIPLOMACY AND PEACE

On the 19th of April 1827 the *Porteño* minister M. J. García was given the task of undertaking a new mission to Rio de Janeiro, this time to attempt to arrive at some preliminary arrangement with the Brazilian government for an armistice. This was partly due to the British mediation begun in 1826, and partly due to exhaustion

---

[1] Tasso Fragoso, *op. cit.*; D. Carneiro, *op. cit.*; Salterain y Herrera, *Lavalleja*, t. xxvi, pp. 129-40.

in Buenos Aires. García was instructed to accept terms honourable to both sides, so long as the Provincia Oriental were 'restored' to the United Provinces or were made 'a separate, free and independent State under the forms and rules which its own inhabitants should choose and sanction'.[1] It was true that Buenos Aires desired the possession of the province, but she would accept its erection into a completely independent buffer state so long as she gained peace in which to solve her disputes with the other provinces. Thus the solution of the ancient conflict over the possession of the Banda Oriental was suggested by centralists in Buenos Aires under pressure from federalists in the Argentine interior. It is doubtful whether Artigas would have wished such a solution, which he would have realised would weaken the River Plate countries.

But Rivadavia was forced to attempt to free himself of the incubus of the war with Brazil, and García was the very man to help him. García had for years feared the influence of that nest of federalists, the Provincia Oriental, and had in fact strongly opposed going to war to rescue her from Brazil. García went too far, however, in his zeal: on the 24th of May 1827 he signed a treaty in Rio de Janeiro in which he renounced all the United Province's claims on the Provincia Oriental and recognised the territory as a part of Brazil, with the name of the Provincia Cisplatina. This was a step which proved fatal to the centralist régime in Buenos Aires. The *Porteños* believed that they had won the war, as the government's propaganda had told them, and they did not wish to lose its fruits. A mob stoned Rivadavia's house and howled for García's blood. Alvear and the army, and of course the Orientals, prepared to resist the execution of the treaty; and in June Rivadavia declared it null and threw all the blame on his minister. The President then resigned in the face of public opinion and the federalist movement, and the United Provinces tumbled into governmental anarchy once more as the centralists lost their prestige.

[1] De Gandía, *Los treinta y tres orientales*, pp. 245 ff.

Manuel Dorrego, the leader of the federalist party in the province of Buenos Aires, became head of the government and abolished the centralist national constitution. The clock was put back seven years, and the United Provinces became again merely a loose collection of allied states under their own caudillos. In this fashion the Provincia Oriental regained its autonomy, and the ideas of Artigas seemed to have gained a permanent triumph, although men of public affairs at this time considered him to have been more a brigand than a statesman. The centralist Alvear lost his command of the United Provinces' army at the Brazilian front, and Lavalleja was appointed to succeed him. Lavalleja, following the prevailing federalist mood, lost no time in dismissing the House of Representatives of his province which had by now shown centralist sympathies. After this, Lavalleja ruled as a dictator, and in doing so lost much support among his people and stored up troubles for the future politics of his country.

In Buenos Aires opinion favoured making peace with Brazil. The patriot army spent a year concentrated round Melo, in the north of the Provincia Oriental, out of contact with the enemy and mined from within by jealousies and political manoeuvring. Brazil too was ready for peace, even though Dom Pedro had sworn to avenge the insult to his honour of the republican victory at Ituzaingó. The Brazilian army stayed in Rio Grande do Sul, slowly reorganising in preparation for a possible offensive in the future.

Lecór had remained inactive and besieged in Montevideo, which held out, as did Colonia, against the army of the United Provinces.[1] These two towns contained some five thousand troops between them. In November 1827 Lecór took over the command of some ten thousand Brazilian troops which were being collected in Rio Grande, and at once proceeded to upset the careful plans prepared by the active German chief of staff, Brown.

[1] Besides the works cited previously in this chapter, see Zum Felde, *op. cit.* pp. 100–9, and L. A. de Herrera, *La Misión Ponsonby*, for the final phase of operations and the peace.

This threat was faced by Lavalleja with some six thousand men at the most. But no decisive action took place, as both sides contented themselves with making what amounted to large-scale raids across the border.

While this pantomime was being enacted, the Brazilians left the western side of the theatre of war almost without troops, and Rivera came back on the scene. He made an easy and spectacular conquest of the Eastern Misiones territory, after having stood aside from the war since his rebellion. His friend Estanislao López of Santa Fe had supported him, and when, early in 1828, Rivera decided to take a hand again in the liberation of his country, Dorrego let him have supplies and welcomed his activity. With men from the Littoral and some from the Provincia Oriental, Rivera crossed the River Uruguay, to the surprise and consternation of Lavalleja, who vainly sent troops to try to stop him. Rivera advanced with his thousand irregulars up the line of the Uruguay, and in April 1828 crossed the River Ibicuy into Brazilian territory. The sparse Brazilian garrisons melted away, as did the local authorities of the district, and Rivera established himself as lord of that part of the frontier. He refused a specious Argentine offer to give him respectability as second-in-command of the Army of the North under Estanislao López's leadership. Rivera had decided that he would not owe obedience to Buenos Aires: he was playing for higher stakes.[1]

Rivera won his gamble at the peace of August 1828 which ended the war. The Provincia Oriental became entirely independent, but as part exchange the Misiones territory which Rivera had occupied was returned to Brazil. After this, Rivera returned to the Provincia Oriental sure of a place among the leaders of the country, since many people believed that he was the only Oriental leader who had been able to inflict real damage on Brazil, and that he had forced the Brazilians to make the province free in order to regain what he had conquered. As they retired from the

[1] De-María, *op. cit.* vol. I, pp. 122–32; Salterain y Herrera, *Lavalleja*, t. XXVI, pp. 176–86.

Misiones, his men followed the custom of the country and sacked the lands they were leaving. In December 1828 Rivera received the title of *Digno y Benemérito* from a grateful people, and was restored to favour. He was the natural leader of one of the two parties already forming while the Provincia Oriental was struggling for existence, and which were now ready to dispute the government of the new state. Lavalleja, who resented Rivera's rebellion and his later success, was the leader of the opposition to the Hero of the Misiones, as Rivera has been called. These two parties have continued, with varying programmes, to the present day, and were responsible for the many civil wars and other political upheavals for which Uruguay was noted until the last half-century. They were personal parties, and therefore they carried personal emotion into the government of the country, with violent results.

The peace of 1828 and the erection of the Provincia Oriental into a separate state came about through the British mediation in the war between Brazil and the United Provinces. British commercial interests in the Plate region were threatened by the continuance of hostilities with their attendant disruption of industry and trade.[1] Britain had gained considerable influence over the governments at Buenos Aires and in Rio de Janeiro in the years since 1807, when the Portuguese Court had sailed under British protection to Brazil, and it was natural that this influence should be used to bring the peace which both Brazil and the United Provinces secretly desired from early in 1827. If peace could only be gained by removing, as a governess might, the apple of discord from the grasp of both contenders, then Britain must play the role of governess, decided the British Foreign Secretary, Canning. And therefore Uruguay was created, and both the United Provinces and Brazil were left without the prize for which they and Spain and Portugal had striven for many years. The Orientals, to the

[1] Letter of Woodbine Parish to Canning, 6 August 1825, published as doc. no.35 in Webster, *op. cit.* Webster's work includes the essential documents in the Foreign Office archives on the British mediation led by Ponsonby.

surprise of many, embarked on an independent career when their country was still better fitted politically, racially and economically to become a province in the loose confederation which Artigas had so rightly envisaged.[1] In fact, Uruguay did not shake herself loose from involvement in Argentine internal politics until the fall of the Argentine dictator Rosas in 1851.

The British mediation had been foreshadowed by Lord Strangford's efforts between 1808 and 1815 to protect the Banda Oriental from Portuguese covetousness, and by Britain's half-hearted support of the mediation offered by the European powers at Paris in 1817 after Lecór's invasion of the Provincia Oriental. Both of these interventions had been undertaken for the purpose of defending Spain's rights over her insurgent colonies against Portuguese aggression rather than for the sake of the Spanish American patriots themselves, even though there was in Britain a considerable body of opinion sympathetic towards the latter. Castlereagh, in pursuit of this policy, had even threatened to re-move British protection from the Portuguese possessions unless Dom João acceded to the mediation. One result of this had been the cooling in 1819 of the secret relations between Rio de Janeiro and Buenos Aires, which had at the time worried the *Porteños*. But in fact Spain had quibbled over the terms of the mediation, and then had been unable to send forces to take over Montevideo from the Portuguese, so that Lecór had remained in possession.

When the outbreak of war between the United Provinces and Brazil threatened in 1825, Woodbine Parish, the newly-arrived British consul in Buenos Aires, was quick to report to Canning the effects he feared such a war might have on British trade in the region. Rivadavia, at that time representative of the United Provinces in London, tried to gain Britain's support by alleging that Strangford had guaranteed the 1812 armistice whereby Portugal had withdrawn from the Banda Oriental, but Canning

[1] See Herrera, *Ponsonby;* Webster, *op. cit.* vol. I, Introduction, section VIII; and P. Blanco Acevedo, *Centenario de la independencia,* especially chaps. VII-X.

refuted the suggestion and refused to enter the war.[1] He desired to stop it by peaceful means.

The war did in fact create havoc among British interests in the region owing to the blockade of Buenos Aires and the privateering, and Canning sincerely feared also that Brazil, the one monarchy in Latin America, might be overwhelmed by a coalition of the Spanish-speaking republics, and that this would endanger the link he had helped to forge between the Old World and the New. Both the United Provinces and Brazil suggested that British mediation would be helpful, and therefore Canning sent out Lord John Ponsonby in 1826 with a suggestion that to end these dangerous disturbances Dom Pedro should cede Montevideo to the United Provinces in return for an indemnity. If Dom Pedro could not accept this solution, he might erect the Provincia Oriental into a small independent state on the model of a town of the Hanseatic League. It is possible that the latter idea had been suggested to Canning by Sarratea, on a mission in London, and at any rate it was a solution which the Argentine government had considered.[2] Canning offered that Britain would guarantee the freedom of navigation of the River Plate if the Emperor of Brazil accepted the first alternative, but not in the second case, since he clearly was not fully convinced of the Provincia Oriental's capacity to survive as a separate state. He cleverly avoided the question of the 'rights' of Brazil or of the United Provinces to the possession of the Banda Oriental, by pointing out that boundaries in Latin America were safer settled as they had stood in 1810, or, failing that, then the only country with rights over the Banda Oriental was Spain. In this way he placed the negotiation on the

[1] He was at pains to inform himself. All the antecedents were summarised in the report in P.R.O., F.O. 97/76, which clarifies the problem up to 1824. A study of Strangford's correspondence in the P.R.O. shows that he did not guarantee the armistice of 1812, although perhaps the Argentines sincerely believed that he did. See also Webster, *op. cit.* doc. no.39.

[2] Letter of Ponsonby to Canning, Rio de Janeiro, 26 March 1826, in Herrera, *Ponsonby*, vol. II, pp. 23-6. Herrera uses the F.O. archives in the P.R.O. as his source. See also letter of Canning to Ponsonby, 28 February 1826, in Webster, *op. cit.* doc. no. 44.

practical level of expediency, setting aside embarrassing questions which migh exacerbate warlike feelings.[1]

Ponsonby, already a respectable figure of some fifty-five years of age, was as firm as Canning about the need for peace. He was 'a gentleman, giving the expression all its strength, and to his manners, which are as civil as they are amiable, he adds the virtues of frankness and rectitude'; thus Trápani, the Oriental who had the most to do with him, wrote to Lavalleja in 1827.[2] Ponsonby was, however, a proud member of an ancient noble family, and therefore not the best choice for a delicate mission to new countries peopled and governed by men very different from those he knew. Indeed, a man of his rank and services would hardly have been sent on such a mission had there not been, according to the Court gossip of the day, another reason. It was said that, with his fine looks and presence, he was a too dangerous rival of the King's over a certain lady. At all events, Ponsonby made it clear in private letters to his friends that he hated his exile in Buenos Aires, although no sign of his feelings appeared in his official correspondence or in his dealings with the local people. He was a sybarite, accustomed to the best of society and comfort, and although he could enjoy the tropical delights of Rio de Janeiro he felt himself frozen, physically and mentally, in the cooler and ruder climate of Buenos Aires. 'No one has ever seen such a disagreeable place as Buenos Aires . . . Never did any place displease me so much and I sigh when I think that I may stay here. I always have Italy in my thoughts, to increase my mortification in this district of mud and rotten bones . . . Nothing good except meat. It is April here and I have already seen frost.' And Ponsonby never really got used to the political *milieu*, with its sudden changes and its strident republicanism, 'republican boasting in all its vigour. An intolerable place.'[3]

---

[1] Herrera, *Ponsonby*, vol. II, pp. 16-22, instructions of Canning to Ponsonby, 18 March 1826. Doc. no. 45 in Webster, *op. cit.*

[2] Herrera, *Ponsonby*, vol. I, p. 96.

[3] Correspondence, *ibid.* pp. 347-9.

Ponsonby was perhaps too frank and straight-dealing to make himself popular with the two governments which he eventually persuaded to free the Banda Oriental; at any rate, he left South America after the successful completion of his mission unpopular at both Buenos Aires and Rio de Janeiro, but regarded with admiration by some of the better-informed Orientals, such at Trápani and Lavalleja. He had had the perspicacity to see from his early days there that the only possible solution in view of the pride of both the big countries was the emancipation of the little one.

The British mediator reached Rio de Janeiro in May 1826 and stayed there before going on to Buenos Aires, discussing until August with the Brazilian government the suggestion of Canning. He argued not on the basis of abstract justice but on that of the actual utility of the Banda Oriental to Brazil, and denied that the Emperor's honour was at stake or that the 'natural frontier' of the River Plate was essential to the Empire. At first Dom Pedro refused either solution proposed, and instead offered peace on the generous conditions that Brazil should retain the territory in dispute, and in return should recognise the existence of the United Provinces as a state. Ponsonby objected that he could not be the bearer of such terms to Buenos Aires, where they were more likely to exacerbate hostility than soothe it, so Dom Pedro qualified them by offering the added inducements that he would make Montevideo a free port and a refuge for Argentine ships without any payment, and would sign a treaty of peace, commerce and navigation with the United Provinces on this basis. Ponsonby finally agreed to proceed to Buenos Aires to offer these terms, since they were at least an offer of peace and could be used to keep the negotiation in being, whereas the first offer would have brought its immediate end. He saw from the state of Brazil that peace was essential to her, even though Dom Pedro himself was not yet prepared to give anything away for its sake. Thus the mediator left Rio de Janeiro already decided that the independence of the Banda Oriental was necessary to end the war, and that the Orientals were fit to rule themselves, just as they were fit to fight for themselves.[1]

Ponsonby reached Buenos Aires on the 16th of September 1826, and spent two years there leading the arduous negotiations towards the only possible end, independence for the Banda Oriental. President Rivadavia scornfully rejected the Brazilian proposition, and at first seemed interested in the independence of the Banda Oriental as the answer. This proposal received ever stronger support from Ponsonby, who made a draft formula on this basis. But Rivadavia, advised by his minister Cruz, shied away from the scheme when Ponsonby made it clear that Britain would not guarantee the existence of the new state, although García supported it, ever willing to be rid of the Banda Oriental.

Yet in a despatch written to Canning in October, Ponsonby expressed his formed opinion that it was an indisputable truth that it was almost as distasteful to the Orientals to be under Buenos Aires as to be under Brazil, and that independence was their most ardent desire. Even in the midst of a common war against Brazil, some Orientals were resisting *Porteño* troops.[2] And besides, as Ponsonby remarked, the Orientals were as civilised as the *Porteños*, and perfectly capable of governing themselves. Meanwhile the war dragged on, ruinous to both sides; and also the Argentine interior, especially Córdoba under Bustos, stirred in a federalist revival which augured ill for Rivadavia.

García's influence and the poor state of the country prevailed to the extent that Ponsonby was authorised at the end of October to approach the Brazilians with the independence proposal, though he was to do it unofficially, through Gordon, the British minister at Rio de Janeiro. The British guarantee was not insisted upon, although something was still hoped for; but Canning was not prepared to give any guarantee, and in November ordered Ponsonby

[1] Documents *ibid.* vol. II, pp. 23-63.
[2] Documents *ibid.* vol. II, pp. 67-120, especially despatches of Ponsonby to Canning 2 and 20 October 1826, pp. 73-80, 88-95, docs. nos. 50 and 51 in Webster, *op. cit.*

to let the mediation drift and wait for the progress of the war to make the contenders more desperate for peace.[1] Dom Pedro remained adamant, on his part, about retaining the Banda Oriental, and in December made his excursion to Rio Grande do Sul to activate the war.

Yet by early February 1827 it was Gordon's impression that Dom Pedro had changed his mind, possibly impressed by what he had found in Rio Grande, and was now prepared to negotiate for peace, it was hoped on the basis of the independence of the Banda Oriental. Rivadavia stood by his verbal promise too, even after the victory of Ituzaingó on the 20th of February. He realised that the only way to save his régime from being overwhelmed by the federalists was to make peace with Brazil and turn his troops against his internal enemies, and it was clear that public opinion would never accept Brazil's retention of the Provincia Oriental. Accordingly García was sent to Rio de Janeiro with instructions to sign the preliminaries of a peace on the basis decided upon. But Dom Pedro had changed his mind again, stung by defeats on land and sea, and there took place the fiasco of May 1827, when García recognised the Banda Oriental as Brazilian, and which led to Rivadavia's fall and an unfruitful extension of the hostilities. García was not entirely to blame, since Gordon had urged the terms on him as the only way of gaining peace, and he himself was convinced that the Banda Oriental, if free, would merely cause further trouble to the United Provinces.[2]

The 'admirable Trápani', Lavalleja's confidential agent in Buenos Aires, was engaged from early in 1827 in winning the good will of Ponsonby for the Banda Oriental, and no doubt Trápani's private interviews influenced the British mediator's attitude towards Oriental independence.[3] By June, Ponsonby regarded Lavalleja as the man destined to play the most important

[1] Doc. no. 52 in Webster, *op. cit.*

[2] Herrera, *Ponsonby*, vol. II, docs. pp. 123-86.

[3] On Trápani's part, see *ibid.* vol. I, pp. 412-81, and Blanco Acevedo, *Informe*, pp. 149-56, 179-240.

part in the Banda Oriental, and was pondering the question of a constitution for the state to be. He realised that any form of monarchy would be unacceptable, but hoped that an 'aristocratic' government would be possible, 'uniting political power to property'. Ponsonby was further impressed by a rumour that Lavalleja meant to unite Rio Grande do Sul with the Banda Oriental, and so to harm Brazil further. In fact, this was Rivera's idea, but Trápani must have changed the names to make more capital from it and spur the mediator to greater efforts.

Vicente López took over the government of Buenos Aires temporarily, and Ponsonby was able to convince him of Britain's good faith, which was impugned by many who believed that she was undertaking the mediation for some sinister purpose of her own.[1] When Dorrego and the federalists came to power, the British mediator at first found the atmosphere more congenial, and was able to persuade the new government to leave open the possibility of a peace on the former basis of Oriental independence. Both Ponsonby and Gordon worked hard on the governments to which they were accredited, but there were months of vacillation on the part of both Buenos Aires and Rio de Janeiro before negotiations could be opened again in April 1828. By then, both sides were thoroughly exhausted and their pride chastened. The only hostilities being carried on were those at sea, where fleets and corsairs, led, officered and partly manned by British subjects, fought each other or preyed on legitimate British trade.

Meanwhile the Orientals had impressed the negotiators still more with their determination to be free, as Lavalleja governed independently in fact after the federalist triumph in Buenos Aires. Ponsonby permitted himself to send advice to Lavalleja through Trápani's correspondence, concerning political affairs between his government and Dorrego's. Also, as Ponsonby noted, the Orientals seemed to prefer British influence to any other. They gained most of their comforts and many of their pleasures from

[1] Herrera, *Ponsonby*, vol. II, docs. pp. 181-259.

England, and their richest landowners expected British immigration to bring them wealth and progress in the near future. By January 1828, Ponsonby foresaw in an independent Banda Oriental a useful buffer state: indeed, this was the first time the idea was put forward. Such a state would be beneficial to Britain's interests and to the whole peace of the world. His conviction was strengthened when Lavalleja, well advised, promised him that he would not allow his side to turn the war into a crusade of republics against monarchy in South America.

In February 1828 the British Government decided to transfer Ponsonby from the legation in Buenos Aires to that in Rio de Janeiro, and Woodbine Parish was left as chargé d'affaires in Buenos Aires. The change took place in July. It accelerated the negotiations for peace which were made possible by the decision Dom Pedro had taken in January to treat on the basis of the independence of the Banda Oriental after all. Lavalleja patiently waited for peace, resisting the temptation to join forces with revolutionary elements inside Brazil in an attempt to force the issue. In March, Buenos Aires had agreed to negotiate on the basis suggested by Brazil, and then Lavalleja agreed, at Gordon's suggestion, to suspend hostilities. The General at the same time expressed approval of the terms proposed, with the remark that they were what he had been fighting for since 1825, and if they had been offered him then, he would have accepted them.[1] If this were so, he had kept his wishes very secret.

However, Dorrego wavered about making peace after having given his promise to Ponsonby, and Rivera's spectacular conquest of the Eastern Misiones after April 1828 caused the Argentine leader to hope again for complete victory and possession of the Banda Oriental. But this hope was illusory, for at this time an English observer found that the Brazilian army was superior in numbers, equipment and training to that of the patriots, whose only advantages were superiority in numbers of horses and in

[1] *Cit.* in Blanco Acevedo, *Informe*, p. 203.

spirit, since at least half were Oriental irregulars fighting for their country.[1] And a great majority of Argentines desired peace on the not dishonourable basis of the independence of the Banda Oriental, so that Ponsonby was able to keep the unwilling Dorrego to his word. Dom Pedro was kept up to the mark by Gordon, even though the Empire's few friends in Montevideo, led by García de Zúñiga, now Governor, implored the Emperor not to abandon them.

Early in August the Buenos Aires plenipotentiaries, Generals Balcarce and Guido, arrived in Rio de Janeiro, followed about a fortnight later by Ponsonby.[2] The two sets of plenipotentiaries had already begun their discussions, but Ponsonby's intermission was needed to secure the acceptance of a few matters of secondary importance, especially by the Argentines, before the preliminaries of peace were signed on the 27th. The most important of these details was the return of the Eastern Misiones to Brazil, which Dom Pedro made a *sine qua non* of peace. After this Ponsonby spared no efforts to persuade Dorrego of the need for ratification of the preliminaries, even threatening that failure to ratify would be taken as an insult by the British Government, with the repercussions which would spring to the Argentines' imaginations. He also wrote to Lavalleja to explain the terms, putting special emphasis on the need to sacrifice the Eastern Misiones or lose both peace and independence. Both patriots gave their assurances that they would do all in their power to implement the treaty, which was in fact ratified by the Congress of the United Provinces in Santa Fe on the 4th of October 1828.

This Preliminary Convention of Peace of August 1828 itself ratified the freedom which the Orientals had enjoyed since the previous year. It left unsolved the question of the exact frontiers of the new state, but this was no obstacle to peace. The solution was

---

[1] Report of the envoy Fraser after visits to Lecór, Lavalleja and Buenos Aires, written to Gordon, 13 April 1828, Herrera, *Ponsonby*, vol. II, pp. 266–74. For this phase of the negotiations see documents, *ibid.* pp. 259–336.

[2] Documents *ibid.* vol. II, pp. 330–36.

not, in fact, found until the early years of this century. The Convention's articles were simple and to the point. In the first two, Brazil and the United Provinces both declared the independence of 'the Province of Montevideo, today called Cisplatine', so that it should erect itself into a state independent of any other nation and under whatever form of government it should wish. Both the powers promised to defend the new state for whatever time should be laid down in the definite treaty of peace. The present government of the Banda Oriental, as soon as the ratifications of the Convention had been exchanged, should immediately call for the election of deputies, as also should the present government of the city of Montevideo, proportional to the numbers of inhabitants of the various districts; and these deputies should be elected and should meet at a place at least ten leagues distant from the influence of troops belonging to any nation, and should there establish a Provisional Government. This government should rule the province and Montevideo until the installation of a permanent government under the provisions of a national constitution. The same deputies would write the country's constitution, which would be inspected before its final adoption by agents of the two contracting powers, with the sole aim of assuring that nothing in it constituted a threat to the security of their countries. Both powers promised to protect the new state up to its final establishment by constitution, and for five years thereafter, against disturbance by civil war. The other articles were concerned with details about the release of prisoners of war, evacuation of troops and other technical matters.

The news of the peace was welcome to most people in the United Provinces, but it left some embittered. Alvear and Lavalle, centralists who had fought in the war against Brazil, rose in revolt against Dorrego, who was caught and shot out of hand in November. This atrocity put the worst representatives of the centralists in power in the province of Buenos Aires: 'Alvear, as a soldier and as a man, is beneath disdain. General Lavalle has the

reputation of a brave soldier, but is considered weak and vain'
wrote Ponsonby. The other provinces, with their federalist ideas,
were set against the *Porteños* once more.[1] This was the starting
point for years of bitter internal struggle, leading first to the
dictatorship of Rosas before the elaboration of a compromise between centralists and federalists. This finally led on towards the
settlement of the Argentine constitutional problem fifty years
after these events.

Ponsonby was shocked as never before at Dorrego's 'horrible
murder', and refused to have anything to do with the 'usurping
government'.[2] His attitude might have been fatal to the peace,
since a full treaty had still to be made; but he would only deal with
a legitimate government of the United Provinces, and advised the
election of one to replace the murderers. However, the British
Foreign Secretary, Lord Aberdeen, instructed Ponsonby not to
stand on ceremony in this fashion, but instead to continue to pro-
mote the final pacification. But since his main task of bringing peace
was completed, Ponsonby took an early opportunity of returning
to England on the grounds of ill-health. He sailed on the 28th of
June 1829 on sick leave, but never returned to his post in Rio de
Janeiro. He was followed by the hatred of most of those he had
tried to help. His firmness had injured many men of greater
sensibility and lesser honesty; but he had been guided by a clear
view of the situation of the Banda Oriental, and he had earned the
future gratitude of a new nation.

It remained for the new state to give itself a constitution. Since
late in 1827 the government of the province had been in the hands
of Orientals except for Montevideo and Colonia, which were held
by the Brazilians until the peace.[3] Therefore even while the war
dragged on, the country underwent the beginning of a reconstruction. The government was meanwhile established at Durazno,

[1] Letters of Ponsonby to Aberdeen, 29 December 1828 and Ponsonby to Parish, 5
January 1829, *ibid.* vol. II, pp. 336–42.
[2] Documents *ibid.* vol. II, pp. 342–54.
[3] Blanco Acevedo, *Informe*, pp. 174 ff.

with the treasury department at Canelones and the customs at the port of Maldonado. The country districts even began to recover to some extent from the effects of the invasions and occupations of the past years. Dorrego treated Lavalleja as an equal, since they were both simply governors of their respective provinces, and moreover Lavalleja commanded the republican army facing the Brazilians. But even Dorrego tried to stir up trouble between Lavalleja and Rivera, setting them against each other over the campaign in the Eastern Misiones.

But Lavalleja was consulted before the final negotiations as to whether the Oriental people would accept the proposed terms of peace, and he received from both Ponsonby and Gordon the respect due to the head of a national government and the commander of a victorious army. In the negotiations themselves neither Lavalleja nor the Oriental people was directly represented, probably owing to a last-minute hope of Dorrego's that Rivera's victories might make Brazil allow the Provincia Oriental to become one of the United Provinces. But Ponsonby was well informed of the Orientals' aspirations, and in any case Brazil did not relax to that extent. However, from the date of the receipt (28th of September 1828) of Ponsonby's letter to Lavalleja announcing the signing of the preliminary convention, the Orientals considered themselves as independent.

In October Lavalleja resigned the command of the patriot Army of Operations against Brazil, thus cutting all links with the United Provinces, whose government was legally responsible for that army. An elected Constituent and Legislative Assembly met in November in San José. When they came to elect a governor for the new state, they were confronted by a situation which had been in preparation for over three years: Rivera was now a national hero with a large and enthusiastic following, which seemed likely to be ready to start a civil war if the less flamboyant Lavalleja were elected. Therefore they chose a man respected by all, one who had been born in Argentina, but had at one time been active in the

Banda Oriental: General Rondeau. Since he was not in the country, they elected the loyal administrator Joaquín Suárez as interim governor. In this way the civil wars which tore Uruguay for seventy years were postponed until the next decade.

A commission was given the task of drawing up the constitution; and here again the beginnings of future difficulties were seen to grow out of past conflicts. Two tendencies at once became apparent, the federalist, led by Santiago Vásquez, and the more Europeanised and centralist, led by José Ellauri. The democratic and republican constitution approved by the Assembly in December 1829 and publicly adopted on the 18th of July 1830 turned out to be liberal and centralist, although with certain provisions suitable only for a federal state. The most important of these was the election of an unnecessary Senate on the basis of one Senator for each Department. In a way, this document showed symptoms of a fault common in Latin American constitutions: the written charter often does not correspond to the manner in which the country is actually governed. Uruguay was a small state with a centralised government, but with strong personalist parties aligned behind mutually suspicious and hostile caudillos. Nevertheless, this constitution brought into being the Oriental State of the Uruguay, whatever problems it created or left unsolved. A feeling of Uruguayan individuality had grown up over the last fifty years, and now at length the people were given the chance of proving whether they could become a nation.[1] Few men even twenty years before would have dared to prophesy that the Banda Oriental would eventually become a completely independent state. Artigas himself had hoped not for this, but for a place for his homeland among a confederated United Provinces. But the forces engaged in the struggle for the possession of the key to the River Plate had proved too well-matched for either to win a clear victory, and furthermore the Orientals had proved in many years of bitter

---

[1] The beginning of Uruguay's independent career is well shown in J. E. Pivel Devoto, *Uruguay independiente*, chaps. v and vi.

struggle that they were fit to hold that key themselves. Their great spirit and their love of freedom were to bring them with dignity through many future trials.

CHAPTER X

THE LAST YEARS OF ARTIGAS

THE man who had done more than any other person to foster the feeling of nationhood in the Orientals, José Artigas, lived on after 1820 in obscure exile in Paraguay.[1] The Dictator Francia refused to change his own policy of maintaining Paraguay aloof from the rest of the world; and indeed there was no reason why he should risk the peace and comparative prosperity of his country to help a defeated revolutionary leader whose country was occupied by the power of Portugal and Brazil and whose own lieutenant caudillo Ramírez had just driven him out.

Before crossing into Paraguay, Artigas had ordered his faithful follower Colonel Latorre to wait, as he would return with help; and Latorre and other *artiguistas* waited many years in hope. Eventually many of the soldiers of Artigas joined the campaign against the Brazilians from 1825 onwards and, recalling their *Jefe's* ideals and the *Patria Vieja*, though critical of his defeats, they helped to found the new Fatherland of 1828. However, Artigas was not allowed to leave Paraguay, even when Ramírez claimed his extradition to face trial. Instead, he was sent to a quiet exile seventy-six leagues from Asunción, at San Isidro Labrador, gen- erally known as Curuguaty from the river on which it stands. It was a small town which was the head of a district famous for the *hierba mate* it produced.

Artigas was supplied by Francia with shelter, food and clothing, as were the few men who had been his escort, and all were given farms to work for themselves. At San Isidro Artigas passed a quarter of a century amidst the jungle and the great *hierba* forests, no doubt pondering the mutability of human fortune. For ten

[1] See D. Hammerly Dupuy, *Rasgos biográficos de Artigas en el Paraguay*; Salterain y Herrera, *Artigas en el Paraguay*; C. Pastore, *Artigas en el Paraguay*, pp. 21-33; J. Stefanich, *Artigas, Francia y el Paraguay*, pp. 382 ff.

years Francia gave him money, and he worked his farm, building himself a four-roomed house of bricks and sun-baked mud and living there with his old black servant and his dog. Since Artigas farmed successfully and had no luxuries, the money was enough for him to indulge in charitable acts towards the poor, until at length Francia heard of them and stopped the pension.

In 1831 Artigas received a visit from the French scientist Bonpland, another of Francia's detainees, but one who was about to be released. Bonpland took the opportunity of presenting the old hero with a copy of the Uruguayan constitution, which had been printed in Montevideo the previous year, and Artigas reverently kissed the book and thanked God for allowing him to live to see his country independent and with a constitution.[1]

In this exemplary retirement Artigas was disturbed at the death of Francia in 1840. In the fears and confusion of the change, the provisional government which took office decided that Artigas, then aged seventy-six, was a threat to the public peace and security, and had him imprisoned in chains in San Isidro for six months. Artigas' crops and cattle were abandoned, and he had to begin again from nothing on his release. Even this must have been less bitter to the old general than imprisonment itself. It was the rise to power of Carlos Antonio López as one of the two Consuls of Paraguay in 1841 which gave Artigas his freedom. The Consuls were disposed to be friendly towards Uruguay, and as a gesture offered Artigas his liberty to return there if he wished. But Artigas preferred to finish his days, which, he said, must now be few, in Paraguay. Since his imprisonment Artigas was so sunk in poverty that the Consuls decided to provide him with money and clothes.

Artigas' countrymen had made some efforts themselves to gain his release by Francia, but with no success. Apart from others, Rivera, although refusing to go to war with Paraguay over the *Jefe's* fate, was interested enough to open negotiations by

---

[1] De-María, *op. cit.* vol. I, *General Don José Gervasio Artigas*, pp. 13-70. See p. 61.

correspondence in 1832. Lavalleja made no move. Indeed most of the public men of the Banda Oriental were too much occupied in rivalry with each other to bother about the fate of a leader who had so manifestly failed in battle. It was not until the 1840s that some realisation of Artigas' true stature penetrated Uruguay again. After Francia's death one of Artigas' old captains, Cabrera, was released and returned to Uruguay with the message that Artigas would like to see his son José María before he died. José María Artigas was then thirty-five, a lieutenant-colonel of cavalry, and he took the decision to go to Paraguay and, if necessary, stay there with his father. But instead of allowing him to go, Rivera, then President of Uruguay, sent a mission to the new Consuls asking for the release of all the prisoners. It was this mission which motivated the offer which Artigas refused. At that time there was great enthusiasm in Uruguay for the old *Jefe*, seen now in perspective as the founder of the country's freedom. Why Artigas refused can only be guessed: it seems likely that he realised that he had lost touch with affairs in his own country and had no wish to be there as a useless show-piece, or worse, to have his name and prestige used to support some party.

Carlos Antonio López, who became President of Paraguay in 1844, showed great admiration for Artigas, and even offered the old man a post as 'instructor to an army of the republic', possibly forgetting Artigas' eighty years in his enthusiasm. At all events, he succeeded in 1845 in bringing the old man from San Isidro to live in a small house on his country estate near Asunción. Here the President himself and the Brazilian Minister were Artigas' kindly neighbours. López treated Artigas very cordially, seeing him frequently and supplying all his needs. The López family often received friendly visits from the old man, and gave affectionate parties for him on his birthdays.

For three months in 1846 Artigas' son José María stayed with his father, having at length persuaded the Uruguayan government to grant him leave despite the war in which his country was engaged.

José María failed to persuade his father to return with him to Uruguay. Artigas refused to allow himself to become the figurehead of one or other of the rival parties indulging in civil wars which saddened his last years. In these declining years, Artigas received visits from various foreign travellers, mostly soldiers curious to see the once feared *Jefe* in retirement. To one of them, the Argentine General José María Paz, Artigas declared his motives for the disastrous struggle against the *Porteño* Directory:

I did nothing but reply with war to the shady manoeuvres of the Directory and to the war which it was making on me because it considered me the enemy of centralism, which then was only one step away from royalism. Taking the United States of America as a model, I wanted the autonomy of the Provinces, giving each state its own government, constitution, flag and the right to elect its representatives, its judges and its governors from among the citizens native to each state. This was what I had claimed for my province and for those which had proclaimed me their protector. To do this would have been to give everyone his own. But the Pueyrredóns and their acolytes wanted to make of Buenos Aires a new Imperial Rome, sending its proconsuls as military governors of the provinces and to despoil them of all public representation, just as they did when they rejected the deputies to Congress which the people of the Banda Oriental had chosen, and when they put a price on my head. [1]

It was as clear and succinct a statement of Artigas' ideas as was ever made.

Artigas' health was excellent, except for the rheumatic pains natural after his years of campaigning, and of which he had complained in the early years of the century when he wished to retire from active service in the Spanish army. His birthday was celebrated as usual on the 19th of June 1850 by the López family, and for his eighty-six years the old man was cheerful and lively. But in the spring he fell seriously ill and received help and attention from his patrons, among whom and in whose country house he died after a few days, in the early hours of the 23rd of September,

---

[1] Interview of Paz with Artigas, *cit.* De-María, *op. cit.* vol. I, p. 64.

exactly thirty years after his entry into Paraguay.[1] But his remains were not allowed to rest where he had found peace. In 1855 the Uruguayan government had them brought back to Montevideo to be re-interred with great pomp.

Poets wrote verses, orators spoke, the General Assembly of Uruguay named a remote township on the Yaguarón after the hero, but the only fitting memorials to Artigas are the existence of a free Uruguay, and the liberal forms of government which were established there and in Argentina. No man worked and fought harder than Artigas for Uruguay's freedom. Although it must be remembered, as Blanco Acevedo pointed out,[1] that 'Artigas was not a cause, but a consequence', yet the *Jefe* cannot be dismissed as a mere fortunate caudillo. It would be unjust to dwell only on the fact that the early nineteenth century saw the eruption and clashing in the River Plate region of the many forces which led to revolution, to a climax in the struggle between Spain and Portugal over the boundaries of their possessions, and to the aspiration for political, economic and social systems in tune with the nature of the local peoples and their way of life.

Undoubtedly Artigas became a hero because these circumstances existed. But he was without question of greater stature than any of the men who surrounded him. Neither Rivera nor Lavalleja showed such determination, such constancy, nor such originality as did Artigas. Lesser men than these seemed fickle as they strove to find their way through the labyrinth of River Plate politics: García de Zúñiga, Bianqui, Herrera, even Larrañaga. We find no man other than Artigas capable of leading the revolution of the Banda Oriental and forming the Federal League at the same time as offering a consistent and reasonable political doctrine. Against his opponents, Artigas stands out with the authority of his honesty of purpose. It is true that he represented the typical strong man dear

[1] Obituary of Artigas in *El Paraguayo Independiente*, Asunción, 28 September 1850 (facsimile edition published by the Instituto Histórico y Geográfico del Uruguay, Montevideo 1950).

[1] Blanco Acevedo, *Informe*, p. 37.

to the peoples of the River Plate: he was a caudillo, but one whose family background of leadership gave him uncommon insight into his country's needs and conditions. He was always on the weaker side, and was frequently defeated. But, a realist, he worked out a system of government suited to those peoples in their peculiar surroundings; and he never admitted defeat, but fought on, with ferocity and with hope. In this determination and resilience Artigas bears comparison with his great contemporary, Bolívar, who was so different in many ways, but so like him in this. As an enemy observer reported to the Spanish government in 1819: 'It is necessary to confess in honour of truth that Artigas, once he has taken sides, is constant in sustaining his part.'[1] His quiet humility and manual labour in his last thirty years bear witness to his strength of character as much as do his ten years of bitter struggle.

[1] Report of Magariños to Exmo Sor. Conde de Calderon, Capitan General del Ejercito destinado ala Pacificacion del Rio de la Plata, d. Madrid 30 August 1819, in A.G.I., Seville, Indiferente General, legajo 1568.

APPENDIX I

(See p. 227, note 1)

Reglam.^{to} Provisorio dela Provincia Oriental para el fomento desu Campaña y Seguridad desus hacendados.

Prim.^{te} ElSōr Alcalde Provincial ademas desus facultades ordinarios, queda autorizado p.^a distribuir terrenos y velar sobre la tranquilidad del vecindario, siendo el Juez inmediato en todo el Orden dela Presente instruccion.

2.ª En atencion ala basta extencion dela Campaña podrà instituir tres Subtenientes de Prov.ª, señalandoles su jurisdiccion respectiva, y facultandolos Seguir este reglam.^{to}.

3.ª Uno deberà instituirse entre Uruguay, y Rio-Negro; Otro entre Rio-negro, y Yý: Otro desde Sta Lucia, hasta la costa dela mar quedando el Sōr Alcalde Provincial, con la Jurisdiccion inmediata desde el Yý, hasta Sta Lucia.

4.ª Si para el desempeño detan importante Comision hallare el Sōr Alcalde Provincial, y Subtenientes de Provincia necesitarse de mas Sugetos, podrà cada qual instituir en sus respectivas Jurisdicciones, Jueces Pedaneos, q.^e ayuden à executar las medidas adoptadas p.^a el entable del Mejor Orden.

5.ª Estos comisionados daràn cuenta à sus respectivos Subtenientes de Provincia: estos al Sōr Alcalde Provincial de quien recibiràn las Ordenes precisas. Este las recibirà del Gobierno de Montev.º y por este Conducto seràn trasmisibles Otras qualesquiera, q.^e ademas delas indicadas, en esta instruccion, se crean adaptables àlas Circunstancias.

6.ª Por ahora el Sōr Alcalde Provincial, y demas Subalternos se dedicaràn à fomentar con brazos utiles la poblaciòn dela Campaña, p.^a ello revisarà cada uno en sus respectivas Jurisdicciones los terrenos disponibles, y los Sugetos dignos de esta gracia, con prevencion, q.^e los mas infelices seràn los mas privilegiados. En conseq.^a los Negros libres, Los Sambos deesta clase, los indios, ylos criollos Pobres, todos podràn ser agraciados con suertes de estancia, si con su trabajo, y hombria de bien, propenden à su felicidad y dela Provincia.

7.ª Seràn igualm.^{te} agraciadas las Viudas pobres si tubieren hijos. Seràn igualm.^{te} preferidos los Casados àlos americanos Solteros, y estos à qualquier extrangero.

8ª Los Solicitantes Sepersonaràn ante el Sōr Alcalde Provincial ò delos Subalternos delos Partidos, donde exigieren el terreno pª su poblacⁿ Estos daràn su informe al Sōr Alcalde Prov! y Este al Gobierno de Montevideo dequien se tendrà la legitimacion dela donacion, y la marca, qᵉ deba distinguir las haciendas del interesado en loSucesivo. Para ello al tiempo depedir la gracia se informarà Si el Solicitante tiene ò no Marca: Si la tiene serà archivada en el libro de Marcas, y deno sele darà en la forma Acostumbrada.

9ª El M. Y. C. Gobernᵒ.ʳ deMontev? despacharà estos rescriptos enla forma qᵉ estime mas conveniente. Ellos, y las marcas seràn dados graciosamᵗᵉ y Se obligarà al Regidor encargado de Propios de Ciudad, lleve una razon exacta deEstas donaciones dela Provincia.

10ª Los agraciados seràn puestos en posesion desde el momento, qᵉ se haga la denuncia por el Sōr Alcalde Provincial, ò por qualquiera delos Subalternos à Este.

11ª Despues dela posesion seràn Obligados los agraciados por el Sōr Alcalde Provincial, ò demas Subalternos à formar un Rancho, y dos Corrales en el termino preciso de dos meses, los qᵉ cumplidos, si se advirtiese Omision, sele reconvendrà pª qᵉ lo efectue en un mes mas el qual cumplido, si se advierte la misma Negligencia, serà aquel Terreno donado à Otro Vecino mas laborioso, y benefico àla Provincia.

12ª Los terrenos repartibles, son todos aquellos de Emigrados, malos Europeos y peores Americanos qᵉ hasta la fha no se hallan indultados por el Xefe dela Provincia pª poseer sus antiguas Propiedades.

13ª Seràn igualmᵗᵉ repartibles todos aquellos terrenos qᵉ desde el año de 1810, hasta el 1815, enqᵉ entraron los Orientales ala Plaza de Monte-video, hayan sido vendidos, o donados por el Gobierno de ella.

14ª En esta clase de terrenos habrà la excepcion siguiente: Si fueron donados, ò vendidos à Orientales ò à extraños: Si àlos primeros Seles donarà una Suerte de Estancia conforme al presente Reglamento: Si alos Segᵈᵒˢ todo disponible enla forma dicha.

15ª Para repartir los terrenos de Europeos, y malos Americanos setendrà presente si estos son casados ò solteros. De estos todo es dis-ponible. De aquellos se atenderà al numero de sus hijos, y con concepto àqᵉ estos no sean perjudicados, Seles darà lo bastante pª qᵉ puedan man-tenerse en lo succesivo, siendo el resto disponible, Si tubiese demasiados terrenos.

16ª La demarcacion delos terrenos agraciables sera legua y media de frente, y dos de fondo, en la inteligencia qᵉ puede hacerse mas ò

menos extensiva la demarcacion segun la localidad del terreno, en el
qual siempre se proporcionara aguadas, y silo permite el lugar linderos
fixos; quedando al Zelo delos Comisionados, economizar el terreno en
lo posible, y Cortar enlo Succesivo desabenencias entre Vecinos.

17ª Sevelarà por el Gobierno, el Sõr Alcalde Provincial, y demas
Subalternos pᵃ qᵉ los agraciados no posean mas qᵉ una Suerte de Estanᵃ:
Podran ser privilegiados sin embargo, los qᵉ no tengan mas qᵉ una
suerte deChacra: podràn tambien ser agraciados los Americanos qᵉ
quisiesen mudar de posicion, dexando la qᵉ tienen à beneficio dela
Provincia.

18ª Podràn reservarse Unicamᵗᵉ pᵃ beneficio dela Provincia el
Rincon de Pande-Azucar, y el del Serro pᵃ mantener las Reyunadas desu
Servicio. El Rincon del Rosario por su extencion puede repartirse asi al
lado de Afuera entre algunos agraciados, reservando en los fondos una
extencion bastante à mantener cinco ò seis mil Reyunos de los dhos - - - -

19ª Los agraciados, ni podràn enagenar, ni vender estas Suertes de
estancia ni contraher sobre ellas debito alguno baxo la pena de nulidad,
hasta el arreglo formal del Provincia, enqᵉ ella deliberarà lo Convenᵗᵉ.

20ª El M. Y. Cabᵈᵒ ò quien el comisione me pasarà un estado del
numᵒ de agraciados ysus posiciones pᵃ mi conocimᵗᵒ.

21ª Qualqʳ terreno anteriormᵗᵉ agraciado entrarà en el Orden del
presente Reglamᵗᵒ debiendo los interesados recavar por medio del Sõr
Alcalde Provincial su legitimacion enla manera Arriba expresada del
M. Y. Cᵈᵒ de Montevᵒ.

22ª Para facilitar el adelantamᵗᵒ deestos agraciados quedan facultados
el Sõr Alcalde Provˡ y los tres Subtenˢ deProvᵃ quienes unicamᵗᵉ
podràn dar licencia pᵃ qᵉ dhos agraciados se reunan, y saquen animales
asi bacunos, como cabalgares delas mismas estancias delos Europeos ò
malos Americanos qᵉ se hallen ensus respectivas Jurisdicciones. En
manera alguna se permitirà qᵉ ellos por si solos lo hagan: siempre seles
señalara un Juez Pedaneo, ù Otro Commisionado pᵃ qᵉ no destrozen las
haciendas enlas Correrias; y qᵉ las qᵉ se tomen se distribuyan con
igualdad entre los Concurrentes, debiendo igualmᵗᵉ celar asi el Alcalde
Provˡ como los demas Subalternos, qᵉ dhos ganados agraciados no sean
aplicados à otro uso qᵉ el de amanzarlo, caparlo, y Sugetarlo à rodeo.

23ª Tambien prohibiran todas las matanzas àlos hacendados, sino
acreditan ser ganados desu Marca, de lo contrario seràn decomisados
todos sus productos y mandados à disposicion del Gobierno.

24ª En atencion ala escases de ganado qᵉ experimenta la Provᵃ se prohibirà toda tropa deganado p.ª Portugal. Al mismo tiempo q.ᵉ se prohibirà alos mismos hacendados la matanza del embrage, hasta el Restablecim.ᵗᵒ dela Campaña.

25ª Para estos fines como p.ª desterrar los bagamundos, Aprehender malhechores, y desertores, sele daràn al Sor Alcalde Provincial Ocho hom.ˢ y un Sarg.ᵗᵒ y Àcada then.ᵉ de Prov.ª quatro Soldados y un cabo. El Cab.ᵈᵒ Deliberarà, si estos deberàn ser de los vecinos q.ᵉ deberàn mudarse mensualm.ᵗᵉ ò de soldados pagos q.ᵉ hagan de esta Suerte su fatiga.

26ª Los t̄h̄es deProv.ª no entenderàn en Demandas, esto es privativo al Sōr Alc.ᵈᵉ Prov.ˡ y alos Jueces delos Pueblos, y Partidos.

27ª Los Destinados à esta Comis.ⁿ no tendràn Otro exercicio q.ᵉ distribuir terrenos y propender asu fom.ᵗᵒ velar sobre la aprehension delos vagos Remitiendolos, ò a este Quartel Gr̄al, ô al Gobierno de M̄.º p.ª el serv.º delas armas, En conseq.ª Los hacendados daràn papelet.ˢ asus Peones y los q.ᵉ se hallaren sin este Requisito y sin otro exercis.º q.ᵉ vagar seràn remitidos en la forma d̄h̄a.

28ª Seràn igualm.ᵗᵉ remitidos à este Quart.ˡ Gr̄al – los Desertores con Armas ò sin ellas q.ᵉ sin licencia de sus Xefes se encuentran en alg.ª deestas Jurisdicc.ˢ

29ª Seràn Ygualm.ᵗᵉ remitidos por el Subalterno al Alc.ᵈᵉ Prov.ˡ qualq.ª q.ᵉ cometiere algun homicidio, Muerte ò violencia con qualqu.ʳ vecino en su Jurisdic.ⁿ. Al efecto lo remitirà asegurado ante el Sōr Alcalde Prov.ˡ y un oficio insinuandole del hecho con este Oficio, [*sic*] q.ᵉ servirà de Cabeza de proceso ala Causa del Delinquente, Lo remitira el Sor Alc.ᵈᵉ Prov.ˡ al Gobierno de Mont.º p.ª q.ᵉ este tome los informes consiguientes y proceda al castigo Segun el Delito.

APPENDIX II
(See p. 332, note 4)

Number of ships entering and leaving Montevideo:

Year	Events	Totals IN	Totals OUT
1806	English blockade 9 December 1806 to 3 February 1807	79	92
1807	excluding the English occupation 3 February to 9 September	18	14
1808		58	51
1809		141	134
1810		231	191
1811	revolution of the Banda Oriental February	191	176
1812	hostilities in the Plate	103	125
1813	,, ,, ,, ,,	77	88
1814	fall of Montevideo to Alvear 23 June	38	40
1815	fall of Montevideo to Artigas 27 February	60	73
1816	Portuguese invasion August	85	74
1817	Montevideo occupied by the Portuguese 18 January	231	204
1818		260	262
1819		352	270
1820		270	255
1821	Provincia Oriental takes name Estado Cisplatino September	359	421
1822	Dom Pedro declares independence of Brazil September	429	231
1823		253	88
1824	Estado Cisplatino swears allegiance to Brazilian Constitution May	303	111
1825	unrest in the province. Revolution against Brazil starts 19 April. War between Brazil and Argentina December	113	
1826	hostilities in the Plate	55	
1827	,, ,, ,, ,,	68	
1828	peace between Brazil and Argentina 27 August. Uruguay free in fact	107	
1829		145	

380

Extracted from Arch. Adm., libro 95 (ships entering 1806 to August 1818), libro 99 (ships entering August 1818 to 1824), libro 96 (ships leaving 1906 to 1815), libro 100 (ships leaving 1816 to 14 November 1833).

SOURCES

I list here only the material which I have used and cited in the footnotes to the text, since it is not my intention to make a complete bibliography of this subject (see M. J. Ardao and A. C. de Castellanos, *Bibliografía de Artigas*, t. I, Montevideo 1953, further vols. to be published).

Manuscript Collections

Argentina

Archivo General de la Nación, Buenos Aires; División Colonial, Sección Gobierno and División Nacional, Sección Gobierno.

Great Britain

Public Record Office; archives of the Foreign Office, the War Office and the Admiralty.

Spain

Archivo General de Indias, Seville; Audiencia de Buenos Aires and Indiferente General.

Uruguay

Archivo General de la Nación, Montevideo; Fondo ex-Archivo Administrativo and Fondo ex-Archivo y Museo Histórico Nacional.

Museo Histórico Nacional, Montevideo; Biblioteca Pablo Blanco Acevedo, Documentos del Consulado de Comercio and Correspondencia de Artigas.

Printed Collections

Archivo General de la Nación, Buenos Aires, *Correspondencia de Lord Strangford y de la estación naval británica en el Río de la Plata con el gobierno de Buenos Aires 1810-1822*, Buenos Aires 1941.

Archivo General de la Nación, Buenos Aires, *Documentos referentes a la guerra de la independencia y emancipación política de la República Argentina y de otras secciones de América . . ., t. I, Antecedentes . . .*, Buenos Aires 1914.

Archivo General de la Nación, Buenos Aires, *Papeles del Archivo*, Buenos Aires, 1942.

Archivo General de la Nación, Montevideo, *Correspondencia del Gen. José Artigas al Cabildo de Montevideo (1814-1816) y correspondencia oficial en copia. Gobernantes argentinos, Artigas y Otorgués al Cabildo de Montevideo (1814-1816)*, Montevideo 1946.

Sources

J. J. Biedma and A. S. Mallié (eds.), *Acuerdos del extinguido Cabildo de Buenos Aires*, serie IV, t. III and IV, Buenos Aires 1926–.

Comisión Nacional Archivo Artigas, *Archivo Artigas*, vols. I –, Montevideo 1950 –, continuing. This collection is to include all documents connected with Artigas that can be found. It has reached vol. IV (1811), so far, and the whole series promises to be of great utility to the student.

Comisión Nacional de Homenaje a Artigas, *El Congreso de Abril de 1813, a través de los documentos*, Montevideo 1951.

Correspondencia del Virrey Francisco Xavier de Elío, in *Revista del Instituto Histórico y Geográfico del Uruguay*, t. II, no. II, pp. 897-1031, Montevideo 1922.

Documentos para la historia argentina (Universidad de Buenos Aires, Facultad de Filosofía y Letras), Buenos Aires 1913–.

Documentos para servir al estudio de la independencia nacional, Instituto Histórico y Geográfico del Uruguay, 2 vols., Montevideo 1938.

Edición conmemorativa del centenario de 1825, in *Revista del Instituto Histórico y Geográfico del Uruguay*, t. X, pp. 281-500, Montevideo 1933.

A. Fernández (ed.), Museo Histórico Nacional, *Exodo del pueblo oriental*, Montevideo 1930.

C. L. Fregeiro (ed.), *Artigas. Estudios históricos. Documentos justificativos*, Montevideo 1886.

L. A. de Herrera (study and ed.), *La Misión Ponsonby*, 2 vols., Montevideo 1930.

Junta Departamental de Montevideo, *Documentos relativos a la Junta montevideana de 1808*, t. I, Montevideo 1958.

A. Lamas (ed.), *Colección de memorias y documentos para la historia y la jeografía de los pueblos del Río de la Plata*, Montevideo 1849.

Museo Mitre, *Contribución documental para la historia del Río de la Plata*, 5 vols., Buenos Aires 1913.

E. M. Narancio (ed.), *Contribución documental para la historia de Artigas y del movimiento de 1815*, in República Oriental del Uruguay, *Anales de la Universidad*, entrega no. 164, pp. 123-232, Montevideo 1949.

N. Piñeiro (ed.), *Mariano Moreno, escritos políticos y económicos*, Buenos Aires 1915.

J. E. Pivel Devoto and R. Fonseca Muñoz (eds.), Ministerio de Relaciones Exteriores, *Archivo histórico diplomático del Uruguay*, t. III, *La diplomacia de la Patria Vieja (1811-1820)*, Montevideo 1943.

Sources

E. Ravignani (ed.), *Asambleas constituyentes argentinas* (Instituto de Investigaciones Históricas de la Facultad de Filosofía y Letras), 6 vols., Buenos Aires 1937-9.

E. Ravignani (ed.) *Comisión de Bernardino Rivadavia ante España y otras potencias de Europa, 1814-1820,* (Instituto de Investigaciones Históricas de la Facultad de Filosofía y Letras), 2 vols., Buenos Aires 1933-6.

Registro oficial de la República Argentina, de 1810 a 1873, 6 vols., Buenos Aires 1879-84.

L. M. Torterolo (ed.), *Artigas y el Cabildo de Corrientes. Documentación interesante,* in *Revista del Instituto Histórico y Geográfico del Uruguay,* t. IV, no. 1, pp. 137-75, Montevideo 1925.

C. K. Webster (ed.), *Britain and the independence of Latin-America, 1812-1830,* 2 vols., London 1938.

Books and Articles

E. ACEVEDO, *José Artigas. Su obra cívica. Alegato histórico,* edición oficial, 3 vols., Montevideo 1950.

ANON., *Apuntes historicos sobre la Banda Oriental del Rio de la Plata, desde el descubrimiento de ese territorio hasta el año de 1818...,* Montevideo 1818?

ANON. (P. F. Sáenz de Cavia), *El Protector nominal de los Pueblos Libres, D. José Artigas clasificado por El Amigo del Orden,* Buenos Aires 1818.

O. ANTÚNEZ OLIVERA, *Artigas como militar,* in E. M. Narancio (ed.), *Artigas. Estudios publicados en 'El País' como homenaje al Jefe de los Orientales en el centenario de su muerte. 1850-1950,* pp. 163-82, Montevideo 1951.

F. A. ARCE, *La formación de la Liga Federal,* in E. M. Narancio (ed.), *Artigas,* pp. 85-97, Montevideo 1951.

F. A. ARCE and M. DEMONTE VITALI, *Artigas, heraldo del federalismo rioplatense,* Paraná 1950.

M. J. ARDAO and A. C. DE CASTELLANOS, *Artigas, Su significación en los orígenes de la nacionalidad oriental y en la Revolución del Río de la Plata,* Montevideo 1951.

H. ARREDONDO, *Civilización del Uruguay. Aspectos arqueológicos y sociológicos 1600-1900,* t. I, Montevideo 1951.

Sources

F. DE AZARA, *Memoria sobre el estado rural del Río de la Plata y otros informes*, ed. Buenos Aires 1943.

F. DE AZARA, *Voyages dans l'Amérique méridionale, depuis 1781 jusqu'en 1801*, ed. C. A. Walckenaer, 4 vols., Paris 1809.

L. E. AZAROLA GIL, *Los orígenes de Montevideo, 1607-1749*, Buenos Aires 1933.

H. D. BARBAGELATA, *Sobre la época de Artigas*, Montevideo, n.d.

L. BARBAGELATA, *Artigas antes de 1810*, 2nd. ed. Montevideo 1945.

F. BAUZÁ, *Historia de la dominación española en el Uruguay*, 3 vols. in 2, ed. Montevideo 1929.

A. BERAZA, *Los corsarios de Artigas (1816-1821)*, Montevideo 1949.

M. BLANCA PARÍS and Q. CABRERA PIÑÓN, *Estudios en torno al origen del Estado Oriental: las relaciones entre Montevideo y Buenos Aires en 1811. El virreinato de Elío. Revista de la Facultad de Humanidades y Ciencias*, año I, no. 2, pp. 37-99, Montevideo December 1947; año II, no. 3, pp. 189-304, August 1948.

P. BLANCO ACEVEDO, *El gobierno colonial en el Uruguay y los orígenes de la nacionalidad*, 3rd. ed., Montevideo 1944.

P. BLANCO ACEVEDO, *El federalismo de Artigas y la independencia nacional*, 2nd ed., Montevideo 1950.

P. BLANCO ACEVEDO, *Informe sobre la fecha de celebración del centenario de la independencia*, 2nd ed., Montevideo 1940.

L. A. DE BOUGAINVILLE, *Viaje alrededor del mundo por la Fragata del Rey la 'Boudeuse' y la Fusta la 'Estrella' en 1767, 1768 y 1769*, Spanish translation, 2 vols., Madrid 1921.

M. BURGIN, *The economic aspects of Argentine federalism, 1820-1852*, Cambridge, Mass. 1946.

R. D. CAMPOS, *Brigadier General Doctor Thomás García de Zúñiga. Grandes hombres en la Provincia Oriental. 1781-1843*, Montevideo 1946.

A. CAPILLAS DE CASTELLANOS, *La lucha contra el centralismo y el Tratado del Pilar*, in E. M. Narancio (ed.), *Artigas*, pp. 201-14, Montevideo 1951.

C. CARBAJAL, *La penetración luso-brasileña en el Uruguay*, Montevideo 1948.

D. CARNEIRO, *História da Guerra Cisplatina*, Rio de Janeiro 1946.

Sources

CONCOLORCORVO, *El Lazarillo de ciegos caminantes desde Buenos Aires hasta Lima*, ed. Paris 1938.

T. B. DAVIS, JR., *Carlos de Alvear, man of revolution*, Durham, N. C., 1955.

I. DE-MARÍA, *Rasgos biográficos de hombres notables de la República Oriental del Uruguay*, ed. J. E. Pivel Devoto, 4 vols., Montevideo 1939.

L. A. DEMERSAY, *Histoire physique, économique et politique du Paraguay et des établissements des Jésuites*, t. I, t. II, pt. I, Paris 1860-64; *Atlas*, livr. 1-4, Paris 1860-63.

A. DEMICHELI, *Formación contitucional rioplatense*, 3 vols., Montevideo 1955.

E. FAVARO, *Dámaso Antonio Larrañaga, su vida y su época*, Montevideo 1950.

E. FAVARO, *El Congreso de las Tres Cruces y la Asamblea del Año XIII, antecedentes y consecuencias*, Montevideo, 1957.

F. FERREIRO, *Orígenes uruguayos*, Montevideo 1937.

TASSO FRAGOSO, *A batalha do Passo do Rosario*, Rio de Janeiro, 1922.

N. FUSCO SANSONE (ed.), *Vida y obras de Bartolomé Hidalgo*, Montevideo 1944.

E. DE GANDÍA, *Los treinta y tres orientales y la independencia del Uruguay*, Buenos Aires 1939.

E. DE GANDÍA, *Las ideas políticas de Mariano Moreno. Autenticidad del plan que le es atribuido* (Publicaciones del Instituto de Investigaciones Históricas, no. XCVI), Buenos Aires 1946.

A. GILLESPIE, *Gleanings and remarks collected during many months of residence at Buenos Ayres and within the upper country*, Leeds 1818.

M. GIMÉNEZ FERNÁNDEZ, *Las doctrinas populistas en la independencia de Hispano-América*, in *Anuario de Estudios Americanos*, t. III, pp. 519-665, Seville 1947.

A. I. GÓMEZ FERREYRA, S.J., *La Invasion Inglesa vista desde Montevideo*, in *La Reconquista y Defensa de Buenos Aires*, Buenos Aires 1947, pp. 137-48.

A. D. GONZÁLEZ, *Las primeras fórmulas constitucionales en los países del Plata (1810-1813)*, Montevideo 1941.

J. C. GONZÁLEZ, *La misión de Juan Manuel de Figueiredo a Buenos Aires en 1821*, in *Revista Histórica*, año LII (2a. ép.), t. XXVIII, Montevideo July 1958, pp. 195-233.

Sources

W. Gregory, *A visible display of Divine Providence; or, the Journal of a captured missionary. . .*, London 1800.

D. Hammerly Dupuy, *Rasgos biográficos de Artigas en el Paraguay*, 'in'–

E. M. Narancio (ed.), *Artigas*, pp. 285-98, Montevideo 1951.

S. G. Hanson, *Utopia in Uruguay*, New York 1938.

C. H. Haring, *The Spanish Empire in America*, New York, 1947.

J. S. Torres Homem, *Annaes das guerras do Brazil com os estados do Prata e Paraguay*, Rio de Janeiro 1911.

R. A. Humphreys, *Liberation in South America, 1806-1827. The career of James Paroissien*, London 1952.

Instituto Histórico y Geográfico del Uruguay, *El Paraguayo Independiente*, Asunción 28 de septiembre de 1850 (edición facsimilar), Montevideo 1950.

Junta de Historia y Numismática Americana, Publicaciones de la Filial de Rosario no. 3, *Diario de Don Manuel Ignacio Diez de Andino, crónica santafecina, 1815-1822*, ed. J. L. Busaniche, Rosario 1931.

D. A. Larrañaga, *Viaje de Montevideo a Paysandú*, ed. Padre B. M. Vidal, Montevideo 1930.

R. Levene, *Ensayo histórico sobre la Revolución de Mayo y Mariano Moreno*, 2 vols., Buenos Aires 1920-1.

R. Levene, *Los primeros documentos de nuestro federalismo político*, in *Humanidades*, Publicación de la Facultad de Humanidades y Ciencias de la Educación, Universidad de la Plata, t. XXIII, pp. 11-50, La Plata 1933.

R. Levene (ed.), *Los sucesos de mayo, contados por sus actores C. Saavedraa, M. Belgrano, M. Rodríguez, etc.*, Buenos Aires 1928.

R. Levene (ed.), *Historia de la nación argentina desde sus orígenes hasta la organización definitiva en 1862*, 10 tomes in 14 vols., 1936-50.

V. F. López, *Historia de la República Argentina, su origen, su revolución y su desarrollo político*, 10 vols., Buenos Aires 1887.

E. Loza, *La campaña de la Banda Oriental (1810-1813)*, in H.N.A., vol. V, section 2, chap. XV, Buenos Aires 1939.

J. Luccock, *Notes on Rio de Janeiro and the Southern parts of Brazil; taken during a residence of ten years in that country, from 1808 to 1818*, London 1820.

J. Maeso, *Los primeros patriotas orientales de 1811 . . .* , Montevideo 1888.

Sources

C. A. MAGGI, 'La Redota' (el Exodo), in E. M. Narancio (ed.), Artigas, pp. 61-8, Montevideo 1951.

M. V. MARTÍNEZ, Andresito, caudillo guaraní, drama de su raza y drama de su vida, Montevideo 1949.

R. DE MENDONÇA, História da politica exterior do Brasil, 10. tomo, (1500-1825), México 1945.

H. MIRANDA, Las instrucciones del año XIII, 2nd ed., Montevideo 1935.

B. MITRE, Historia de Belgrano y de la independencia argentina, ed. 4 vols., Buenos Aires 1927.

D. L. MOLINARI, Antecedentes de la Revolución de Mayo, III (Facultad de Filosofía y Letras, Publicaciones del Instituto de Investigaciones Históricas, no. XXXII), Buenos Aires 1926.

E. M. NARANCIO, El origen del Estado Oriental, in República Oriental del Uruguay, Anales de la Universidad, entrega no. 162, Montevideo 1948.

E. M. NARANCIO, El Reglamento de 1815, in E. M. Narancio (ed.), Artigas, pp. 135-47, Montevideo 1951.

E. M. NARANCIO (ed.), Artigas. Estudios publicados en 'El País' como homenaje al Jefe de los Orientales en el centenario de su muerte. 1850-1950, Montevideo 1951.

M. W. NICHOLS, The Gaucho. Cattle hunter. Cavalryman. Ideal of romance, Durham, N.C., 1942.

M. DE OLIVEIRA LIMA, Dom João VI no Brasil 1808-1821, 2nd. ed., 3 vols., Rio de Janeiro 1945.

C. PASTORE, Artigas en el Paraguay, in Artigas. Homenaje en el centenario de su muerte, ed. Instituto Histórico y Geográfico del Uruguay, Montevideo 1952.

J. PÉREZ, Ramírez y Artigas, elevación y ocaso, La Plata 1949.

C. PINTOS DIAGO, Leonardo Olivera, el señor del este, Montevideo 1945.

J. E. PIVEL DEVOTO, Uruguay independiente, in A. Ballesteros y Beretta (ed.), Historia de América y de los pueblos americanos, t. XXI, Barcelona 1949.

J. E. PIVEL DEVOTO, Raíces coloniales de la revolución oriental de 1811, Montevideo 1952.

Sources

J. E. PIVEL DEVOTO, *El Congreso Cisplatino (1821)*, in *Revista del Instituto Histórico y Geográfico del Uruguay*, t. XII, pp. 111-424, Montevideo 1936.

J. E. PIVEL DEVOTO, *Prólogo*, in *Archivo Artigas*, vol. II, pp. VII-LXXXI, Montevideo 1951.

J. E. PIVEL DEVOTO, *Prólogo*, in *Archivo Artigas*, vol. III, pp. VII-CXLII, Montevideo 1952.

ROCHA POMBO, *História do Brasil*, 5 vols., Rio de Janeiro 1935.

E. RAVIGNANI, *Historia constitucional de la República Argentina; notas tomadas por . . . Propotnik y Sicard*, 3 vols., Buenos Aires 1930.

E. RAVIGNANI, *El Virreinato del Río de la Plata (1776-1810)*, in H.N.A., t. IV, 1, 1, chap. I, Buenos Aires 1938.

J. A. REBELLA, *'Purificación'. Sede del protectorado de 'Los Pueblos Libres' (1815-1818)*, in *Revista del Instituto Histórico y Geográfico del Uruguay*, t. X, pp. 172-280, Montevideo 1933.

J. P. and W. P. ROBERTSON, *Letters on Paraguay: comprising an account of a four years' residence in that republic under the government of the dictator Francia*, 3 vols., London, 1838-9.

J. P. and W. P. ROBERTSON, *Letters on South America; comprising travels on the banks of the Paraná and the Río de la Plata*, 3 vols., London 1843.

E. DE SALTERAIN Y HERRERA, *Monterroso, iniciador de la Patria y secretario de Artigas*, in *Revista Nacional*, t. XXXVI, año IX, no 106, pp. 85-130, Montevideo 1947.

E. DE SALTERAIN Y HERRERA, *Artigas en el Paraguay (1820-1850)*, 2nd ed., Montevideo 1950.

E. DE SALTERAIN Y HERRERA, *Lavalleja. La redención patria*, in *Revista Histórica*, año L (2a. ép.), t. XXV, nos. 73-5, Montevideo March 1956, pp. 1-191, t. XXVI, nos. 76-78, Montevideo October 1956, pp. 1-186, and año LI (2a. ép.), t. XXVII, nos. 79-81, Montevideo January 1957, pp. 1-216.

J. SARRAILH, *L'Espagne éclairée de la seconde moitié du XVIIIᵉ siècle*, Paris 1954.

J. STEFANICH, *Artigas, Francia y el Paraguay*, in *Artigas. Homenaje en el centenario de su muerte*, ed. Instituto Histórico y Geográfico del Uruguay, Montevideo 1952.

BB2

Sources

J. STREET, *Lord Strangford and Río de la Plata, 1808-1815*, in *The Hispanic American Historical Review*, vol. XXXIII, pp. 477-510, Durham, N.C., November 1953.

J. STREET, *La influencia británica en la independencia de las Provincias del Río de la Plata, con especial referencia al período comprendido entre 1806 y 1816*, in *Revista Histórica*, año XLVII (2a. ép.), t. XIX, nos. 55-7, Montevideo September 1953, pp. 181-257; año XLVIII, t. XXI, nos. 61-3, Montevideo July 1954, pp. 329-91; año XLVIII, t. XXII, nos. 64-6, Montevideo August 1954, pp. 1-83; año XLIX, t. XXIV, nos. 70-2, Montevideo August 1955, pp. 226-317.

J. TORRE REVELLO, *Los gobernadores de Buenos Aires (1617-1777)*, in H.N.A., vol. III, part 2, chap VIII, Buenos Aires 1937.

J. M. TRAIBEL, *La Liga Federal. (Informe de una investigación histórica en los archivos de las Provincias Argentinas de Entre Ríos y Santa Fe)*, República Oriental del Uruguay, *Anales de la Universidad*, entrega no. 160, pp. 93-164, Montevideo 1947.

J. M. TRAIBEL, *Artigas antes de 1811*, in E. M. Narancio (ed.), *Artigas*, pp. 19-41, Montevideo 1951.

J. M. TRAIBEL, *El Congreso de Oriente*, ibid. pp. 99-110, Montevideo 1951.

A. ZUM FELDE, *Evolución histórica del Uruguay*, 3rd ed., Montevideo 1945.

INDEX

Artigas, José Gervasio (*continued*)
relations with the General Constituent Assembly of the United Provinces, 175-83; his economic views, 181, 216, 222, 224-32, 233; struggle for independence from Buenos Aires, 189-99, 206-13; his government of the Provincia Oriental, 213-42; his views on agriculture, 217, 231-2, and on country settlement, 225-30, 376-9, and on foreign trade, 236-7, 239-40, 270-1, 273, 277-8, and on education and religion, 241-2

As *Protector de los Pueblos Libres*, 233, 244-66, 269, 270-4, 279, 281, 291, 326; his appearance and way of life, 260-1, 271-4; and the Portuguese invasion (1816), 281, 282, 287, 290-311; his declining influence in the Federal League, 311-28; his defeat and exile, 325-8; persistence of his ideas, 353, 368, 370, 372, 374; his declining years and death, 370-4; his stature, 374-5

Artigas, José María, legitimate son of José Gervasio, 76, 258, 372-3

Artigas, José Nicolás, brother of José Gervasio, 49

Artigas, Juan Antonio, grandfather of José Gervasio, 44-6

Artigas, Manuel, brother of José Gervasio, 49, 61n

Artigas, Manuel, natural son of José Gervasio, 51

Artigas, Manuel, cousin of José Gervasio, 128, 133

Artigas, Manuel Francisco, brother of José Gervasio, 49, 133, 192, 203, 247, 248, 250, 292, 293, 308

Artigas, Martín José, father of José Gervasio, 45-6, 47, 49

Artigas, Martina Antonia, sister of José Gervasio, 49

Asencio, Arroyo (stream), 129

Asunción, 4, 5, 269, 370, 372

Attila, 317

Auchmuty, Sir Samuel, 89, 93

Ávalos, 325

Ávalos, Pact of, 326

Avilés, Gabriel de, Marqués de, 56

Ayacucho, 339

Ayuí, Arroyo (stream), 153, 162, 164, 169

Azara, Félix de, 12, 13, 14, 54; scheme for settlement of Banda Oriental, 57-61, 69, 121, 123, 225, 227

Azara, Nicolás de, 60n

Badajoz, Treaty of, 63, 78

Bagé, 350

Balcarce, Juan Ramón, 317-8, 334, 340, 364

Balcarce, Marcos, 313

Baldenegro, Eusebio, 249, 307

Banda Oriental, discovery and early settlement, 4-9; disputed between Spain and Portugal, 1-3, 15, 17, 19-22; natural resources and products, 2, 4, 6, 31, 34; cattle, 2, 4, 6-8, 16, 29, 67, 214-5, 230; cattle industry, 6-8, 28, 29-32, 49, 59, 226-7, 332, social effects of, 8-10, 32, protection of cattle, 29-30, 54, 61, 226, 229; social conditions, 9, 10-15, 24, 29, 32, 43, 48, 58, 120; and domination by Buenos Aires, 7, 28, 34, 181; illicit trade with Brazil, 15, 29, 50, 54, frontier with Brazil, 24, 45, 57, 66-7, 122-3; Portuguese attempts to annex, 8, 10, 15-17, 20, 62-3, 102-4, 136-46, 158-61

Authority of Buenos Aires in, 41-2, 120, 121-2; administrative

Banda Oriental (*continued*)
divisions, 41-3, 61; state of disorder in, 51-7, 58, 78-9, 93, 118; economic difficulties, 59

Emancipation of, 44, 106-7, 117, 118-36, 147-61, 164, 168-9, 178; unity of, 120-1, 124, 165; federalism in, 154, 156-8, 163-5, 168-70, 174-88; named Provincia Oriental, 180. *See also* Montevideo; Provincia Oriental; *and* Uruguay

Barbacena, Felisberto Caldeira Brant Pontes, Marquês de, 350

Baron's Club, the, 335

Barreiro, Miguel, 126, 146, 176, 178, 187, 203; Artigas' delegate in Montevideo, 219, 222, 235-6, 263-5, 295, 299-301, 304, 306

Barú, Matías, 327

Basualdo, Blas, 206, 249, 258

Batoví, 54; plan for settlement, 57-61, 67, 121; surrendered to Portuguese, 62

Bauzá, Francisco, 9

Bauzá, Pedro Celestino, 125

Bauzá, Rufino, 209-10, 307

Bedoya, 315

Belén, 151, 198, 248

Belgrano, Manuel, 112, 130, 132, 133, 211, 280, 313, 318-9

Benavídez, Venancio, 129, 133, 135

Beresford, William Carr, 80, 81-2, 91, 275

Bianqui, Jerónimo Pío, 305, 333, 335, 374

Blanco Acevedo, Pablo, 374

Bolívar, Simón, 220-1, 259, 339, 375

Bolivia, 17

Bonaparte, Joseph, 100

Bonaparte, Napoléon, 62, 88, 100, 101, 104, 138

Bonpland, Aimé, 244, 371

Bourbons, the, 19

Boves y de la Iglesia, José Tomás, 221

Bowles, William, 236, 277-8

Braganzas, the, 288, 320, 336

Brazil, 1, 19, 98, 277, 316, 329, 370; exploitation of Banda Oriental, 8; illicit trade with Banda Oriental, 15, 29, 30, 50, 54, 66, 238; her boundaries, 22, 232; unrest on her frontier with Banda Oriental, 57, 66-7, 284, 286; incorporation of Banda Oriental into, 330, 334, 335-7, 338; independence of, 334, 335, 336, 337; war with United Provinces over Provincia Oriental, 344, 346, 349-51, 353-4; peace negotiations, 351-2, 353, 355, 357-64, 367

British merchants, interest in trade with the Plate region, 88-9, 91, 92-3; trade opened to them, 105-6, 236; influence on local politics, 117, 138; and Provincia Oriental, 236-8

Brown, Gustavo Henrique, 353

Brown, William, 199, 256, 259, 263, 349

Buenos Aires, 1, 5, 10, 358; domination of Banda Oriental, 6-8, 28, 29, 31, 34, 41-3, 60, 121-36; Cabildo of, 7, 19, 95, 96, 99, 103, 107, 108-9, 112, 143, 256, 258, 323; Audiencia of, 17, 18, 90, 107, 108, 116; commercial affairs, 18-9, 24, 25, 34-41, 105-6; Consulado of, 35-41, 43, 96, 97, 99; neglect of Banda Oriental, 78-9; population, 80; English occupation of, 80-2, and Reconquest, 82-3; her part in the second English Invasion, 88, 89, 90, 91-2; her hostility towards Montevideo, 93-8, 99, 101, 103, 104, 107, 110; revolution, 87-8, 99, 105, 106-17
Reaction to Portuguese schemes,

Chaná Indians, 5, 6
Charcas, Audiencia of, 22
Charles III, of Spain, reforms of in the Plate region, 28, 30-2
Charles IV, of Spain, 100-1
Charrúa Indians, 4, 56, 66, 67, 119n
Chiclana, Feliciano, 307
Chile, 89, 91, 134, 166, 281, 305, 307, 319; trade with the Plate region, 34, 253
Church in the Banda Oriental, the, 43, 58, 224, 242
Chuy, River, 346
Cisneros, Baltasar Hidalgo de, 109-11, 113, 116
Colonia del Sacramento, see Colónia do Sacramento
Colonia del Sacramento, Department of, 232
Colónia do Sacramento, under Portuguese rule, 10, 17-9, 21, 22, 24; taken by Spain (1777), 22-4; as Colonia del Sacramento, 42, 58, 118, 121, 125, 126, 128, 131, 133, 134, 135, 147, 181, 206, 209, 216, 236, 237, 238, 239, 285, 286, 292, 303-4, 307-8, 341, 343, 345, 346, 353, 366
Concolorcorvo, 15
Congreso Cisplatino, 333-5
Congreso de abril de 1813, 175-83, 187, 192
Congreso de la Capilla de Maciel, 191-3, 203
Congreso de la Panadería de Vidal, 143, 156
Congreso de la Quinta de la Paraguaya, 146, 147, 148, 156, 176
Congreso de Oriente, 254, 262-5
Congress of the United Provinces of the River Plate (1828), 364
Congress of Tucumán, 257, 280, 281, 287-90, 293, 299, 300, 301, 315, 320, 323

Congress of 1825 (Oriental), 342, 344, 353
Connecticut, Constitution of, 185
Constituent and Legislative Assembly of the Provincia Oriental (1828), 367-8
Constituent Congress of the United Provinces of the River Plate (1824), 340-1, 342, 345, 347
Constitution, Argentine, of 1826, 347, 349, 353
Constitution, Uruguayan, of 18 July 1830, 368, 371
Consular government of Paraguay, 371, 372
Contraband, in the River Plate region, 17, 18, 19, 30, 36, 37; British, 19, 30, 93, 96, 97; Portuguese, 30, 54; in Montevideo, 30, 54; Artigas' part in, 49-50; in Banda Oriental, 123, 217, 224, 235, 238; in the Littoral Provinces, 275
Contrat Social, of Rousseau, 156, 177
Córdoba, city, 18, 81, 82, 179; Cabildo of, 254
Córdoba, province, 183, 263, 264, 314, 317, 318, 321; federalism in, 245, 252, 257, 313, 322, 360; declining influence of Artigas in, 281
Correa, Gervasio, 250, 312, 313, 321, 326
Corrientes, city, 246, 247, 251, 268, 274, 327; Cabildo of, 254-6
Corrientes, province, 247, 261, 273, 292, 296, 309; federalism in, 183, 204, 210, 244-50, 252, 268, 274, 311, 315, 325, 326, 340; life in, 274-7
Corrientes, River, 327
Corumbé Hills, 297
Council of Regency, in Spain, 111, 115, 121, 124
Creoles, scorn of for Spaniards, 53, 70; of Buenos Aires, their reaction

Maldonado (*continued*)
205, 216, 236, 237, 238, 239, 286, 304, 316, 336, 346, 367
Maldonado, Department of, 232
Maldonado, Sierras de, 41
Maldonado Chico, Arroyo (stream), 8
Maldonado Grande, Arroyo (stream), 8
Mandisoví, 327
Mangueira, Laguna, 297
Manoel Riveiro, Bento, 308, 313
Marcha Oriental, the, of Bartolomé Hidalgo, 149-50
Martínez, Juan José, 333
Massachusetts, Declaration of Rights of, 184; Constitution of, 185
Mediating Powers, the, 305, 306, 329, 356
Medina, Francisco, 31
Melián, José, 249
Melo, 62, 292, 353
Melo, Francisco, 125
Melo de Portugal, Pedro, 53
Memoria sobre el estado rural del Río de la Plata, of Azara, 58-61
Méndez, Bautista, 245, 268, 272, 277, 311, 315, 326, 327
Méndez, Juan, 187
Mendoza, city, 281, 319
Mendoza, province, 322
Menna Barreto, Gaspar Francisco, 297
Mercedes, 121, 129, 132, 133, 147, 209, 218
Merim, Laguna, 296
Meseta de Artigas, 271
Mexico, 9, 89
Minas, 131, 133
Miranda, Francisco de, 79-80, 81
Misiones, district, 41, 49, 57, 64, 148, 165, 166, 198, 242, 273, 295, 308, 315, 325, 326, 327; invasions by Portuguese, 19, 62-3, and reaction of Banda Oriental, 62-3; Artigas'

Misiones, district (*continued*)
attempts to recover, 65, 152, 180-1, 284-5, 292, 297, 306, 308-9; capture by Rivera, 354-5, 363, 367; returned to Brazil, 364
Missions, Franciscan, in Banda Oriental, 5; Jesuit, in Paraguay, 5, 21, 181, Spanish campaign against, 21
Mitre, Bartolomé, 255
Monteagudo, Bernardo, 207
Monterroso, Fray José Benito, 125, 126, 178
Montes de Oca, Luciano, 312, 313
Monteverde, Domingo de, 221
Montevideo, 17, 20, 22, 24-33; foundation, 10, 20-1, 44-5; strategic importance, 20, 27, 35, 117, 131, 136; population, 20, 24, 26, 39, 44, 80; commercial importance, 24, 29, 31, 32, 34-5, 98, 122; life in, 24-7, 33; architecture, 27; as administrative centre, 28, 34, 41, 120, 122; development of Banda Oriental, 28-9, 39, 42; reaction against domination by Buenos Aires, 29, 35-43, 78-9, 84-5, 86, 92-3, 94, 96-8; trade with Peru, 31, with Cuba, 32; commercial rivalry with Buenos Aires, 34-41, 43, 105-6; as a port, 34-5, 38, 39-41; independence from Buenos Aires, 41, 43, 85, 86, 97, 98, 101, 105-6; limits of jurisdiction, 41-3; education in, 47-8; in Reconquest of Buenos Aires, 82-7; English occupation, 89-93
Hostility towards Buenos Aires, 99, 101, 103, 104, 108, 109; loyalty to Spain, 102, 103, 104-5, 106, 108-9, 113-7, 122, 123-4, 136-7, 141; reaction to revolution of Buenos Aires, 113-7; as capital of Viceroyalty, 124; emancipation party in, 125; and Portuguese schemes,

Rivarola, Francisco Bruno de, 178, 179, 259-60, 261
Riveiro, Bento Manoel, 308, 313
Rivera, Bernabé, 308, 333
Rivera, Fructuoso, 131; officer of Artigas, 171, 198, 206, 208, 209-10, 219, 226, 292, 293, 297, 298, 306, 308, 309, 310; submits to Portuguese, 310-1, 333, 334, 335, to Brazilians, 337, 338; supports liberation movement, 339, 340, 343-6, 347-8; for complete independence, 348, 354-5, 362, 363, 367; national hero, 367; and Artigas, 371-2, 374
Robertson, James Parish, merchant, 6, 10, 27; in Corrientes, 247; in Santa Fe, 250-2; and the federalists, 269-74
Robertson, William Parish, in Santa Fe, 267; in Corrientes, 268-9, 276
Robertson, James Parish and William Parish in the federal provinces, 246-7, 267, 269, 271, 274-7, 311
Rocamora, Tomás de, 65-6, 69-71
Rocha, town, 292
Rocha, Laguna de, 8
Rodríguez, José Francisco, 279, 280
Rodríguez, Martín, 334, 340, 341, 346, 348
Rodríguez Peña, Nicolás, 202, 205
Rondeau, José, school-fellow of Artigas, 47; and revolution, 119-20, 127-8, 132, 166; and Banda Oriental, 133-4, 135, 136, 143, 146, 147, 150, 165, 169, 170, 171, 173, 174, 175, 179, 187, 188; and *Congreso de Maciel*, 190-3; and siege of Montevideo, 193-9; as Supreme Director of United Provinces, 257, 262, 320-1; against Artigas and federalism, 321-3; Governor of Provincia Oriental (1828), 367-8
Rosario, 280, 318, 319

Rosas, Juan Manuel de, 120, 167, 356
Rousseau, Jean-Jacques, 156, 177
Ruiz Huidobro, Pascual, 66-8, 77, 82-3, 94

Saavedra, Cornelio, 112
Sáenz, Bernabé, 333
Sáenz de Cavia, Pedro Feliciano de, 47, 116, 208, 316-7
Saint Catharine's Bay (Bahia de Santa Catarina), 286
Salazar, José de, 113, 115, 116-7, 126, 127, 131, 141
Salcedo, Marcos, 178, 179
Salta, 280
Salto, 151, 218
Samaniego, Gregorio, 250, 312, 313
San Carlos, 121, 133, 238, 292
San Gabriel de Batoví, *see* Batoví
San Ildefonso, Treaty of, 22
San Isidro Labrador, *alias* Curuguaty, 327n., 370-2
San José, 126, 133, 144, 147, 178, 367
San José, Department of, 232
San Juan, 322
San Juan Bautista, 178
San Luis, 322
San Martín, José de, 119, 148, 165-6, 280, 281, 307, 311, 319
San Miguel, 296
San Nicolás, 317, 318
Sánchez, Isabel, 51
Santa Ana, 297, 303, 349
Santa Catarina, Island of, 22, 296
Santa Fe, city, 248, 250-1, 254, 265, 267, 268, 269-70, 280-1, 318; Cabildo of, 265, 314
Santa Fe, province, 6, 183, 256, 261, 263, 264, 265, 266, 296, 337, 338, 339, 354; federalism in, 244-5, 248, 250-1, 253, 254, 257, 267-8, 340; trade of, 253, 268, 314; struggles with Buenos Aires, 265, 279-81, 291, 294, 311;

Santa Fe (*continued*)
  declining influence of Artigas in, 314, 317-35
Santa Lucía, district, 131, 170, 292
Santa Lucía, River, 171, 193, 292
Santa Tecla, 42, 47, 58, 67, 121
Santa Teresa, 42, 292, 295, 296, 298, 346
Santiago del Estero, 313-4
Santo Domingo Soriano, 5, 24, 49, 121, 122, 129, 130, 132, 144, 178, 235, 292, 343, 345; Cabildo of, 337
Santo Domingo Soriano, Department of, 232
Santo Tomé, Pact of, 280
São Borja, 292, 295, 297
São Vicente, 16, 20
Sarandí, battle of, 245
Sarmiento, Domingo F., 9
Sarratea, Manuel de, 140, 141, 146, 158, 195, 211, 357; intrigues against Artigas, 162-4, 167-74, 176, 188, 259, against Pueyrrecón, 322; Governor of Buenos Aires, 323, 340; and fall of Artigas, 323-5, 326
Saucesito, Arroyo (stream), 313
Seville, 100, 105, 108; Junta of, 102
Sierra, Santiago, 187
Silveira, Bernardo de, 298
Sipe Sipe, 279
Smith, Sir William Sidney, 107
Sobremonte, Rafael de, Marqués de, 62-4, 68, 69, 73, 80-1, 82, 85, 87, 88, 89, 90, 121, 227
Sociedad Patriótica, the, 184, 196
Soler, Miguel Estanislao, 132, 206, 208, 209, 210, 212, 259, 340, 350
Solís, Juan de, 4
Solís Grande, Arroyo (stream), 8
Soria, Joaquín de, 117
Soriano, *see*, Santo Domingo Soriano
Sotelo, Pantaleón, 292, 297
Southern Star, La Estrella del Sur, The, 91

Souza, Diogo de, 141, 142, 143, 146, 158, 159, 160
Souza Coutinho, Rodrigo de, 102-3, 138-9, 140, 142
Spain, 4, 99, 255, 277, 282, 284, 286, 305, 306, 328, 333, 355, 356, 357, 374; empire in America, 2, 5, 16, 22; reaction to Portuguese expansion, 16-7, 19, 20, 21, 22-4; trade system, 18, 30-1, 33, 36; policy towards Montevideo, 34-5, 42, 87, 97; declining authority in the Plate region, 35, 105, 107-8, 110, 111-2, 131; attempts to recover Banda Oriental, 329, 331
Staples, Robert Ponsonby, 277-8
Stock-raisers of Montevideo, Guild of, 64, 68-9, 71-2, 75, 78-9
Strangford, Percy Clinton Sydney Smythe, Viscount, British Minister in Rio de Janeiro, and Portuguese designs on Banda Oriental, 103, 104, 107, 135, 137-42, 145, 146, 158-61, 265, 284, 306, 356; and revolution in the Plate region, 106, 113, 117, 139-40, 146, 162, 195-6, 204, 211, 282
Suárez, Joaquín, 125, 368

Tacuarembó, district, 338
Tacuarembó, Arroyo (stream), 41
Tacuarembó Chico, Arroyo (stream), battle of, 309, 323, 325
Tagle, Gregorio, 287, 322
Tarragona, Juan Francisco, 265
Telégrafo Mercantil, 39
Thirty-three Orientals, the, 341, 342
Tordesillas, Treaty of, 16
Tranquillising parties, 169
Trápani, Pedro, 341, 342, 344, 358, 359, 361-2
Treaties of May 1816, the, 280-1
Treaty of Badajoz, 63, 78

2553851

Made in the USA